The M & E Higher Business Education Series

Practical Business Law

General Editor

Dr Edwin Kerr
*Chief Officer, Council for National
Academic Awards*

Advisory Editors

K. W. Aitken
*Vice-Principal, South-East
London College*

P. W. Holmes
*Director, Regional Management
Studies Centre, Bristol Polytechnic*

Other titles in the same series:
*Financial Accounting
Human Behaviour in Organisations
Quantitative Approaches in Business Studies*

The M & E Higher Business Education Series

Practical Business Law

A. Arora

LLB, PhD

Barrister, Lecturer in Law,
University of Liverpool

Macdonald and Evans

Macdonald & Evans Ltd
Estover, Plymouth PL6 7PZ

First published 1983

© Macdonald & Evans Ltd 1983

British Library Cataloguing in Publication Data

Arora, A.
    Practical business law.—(The M&E higher business
    education series)
    1. Commercial law—England
    I. Title
    344.206'7   KD1629

    ISBN 0-7121-0463-1

Phototypesetting by
Anneset, Weston-super-Mare
Avon
and printed in Great Britain by
J. W. Arrowsmith Ltd
Bristol

Foreword

In recent years business practice has been undergoing major and fundamental changes for a variety of economic, social and technological reasons. In parallel with these changes the developments of education for business at all levels have also been extensive and far-reaching. In particular this is true at the advanced levels for courses leading to (*a*) the first degrees of the Council for National Academic Awards and of the universities, (*b*) the higher awards of the Business Education Council and its Scottish equivalent, and (*c*) examinations of the relevant professional bodies. Many such courses are now offered in educational institutions which include the polytechnics, the universities, the colleges and institutes of higher education, the further education colleges and the Scottish central institutions. In addition to these developments in curricular design there have also been important advances in educational and teaching methods.

Macdonald & Evans already has a large involvement in meeting the needs of students and staff in business education through its BECBOOK and HANDBOOK series. It has now decided to complement these with its Higher Business Education series.

The series is intended to be one of major educational significance which will cover all important aspects of higher business education. It will be designed for student and staff use with all of the advanced courses at all of the educational institutions mentioned above. Each book will have both a planned part in the series and be complete in itself and, in it, a thematic and problem-solving approach will be adopted, thus bringing a body of theory to bear on business problems—a major feature of the whole series.

The editorial team have chosen authors who are experienced people from technological institutions and from professional practice and will collaborate with them to ensure that the books are authoritative and are written in a style which will make them easy to use and will assist the students to learn effectively from such use.

The editorial team will welcome criticisms on each of the books so that improvements may be made at the reprint stages to ensure a closer achievement of the objectives of the books and the entire series.

Edwin Kerr
General Editor

Preface

The aim of this book is to outline the law relating to the commonest and most important commercial transactions, and to include sufficient detail to enable the student to understand the practical working of the law. The subject can readily be divided into:

(*a*) the general rules relating to all commercial contracts;

(*b*) the law governing both domestic and international transactions in goods;

(*c*) the law relating to ancillary transactions such as banking and insurance;

(*d*) the law governing commercial associations; and

(*e*) the law of employment which, because of its wider implications, is now often treated as a separate subject.

This book has been written for students who are concerned with commercial law, not as prospective lawyers, but incidentally to their main areas of study, in particular for those taking business studies at degree level or the BEC Higher National Diploma, as well as for those taking professional examinations in insurance, banking and the import/export trade. The law is therefore dealt with as an aspect of the transactions with which students are familiar, in the context of their economic and commercial impact, and a knowledge of this context is assumed.

The book is therefore divided into five separate parts dealing with the separate but interdependent areas of the law outlined above. Part I of the book is a general section in which the law of contract and commercial agency are dealt with. The next part deals with the law relating to transactions in goods—both domestic and international sales are here considered. The text then goes on to deal with other transactions in goods, namely hire-purchase and credit agreements. Part III of the book deals with transactions which are ancillary to trading such as insurance and banking. Part IV of the book deals with the law relating to commercial associations which are employed to carry on business undertakings. This part therefore deals with company and partnership law. The final chapter of the book deals with the law of employment which is an essential adjunct to commercial operations.

Finally, I would like to express my thanks to Professor R. R. Pennington for his valuable assistance and encouragement in the preparation of the book. I would also like to express my thanks to Mr Robert Upex for his helpful comments on the labour law chapter. My thanks are also due to Mr Peter Holmes and Mr David Sutherland, and to Miss Yolanda Chan and her colleagues at Liverpool University for typing the manuscript.

The law is set out as it stood on 1st January 1983.

1983   AA

Contents

PART III   ANCILLARY TRANSACTIONS

PART IV   COMMERCIAL ASSOCIATIONS

Table of Cases

Table of Statutes

CHAPTER ONE

Introduction: An Outline History of Commercial Law

Commercial law had its origins in the customary practices of the merchants in the middle ages. In particular the merchants from abroad brought with them their own practices in relation to the sale of goods and loans which they made to the monarchs of their country. For example, the modern law on bills of exchange and agency in particular are derived from the practices of merchants coming to this country from abroad. The wealthy merchants of Italy issued receipts in return for deposits left with them, and in time these receipts were recognised by other merchants and negotiated if the holder required immediate cash. The merchant who received the receipt either kept it and produced it before the depositor when he required cash or renegotiated it. Similarly, the practice developed that these merchants sent trusted employees abroad to conduct business for them and they thereby developed the rules of agency law.

The practice developed that disputes in relation to purely domestic transactions were settled by the market and fair courts which were held in towns and cities throughout the country for the duration of the fairs. Where however the dispute involved merchants of different countries it would be settled by the international fair courts and counsular courts. The rules of mercantile custom applied only to transactions between merchants and were not part of the common law. Until the sixteenth century the common law courts had no mercantile law jurisdiction and only a rudimentary law of contract.

In the sixteenth and seventeenth centuries the common law courts at Westminster began to assume jurisdiction in mercantile cases in competition with the Court of Admiralty, and the local fair and market courts declined since the common law courts gave more effective justice to merchants. One of the problems the local fair and market courts had was that they were ineffective at enforcing decisions given by them since they were only enforcable against the unsuccessful party if he was resident or had assets in the same district. The local courts were therefore ineffective if the person against whom a judgment was given had moved or transferred his assets to another locality. Moreover, the common law courts made themselves attractive by adopting the rules of mercantile custom where the common law differed from it. This resulted in the wholesale adoption of mercantile custom as part of the common law in the latter half of the seventeenth century, particularly in relation to sale of goods and bills of exchange. Moreover, the requirement that both the parties should be merchants was disregarded by the common law courts and so no separate system of commercial law applicable only where both parties were merchants ever evolved, as it did in other countries in Europe.

In the eighteenth and nineteenth centuries the rules of mercantile law were elaborated by logic, analogy and deduction. At the end of the nineteenth century parts of mercantile law were codified by statute, but without affecting or altering the rules of the common law which were not inconsistent with the statutory codification. In particular at this time the law of bills of exchange, partnership and sale of goods was embodied in Acts of Parliament. In the twentieth century the rules of commercial law have been affected extensively by statutory enactments particularly designed to protect the rights and interests of the consumer.

PART ONE

General Rules

CHAPTER TWO

The Principles of Contract Law

OBJECTIVES

It is proposed in this chapter to deal with the law relating to contracts in general. In particular the chapter deals with:

(a) forms of contracts and the essentials of a valid contract, including:
  (i) offer;
  (ii) acceptance;
  (iii) consideration;
  (iv) variations of the terms of a contract;
  (v) estoppel;
  (vi) privity of contract;

(b) contents of a contract, including express and implied terms and standard form contracts;

(c) exclusion clauses and the Unfair Contract Terms Act 1977;

(d) capacity of persons to contract;

(e) mistake, misrepresentation and illegal contracts;

(f) performance and discharge of contractual obligations;

(g) frustration of a contract;

(h) remedies for breach of contract.

DEFINITION OF A CONTRACT

A contract is an agreement between two or more persons which gives rise to legally recognised and enforceable rights under the law. A contractual undertaking is generally based on the parties reaching an agreement whereby one or both is obliged either to do a certain act or to refrain from doing an act, and the failure of either of them to fulfil his obligations enables the other party to sue him for breach of contract.

Form of contracts

A simple contract can either be wholly written, wholly oral or partly in writing and partly oral; in some cases a contract may be inferred from the conduct of the parties.

There are, however, certain statutory exceptions to the general rule that a contract may be in any form the parties wish. Some of these statutes require the contract to be by deed (i.e. to be both signed and sealed), to be in writing or alternatively merely to be evidenced in writing by a memorandum or note of the terms of the contract.

Contracts under seal

A contract made without consideration (for example, a gratuitous promise by a member of a family to work in the family business without a salary or other remuneration), or a contract for a lease of land for more than three years must be made under seal in order to be valid (*see* Law of Property Act 1925, ss. 52, 54(2)). Nevertheless a written but unsealed agreement for the grant of a lease for more than three years which is not under seal may be enforced in equity as an agreement to enter into a contract or lease.

Contracts in writing

A number of Acts of Parliament require certain types of contracts to be in writing; for example, certain contracts of insurance. Bills of exchange and promissory notes, both of which give rise to contractual obligations, must also be in writing. The statutes dealing with these contracts may also require the form of the relevant contract which it governs to be in a particular form and the result of non-compliance will vary under each statute.

Contracts evidenced in writing

The Statute of Frauds 1677 required five different types of contracts to be entered into in writing or at least to be evidenced by a written note or memorandum of their terms. The only kinds of contract still affected by this requirement are contracts of guarantee and contracts for the sale or disposition of land. (Contracts for the sale of land are now governed by the Law of Property Act 1925, s. 40.) The memorandum or note which evidences the terms of the agreement must identify the parties to a contract and the capacity in which they enter into the contract and the subject–matter of the contract must be identified; thus in the sale of land it may be sufficient to identify the property by stating its location. In *Plant* v. *Bourne* (1897) a memorandum which described the subject–matter of the case as "24 acres of land at Totmonslow" was held to be a sufficient description. The memorandum must also state the consideration and the material terms of the contract; for example a memorandum evidencing an agreement for a lease must state the duration and the date of commencement of the lease and the rent payable. Finally, the memorandum must be signed by the parties or at least by the one of them who is sued on the contract.

The statutory requirement of a memorandum does not affect the validity of a contract, but merely renders the contract unenforceable by action unless the agreement has been evidenced in writing and signed by the defendant. It is therefore possible to reduce the agreement to writing at any time before an action is brought.

The memorandum need not be a single document or be formally prepared for the purposes of satisfying the Statute of Frauds. A document, if it can be shown to evidence the agreement, although it clearly does not contain the whole of the contractual terms agreed between the parties, may refer to some other document, and the two documents may be read together to convey a complete picture of the contract. If, however, the document contains no reference to any other document and the connection can only be made by oral evidence showing that the documents form a connected series, the court will not allow the documents to be read together unless they are clearly related to each other by the function they fulfil. In *Timmins* v. *Moreland Street Property Co* (1958), the purchasers of a house sent to the vendor a cheque for £3,900 payable to the vendor's solicitor. The vendor gave a receipt for the amount which was signed by him alone. The purchasers countermanded the cheque, and in an action by the vendor for breach of a contract, the court held that the action could not succeed since the cheque could not be examined with the receipt as evidence of the agreement. The cheque in favour of the vendor's solicitor could not be read together with the receipt or any other document, because there was no reference to the transaction for which the cheque was given in the body of it and so it was not necessarily related to the receipt. On the other hand in *Pearce* v. *Gardner* (1897), a letter which was headed "Dear Sir" but omitted the name of the person to whom it was addressed was read together with the envelope in which it was sent as evidence of the identity of the seller in an action for breach of a contract to sell gravel lying in a bed (i.e. an interest in land) to the plaintiff.

The terms of a contract required under the Statute of Frauds 1677 to be evidenced in writing cannot be effectively varied by a subsequent oral agreement or by a document which fails to comply with the Statute itself, but it is possible for the parties to agree orally to terminate the agreement.

ESSENTIALS OF A VALID CONTRACT

A contract which is to be held valid and enforceable in law must:

(*a*) involve an offer and acceptance of the offer;

(*b*) provide for valuable consideration given by the parties to each other unless it is made under seal;

(*c*) be the result of an intention by the parties to create legal relations between themselves;

(*d*) be entered into by parties who have the necessary capacity to enter into the contract;

(*e*) involve the genuine consent of the parties to terms of the contract; and

(*f*) be legal and actually susceptible of performance.

The offer of a contract

The parties to a contract must reach an agreement which is final and certain. An agreement consists of an unconditional acceptance by the offeree (the person to whom the offer is made) of the offer made by the offeror (the person making the offer).

Offer

An offer expresses the willingness of the offeror to be bound by the terms of the offer if it is accepted by the offeree. An offer can be made to a particular individual and only he can then accept it, or an offer can be made to a group of individuals and in such a case any member of the group can accept in conformity with its terms, or an offer can be made to the world at large, in which case any person who has notice of the offer may accept it. In *Carlill v. Carbolic Smoke Ball Co* (1893), the defendant company advertised that if anyone caught influenza after using its medical smoke balls, the company would pay £100 to that person. The plaintiff, having used the smoke balls, contracted influenza and brought an action for the recovery of £100. The court held the plaintiff's action was admissible and held that the offer was a general offer, capable of acceptance by anyone who complied with its terms. The plaintiff having done this by using the defendant's smoke ball was entitled to recover the amount advertised when she subsequently contracted influenza.

An offer may be made expressly or be implied from the conduct of the offeror.

An offer must be distinguished from an invitation to treat or negotiate terms. An offer must be definite so that it is capable of acceptance. It must be distinguished from a situation where the person who takes the first step is in fact not making an offer but inviting another person to do so. It is then said to be an invitation to treat which the person who makes the first overtures can then accept. For example, in *Fisher* v. *Bell* (1961) it was held that the display of goods in a shop window is not an offer to sell those goods, but an invitation to the public to make an offer for them. Similarly, in *Pharmaceutical Society of Great Britain* v. *Boots Cash Chemists (Southern) Ltd* (1953) it was held that the display of goods on a shelf in a self-service shop was an invitation to the public to make an offer for them.

The question whether a statement is an offer or an invitation to treat depends primarily on the intention with which it was made, but the following situations have been established in law as producing the result that only "an invitation to make an offer" is being made.

Auction sales
At an auction the rule generally is that an offer is made by the bidder and accepted by the auctioneer who signifies his acceptance of the highest offered price by the fall of the hammer. An auctioneer is under no obligation to sell the goods and can withdraw them at any time before his acceptance of the highest bid. An offer made at an auction lapses when a higher offer is made by another bidder.

Display of goods for sale
The display of goods in a shop window is not an offer to sell the goods but an invitation to customers to make an offer (*see Fisher* v. *Bell* (1961)).

Advertisements
An advertisement of a willingness to contract is not an offer. For example, in *Partridge* v. *Crittenden* (1969) it was held that a newspaper advertisement which states that goods are for sale is not an offer, and an advertisement that an

auction will be held is not an offer to hold the auction made to members of the public who attend in order to bid: *Harris* v. *Nickerson* (1873). Advertisements of rewards for the return of stolen property and the advertisement of other unilateral contracts are offers capable of acceptance by performance of the act called for by the offer.

Sale of shares

A company which invites members of the public to subscribe for its shares is not making an offer, but is asking for members of the public to make an offer to acquire these shares on the terms indicated in the invitation.

Duration of an offer

An offeror may state expressly that an offer will be held open for a specified length of time, and it is then capable of acceptance at any time during that period. If no time for acceptance is specified, an offer remains open for a reasonable length of time, the length of which is a question of fact in each particular case.

Termination and withdrawal of an offer

An offer can be withdrawn at any time before it is accepted, but in order for the withdrawal to be effective it must be communicated to the offeree before he accepts the offer. Merely posting a letter giving notice of the withdrawal of the offer is insufficient. The notice of withdrawal must actually reach the offeree. In *Byrne* v. *Van Tienhoven* (1880), the defendants posted an offer to sell tinplate to the plaintiffs in New York on 1st October. They then posted a letter of withdrawal on 8th October which did not reach the plaintiffs until 20th October. The plaintiffs on receiving the offer on 11th October accepted it immediately, and confirmed their acceptance by post on 15th October. The court held there was a binding contract and that the withdrawal of the offer was ineffective since it did not reach the offeree in New York until after he had accepted the offer.

Where notice of the withdrawal of an offer by the offeror does not reach the offeree due to his own negligence (e.g. where the offeree fails to notify his change of address and the notice of withdrawal is sent to the offeree's previous address), or alternatively if the notice of withdrawal does reach the offeree but he fails to read it, the revocation of the offer is effective from the date when notice should have reached the offeree, and he cannot subsequently purport to accept the offer.

The withdrawal of an offer, whilst it must be communicated to the offeree, need not be communicated by the offeror personally. It is effective if the offeror's withdrawal of his offer is communicated to the offeree by a reliable source. In *Dickinson* v. *Dodds* (1876) it was held that an offer to sell land could not be accepted after the offeror had to the knowledge of the offeree agreed to sell the land to a third party.

Rejection of an offer

An offer is terminated when it is rejected by the offeree. A qualified or conditional acceptance is equivalent to a rejection of it (for example, an acceptance of an offer to sell goods where the acceptance is conditional on the buyer's being able to borrow the price). An offer is also rejected by the offeree when he purports to accept it but his acceptance is accompanied by new terms which amount to a counter–offer. In *Hyde* v. *Wrench* (1840) the defendant offered to sell a farm for £1,000. The plaintiff offered to buy it for £950, and when that counter–offer was rejected he purported to accept the original offer. The court held that by offering to buy for £950 the plaintiff was making a counter–offer, the effect of which was to reject the original offer which he could not subsequently accept. However, an inquiry by the offeree to determine whether the offeror would vary the original terms does not amount to a counter–offer. In *Stevenson, Jacques & Co* v. *McLean* (1880) the defendant offered to sell a quantity of iron to the plaintiffs, who asked whether they could take delivery over a period of four months. It was held this did not amount to a counter–offer, and the inquiry by the plaintiffs was merely a request for information.

A rejection of an offer by the offeree must actually be communicated to the offeror, and once the rejection has reached him the offeree cannot purport to accept the offer, although the subsequent letter of acceptance is posted by the offeree before the earlier letter of rejection has reached the offeror.

Lapse of time

An offer which expressly states that it is only capable of acceptance within a limited time must be accepted during that time and cannot be accepted after that time has expired. In *Tinn* v. *Hoffman & Co* (1873) it was held that an offer which stipulates that it must be accepted by return of post must be accepted either by return of post or by some other equally expeditious method. If an offer does not specify the time within which it is to be accepted, it will lapse unless accepted within a reasonable time. In *Ramsgate Victoria Hotel Co Ltd* v. *Montefiore* (1866) the defendant applied for allotment shares by the plaintiff company in June 1864, but the company did not allot any shares to him until the following November. It was held that although the defendant had not withdrawn his application he was not bound to accept them because the shares were not allotted to him within a reasonable time.

What is a reasonable time depends on the method by which the offer is communicated and the nature of the subject matter; for example in the case of perishable goods if the offeree is to accept an offer to sell them to him, he must do so expeditiously.

Occurrence of a condition

An offer which expressly provides that it will terminate on the occurrence of a certain event will terminate automatically if and when that event occurs.

Death

The death of the offeror itself does not terminate the offer unless the contract is one which involves personal service (e.g. an offer of employment) or involves personal relationships (e.g. an offer to marry).

Acceptance of an offer

In order for the parties to reach an agreement, the offeree must assent to the terms of the offer unconditionally either within a reasonable time or within the time specified in the contract. If the terms of the offer require acceptance to be in a specified mode, that method must be used (e.g. by telex or other specified method).

Unconditional acceptance

An acceptance will not be valid if it is conditional or if it amounts to a counter–offer. Thus in *Tinn* v. *Hoffman & Co* (1873) it was held that an offer to sell 1,200 tons of iron is not accepted unconditionally if the acceptance is of 800 tons. In *Northland Airlines Ltd* v. *Dennis Ferranti Meters Ltd* (1970), it was held that an acceptance is also ineffective if it introduces another new term which the offeror can either accept or reject. If, however, the effect of a conditional acceptance is that an independent third party has to do a certain act (e.g. fix the price under a contract of sale), then the acceptance is valid because the parties are in agreement as regards the main terms of the contract, and the appointment of a person to fix the price merely provides for the carrying out of the contract.

Time of acceptance

The general rule is that the acceptance of an offer must be communicated to the offeror or to his authorised agent and it is effective from the moment of communication. Thus if an oral acceptance is not heard by the offeror because of the noise of an aircraft flying overhead, or is spoken into a telephone after the line has gone dead so that the offeror does not hear it, there is no valid communication of the acceptance and therefore no contract.

Method of acceptance

An offeree may communicate his acceptance of an offer in one of a number of ways and, provided that the acceptance is actually brought to the notice of the offeror, it is valid.

If the terms of the offer require a specific method of acceptance, then the offeree must comply exactly with that method and acceptance by any other means will be ineffective. In *Quenerduaine* v. *Cole* (1883) the offeror required an immediate reply to his offer, and the court held this would implicitly require a reply by telex or other equally efficient method.

Where the offeror does not state the method of acceptance to be employed the offeree must accept the offer within a reasonable time and by a reasonably expeditious method; for example, an offer made by post generally implies that the acceptance must also be communicated by post or by another equally speedy method (*see Manchester Diocesan Council for Education* v. *Commercial and General Investments Ltd* (1970)).

The offeror cannot make the silence of the offeree serve as an implied expression of his acceptance. There must generally be a positive act on the part of the offeree indicating his acceptance. In *Felthouse* v. *Bindley* (1862) the court held that an offer which by its terms would be treated as accepted if it were not rejected by a certain date did not impose an obligation on the offeree to reply, and his failure to do so did not amount to an implied expression of his assent to the offer.

In the case of unilateral contracts the offeree accepts by performing the act required of him (e.g. finding lost property). In such cases it has been determined in *Carlill* v. *Carbolic Smoke Ball Co* (1893) and confirmed in *Errington* v. *Errington* (1952) that it is unnecessary for the offeree to communicate his acceptance before performing his part of the bargain, and performance of the act called for is a sufficient acceptance of the offer.

Postal acceptance

Where the terms of the offer either expressly or implicitly permit the offeree to accept it by post, the rule that acceptance is only valid when communicated to the offeror is modified, and provided the letter of acceptance is properly posted (i.e. properly addressed and stamped), acceptance takes place at the time of posting, not when the letter reaches the offeror. This is because the Post Office is treated as the agent of the offeror to receive the acceptance on his behalf. In *Holwell Securities Ltd* v. *Hughes* (1974) it was held that if the offeror wants acceptance to become effective only on his receipt of the letter of acceptance, he must say so expressly in his offer. Otherwise the postal rules will apply and the acceptance of the offer will be effective at the time the letter is posted; even though the letter is lost in the post and never reaches the offeror (*see Household Fire Insurance Co* v. *Grant* (1879)). To be effective immediately the letter of acceptance must be properly posted, and so if the offeree merely hands the letter to a postman on his delivery round, the letter is not properly posted because a postman on a delivery round is not authorised to receive mail; the acceptance becomes effective only when the postman actually hands the letter to the Post Office.

Once the letter of acceptance has been posted the offeror cannot revoke the offer. In *Byrne* v. *Van Tienhoven* (1880) the court held that a letter of revocation which reached the offeree after he had posted his acceptance of the offer was ineffective.

Instantaneous communication

An acceptance which is by some instantaneous method of communication, i.e. by telephone or by telex, is ineffective until it is actually communicated to the offeror. The rules relating to postal acceptance do not therefore apply. It is for the offeree to ensure that the acceptance actually reaches the offeror, but an offeree is not responsible for any act or omission on the part of the offeror which delays the notice coming to his attention. In *Entores Ltd* v. *Miles Far East Co* (1955) the court held that an acceptance communicated by some instantaneous method (in that case by telex) is effective when the telex machine prints the acceptance at the offeror's place of business. But if the telex machine is not manned at the time or does not have any ink so that the acceptance is not printed, then the offeror is responsible for the negligence and the acceptance is valid. The rule is the same where a telephone or other instantaneous method is used to convey acceptance.

Defective postal communication
Where the letter of acceptance is delayed due to the fault of the offeree (e.g. it is misdirected), the acceptance is effective only when it reaches the offeror, and the offeror can revoke the offer at any time before the acceptance actually reaches him.

Revocation of an acceptance
The question which arises here is whether an acceptance by post which takes effect immediately on proper posting can be revoked by a quicker means of communication where the notice of revocation reaches the offeror before the acceptance (*see Wenkheim* v. *Arndt* (1873)). The view has been expressed that where the revocation of an acceptance reaches the offeror before the letter of acceptance, he has not suffered any detriment and therefore the offeree can revoke; but the better view is that since the Post Office is treated as an agent of the offeror to receive the acceptance on his behalf, a revocation of the acceptance cannot be effected at all after the letter of acceptance has been posted.

Acceptance in ignorance of offer
An acceptance can only be valid if the person purporting to accept was at the time of the acceptance actually aware of the offer (*see R.* v. *Clarke* (1927)). A mere coincidence of intentions on the part of two persons so that they have a mutual desire to enter into a contract on identical terms is insufficient and cannot amount to an acceptance of an offer since no offer has in fact been communicated to any offeree for consideration. Thus there is no binding agreement if the offeror writes to the offeree offering to sell his car to him for £500 and the offeree simultaneously writes to the offeror to buy his car for £500.

Certainty of terms
An agreement will not be binding if it lacks certainty, either because it is vague or because it is incomplete. The courts will try to give effect to the agreement in the light of what is reasonable. Thus in *Hillas & Co Ltd* v. *Arcos Ltd* (1932) a contract for the sale of timber said it must be of "fair specification". It was held that since there had been a course of previous dealings between the parties and

they were aware of trade custom, a standard of reasonableness would be applied to resolve the vagueness.

Where the agreement is so vague that the courts cannot reasonably give effect to it or discover the intentions of the parties, the courts have refused to give effect to the agreement (*see May and Butcher* v. *R.* (1934)), but if the lack of certainty is merely due to the fact that the parties have not agreed on a price, the court may hold that a reasonable price must be paid since this is presumed to be the parties' intention (*see Foley* v. *Classique Coaches* (1934)). The courts will ignore a phrase which is meaningless and adds nothing to the contract (*see Nicholene Ltd* v. *Simmonds* (1953)).

Consideration

An agreement is not binding on the parties as a contract unless it is either made under seal or is supported by consideration. Consideration has been defined as "some right, interest, profit or benefit accruing to one party, or some forbearance, detriment, loss or responsibility given, suffered or undertaken by the other." Consideration can therefore simply be said to be the price one party has to pay to obtain the promise of the other that he will do or refrain from doing a certain act. Consideration is thus a benefit to one party and a detriment to the other.

Consideration can thus take one of two forms:

(*a*) Performance by one party of the act requested by the offeror will be valid consideration, as well as a valid acceptance in a unilateral contract; e.g. the use of the smoke ball in *Carlill* v. *Carbolic Smoke Ball Co* (1893) and the consequent inconvenience in using it was held to be sufficient consideration. The consideration given by the offeree is then said to be executed.

(*b*) Both parties promise to do or to refrain from a certain act in the future; e.g. a promise to supply certain goods in return for payment for those goods at the time of delivery. This is known as executory consideration, since the contract is made by the exchange of promises and the consideration will become executed only when the parties perform their respective obligations.

A number of rules have been established to determine whether consideration for a contract exists.

(*a*) *Consideration need not be adequate.* The courts will not enforce a simple contract unless some consideration has been given for the other party's promise, but the consideration need not be as valuable as that promise (e.g. a contract for the sale of a car worth £1,000 for a price of £500). The courts will not estimate the monetary value of the obligations of each party and pronounce on whether the benefit conferred on or detriment suffered by the plaintiff is equal in value to the benefit conferred on or the detriment suffered by the defendant. In *Chappell & Co Ltd* v. *Nestle Co Ltd* (1960) the court held that a promise by a chocolate manufacturer to supply records on a customer's sending him 1s. 6d. and three chocolate wrappers was enforceable as a contract, even though the records had a retail price far in excess of 1s. 6d. The court went as far as saying that the chocolate wrappers on their own might have been held to be sufficient consideration, but this is doubtful since they do evidence the fact that a certain quantity of chocolate has been bought. The courts are therefore not concerned with the sufficiency of consideration, unless the use of a nominal consideration in fact amounts to a deliberate attempt to evade the rule requiring valuable consideration for a contract to exist.

(b) *Past consideration.* The consideration for a contract must be given in return for a promise on the part of the other party. Thus if A digs B's garden, and B then promises to pay £5, the consideration given is past since the work was not done in return for a promise already made, and B cannot enforce the subsequent offer to pay him £5. However, if the giving of the consideration and the promise of the other party form substantially one transaction or are contemporaneous, there is valid consideration. Thus where a purchaser buys goods and is required to send a registration card to the manufacturer to take the benefit of the manufacturer's guarantee, the sale and giving the guarantee are substantially a single transaction and the manufacturer is contractually bound by the guarantee. Past consideration is, exceptionally good consideration for the issue of a bill of exchange or cheque given in satisfaction of an existing debt or liability.

(c) *Consideration must be legal.*

(d) *Inadequate consideration.* Where there is an existing or moral duty on one of the parties to do a certain act, a promise of reward by the other party in order to induce him to do the same act cannot be enforced in law. In *Collins* v. *Godefray* (1831), the court held that a promise by a witness to give evidence in legal proceedings in return for a promise by a party to the proceedings to make a payment to the witness did not give rise to a contract since the witness was already bound by the general law to attend and give evidence. Similarly, in *Stilk* v. *Myrick* (1809) it was held that a promise by a shipowner to pay extra wages to the remaining crew of a ship after two of the crewmen had deserted could not be enforced by a member of the crew, since the remaining crew were already contractually obliged to work the ship home. A promise made out of love and affection is similarly unenforceable, since there is no valuable consideration given by the person who enjoys the position of affection.

VARIATION OF THE TERMS OF A CONTRACT

A variation of the terms of a contract must be supported by fresh consideration and unless new consideration is given in addition to that originally promised the variation has no contractual effect. Thus a buyer who has contracted to buy goods for £500 is not bound by a subsequent promise to pay £600 for them instead unless the seller also promises something in addition to his original obligation. The performance of a contract in a method different from that required under the terms of the original contract will not be sufficient consideration; for example, the part payment of an existing debt at an earlier date will not discharge the debtor from his liability to pay the balance remaining and the creditor can subsequently claim payment of the balance outstanding. However, if the part payment of the debt is accompanied by fresh consideration (e.g. payment at an earlier date than the date on which payment falls due plus the payment of a gift), there will be sufficient consideration and the creditor cannot claim performance under the original contract. An effective variation of the terms of the contract supported by new consideration is binding and neither party can revert to the original terms.

Waiver of the terms

A variation of the terms of the contract may be given limited effect if it can be treated as a waiver by one of the parties of his legally enforceable rights. A party can agree to waive his strict rights before the contract is performed by the other party or after a breach of the contract by that party. However, the effect of a waiver is not to vary the contractual terms, but if the parties actually carry out the contract in accordance with the waiver, neither party can claim that it has been broken. But if the party for whose benefit the terms of the original contract were waived does not perform the contract in accordance with the waiver, it was held in *Charles Rickards Ltd* v. *Oppenheim* (1950) that on giving reasonable notice the party granting the indulgence can retract. For example, if under a contract of sale goods are to be delivered by one consignment and the buyer agrees to take delivery by instalments he can insist on all the goods being delivered as a single consignment if the seller fails to deliver the first instalment on time.

Estoppel

A variation of the terms of the contract which is ineffective at common law because of a lack of consideration may nevertheless be effective in equity by reason of estoppel. The rule of estoppel is based on the premise that a party who either expressly or by his conduct induces the other party to the contract to believe that the strict terms of the contract will not be enforced with the result that the other party to the contract relies on the inducement to the effect that the terms of the original agreement will not be strictly enforced, the party who is responsible for the inducement cannot without first giving reasonable notice enforce the terms of the original contract. The party inducing the departure from the contract will be held to be estopped or legally prevented from enforcing the original terms of the contract in that situation. The essentials for estoppel to operate are as follows:

(*a*) There must have been a representation either by conduct, expression or implication. In *Hughes* v. *Metropolitan Railway* (1877) a landlord by his conduct induced his tenant to believe that he would not enforce the repairing covenant in the lease during negotiations by the tenant for the sale of the lease, and it was held that the landlord could not subsequently sue the tenant for breaches of the covenant during that time. In *Central London Property Trust Ltd* v. *High Trees House Ltd* (1947) there was an express variation of the terms of the contract. The facts of the case were that the plaintiff landlord agreed with the tenants in a block of flats he rented that for the duration of the war, they would not have to pay the full rent. On the termination of the war, however, he brought an action to recover the arrears of rent for the period of the war during which he had agreed to waive his rights to the full rent and he further sought a declaration that he could claim full rent for the future. The court held the plaintiff was estopped from recovering the arrears of rent for the duration of the war, because he had expressly waived his strict rights under the contract. However, the court held that he could recover the full rent for the future on giving reasonable notice to the tenants of his intention to enforce his strict rights.

(b) The party to whom the statement is made must have relied on the other party's representation that his strict rights under the contract would not be enforced and the first party must thereby have suffered some detriment.

(c) It must be inequitable for the representor to go back on the representation.

The rule of equitable estoppel only suspends the rights of the representor. However, he can on giving reasonable notice enforce his original contractual rights strictly in the future, and he is only precluded from suing for damages for past breaches.

INTENTION TO CREATE LEGAL RELATIONS

A valid agreement which is supported by consideration will only be enforced by the courts as a contract if the parties intended their agreement to have legal consequences and to be legally binding. The courts are more likely to hold that the parties intended their agreement to have legal effect where an agreement is entered into at arm's length. However, the parties can expressly negative any suggestion that the agreement is intended to be legally binding. Thus in *Rose and Frank Co* v. *J. R. Crompton and Brothers Ltd* (1923) an agreement was entered into which was stated to be binding in honour only and not intended to be subject to the jurisdiction of the courts. The court held that whilst the parties cannot exclude the jurisdiction of the courts to enforce a contract by an express agreement, they can prevent their agreement being a contract by showing that it was not intended to have legal consequences and the courts would not therefore enforce it.

Whilst social and domestic arrangements are not usually intended to create legally binding agreements (e.g. accepting an invitation to dinner) the courts may nevertheless hold such an agreement to be enforceable and give legal affect to it where the parties clearly intended it to be binding on them. The rule is that if the agreement between the parties does not relate to a purely domestic situation, and is not connected with the routine management of the household, then the courts may hold it legally binding. In *Simpkins* v. *Pays* (1951), three ladies who lived in the same house entered a fashion competition and agreed that if they won the prize money it should be shared between them. The court held the agreement was intended to be legally binding. In *Jones* v. *Padavatton* (1969) a similar agreement between a mother and daughter was held to be legally binding.

PRIVITY OF CONTRACT

Only the parties to a contract may sue or be sued on it. The rule therefore is that only a person who has given consideration under the contract may bring proceedings to recover the benefit of the contract. In *Dunlop Pneumatic Tyre Company Ltd* v. *Selfridge & Co Ltd* (1915) a tyre manufacturer sold tyres to a wholesaler on the condition that upon their resale to a retailer the wholesaler would not only sell the tyres at the manufacturer's recommended wholesale price but also obtain a promise from the retailer that he too would resell them to the public at the manufacturer's recommended retail price. The wholesaler obtained such an assurance from a retailer who resold the tyres supplied to him at less than the manufacturer's recommended retail price. It was held that the manufacturer could not bring an action against the retailer since the manufacturer was not a party to the promise given by the retailer to the wholesaler. Similarly in *Scruttons Ltd* v. *Midland Silicones Ltd* (1962) the House of Lords held that the stevedores could not take the benefit of an exclusion clause entered into between the carriers and charterers of a ship when the stevedores negligently damaged the cargo when unloading it, unless they could show that there was a separate contract between the shipowners and themselves. In *Satterthwaite & Co Ltd* v. *New Zealand Shipping Co Ltd* (1971), however, stevedores were held to be entitled to the protection of an exclusion clause included in a contract between the carrier and the shipper of goods on the ground that the stevedores had given valid consideration by unloading the goods.

A number of statutory and common law exceptions have been developed to the doctrine that only a person who is a party to a contract and has given consideration under it can enforce the contract. Such exceptions have been made in the case of resale price maintenance agreements, life-, fire- and motor–insurance policies, and at common law negotiable instruments can be sued on by persons who for the time being are entitled to the benefit of them although they are not the original parties to the instrument.

COLLATERAL CONTRACTS

A contract between two parties may be accompanied by an independent and separate contract between one of the parties to the main contract and a third party relating to the same subject–matter. In *Shanklin Pier Ltd* v. *Detel Products Ltd* (1951) the plaintiffs employed contractors to paint a pier and relied on a promise made to them by the defendants that the paint would last for seven years, and so instructed the contractors to buy the paint from the defendants. The paint, in fact, was unsuitable and lasted three months. It was held that whilst the main contract for the sale of the paint was between the defendants and the contractors, the plaintiffs were entitled to succeed in their action on a collateral contract which existed between them and the defendants.

THE CONTENTS OF A CONTRACT

Express terms

Where a contract is in writing, the courts will not generally look beyond the written document, and the contract is governed exclusively by its terms. However, extrinsic evidence is admissible where it is necessary to show the capacity in which the parties contracted (e.g. as principals or as agents for third persons), or to ascertain the correct meaning of the terms of the contract, or to identify the subject–matter of the contract. Extrinsic evidence is also admissible if it is shown that the written contract was not intended to contain all the terms agreed between the parties.

Even where extrinsic evidence is inadmissible to vary, add to or contradict the terms of a written agreement, it may be shown that the parties entered into a contemporary oral agreement which suspended the operation of the written contract or a subsequent oral agreement varying its terms. (*see City & Westminster Properties Ltd* v. *Mudd* (1959)).

Implied terms

Certain types of terms may be implied into a contract to give full effect to the intentions of the parties. Following the decision in *Luxor (Eastbourne) Ltd* v. *Cooper* (1914), terms are implied if in fact they are so obviously necessary to give effect to the contract that the parties must have intended them to apply. Other types of terms may be implied by the law itself (e.g. the implied promise by a seller of goods that he is the owner of them or is authorised to sell them and that the goods he delivers will correspond with the description of them in the contract).

Standard form contracts

Standard form contracts are used in business to expedite the negotiation of transactions which are repeated over and over again (e.g. a manufacturer's standard conditions of sale which are incorporated in each individual contract of sale). However, such conditions may exploit the bargaining strength of one of the parties to the contract by the use of clauses wholly in his own favour, and Parliament has attempted to limit the effect of such clauses, particularly in consumer transactions.

EXCLUSION CLAUSES

A person who wishes to rely on the protection of an exclusion clause must show that it was incorporated into the contract and that the wording of the clause is sufficiently wide to cover the liability which would otherwise be imposed on him to make good the damage or loss suffered by the other party.

Where a written contract is entered into and a person signs a contractual document, it was held in *L'Estrange* v. *Graucob* (1934) that he is bound by the terms even though he has not read the document and is unaware of the terms of the exclusion clause. However, the clause must be set out in a document which has contractual force; so if an exclusion clause is set out in what in fact is a receipt, it will not be binding on the other party. (*See Chapleton* v. *Barry UDC* (1940)).

The party who seeks the protection of an exclusion clause must show that he took reasonable steps to bring it to the notice of the other party. Thus, in *Henderson* v. *Stevenson* (1875), it was held that where an exclusion clause is printed on the back of a ticket it will be ineffective unless there are words on the face of the ticket drawing attention to it or notice is given by some other equally effective means. It was said in *Thornton* v. *Shoe Lane Parking Ltd* (1971) that the more unusual or unexpected the nature of the exclusion clause the more difficult it will be for the party who seeks the protection of the exclusion clause to show that he has taken reasonable steps to bring it to the attention of the other party.

Where the parties have engaged in a course of dealings the exclusion clause may apply and give protection although it was not expressly brought to the attention of the other party in connection with that particular transaction, provided it can be shown that on previous occasions when the parties have dealt with each other the exclusion clause had been incorporated in the contracts made by them. (*See J. Spurling Ltd* v. *Bradshaw* (1956) and *McCutcheon* v. *David MacBrayne Ltd* (1964)).

Construction of exclusion clauses

Exclusion clauses will always be construed narrowly so as to restrict the protection given to the party who relies on it. In order to be valid the wording of the clause must indicate that it is to apply in the particular situation which has arisen. An exclusion clause which seeks to protect against a breach of a minor term of a contract will not be extended to cover a breach of a main term, the breach of which would normally entitle the innocent party to terminate the contract. Nor will a clause which merely gives protection for breach of an implied term of a contract be extended to cover a breach of an express term. In *Suisse Atlantique Société d'Armement Maritime SA* v. *Rotterdamsche Kolen Centrale (The Suisse Atlantique)* (1967) the court held that certain types of breach of contract are so serious that an exclusion clause will not protect the party in breach, and the contract will be treated as terminated by the breach so that the other party may in all circumstances sue for damages. The court held that such serious breaches of contract are of the two following types:

(*a*) *Breach of a fundamental term* where the term which is broken is so fundamental or important that it goes to the core of the contract and the party in breach cannot rely on the exclusion clause; for example, where under a contract of sale something entirely different is supplied from what has been contracted to be sold (*see Karsales (Harrow) Ltd* v. *Wallis* (1956)).

(*b*) *Fundamental breach* where the breach of contract is so serious that the whole basis of the contract has been destroyed; for example, where a carrier of goods delivers them to the wrong person.

The courts until recently had applied the principle that a party who was in breach of a fundamental term or had committed a fundamental breach could not rely on the exclusion clause for protection. In the case of *Securicor Transport Ltd* v. *Photo Production Ltd* (1980) the House of Lords held that whether an exclusion clause is to extend to a breach of a fundamental term or fundamental breach depends on the intention of the parties at the time of contracting. The court will not, however, allow a party to rely on an exclusion clause in circumstances where it would not be fair and reasonable for him to do so, and in deciding this question the court will look at the relative bargaining strength of the parties, the nature of the breach and whether it was a standard form contract.

The question whether an exclusion clause extends to a situation where the breach of contract is due to the guilty party's negligence is again one of construction. An exclusion clause will not protect a party where loss or injury is caused due to his negligence unless the exclusion clause expressly so provides or the guilty party would in any case only be liable if he were negligent and not simply because the other party has suffered loss. However, the courts have recently held that where the wording of the exclusion clause is so wide as to incorporate exemption from liability for negligence then it may be effective for that purpose. Thus, an exemption from liability "for loss caused by any means whatsoever" has been held wide enough to exclude the liability of a carrier of goods for negligence (*see Alderslade* v. *Hendon Laundry* (1945) and *Hair and Skin Trading Co* v. *Norman Air Freight* (1974)).

Unfair Contract Terms Act 1977

The effect of the Unfair Contract Terms Act 1977 is to restrict the ability of a party to exclude his normal liability in contract or tort for personal injury or damage to property. The Act deals with the following situations:

Liability in negligence
(*a*) By s. 2(1) the 1977 Act provides that normal contractual liability for negligence resulting in death or personal injury can no longer be excluded or restricted by a term which is incorporated in the contract or by a notice exhibited to the other party (e.g. a notice on premises which purports to exclude liability for personal injury to visitors who have paid admission fees).

(*b*) Section 2(2) further provides that in the case of any other loss or injury due to negligence a contractual clause or notice which purports to exclude or restrict liability for negligence will only be valid to the extent that it is reasonable, and the factors to be taken into account in deciding whether the exclusion provision is reasonable are set out in s. 11 of the Act. Even if the contractual term satisfies the test of reasonableness, it will be ineffective unless it is properly incorporated in the contract, and as a matter of construction it must be wide enough to cover the loss which has occurred.

(*c*) Section 5 of the Act provides that the liability of a manufacturer for negligence in the production of goods can no longer be restricted by the so called "manufacturer's guarantees" which give the owner specified rights (e.g. the right to replacement or repair of the goods) in place of the manufacturer's normal legal liabilities.

Standard form contracts

The Unfair Contract Terms Act 1977, s. 3, applies where one of the parties to the contract enters into it in the ordinary course of business whilst the other party is a consumer; it also applies when the contract contains standard terms introduced by one party as part of his business practice, and it is then immaterial whether the other party contracts as a consumer. Section 12 of the Act defines a consumer as a person who enters into the contract otherwise than in the ordinary course of business or does not hold himself out as contracting in the course of business. Section 3 provides that the party to the contract whose standard terms are embodied in the contract cannot protect himself from his normal legal liability by an exclusion clause unless the clause satisfies the test of reasonableness. Moreover, by s. 3(2) he cannot exclude his normal liability by provisions which do so indirectly (e.g. by a provision which enables him to perform his contractual obligation in a way which is substantially different from what is reasonably expected under the contract) or by a provision which enables him to fulfil his obligations even though he makes no promise at all (e.g. a contract of sale subject to the condition that delivery will only be made if the seller can obtain the goods). An exclusion clause will therefore be ineffective where there is a fundamental breach which goes to the root of the contract.

In *Rasbora* v. *JCL Marine Ltd* (1971) (a case which would now be decided under the Unfair Contract Terms Act 1977, s. 3), it was held that the manufacturers and sellers of a power boat could not under an exclusion clause avoid liability for damage to the boat and other property when it was destroyed due to electrical manufacturing defects. The clause deprived the buyer of any rights in respect of the quality or condition of the boat other than the right to have defective parts replaced and the sellers' judgment as to whether a part was defective was made conclusive. The court held that the exclusion clause was ineffective because the sale was a "consumer sale" within the Sale of Goods Act 1893, s. 55(7), even though the buyer was a company and therefore the sellers could not exclude the implied condition that the goods should be of "merchantable quality" under s. 14 of the 1893 Act. Moreover, even if the sale had not been a "consumer sale" the exclusion clause would have been ineffective because it was not fair and reasonable (within the Sale of Goods Act 1893, s. 55(4), (5)) to allow the sellers to rely on the clause. The electrical faults which were the cause of the damage to the boat amounted to a fundamental breach on the part of the sellers who were liable to the purchasers.

Test of reasonableness

The Unfair Contract Terms Act 1977, s. 11, sets out the factors to be considered in determining the reasonableness of an exclusion clause and requires the court to have regard to various matters in particular the circumstances which ought reasonably to have been known to the parties at the time the contract was entered into.

CAPACITY TO CONTRACT

Every person over the age of 18 years is presumed to have full capacity to enter into legally binding contracts which can be enforced fully by and against him. However, certain classes of persons are treated as being under a disability, and for their own protection the law does not hold them to be bound fully by their contracts. These persons are minors, persons under mental disability and corporations.

Minors

A person under the age of 18 years is a minor and does not have full capacity to enter into contracts. Contracts entered into by minors are divided into the following categories:

Valid contracts

A minor is bound by contracts entered into by him which are for the supply to him of necessary goods and services, namely those goods supplied and services rendered (e.g. education, legal advice, funeral services) which are reasonably necessary to maintain him in the state, station and degree of comfort to which he is accustomed (*see* the Infants Relief Act 1874, s. 1).

The question which has to be determined is whether it is reasonably appropriate for the minor, however rich, to acquire the goods or services in question having regard to his normal standard of living. It is for the supplier of the goods or services to show that the goods or services in question are actually necessaries. In *Nash* v. *Inman* (1908) a tailor failed to recover the price of eleven waistcoats and other clothes supplied to a wealthy undergraduate because he failed to show that the articles in question were necessary to keep the minor in the style of life to which he was accustomed.

If a contract for goods or services supplied is held to be for necessaries, the minor is only liable to pay a reasonable price for them. Thus a supplier of goods can only recover the normal market value of the goods or services supplied and not the contract price if it is in excess of the normal price.

Loans made to minors

A loan made to a minor cannot be recovered in law except in so far as the money (or some part of it) is used by the minor to purchase necessaries or discharge his liability for necessaries supplied to him. On the other hand, it was held in *Earl* v. *Peale* (1712) that a person who spends money in buying necessaries for a minor at his request is entitled to recover those amounts from the minor.

Service contracts

A minor is bound by a service contract if the contract is for necessaries and also if the contract on the whole is for his benefit.

Where, however, the service contract imposes an obligation on the minor to perform certain services, it will not be enforceable if the contract on the whole is harsh and oppressive. Thus, in *De Francesco* v. *Barnum* (1889) it was held that an employer could not enforce against a stage apprentice a contract which provided that the apprentice could not accept any other professional engagements without the employer's consent, that she would only be entitled to a salary if he actually used her services, that she could be sent abroad at any time and that her contract of employment could be terminated at any time.

Voidable contracts

Certain types of contracts entered into by a minor are binding on both parties, but the minor can set aside the contract by repudiating liability under it before he reaches the age of majority or within a reasonable time after he reaches his majority. If the minor fails to repudiate the contract, it is binding on him and can be enforced against him. The other party to the contract, if he is of full age, cannot avoid the contract. There are four types of contract which will bind the minor if not repudiated before he reaches majority or within a reasonable time thereafter:

(*a*) *Contracts concerning land.* A minor who enters into a contract to buy or to acquire an interest in land or to take a lease of any premises is bound by it unless he repudiates the contract. Similarly, a minor who contracts to sell land or to grant a lease or any premises is bound by the contract unless he repudiates it before reaching the age of majority or soon after.

(*b*) *Shares in companies.* A minor who agrees to subscribe for or to buy shares in a company is bound by the contract and is bound to pay for the shares unless he repudiates the contract.

(*c*) *Partnership.* A minor can enter into a partnership agreement but he cannot be made liable to creditors of the firm for partnership debts until he reaches his majority. If he does not repudiate the partnership agreement before he reaches majority or within a reasonable time afterwards he will be bound by the partnership agreement.

(*d*) *Marriage settlements.* A marriage settlement entered into by a minor is binding on him unless he repudiates it before or within a reasonable time after attaining his majority.

Rules relating to repudiation

A minor can repudiate a voidable contract either before he reaches majority or within a reasonable time thereafter, otherwise he loses the right to repudiate. The act of repudiation relieves the minor from any liability for the future. A minor cannot recover amounts paid by him under the contract before repudiation unless there has been a total failure of consideration for his promises (i.e. he has received nothing in return).

Void contracts

All other contracts entered into by a minor, in particular contracts for the supply of goods which are not necessaries, are void and cannot be enforced against him.

Persons under mental disability

A contract entered into by a person who is mentally ill and who is incapable of understanding the nature of the contract and giving genuine consent is voidable by him if the other party to the contract was aware of his mental condition. A mentally ill person must nevertheless pay a reasonable price for necessary goods and services supplied to him. A contract entered into by a mentally disordered person at a time when he was suffering from the disability can be ratified or confirmed by him when he recovers from his disability and the contract then becomes binding on him.

A person who enters into a contract in a state of drunkenness can avoid the contract if, at the time he entered into it, he was incapable of understanding the nature of the obligations he undertook. Such a person can ratify a voidable contract when he becomes sober, and even without ratification he is liable to pay a reasonable price for necessaries supplied to him.

Corporations

A company formed by Act of Parliament or under the Companies Acts 1948–1981 has capacity to enter into contracts and to bind itself by contracts only for the purpose of carrying on the kind of business it is authorised to carry on by its constitution. Moreover, the company's memorandum may expressly limit the power of a company or its board of directors to enter into certain types of contracts. If the company acts beyond its powers or in defiance of such limitations it is acting ultra vires and at common law the contract was void. The European Communities Act 1972, s. 9(1), however, now gives an innocent third party who enters into a contract with a company in good faith his normal remedies against the company unless he was aware that the company or its directors were exceeding their powers in entering into the contract.

MISTAKE, MISREPRESENTATION AND ILLEGAL CONTRACTS

Mistake

A mistake on the part of the parties to a contract will not generally invalidate it. Certain types of mistake, however, are regarded as being so fundamental that they may operate to nullify consent and so prevent a contract being made at all. At common law the effect of a mistake on the part of either or both of the parties is that the contract will be held to be void. A mistake can be fundamental if it is one of the following kinds.

(*a*) *Mistake as to the existence of the subject matter.* There is no contract where either one or both of the parties are mistaken as to the existence of the subject–matter of the contract. There is such a mistake if goods are sold in the belief that they still exist when in fact they have been destroyed.

(b) *Mistake as to the identity of the subject–matter.* There is no contract if the parties intend the contract to relate to different subject–matters. For example, in *Raffles* v. *Wichelhaus* (1864), the plaintiff sold 125 bales of cotton described as on board a steamship named "Pearless from Bombay" and, unknown to either the buyer or seller, there were two ships in Bombay of the same name but sailing at different times and the seller had one ship in mind and the buyer the other ship. The court held that there was no agreement between the parties.

Where both parties make the same mistake the court may hold the contract to be valid because despite the mistake, both parties contract about the same subject–matter. In *F. E. Rose (London) Ltd* v. *W. H. Pim Jnr & Co Ltd* (1953) a buyer agreed to buy horsebeans from the seller under the description feveroles which both of them understood to mean horsebeans even though a feverole is a different kind of bean. The court held there was a valid contract since the parties were in fact agreed on the subject–matter of the contract (i.e. horsebeans).

(c) *Mistake as to identity.* A mistake as to the identity of the parties may be held to negative consent. Thus where a seller intends to make an offer to B the contract will be void if C accepts the offer by inducing the seller to believe that he is really B. However, it may be difficult to prove mistake as to identity if the parties are in each other's presence at the time of contracting. Where the parties enter into a contract when both are personally present there is a presumption that the parties enter into the contract with each other irrespective of their correct names. In *Phillips* v. *Brooks Ltd* (1919) a rogue agreed to purchase jewellery from the plaintiff, and as he was about to make payment by cheque, he represented that he was Sir George Bullough and gave the real Sir George Bullough's correct address. The plaintiff checked a directory which showed Sir George Bullough as living at that address and allowed the rogue to take the jewellery in return for a cheque on which he had forged Sir George Bullough's signature. The cheque was dishonoured, and the plaintiff claimed that there was never a valid contract between him and the rogue, and so the rogue could not pass a title to the jewellery to a third party to whom he had resold it. The court held the plaintiff sold and intended to sell the jewellery to the person who came into the shop and therefore there was no mistake as to identity when the contract was made (*see also Ingram* v. *Little* (1961) for further discussion of these issues). Similarly, in *Lewis* v. *Averay* (1972) it was held the plaintiff intended to contract with the person before him when he sold a car to a rogue who represented himself to be Richard Green, the actor. The court held there was no mistake as to identity since the plaintiff intended to contract with the person before him.

Where the parties enter into a contract by correspondence and are not in each other's presence when the contract is concluded, mistake as to identity can avoid the contract. In *Cundy* v. *Lindsay* (1878) a rogue called Blenkarn ordered goods by post and signed the letter containing his name so that it looked like "Blenkiron & Co", a respectable firm known to the plaintiffs. The plaintiffs sent the goods at the address given by the rogue but the rogue failed to pay for them. He then sold the goods to a third party and in an action by the plaintiffs the court held there was no valid contract between the parties. The plaintiffs did not intend to deal with Blenkarn but with Blenkiron & Co, and as there was no sale to Blenkarn he could not pass a valid title to the goods to the third party.

However, a mere mistake as to the credit–worthiness or other attributes of one of the parties is not sufficient to avoid the contract. In *King's Norton Metal Co Ltd* v. *Edridge Merrett & Co Ltd* (1897) the plaintiffs received an order for goods from "Hallam & Co" which was described on the letterhead as a substantial business with various retail outlets throughout the country. In fact the business name "Hallam & Co" was used as an alias by a rogue and there was no substantial business carried on by any real firm called "Hallam & Co". The plaintiffs supplied goods on credit to "Hallam & Co" and the rogue resold them to the defendants but failed to pay for them. The court held there was a valid contract of sale since the plaintiffs intended to contract with the writer of the letter, and the only mistake on the part of the plaintiffs was as to his credit–worthiness, not his identity, and this was insufficient to avoid the contract.

(*d*) *Mistake as to the terms of the contract.* A mistake as to the terms of a contract may negative the consent of the parties and so prevent a contract existing. In *Hartog* v. *Colin & Shields* (1939) it was held that if A offers to sell rabbit skins at a fixed price per piece and B accepts the offer at the same price per pound, believing that to be what A offered there is no binding contract. However, mistake as to the quality of the goods contracted for will not avoid the contract. In *Smith* v. *Hughes* (1871) it was held the sale of oats which the purchaser believed to be old oats although the seller simply offered to sell oats could not be set aside unless the purchaser could also show that he honestly believed that the seller was offering to sell the oats as being old oats.

Fundamental mistake does not nullify consent

At common law although there has been a fundamental mistake there are a number of situations where it will not avoid the contract. Thus where one party in fact asserts the existence of the subject–matter the plaintiff can recover damages unless the goods or subject–matter existed at one time but have since perished: *see McRae* v. *Commonwealth Disposals Commission* (1950). If the subject–matter never existed at all (e.g. if the defendant contracts to sell a ship by name and as being at a certain place and there is in fact no ship there) there is a valid contract and the seller will be guilty of a breach of it when he fails to make delivery.

Mistake in equity

Equity may give relief to a person in a number of situations where the common law fails to provide a remedy; for example, where the mistake is not fundamental, or where there is a mistake which affects the value of the thing sold. In *Re Garnett* (1885) the testator left half of his estate to his sister and the other half to be divided equally between his two nieces. The nieces released their interest to the sister for £10,500 believing that to be its real value when in fact the interest the two nieces had in the land was worth substantially more. It was held the sale would be set aside. Equity may also set aside an agreement entered into under a mistake of law (*see Allcard* v. *Walker* (1896)) or as to the existence of a private right (*see Cooper* v. *Phibbs* (1867)). Moreover the remedies available in equity are wider than at common law, which will merely declare the contract void for lack of consent.

Mistake in signing documents

A party who signs a document is bound by the legal obligations embodied in it regardless of whether he read the document. Where a party signs a document which turns out to be entirely different from the document he believed he was signing, however, he can plead that the document is not binding on him. The plea is not available to a person who negligently failed to inquire into the nature or effect of the document, but has been applied to assist persons who due to some infirmity did not appreciate the nature of the document executed. Thus in *Foster* v. *Mackinnon* (1869) an elderly and nearly blind man was induced to endorse a bill of exchange under the belief he was executing a guarantee similar to the one he had executed on previous occasions. It was held the document should be set aside because it was executed under a mistaken belief as to its character even though to a person with normal sight its character would have been readily apparent. On the other hand, in *Saunders* v. *Anglia Building Society* (1971) an old lady signed a document which she thought was a deed making a gift of her house to her nephew when in fact the document amounted to a transfer of the house to her nephew's business associates. The court held that it could not set aside the transaction because the document she intended to execute was not fundamentally or radically different from the one she in fact signed, and she could easily have seen from the beginning of the document that the transfer was expressed to be made to a person other than her nephew.

Misrepresentation

A misrepresentation is a false statement of fact made by one party to a contract to the other during negotiations for the contract; to entitle the other party to relief the misrepresentation must induce him to enter into the contract. Mere sales talk or exaggerated commendations of the value of goods or services do not afford any grounds for relief. Thus to describe land as "fertile and improvable", as was done in *Dimmock* v. *Hallett* (1866), is a mere commendation and does not provide a ground for relief if the land is barren. A statement which constitutes an effective misrepresentation must satisfy the following requirements.

(*a*) *It must be a statement of fact.* A misrepresentation must be a misstatement of fact, as distinct from an expression of opinion or intention or a statement of law. A misstatement of opinion or of intention, however, may involve an implicit statement of fact and thus be a ground for avoiding the contract. This is so if it can be shown that a person who expressed the opinion or intention did not honestly believe in it or intend to do the act stated. In *Smith* v. *London & House Property Corporation* (1884) the vendor of certain property described the tenant as "most desirable" when in fact he knew that the tenant was in arrears with rent. The purchaser was held entitled to rescind the contract because, the court said, the vendor could not possibly have entertained the opinion he expressed. (*See also Brown* v. *Raphael* (1958).)

(*b*) *The statement must induce the other party to contract.* If the misrepresentation is to be a ground for relief it must have operated on the mind of the representee and actually induced him to enter the contract. If, therefore, the representee was unaware of the statement or if he was not induced to enter into the contract by the statement's being made he has no remedy. Thus in *Horsfall* v. *Thomas* (1862) the seller sold a gun which exploded after being used a few times. The buyer alleged the contract was entered into due to the fraudulent misrepresentation of the seller that the gun was sound, but the court rejected the claim since the buyer had examined the gun and relied on his own inspection and not the seller's statement. However, in *Redgrave* v. *Hurd* (1881) a solicitor who induced an innocent party to enter into a partnership by a false statement was held guilty of misrepresentation and the innocent party was entitled to have the contract set aside.

Whilst the misrepresentation need not be the sole inducement to enter into the contract, it was said in *Edgington* v. *Fitzmaurice* (1885) that it is sufficient if it can be shown to be one of the factors which induced the innocent party to enter into the contract. The misstatement must also be material and must have been effective in inducing the contract. It must be reasonable to conclude that, had the innocent party known of the true state of affairs, he would not have entered into the contract.

Types of misrepresentation
The type of remedy which becomes available for misrepresentation depends on the type of misstatement made by the misrepresenter and his state of mind at the time he made the statement.

Innocent misrepresentation
A statement made by a person in the belief that it is true, when in fact it is not, is an innocent misrepresentation. The representer does not act fraudulently even though he may have made the statement negligently. At common law an action for damages did not lie for a mere innocent misrepresentation unless the misrepresentation had become a term of the contract by being repeated in it.

Negligent misrepresentation
A negligent misrepresentation is one which is made carelessly, or without reasonable belief in its truth. Prior to the Misrepresentation Act 1967 a

negligent misrepresentation did not entitle the person to whom it was made to claim damages unless a duty of care was owed to him by the other party to advise him carefully because of the special personal relationship between them under the rule in *Hedley Byrne & Co Ltd* v. *Heller & Partners Ltd* (1964). The Misrepresentation Act 1967, however, has reduced the importance of establishing a special duty of care and s. 2(1) of the Act provides that where a person has entered into a contract as a result of a misrepresentation made to him, then the person making the representation is liable to him for his consequential loss in the same way as though the statement had been made fraudulently.

Fraudulent misrepresentation

A representation is a fraudulent one if it is made in the absence of an honest belief that it is true. In *Derry* v. *Peek* (1889) it was said that in order to show fraud it must be established that a false statement was made (*a*) knowingly, or (*b*) without belief in its truth or (*c*) recklessly whether it be true or false. A plaintiff who alleges fraud on the part of the other party must show the absence of an honest belief by the other party in the statement he made. The facts of *Derry* v. *Peek* were that a company issued a prospectus, stating that it had power under an Act of Parliament to use steam power for operating its tramway cars. The consent of the Board of Trade was in fact required before this could be done; when it was applied for, the Board of Trade refused to give consent. In an action brought by a plaintiff who had subscribed for shares in the company the directors pleaded that they had reasonable grounds to believe that the statement was true and in fact believed it to be true. It was held that the directors were not liable for fraudulent misrepresentation since they honestly and reasonably believed in the truth of what the prospectus said.

Remedies for innocent and non–negligent misrepresentation

The remedy of damages for innocent misrepresentation was available neither at common law or at equity. Prior to the Misrepresentation Act 1967, therefore, a misrepresentation which induced the other party to enter the contract gave the innocent party only a right to rescind the contract, but not to recover damages unless the misrepresentation had become a term of the contract. The Misrepresentation Act 1967, s. 2(2), however, provides that the court may in its discretion award damages instead of rescission, if an award of damages would be just and equitable. A separate right to claim damages is now given under s. 2(1) of the same Act where the misrepresentation, although innocent, was made negligently.

An innocent party who wants the contract set aside for misrepresentation may either rescind it by communicating his intention not to be bound by the contract to the party responsible for the misrepresentation or alternatively by obtaining an order of the court. He must do one or other of these things within a reasonable time after discovering the falsity of the misrepresentation and within a reasonable time after the contract is made.

The court will refuse to make an order for rescission in the following cases:

(*a*) where there has been an innocent misrepresentation if the parties cannot be restored to their original position;

(*b*) where the innocent party, either expressly or by his conduct, affirms the contract after he gains knowledge of the untruth of the statement made to him;

(*c*) where an innocent third party has acquired rights in the subject–matter of the contract before the innocent party exercises his right to rescind;

(*d*) where there has been a fraudulent misrepresentation; the innocent party can rescind within a reasonable time after he has actual knowledge of the fraud, however long that may be after the contract was entered into.

In the case of innocent misrepresentation, lapse of time is a bar to rescission if the innocent party fails to rescind within a reasonable time after the contract was made, even if he does not discover the falsity of the misrepresentation within that time. In *Leaf* v. *International Galleries* (1950) the vendor of a painting represented it to be by Constable and the purchaser sought to rescind the contract five years later when he discovered the misrepresentation. The court held that the purchaser could not rescind the contract. In the case of an innocent misrepresentation the contract must be rescinded within a reasonable time from the time of the misrepresentation, whilst in cases of fraudulent misrepresentation time does not run until the fraud is discovered.

Remedies for negligent misrepresentation

Where the defendant was under a duty to exercise reasonable care in making statements to the other party in negotiating a contract, the innocent party can, in addition to rescinding the contract, claim damages from the defendant at common law on the principles set out in *Hedley Byrne & Co Ltd* v. *Heller & Partners Ltd* (1964) and *Esso Petroleum Co Ltd* v. *Mardon* (1976). In any case of negligent misrepresentation an action will also lie under the Misrepresentation Act 1967, s. 2, and the court may in its discretion award damages instead of ordering rescission under s. 2(2). In an appropriate case, therefore, the court may order damages instead of rescinding the contract.

Fraudulent misrepresentation

An innocent party who has been induced to enter into a contract due to fraudulent misrepresentation may both rescind the contract and claim damages for his consequential loss. Again, an innocent party can rescind the contract either by a court order or by notifying the party responsible for the misrepresentation. Additionally the innocent party can bring an action at common law for the tort of deceit if he can prove actual loss.

Illegal contracts

A contract although otherwise valid may be unenforceable if it is illegal either because the purpose of the contract is unlawful or the method of performance intended is illegal.

The effects of illegality

A contract the purpose of which is illegal is unlawful and therefore void and neither party can enforce it. For example, in *Re Mohmond and Ispahani* (1921), the plaintiff sold linseed oil to the defendant under the belief that he had the necessary licence required by statute. The defendant rejected the goods and it was held that the contract of sale of linseed oil was illegal and the plaintiff had no cause of action. Any money or goods transferred between the parties to an illegal contract cannot be recovered by the payer or transferor. However, property may be recoverable if the true owner can prove his title to it without relying on the illegal contract. Thus, in *Bowmakers Ltd* v. *Barnet Instruments Ltd* (1945) the plaintiffs succeeded in an action for wrongful conversion of certain machine tools which they owned but which had been hired out to the defendants under an illegal hiring contract. The court held that the action was based by the plaintiffs on their title to the goods and was not to enforce the unlawful agreement between the parties. Consequently there was no obstacle to the action proceeding. (*See also Singh* v. *Ali* (1960).)

A contract which is lawful at its inception may be carried out in an unlawful manner; in such a case, whether an innocent party who enters into the contract or lawfully performs his part of the contract can maintain an action depends largely on the purpose of the rule of law or the statute which makes performance of the contract in a certain manner unlawful. Moreover, an innocent party who refuses to participate in the illegality is not deprived of his rights.

Contracts made illegal by statute

Certain types of contract are made illegal by various statutes and in such cases the statute imposes the penalty for example, any agreement to bring a person into the country so as to avoid going through immigration control would be contrary to the Immigration Acts and illegal.

Contracts illegal at common law

The courts have at common law held certain types of contracts to be illegal on the grounds of public policy (e.g. contracts entered into between parties where the purpose of the agreement is to commit a crime or tort). For example, an agreement to smuggle whisky into the USA when it was contrary to American law was held in *Foster* v. *Driscoll* (1932) to be illegal in English law. Contracts are illegal at common law if they are prejudicial to the administration of justice or are contrary to public policy; for example, an agreement not to appear at a court hearing on the question whether a bankrupt should be discharged is unlawful (*see Kearley* v. *Thomason* (1890)). Moreover, an agreement tending towards the maintenance of litigation is illegal unless the party giving financial assistance has a genuine and substantial interest in the case. In *Trendtex Trading Corporation* v. *Crédit Suisse* (1980) it was held that a guarantee by Crédit Suisse to pay the legal costs of an action brought by Trendtex against the Central Bank of Nigeria was not void for maintenance. Crédit Suisse had shown it had a substantial interest in the outcome of the legal proceedings since that was the only possibility it had to recover amounts owed to it by Trendtex. Contracts to defraud the Revenue are also illegal; so, in *Miller* v. *Karlinski* (1945), where the purpose of a scheme between the employer and employee was for the employee to avoid tax on his income, the agreement was illegal. Contracts which tend towards sexual immorality are also illegal. In *Pearce* v. *Brookes* (1866) the owner of a brougham was held not entitled to recover the rent on the hire of the vehicle because he was aware it would be used for the purposes of prostitution.

Contracts void by statute
If a contract is made void by statute neither party can enforce it. For example, the Gaming Act 1845 provides that all gaming and wagering contracts whereby one party is to win and the other to lose on the occurrence of an uncertain future event are null and void, and so neither party can enforce the agreement. The Act renders not only the original agreement itself void but any subsequent promise made by the loser to pay a lost bet on further considerations being provided.

Contracts void at common law
The common law treats the following types of contracts as void:

(*a*) contracts to oust the jurisdiction of the courts; these are void on the grounds of public policy;

(*b*) contracts prejudicial to the status of marriage: in *Herman* v. *Charlesworth* (1905) a contract to pay money by a lady in return for the defendant introducing her to members of the opposite sex with a view to marriage was a marriage brokage contract and illegal;

(*c*) contracts in restraint of trade: (whether it be a restraint on the freedom of an employee to use his skills or set up a rival business) are void if the restrictions are unreasonable. The courts have established a number of requirements which a provision in restraint of trade must satisfy if it is to be given effect. An employer, even in the absence of a covenant in restraint of trade, is entitled to a certain amount of protection against former employees. An employer can thus obtain an injunction to prevent an employee from disclosing or using the employer's trade secrets (*see Printers & Finishers Ltd* v. *Holloway* (1965)) where the information is distinct from the use of his skills by an employee. An employee is justified, however, in disclosing any trade secrets of his former employer if the employer is doing an unlawful act. Otherwise a former employer who wants protection against the employee, either from setting up a rival business or working for a rival employee, can do so if there is an agreement between the employer and employee that he will refrain from doing so. In order for such a covenant to be held enforceable the courts have held:

(*i*) there must be an interest of the promisee meriting protection. An employer cannot restrain an employee from using his skill even though that skill was acquired whilst working for his former employer. In *Herbert Morris*

Ltd v. *Saxelby* (1916) the defendant covenanted with his former employers that he would not work in the fork lift industry in the UK and Ireland for seven years. The court held that the covenant was too wide and therefore void. An employer can only place a restraint on his former employees to the extent necessary to protect himself against the improper use of the employer's trade secrets. To that extent the employer has to show some interest which, if not protected, would result in loss or injury to the employer's business;

(*ii*) the covenant is only valid if it is reasonably necessary for the protection of the covenantee's interest. The covenant must be reasonable, first, with regard to the area in which it is to apply. Thus in *Nordenfelt* v. *Maxim Nordenfelt* (1894), a clause which prevented the vendor of an armaments business from setting up a rival business or from engaging in the same business anywhere in the world was held valid because of the restricted nature of the market and customers. In *Mason* v. *Provident Clothing and Supply Company* (1913), however, a clause preventing a former employee from entering into employment with another employer within a radius of 25 miles of the employer's place of business was held void because it applied to too large an area. Secondly, the time during which the restraint is to apply should not be unreasonable. In *Fitch* v. *Dewes* (1921) a life-long restraint was held invalid;

(*iii*) the activities covered by the restraint must not extend to an activity which is irrelevant to the interest to be protected. In *Attwood* v. *Lamont* (1920) the defendant's contract of employment contained a clause that he should "not, either on his own behalf or for anyone else, work as or enter into business as a tailor, general draper, hatter, haberdasher ..." The court held that the plaintiff, a tailor, could not enforce the covenant because its scope extended beyond the business of a tailor and therefore was void;

(*iv*) the restraint must be reasonable and fair, and the law will have regard to the bargaining strength of the parties. There is an inference that the restraint is unfair if the party imposing it is in a stronger bargaining position. For example, where music publishers entered into a contract with a young, unknown songwriter whereby they were given a copyright to exploit his work anywhere in the world for five years but with a right to terminate the agreement at any time, the court held that the agreement was void because it was an improper restraint of trade. The court said that when one of the parties to the contract is in a weaker position, then there is on inference that the agreement is unfair and it is up to the party seeking to enforce the agreement to show that the terms are not unreasonable;

(*v*) finally, a contract in restraint of trade will be invalid if it is against public policy to give effect to it. A clause may be held invalid even if it satisfies the above requirements, if to give effect to it would be against public policy; where, for example, the effect of the clause is to restrict competition and induce conditions whereby a monopoly is or may be created in the hands of the party imposing the restraint. Thus where an agricultural society changed its rules to prevent members selling any milk produced by them in County Kerry to anyone except the society, the court held that the rules amounted to an unfair restraint of trade and therefore to that extent were void. The effect of enforcing the rules would have been to eliminate or reduce competition and thereby create a monopolistic situation (*see McEllistrim* v. *Ballaymacelligott Co-operative Agricultural & Dairy Society Ltd* (1919)).

PERFORMANCE AND DISCHARGE OF CONTRACT

In order to discharge his obligations under a contract, the method of performance used by a party must comply with the terms of the contract. A failure to perform in accordance with his contractual obligations will give the other party the right to bring an action for damages, or if the breach is of a more serious nature, it will entitle the innocent party to have the contract terminated.

The courts have traditionally divided contractual obligations into conditions and warranties. A breach of a condition amounted to a breach of a term which was fundamental to the contract and entitled the injured party to have the contract set aside and also to sue for damages. On the other hand, a breach of warranty entitled the injured party merely to sue for damages, but not to terminate the contract. In *Hong Kong Fir Shipping Co Ltd* v. *Kawasaki Kisen Kaisha Ltd* (1962) the charterers of a ship repudiated the charterparty contract when the ship broke down for the second time and had to be taken into a dock for repair. The House of Lords held that the charterers had wrongfully repudiated the charter and held that, whilst the terms in a contract are divided into conditions and warranties a contract may contain terms which are in fact neither. The court should not grant relief on the basis of whether the breach is one of condition or warranty, but should look at the type of damage or loss caused as a consequence of the breach and grant a remedy accordingly. These types of terms have often been called "innominate terms".

The order of performance

Certain types of conditions require one party to perform his contractual obligations before the other party, and if the party who is required to initiate performance by fulfilling his part of the contract fails to do so, the other party to the contract need not commence performance. This type of an express term is known as a condition precedent.

The terms of the contract, however, may provide, or it may be implied, that performance must be concurrent or simultaneous, and neither party can then bring an action for breach unless he himself has performed, or is ready to perform his part of the contract. Thus in a contract involving the sale of goods, the delivery of goods and the payment of the purchase price are usually simultaneous.

Alternatively, the promises of the parties under a contract may be completely independent and each party can enforce the other's promise although he has not himself performed his own contractual obligations.

The obligation to perform

The general rule is that performance should be complete and exactly in accordance with the terms of the contract, unless the parties waive or vary their rights to enforce strict compliance.

Where a contract imposes on one of the parties a duty to perform an entire obligation he cannot recover anything for work only partly completed. In *Cutter* v. *Powell* (1795) the widow of a seaman was held not to be entitled to any payment of wages for work done by her husband when he died during a voyage, because under the terms of contract he was only entitled to receive payment on completion of the entire voyage. Similarly, in *Sumpter* v. *Hedges* (1898) a builder who contracted to receive a lump sum payment on the completion of two houses was held not to be entitled to any payment when he failed to complete both houses.

Where, however, a contract imposes severable obligations (e.g. the delivery of goods is to be by instalments), a party who performs a part of the contract can enforce his rights to a proportionate part of the consideration for the whole of his promise.

Where a party has performed the term of the contract substantially but there is a defect as to the quality of the work, it may be possible to recover the amount of the contract minus the cost of correcting the defect (*see Hoenig* v. *Isaacs* (1952)). Similarly, where there has been only partial performance of the contract, the party who has performed partially can recover under a quantum meruit.

Frustration of a contract

Whilst performance of the parties' contractual obligations may discharge a contract, the obligations imposed on the parties may also be discharged where performance becomes impossible due to a frustrating event for which neither party is responsible. Where, for example, the subject–matter of the contract is destroyed (*see Appleby* v. *Myers* (1867) and *Taylor* v. *Caldwell* (1863)) or the performance of the contract becomes illegal (*see Errel Bieber & Co* v. *Rio Tiato Co Ltd* (1918)), the contract is frustrated. It is not mere hardship or inconvenience which frustrates the contract, but the circumstances must arise which mean that if the parties were compelled to perform the contract, they would in fact be performing a wholly different contract from the one they entered into (*see Davis Contractors Ltd* v. *Fareham UDC* (1956)).

The remedies provided by the common law were inadequate to compensate the parties and the Law Reform (Frustrated Contracts) Act 1943 now provides that where a contract is discharged due to frustration:

(*a*) any sums payable under the contract before the frustrating event cease to be payable when the contract is frustrated;

(*b*) any sums already paid under the contract can be recovered; but

(*c*) if a party to whom these amounts were paid or payable had incurred expenses before the frustrating event the court may allow him to retain or recover the expenses already incurred or part of those expenses;

(*d*) the court may award compensation to a party who has conferred benefits on the other party under the contract to the extent of the value of those benefits;

(*e*) rights which accrue in the future cannot be enforced.

Breach of a contract

There is a breach of contract when one of the parties to the contract either fails to perform his obligations when performance becomes due or indicates before the date of performance that he will not perform his obligations under the contract. Where a party repudiates the contract before the date of performance there is an anticipatory breach, and the innocent party can either accept the breach immediately and bring an action for breach of contract, or he can treat the contract as continuing and bring an action for wrongful failure to perform when the date of performance has passed. If the innocent party treats the contract as continuing until the date of performance has actually passed he defers bringing an action at his own peril and may lose his right if circumstances intervene which frustrate the contract (*see Avery* v. *Bowden* (1855)).

Effect of breach

(*a*) Where there is a breach of condition or other innominate term which goes to the root of the contract, the innocent party may treat the contract as discharged and have it set aside and/or sue for damages. Alternatively the injured party can treat the contract as continuing and sue for damages alone.

(*b*) Where the breach is one of warranty or a lesser term the injured party can only bring an action for damages.

REMEDIES FOR BREACH OF CONTRACT

Damages

The only remedy available at common law for breach of contract is an award of damages, which is a monetary sum fixed by the court to compensate the injured party. In order to recover substantial damages the innocent party must show he has suffered actual loss or he will only be entitled to a nominal amount of damages in recognition of the fact that he has a valid cause of action; for example, where the court recognises that the plaintiff has been wronged but for some reason considers that his action is frivolous, with the result that only 1p or 5p damages are awarded.

The injured party can recover such damages as may fairly and reasonably be considered as arising naturally or such damages as may reasonably be supposed to have been in the contemplation of both parties as the probable result of the breach of contract when they entered into the contract. In *Hadley* v. *Baxendale* (1854) it was held that the plaintiffs were not entitled to damages for loss caused to them when the defendants delayed the delivery of a shaft required to keep the plaintiffs' mill working. The court held that the defendants could not foresee that a delay would result in a stoppage of work at the mill. The principle established by this case has been applied in later cases. In *Victoria Laundry (Windsor) Ltd* v.*Newman Industries Ltd* (1949), the defendant failed to deliver a boiler for the plaintiff's laundry and the laundry had to be closed down during a five–month period whilst the plaintiff was awaiting the delivery of the boiler. The plaintiff sought to recover for the loss of the profits it would have earned during the period the laundry had to be closed down and for the loss of certain lucrative dyeing contracts it had entered into. The court held that the test was whether the loss was "reasonably foreseeable" and this depends on the state of the defendant's knowledge at the date of the contract. The defendant in fact knew that the boiler was required for immediate use and therefore could foresee the loss which would result from delay, but he was not liable for the loss of the especially lucrative dyeing contracts since he had no knowledge of them when the contract for the boiler was made; moreover, he could not reasonably foresee that the plaintfiff would enter into contracts yielding especially high profits.

The test of reasonableness contemplated in the rule governing the damages recoverable for breaches of contract is applied on the assumption that the defendant must foresee all likely and expected consequences of his breach of contract.

In *The Heron II* (1967) the plaintiffs chartered a ship from the defendants to carry sugar from Constanza to Basrah with the intention of selling the sugar on arrival at Basrah. The defendant caused the ship to deviate during the voyage and the sugar arrived nine days late at Basrah by which time the price of sugar had fallen. The plaintiffs consequently brought an action to recover the amount they would have received for the sugar had the defendant not deviated from the route. The House of Lords held that although the defendant was not actually aware that the sugar was for sale in Basrah he must have realised that it would be sold on arrival, and since the market price was likely to fluctuate the plaintiff was entitled to recover his loss. The court held that there must be a "very substantial" or "serious possibility" of loss occurring in order to satisfy the test of remoteness in contract. The reasoning in the House of Lords establishing the test of remoteness of damage in contract was followed in *H. Parsons (Livestock) Ltd* v. *Uttley Ingham & Co Ltd* (1978) where the defendants were held liable when they supplied the plaintiffs with a hopper for storing pig food, because the hopper provided only defective ventilation for the food so that it became mouldy and diseased with the result that the plaintiff's pigs died after having contracted a disease from eating the food. The Court of Appeal held the defendants liable for the loss of the pigs on the grounds that the defendants could have contemplated a "serious possibility" that the pigs might become ill or die as a result of the breach of contract.

Mitigation of damages

A party who has suffered a breach of contract is under a legal duty to seek to mitigate his loss and he must take reasonable steps to reduce the loss caused by the breach of contract as far as possible. For example, a buyer who accepts a seller's anticipatory breach is bound to mitigate by buying substitute goods at the current market price. If the market price of the goods exceeds the contract price, he is entitled to recover the difference he has paid.

Penalty clauses

The parties to a contract may agree between themselves on a fixed sum as damages to be paid in the event of breach of contract. If the fixed sum is a genuine pre–estimate of the probable loss which will be caused, then the agreement is binding on the parties even if the actual loss incurred is greater. In *Cellulose Acetate Silk Co Ltd* v. *Widnes Foundry (1926) Ltd* (1933) a contract for the construction of an acetone recovery plant provided that if completion was delayed the contractors were to pay £20 per week by way of penalty. The plant was completed 30 weeks late and the owners suffered loss amounting to £5,850. The court held they could only recover £600, although the parties knew that the owner's loss due to a delay in completion would be in excess of £20 per week. The object of the clause must have been to limit the contractor's liability, and was not merely a penalty for wrongful failure to complete the contract. Similarly, in *Dunlop Pneumatic Tyre Co Ltd* v. *New Garage & Motor Co Ltd* (1905), the payment of £5 per tyre if the defendants sold them in breach of an agreement entered into by them with the plaintiffs was not penal but an attempt to limit the liability of the defendants. In this case, however, the parties could not, because of the uncertainty of the damage likely to be caused, make a genuine pre–estimate of the damages. The sum agreed between the parties is termed "liquidated damages", and it must be distinguished from an amount which operates, not as a pre–estimate of the damages, but as a penalty whose purpose is to deter a party from breaking the contract. A penalty clause is void, and the plaintiff will only be able to recover damages assessed under the normal principles. If the amount of "damages" agreed by the parties is exorbitant or unconscionable in comparison with any actual damage which might arise then the amount will be held to be a penalty and therefore irrecoverable.

Equitable remedies

The equitable remedies for breach of contract are discretionary and will only be granted where damages are inadequate to compensate the plaintiff.

Specific performance

The effect of an order of specific performance is to compel the defendant actually to perform his part of the contract instead of paying damages for not performing it. An order of specific performance will only be granted where damages are an inadequate remedy (e.g. where the contract involves the sale of goods which are unique so that the plaintiff cannot obtain a satisfactory substitute on the open market). A contract for the sale of the Mona Lisa, other conditions being satisfied, will be specifically enforced since the purchaser cannot obtain a substitute. Similarly, contracts for the sale of land or of a house will be specifically enforced since the law regards both as unique. In *Wolverhampton Corporation* v. *Emmons* (1961) the plaintiff corporation acquired land for the purposes of reconstruction and subsequently sold part of it to the defendant, who covenanted to demolish the houses on it and to build new ones. The demolition was carried out and plans for the new houses approved. The court ordered specific performance of the covenant to build since the defendant's obligations were defined precisely and damages would be an inadequate remedy to the corporation. A refusal to grant an order of specific performance would result in the site being left vacant and that would be a loss to the corporation of rents and rates.

The courts will not, however, order specific performance in the following situations:

(*a*) if the contract is for personal services (e.g. a contract of employment where one of the parties is employed to paint a portrait or write a book or to sing at a concert). Moreover, the Trade Union and Labour Relations Act 1974, s. 16, provides that the courts may not make an order of which the effect is to enforce specifically a contract of employment;

(*b*) if the effect of an order would be that the courts would have to supervise in detail compliance with the order. In *Ryan* v. *Mutual Tontine Association* (1893) the courts refused specific performance of an undertaking to have a porter "constantly in attendance";

(*c*) if the contract would not be specifically enforceable against the person asking for specific performance (e.g. where the person seeking the order is a minor).

Injunction

An injunction will only be granted where damages are an inadequate remedy. An injunction can be of a negative character, because it restrains one of the parties from doing a certain act in breach of the contract he has entered into. For example, in *Mason* v. *Provident Clothing & Supply Co Ltd* (1913) it was held that an injunction may be granted to prevent an employee from breaching a covenant in his contract of employment that he will not enter into similar employment within 25 miles of the area where the employers have their business. Similarly, in *Nordenfelt* v. *Maxim Nordenfelt* (1894) an injunction was granted to restrain the vendor of an armaments business from setting up a rival business, and a covenant in the contract of sale which prevented the vendor from entering into the same business anywhere in the world was held valid.

Alternatively the courts may grant a mandatory injunction, which, like an order of specific performance, requires the defendant to do a particular act in order to fulfil his contractual obligations. For example, where an actress enters into a contract to attend drama lessons, the courts may grant an injunction restraining her from doing an act the result of which would be that she would be unable to attend those lessons and be in breach of her obligation under the contract.

PROBLEMS

1. Distinguish an offer from an invitation to treat. When does an offer terminate?

2. What are the rules relating to the method of acceptance of an offer if:

(a) the offeror specifies a method of acceptance;

(b) the offeror tells the offeree that he will take his failure to reject the offer as signifying its acceptance;

(c) the acceptence is by some instantaneous method of communication (e.g. telephone or telex)?

3. Unless a contract is by deed there must be valid consideration on the part of the promisee for a contract to exist. What forms can consideration take? What are the rules relating to valid consideration?

4. Explain the doctrine of estoppel. When will it operate to bind the parties to an apparent agreement?

5. Explain the rule of privity of contract.

6. What is meant by the term "fundamental breach" or "breach of a fundamental term"?

7. What are the rules relating to mistake as to the identity of a person and mistake in signing a document as factors invalidating a contract?

8. What are the rules relating to a misrepresentation inducing a contract? Distinguish between innocent, fraudulent and negligent misrepresentation.

9. What are the remedies for innocent and fraudulent misrepresentation?

10. What contracts are illegal and what is the effect of the illegality?

11. When is a contract frustrated? Does a party who has performed his part of the contract and conferred benefits on the other party before the frustrating event have any right to compensation?

12. Give an account of the common law and equitable remedies for breach of contract.

CHAPTER THREE

Commercial Agency

OBJECTIVES

It is proposed in this chapter to examine the law governing an agency relationship created for commercial purposes. In particular the chapter deals with:

(a) the creation of the agency relationship;

(b) the agent's authority to bind his principal;

(c) the ratification by the principal of the agent's acts;

(d) the duties of the agent to his principal, including the duties arising out of the fiduciary nature of the relationship;

(e) the duties of the principal towards the agent;

(f) the remedies available to both the principal and the agent against each other for breach of their respective obligations;

(g) the different classes of principals and agents;

(h) the legal relationship between the agent and the third party with whom he deals; and

(i) termination of the agency relationship.

THE AGENCY RELATIONSHIP

An agency relationship arises when one person, who is called the agent, is authorised or considered by law as authorised to represent another person, called the principal, in such a way as to be able to affect the principal's legal position. The contract between the principal and agent is subject to the normal rules of contract law, and as such the parties may enter into either a written or an oral contract. In order therefore to constitute one party the agent of another the principal should expressly or implicitly agree that the other shall represent him or act on his behalf, and the party who is to act as the agent must consent to represent the principal in the transaction or negotiations. The parties must normally contract expressly to be bound by the agency relationship, but an agency relationship may also arise by operation of law in two situations, namely an agency by estoppel or agency by necessity.

An agency by estoppel arises where one person (the principal) induces a third person to believe by his words or conduct that a particular person is authorised to act as agent for the principal. The principal cannot subsequently deny the existence of the agency relationship if to do so would prejudice a third person who consequently is treated as being in the same position as though the principal had in fact authorised the agent to act on his behalf. The doctrine of estoppel will operate either where the agent has no authority to represent another as his agent, but the person who is now treated as the principal has conferred all the indicia of an agency on him, or alternatively, the agent may have a real authority to act for the principal, but the latter is estopped by his conduct from denying to a third person that the agent has additional powers. The requirements for estoppel to operate under the normal rules of law have similarly to apply to the agency relationship: there must be a representation (either express or implied) on the part of the principal; there must be a reliance on that representation by the third person; and the third person relying on the representation must alter his position as a result of that reliance.

An agency of necessity arises in situations of urgent necessity, usually from some accident and it is impossible for the agent to contact the person in whose interest he acts. The application of the agency of necessity is restricted in modern times because, due to modern forms of communication, it is rare that the agent or bailee cannot communicate with the person whose interests he seeks to protect. An example of a situation where an agency of necessity will be created is where perishable goods in the custody of a bailee begin to deteriorate. The bailee must then act in good faith and for the benefit of the owner of the goods either by exercising the power to sell the goods which the law confers on him or by taking steps to prevent further deterioration.

Once the agency relationship is established the agent is invested by law with authority to bind the principal as though the principal were acting personally, and if the agent acts within the authority conferred on him, the principal is bound by the contract.

THE AGENT'S AUTHORITY

A principal will only be bound to a third party by contracts entered into if the agent acts within the scope of his authority. If the agent acts outside the authority conferred on him the principal may ratify or confirm his agent's acts and make them binding on him, otherwise the agent may be held personally liable under the contract or other transaction.

Types of authority

The type of authority which the agent has vested in him will depend on the type of agency relationship that exists between the agent and his principal. If the agency relationship is created by an express contract the agent's authority may be written or parol. If there is a written authority given to the agent the ordinary rules of construction will apply and the agent's written authority will be deemed to be conclusive as to the extent of his powers. In such a case the agent will not be deemed to have powers beyond those expressly conferred in the document (*see Robinson* v. *Mollett* (1875)). If the agent derives his authority from the customs of the trade or profession in which he practises, however, he will be deemed to have such authority, although the written authority given to him does not expressly so provide.

If there is any ambiguity relating to an interpretation of the agent's express authority, then, provided the agent acts in good faith and in accordance with a reasonable construction of his authority, he will be treated as having acted within its limits. Thus in *Boden* v. *French* (1851) the sale of coal by the agent at a higher price than authorised by his principal and the grant of two months credit to the buyer was held not to be within the terms of his agency. However, in *Ireland* v. *Livingston* (1872), the acquisition of 400 tons of sugar, which was the maximum the agent could obtain at the specified price, was a reasonable exercise by the agent of his authority to purchase approximately 500 tons of sugar.

Implied, usual and customary authority

An agent may have certain implied authority in addition to any express authority, whether because the express authority conferred on the agent is insufficient to enable him to perform his functions, or because a reasonable interpretation to the agent's express authority may make it necessary to imply certain additional powers on the agent. The implied authority of an agent can therefore be said to be part of the agent's actual authority which the principal has conferred on the agent by implication of law. Generally an agent has implied authority to do everything necessary and incidental to the performance of his express functions; for example, an agent authorised to make a binding contract for the sale of a house is implicitly authorised to sign a written memorandum of the contract of sale to satisfy the Law of Property Act 1925, s. 40.

Usual authority

An agent employed to act for a principal in the ordinary course of his trade, business or profession will implicitly be authorised to do what is usual in that trade, profession or business. The agent's usual authority rests on the objective idea of what is usual in a particular trade, profession or business and the principal is liable for all the acts of the agent which are within the authority usually confided to an agent of that character. If the principal has placed any restrictions on the authority which the agent would usually have in the course of his trade, profession or business, then unless the principal takes reasonable steps to notify a third party who deals with the agent of those limitations, the secret reservation depriving the agent of that authority is ineffective (*see* *Watteau* v. *Fenwick* (1893) and *Edmunds* v. *Bushell & Jones* (1865)).

Customary authority

Where the agent is employed to act for his principal in a certain market or business place, then the agent is implicitly authorised to act in accordance with the usages and customs of that market or business place. Strictly speaking, such customary authority is simply a variety of the agent's usual authority. The custom must be known to the principal or be so notorious that the principal cannot be heard to say that he had no knowledge of it. The custom must also be lawful and reasonable. In *Robinson* v. *Mollett* (1875), the agent, in accordance with a custom of his trade having purchased tallow in large quantities, sold a quantity of it to his principal. The principal refused to accept the tallow when he discovered that what was tendered to him was owned by the agent personally. The principal was held not bound by a custom of the trade of which he had no knowledge and which was in any case unreasonable because of the conflict it permitted between the agent's interests and his duty to his principal.

Agency by estoppel

Where estoppel operates to create an agency relationship the agent has apparent or ostensible authority to bind his principal. Agency by estoppel is not the result of agreement between the principal and the agent. The agent's authority is the product of the principal's conduct or representation that the agent is authorised to act on his behalf. The agent is considered to have such authority as a reasonable third party would understand the agent to have from the conduct or statements of the principal. In *Rimmer* v. *Webster* (1902), the principal executed deeds of transfer of certain bonds with the names of the transferees left blank and the agent filled in the names of a third party as transferee; the third party was held to have a good title to the bonds although the agent acted outside the scope of his actual authority by transferring the bonds to him. In *Fry* v. *Smellie* (1913) it was similarly held that the principal could not recover the bonds which the agent had transferred by completing a blank transfer, because he had vested the agent with all the indicia of a valid title and any secret limitation of the agent's authority could not affect the third party's title.

Agency by operation of law

The authority of an agent depends on what the law presumes the principal would have agreed to the agent doing, if the principal had been in a position to convey instructions to the agent.

RATIFICATION BY THE PRINCIPAL

If the agent has no authority to act for the principal or has merely a limited authority and exceeds it, the principal may ratify the agent's conduct. Once the principal has done this he will adopt the transaction as if he had given prior authorisation to the agent to enter into that contract or transaction. A third party, therefore, who is affected by the agent's conduct will be able to sue the principal on the transaction once the principal has ratified the transaction. Ratification is only effective if the agent whose act is sought to be ratified purported to act for the principal at the time the transaction was entered into, and the principal had capacity to enter into such a transaction himself at that time.

The principal must therefore be in existence at the time the agent entered into the transaction, because the agent cannot purport to act for a non–existent principal. Moreover, the third party must be aware of the fact that the agent is acting for a principal, although he need not be named. In *Watson* v. *Swann* (1862) the agent insured a cargo belonging to the principal in his own name when he failed to obtain insurance cover in his principal's name. It was held that the principal could not ratify the insurance and recover on the insurance policy, the insurers being unaware at the time insurance cover was given that the agent was acting for a principal. The only person who can ratify the agent's acts is the person on whose behalf the act was expressed to be done and the principal must be identified or be capable of identification at the time the contract is entered into (*see Keighley, Maxsted & Co* v. *Durant* (1901)).

The principal can only ratify the acts of his agent if at the time of ratification he was aware of the material facts which may affect his decision whether to ratify and at that time he must have the capacity to ratify. A principal can only ratify those acts of an agent which the principal contracting for himself could legally have entered into personally.

The ratification need not be in writing, and any act or statement which shows an intention to ratify is sufficient; for example, where the agent accepts goods on an approve–or–return basis and the principal retains the goods after the inspection period has expired.

The effect of ratification is that the principal and the other party to the transaction are placed in a directly binding relationship. The principal must ratify the agent's act in full; ratification of a part of an unauthorised act is ineffective.

THE DUTIES OF AN AGENT

The agency relationship imposes a number of duties on the agent due to the contractual nature of the relationship, but in addition to these duties the nature of the fiduciary relationship between the parties imposes further duties on the agent. It is proposed to deal with the agent's duties arising out of contract in the following paragraphs.

The duty to perform his undertaking

The agent is under a contractual duty to perform his obligations and a wrongful failure will mean the agent is liable for breach of contract. In *Turpin* v. *Bilton* (1843) the agent was held liable for a breach of contract when he failed to insure his principal's ship and it was lost. Following *Cohen* v. *Kittell* (1889), however, the agent is not obliged to perform an undertaking which is illegal or void.

If the agency relationship is gratuitous and the agent does not receive a commission or fee for the performance of his duties, he is not obliged to perform the undertaking at all and will not be liable for failing to do so. If, however, the agent performs the undertaking negligently he will be liable for negligence. In *Wilkinson* v. *Coverdale* (1793) the agent was held liable in negligence when the agent performed a gratuitous undertaking to take out an insurance policy, but did so in such a manner that the principal was unable to claim for the loss.

The agent must act in accordance with the authority conferred on him. He must therefore obey any express instructions or act in accordance with the general nature of his business, trade or profession, and must act wholly for the benefit of the principal.

The duty to act with care and skill

An agent will owe a duty to act with reasonable care and skill, regardless of whether the agency is contractual or gratuitous.

Where there is a contractual relationship between the principal and his agent the standard of care required from the agent is such as a normal agent in his position would exercise. If the agent exercises normal skill and care and acts in a reasonable manner he will not be liable in negligence In *Lambert* v. *Heath* (1846) a broker employed to purchase railway stock in the normal course of business was held not liable when it was discovered that the stock he had purchased was not genuine. The agent for reward implicitly undertakes to exercise such reasonable care as is expected from the ordinary competent practitioner of his trade or profession.

If the agent acts in accordance with his express instructions, he is not liable if performance of those requirements does not turn out to be in the best interests of the principal.

Where there is a gratuitous agency the agent must exercise such care as a reasonable man would exercise in respect of his own affairs, but if the agent has held himself out as possessing the skill necessary for a particular undertaking then he must show such skill as is reasonably necessary for that undertaking. In *Shiells* v. *Blackburne* (1789) the agent was held not liable in negligence when, acting as a gratuitous agent, he entered a parcel belonging to the principal together with his own parcels for customs clearance, and due to a mistake by the agent in describing the principal's goods the parcels became liable for forfeiture. It was said that the agent exercised the same standard of care in respect of the principal's parcel as he had shown in respect of his own and he was therefore not liable in negligence to the principal.

The duty not to delegate

The agency relationship is one where the principal reposes trust or confidence in his agent, and the agent is therefore under an obligation to perform his duties personally; unless the agent is permitted either by law or under the contract of employment the appointment of a sub-agent will be a breach of his obligations (*see Allam & Co Ltd* v. *Europa Poster Services Ltd* (1968)).

Where the principal reposes no personal confidence in the agent the maxim that a "delegate cannot sub-delegate" has no application. Alternatively, where the agent personally performs functions which involve the exercise of confidence or the possession of personal attributes then he can only sub-delegate functions of a purely administrative or ministerial character to a sub-agent. The agent cannot, however, sub-delegate duties which require the use of personal skill on his part. Thus in *John McCann & Co* v. *Pow* (1975) an agent who sub-delegated the sale of his principal's house was held disentitled to his commission when the sub-agent sold the house. The sub-delegation consisted not only of purely ministerial acts, but also of the exercise of personal abilities to obtain the best possible price.

If the agent has either express or implied authority to sub–delegate the agent is not in breach of his duty and is entitled to recover his commission. In *De Bussche* v. *Alt* (1878) an agent who obtained the approval of his principal to appoint a sub–agent in Japan to sell a ship was held entitled to recover his commission when the sub–agent sold the ship. In certain cases the principal's consent to sub–delegate may be implied; for example, where a parent company appoints its subsidiary company as an agent it is apparent that the agent itself must sub–delegate and act through its servants or employees. Where sub–delegation is permitted the agent will be liable to his principal for any breaches of duty committed by the sub–agent unless the agent can show he acted reasonably and took due care in appointing sub–agents.

Since there is no contractual relationship between the sub–agent and the principal, the sub–agent cannot sue the principal for his commission (*see Schmaling* v. *Tomlinson* (1815)). Similarly, the principal cannot bring an action against the sub–agents for breaches of duty committed by them (*see Calico Printers' Association Ltd* v. *Barclays Bank Ltd* (1931)).

The duty to respect the principal's title
The agent cannot deny the title of his principal to goods, money or other property held by the agent on the principal's behalf. The possession of the agent is the possession of the principal for all purposes, and the agent would be in breach of his duty if he denied his principal's title to goods or property held by him for the principal.

The duty to account
The agent must account to his principal for all money received for the principal even though the agent receives the money as a result of a void or illegal transaction entered into by the agent.

The agent is under an obligation to keep the principal's money or property separate from his own or that of other clients and to keep proper accounts. The property or money held by the agent for his principal is fixed with a trust and therefore in the agent's bankruptcy his creditors have no claim over it.

AGENT'S DUTIES ARISING FROM THE FIDUCIARY NATURE OF THE AGENCY RELATIONSHIP

In addition to the contractual duties imposed on the agent under the agency relationship, there are certain other duties imposed on an agent by the rules of equity because of the special nature of the relationship between the agent and his principal. The agency relationship is one of confidence where one party places trust in the other and for that reason equity imposes certain fiduciary duties on the agent, in the same way as on a trustee.

The duty not to let his personal interest conflict

Where the agent's position is such that his own private interest may affect the performance of his duty or conflict with that duty, he is under an obligation to disclose all material facts to the principal, so that the principal can choose whether to let the agent continue to act on his behalf. If the agent does not disclose the full extent of his personal interest, the principal is entitled to rescind the transaction and require the agent to account for any profit he has personally made. In *McPherson* v. *Watt* (1877), an agent who was appointed to sell his principal's house purchased it in his brother's name without disclosing the fact that the purchase was for his own benefit. The court refused to grant an order of specific performance on the grounds that the agent had allowed his personal interest to conflict with his duties as an agent. It is immaterial that the contract in fact is a fair one.

Moreover, the agent must not use information acquired by him in the course of his employment as an agent for his personal benefit. Thus an employer can obtain an injunction to prevent his former employee from using information which became available to him in his position as an agent provided the employer can show the agent that he would not have had access to such special information but for his position. In *Boardman* v. *Phipps* (1966) the agent was liable to account for a profit made by him as a result of information he acquired about certain shares whilst acting in his capacity as a solicitor for his principal.

The agent cannot act for both the principal and the third party to the contract unless he makes full disclosure to both parties and they consent to the double agency. In *Fullwood* v. *Hurley* (1928) the agent could not recover his commission from his principal, the purchaser of a hotel, when it was discovered the agent had, unknown to the parties, acted for both the vendor and purchaser in a sale transaction.

The duty not to make a secret profit

The agent must not make a secret profit from acting in that capacity. He must account for all amounts received by him, including any secret profit, and his failure to do so will disentitle him to recover his commission and also make him liable to dismissal. A secret profit includes any financial advantage which the agent receives over and above his commission or agreed renumeration from the principal, without the knowledge of the principal. A bribe or a secret commission given by a third party is a secret profit. Thus, in *De Bussche* v. *Alt* (1878) it was held that an agent appointed to sell a ship in Japan who purchased it himself and resold it at a higher price was liable to account for the profit he made from the resale and he was not entitled to his commission. It is not necessary for the principal to suffer a loss or any damage in order to recover a secret profit. In *Reading* v. *Attorney-General* (1951) it was held that a soldier who used his uniform to smuggle drugs through police barriers was liable to account for the profit (*see also Attorney-General* v. *Goddard* (1929)).

If the principal is aware of the bribe or financial advantage conferred on his agent and either expressly or by acquiescence consents to the agent retaining it, then the profit is no longer a secret profit and the agent is entitled to retain that and recover his commission.

THE DUTIES OF THE PRINCIPAL

The basis of a contractual agency relationship is that both parties owe duties to each other in return for the promises given. The principal owes the following duties to his agent:

The duty to pay remuneration
The principal must pay the agent for his services. The obligation to pay a remuneration or commission to the agent exists only where the obligation is created either expressly or implicitly. If the nature of the obligation shows that remuneration was intended to be paid then the agent can recover a reasonable sum as a quantum meruit. If there is a custom of the trade or profession which entitles the agent to commission, then the agent's commission will be calculated by reference to what is customary in that trade or profession.

However, if the language of the agency agreement shows that the agent was intended to act gratuitously the agent is not entitled to a remuneration. In *Taylor* v. *Brewer* (1813) an agent who agreed to "accept such remuneration as should be deemed right" was held not entitled to any commission. Similarly in *Munro* v. *Butt* (1858) a builder undertook certain work in return for a lump sum payment. The court held he could not recover under a quantum meruit when he abandoned the work whilst it was uncompleted.

The agent is only entitled to receive his remuneration if he has earned it because he is the direct or effective cause of the event on the occurrence of which the principal agrees to pay the agent. Thus the agent must show not only that he has completed his obligations under the agency agreement, but that his acts were essential to make fulfilment possible. In *Burchall* v. *Gowrie and Blackhouse Collieries Ltd* (1910) an agent employed to sell a colliery was held entitled to his commission when he introduced a purchaser to the principal who then proceeded to make the contract behind the agent's back.

It is immaterial for the purposes of remuneration that the principal has derived no benefit from the agent's act, provided the agent has performed his obligations under the agency agreement. If the agent was employed to perform an illegal act, however, and enters into such a transaction he may lose his right to recover commission. According to *Haines* v. *Busk* (1814), the agent will be entitled to his remuneration if he himself does not perform any illegal acts, but the chain of transactions is such that he can only perform his obligation if another has acted illegally. Moreover, if the wrongful or illegal part of the obligation can be severed from the unlawful, the principal will be liable to pay for the value of the agent's lawful acts.

The duty to indemnify the agent

The principal's duty to indemnify his agent for liabilities and expenses incurred by the agent in the performance of his duties may be either express or implied, but the scope of the principal's duty to indemnify depends on the agreement between the parties and the kind of business in which the agent is employed (*see Hippisley* v. *Knee Brothers* (1905)). The agent must act within the scope of his express, implied or usual authority (*see Barron* v. *Fitzgerald* (1840)). In *Bayliffe* v. *Butterworth* (1847) the principal was held to be under an obligation to indemnify his agent when the agent, in accordance with custom, sold the principal's shares to another broker in Liverpool but the principal subsequently failed to deliver them, so that the third party purchased the shares on the open market and claimed the difference in the contract price from the agent, as he was entitled to do by the usage of the market.

There is no duty to indemnify the agent if he acts unlawfully, negligently or otherwise in breach of his duties.

REMEDIES FOR BREACH OF THE PARTIES' DUTIES

Principal's remedies

The principal will have a number of remedies available against the agent where the agent acts in breach of his contractual undertaking or fiduciary duties.

Dismissal

The principal may dismiss the agent without notice when he discovers the agent's misconduct, and the principal is not then liable to pay any compensation. The agent's misconduct can be relied upon as a defence in an action by the agent.

Legal action

In addition to the right of dismissal, if the agent is negligent in the performance of his duties the principal can bring an action for damages against him. If there is a contract between the parties, the principal's action will be for breach of contract.

Remedies available to the agent

The agent can bring an action for breach of contract if the principal fails to pay the agent's agreed remuneration, or he may recover a reasonable sum for work done by suing for a quantum meruit.

Set-off

The agent may be able to set-off any amounts due to him from the principal against such amounts as are held by him on trust for the principal.

Lien

If the principal has failed to discharge his obligation of paying remuneration, the agent can claim a lien over the principal's goods in his possession. The agent can sell these goods to discharge the principal's obligation to him and transfer the balance to the principal.

THE DIFFERENT KINDS OF PRINCIPAL

The rights and liabilities of the parties, including those of the third party, depend on the degree of disclosure of the existence and identity of principal.

A *named principal* is one whose name has been revealed to the third party by the agent, and so that the third party knows that the agent acts in a representative capacity and also knows the identity of the principal.

A *disclosed principal* is one whose existence has been revealed to the third party, but whose exact identity remains unknown. The third party therefore knows that the agent is contracting as an agent, but he is unaware of the principal's identity.

Where the principal is *undisclosed,* the third party is aware neither of the principal's identity nor of the fact that the agent is acting on behalf of someone else. The third party usually enters into the contract in the belief that the agent is contracting on his own behalf.

The type of agent the third party is dealing with will determine the liability of the parties; for example, a disclosed principal can ratify the conduct of his agent, but where the principal is undisclosed the third party intends to contract with the agent and the principal cannot ratify acts by the agent which were not within the limits of the authority actually conferred on him. The agent's intention is therefore important in order to determine the effect between the parties.

Where the agent acts for a disclosed principal
Where the agent has made a contract with a third party on behalf of a disclosed principal who actually exists and has authorised the agent to make the contract, the principal can sue and be sued by the third party. A direct contractual relationship is created between the principal and the third party. The agent is not a party to the contract if he acts within the authority conferred by the principal or within his customary or implied authority.

The principal is not, however, bound by any contract which is outside the scope of the agent's actual, apparent or presumed authority. A third party who has actual or constructive notice of the agent's lack of authority cannot hold the principal liable. Thus if the third party has the opportunity to discover that the agent does not have authority to enter into the contract for his principal and fails to avail himself of that opportunity he is deemed to have constructive notice of the agent's lack of authority. Similarly, if the agent purports to act for his own benefit, that may amount to a notice of an irregularity to the third party.

THE EFFECT OF PAYMENTS MADE TO THE AGENT

Generally, payment to the agent is irrelevant. If, however, the third party conducts himself so as to make the principal believe that the agent has discharged the liability of the principal to a third party, so that the principal reimburses the agent, the third party will not be entitled to payment from the principal although the agent has not in fact discharged the principal's liability (*see MacClure* v. *Schemeil* (1871)).

Where the third party is under an obligation to pay the principal, payment to an agent will not discharge the third party, but there are the following exceptions to this rule:

(*a*) If the agent has authority to receive payment on the principal's behalf, then payment by the third party to the agent will discharge his liability to the principal. The agent may have express, implied or customary authority to receive payments on behalf of his principal. Moreover, if the principal holds his agent out as having the authority to receive payment, then payment by a third party to the principal's agent will discharge the third party.

(*b*) If the agent receives payment, although without any authority, and transfers the amount received to the principal the third party will be discharged from his liability. Where the agent who lacks authority to receive payment fails to hand the money over to his principal, the third party will not be discharged.

(*c*) If the agent is entitled to a lien on goods which belong to his principal, and in pursuance of this authority he sells the goods to a third party who pays the agent, then the third party who pays the agent will be discharged from his liability to the principal to the extent of the value of the goods.

(*d*) The third party will be discharged by payment to the agent if the principal by his conduct leads the third party to believe that the agent is contracting as a principal (e.g. where the principal transfers documents of title to the agent and the agent represents to the third party that he is the true owner of the subject–matter).

THE RELATIONSHIP BETWEEN THE AGENT AND THE THIRD PARTY

Only where the agent makes himself personally liable to the third party can the third party sue the agent; if the third party elects to sue the agent he will be barred from bringing an action against the principal. The election to bring an action against the agent must be clear and unequivocal. In *Calder* v. *Dobell* (1871) the third party invoiced goods in the name of the agent, although he knew that the agent was acting for a principal. The third party subsequently threatened the agent with legal proceedings, but the court did not consider this action sufficient to constitute an election to discharge the principal in subsequent proceedings. The commencement of legal proceedings, however, will in itself amount to an election if it is made with full knowledge of the facts, and if the third party is aware that the agent was acting for a principal.

If the agent has authority to receive payment on behalf of his principal and the agent is indebted to the third party, that third party can set off the amount owed to him from sums which the third party owes to the principal.

A third party can set up fraud or misconduct against an agent in a position where, if the principal himself had been personally responsible, the third party would have been able to pursue the action against the principal. The principal will be liable although the agent was not authorised to make such a representation. In *Refuge Assurance Co Ltd* v.*Kettlewell* (1909) the holder of an insurance policy who was induced by the insurance company's agent to continue to pay premiums by a false representation that she would receive a free policy was entitled to bring an action against the principal although the statement was made without the knowledge or authority of the principal. Similarly in *Lloyd* v. *Grace, Smith & Co* (1911) a third party was held entitled to pursue an action against the principal when his agent was guilty of a misappropriation of the third party's property. An agent does not act fraudulently (and therefore his principal is not liable) if he makes a statement to the third party which (unknown to the agent or his principal) is false, because there is no intention to deceive.

THE EFFECT OF THE AGENCY RELATIONSHIP BETWEEN THE AGENT AND THE THIRD PARTY

An agent will only be personally liable to the third party with whom he deals if a contract entered into by deed is executed in his name and he is a party to it. If a written contract (otherwise than by deed) is entered into, the agent will be personally liable only if he intends to be bound personally. In such a situation the agent will be personally liable even though he acts for a disclosed principal. The agent will not necessarily be personally liable if he has no authority to enter into the contract, but he would in such circumstances be liable for breach of warranty of authority. However, the agent will always be personally liable where he in fact is the principal; in *Kelner* v. *Baxter* (1866) persons who purported to enter into a contract on behalf of a non–existent company were held personally liable to the other party. Finally, the agent will be personally liable under a contract if the parties intend that he should be personally liable; i.e. the agent will be intended to bind himself personally if he signs a contract without any qualification showing that he acts as an agent. If the situation is unclear, however, the court will examine the surrounding circumstances and any written contract together with the custom and usage of the trade.

Implied warranty of authority

Where the agent is not personally liable but has acted without his principal's authority he may be personally liable for breach of warranty of authority if a third party enters into a contract in reliance of his representation that he has authority. The principle laid down in *Collen* v. *Wright* (1857) was that a person who purports to act as an agent implicitly warrants that he has authority to make the contract he enters into, unless he expressly disclaims that authority or the third party has actual knowledge of the agent's lack of authority. Where, therefore, the third party is misled by the agent's misrepresentation of authority, the agent will be personally liable to the third party. In *Collen* v. *Wright* the personal representatives of the defendant who had acted as an agent were held liable to the plaintiff because the defendant had warranted he had authority to act as an agent for the principal. The decision was followed in *Yonge* v. *Toynbee* (1910) and the agents were held liable for breach of warranty of authority when at the time they purported to act for a principal with his authority he no longer had the mental capacity to enter into the contract.

Where the agent acts for an undisclosed principal

An undisclosed principal is one of whose existence the third party is unaware, so that the third party is unaware the agent acts in a representative capacity. In such a situation a person who is not openly a party to a contract may acquire rights and be subjected to liabilities under it. An undisclosed principal can therefore sue and be sued in his own name provided the agent is acting within the actual scope of his authority.

THE POSITION OF THE UNDISCLOSED PRINCIPAL

Generally the undisclosed principal is in the same position as the disclosed principal, but there are two exceptions. If the agent purports to act as the owner or proprietor of the subject–matter of the transaction, then he may implicitly represent that there is no principal and he (the agent) acts for this own benefit. If the agent acts in such a manner he will be treated as having entered into the contract in his own name and parol evidence will not be allowed to show that he acts for an undisclosed principal. In *Humble* v. *Hunter* (1848) an agent who described himself as the "owner" of a ship in a charterparty was treated as implicitly having represented that he contracted in that capacity, and his undisclosed principal, the real owner, could not sue on the charterparty. Secondly, the undisclosed principal may have no rights under the contract even if he is capable of identification by oral evidence. Thus, where an agent induces a third party to enter into a contract for personal reasons, the principal may have no rights under the contract. Moreover, if the identity of the person with whom the third party contracts is material to the contract, then the agent's failure to disclose the existence of the principal may deprive the principal of his right to sue under the contract. In *Said* v. *Butt* (1920) the plaintiff employed an agent to purchase a ticket to the theatre for him, realising that the management would not sell a ticket to him personally. It was held there was no contract between the plaintiff and the theatre manager because the plaintiff's identity was material to the contract and he could not employ an agent to purchase a ticket for him. (Contrast *Dyster* v. *Randell & Sons* (1926).)

The position of the agent

If the agent acts within the scope of his express authority, then no problem arises; but if the agent acts outside the scope of that authority the undisclosed principal cannot ratify the unauthorised act of the agent.

If the agent enters into the contract in such a way that the principal is excluded, the agent is personally bound, and the position is the same as where the principal is a disclosed principal. If the principal is an undisclosed principal, the third party will not have elected to sue the agent with knowledge of the full material facts because the third party is unaware of the existence of a principal, so the third party can bring a further action against the principal when he discovers the existence of the undisclosed principal. Moreover, a third party is entitled to set up against the undisclosed principal any defences he would have against the agent, provided the agent has acted within the scope of his authority. The right to set–off is only available if the debt had accrued before the third party became aware of the existence of the principal.

If the agency relationship is undisclosed a third party who settles amounts outstanding and makes payment to the agent (unaware of the principal's existence) is discharged, if such a payment would have discharged the third party had the agent in fact been the principal and the third party had no notice of the existence of a principal at the time payment is made.

TERMINATION OF THE AGENCY RELATIONSHIP

The agency relationship may be terminated like any other contractual relationship in a number of different ways, as follows:

(*a*) Where the agency relationship is created by agreement the relationship may be determined by both parties agreeing to terminate it. It will also be terminated if one of the parties withdraws from the original agreement, either by giving notice to terminate the agency or by one party renouncing the obligations imposed on him. However, one party cannot terminate the agency agreement where the agent has incurred personal liabilities by acting on behalf of the principal or where the agent has a lien over goods held for the principal;

(*b*) If the principal ceases business and there is no express term in the agency contract relating to the length of service, then termination by the principal of the agent's authority will entitle him to his commission or a reasonable amount as compensation (*see Turner* v. *Goldsmith* (1891)). However, if there is no term in the agency contract relating to the duration of the agency relationship, the agent is not entitled to recover his commission unless the courts can imply such a term into the contract. Once the agent has performed his obligations under the agency relationship, the agent will be entitled to recover the commission or other remuneration, and a later termination of the contract will not deprive the agent of his rights to receive commission;

(*c*) The complete performance by the agent of his contractual obligations will terminate the agency relationship;

(*d*) The agency relationship will be terminated if the subject–matter of the agency is destroyed or if performance of the agency is made impossible by subsequent events (e.g. the death of the agent or frustration of the contract or the bankruptcy of the parties).

The effect of termination

Where notice of termination is necessary, the agent ceases to have any continuing authority and cannot make his principal liable after notice has been given. The notice does not affect the rights already vested in the parties at the time when the notice is given (e.g. the principal can sue the agent for negligence committed by the agent before the agency relationship is terminated, and the agent may sue for remuneration earned before the termination).

Where notice of termination is not required to be given, a unilateral termination by the principal of the agent's authority will not affect a third party provided the agent acts in a manner previously authorised by his principal, and the third party does not have actual notice that the agent's authority had been terminated. If the principal holds out the agent as still having authority to act on his behalf, he will be estopped from denying the agent's authority. If the agent is acting in exercise of an implied or apparent authority, notice of termination of the agent's authority will be necessary. However, such rights as had already vested in the parties before the act of revocation can still be enforced.

PROBLEMS

1. How may an agency relationship be created or arise?

2. Distinguish between the different kinds of authority which an agent may have to bind his principal to a third party.

3. When can a principal ratify the unauthorised acts of his agent?

4. What duties does an agent owe to his principal at common law?

5. What is meant by the expression that the agency relationship is of a fiduciary nature? What fiduciary duties are owed by the agent to his principal?

6. Explain the duties owed by a principal to his agent.

7. What remedies does the principal have against his agent for a breach of the obligations owed to him by the agent?

8. What is meant by the agent's breach of warranty of authority?

9. Distinguish between a disclosed and an undisclosed principal.

10. When does an agency relationship terminate?

PART II

Transactions In Goods

CHAPTER FOUR

Sale of Goods

OBJECTIVES

It is proposed in this chapter to deal with the law relating to the domestic sale of goods, the rules of which are now codified in the Sale of Goods Act 1979. In particular the chapter deals with:

(a) what constitutes a sale; the rules under the Act relating to the price and valuation of goods;

(b) the statutory terms implied under the Act;

(c) exclusion of implied conditions in consumer sales;

(d) passing of title to goods under the contract of sale, including the passing of ownership to specific and unascertained goods;

(e) retention of title clauses;

(f) passing of risk;

(g) sales by a non-owner and protection of sub-purchasers;

(h) obligations of the seller and remedies of the unpaid seller;

(i) remedies of the buyer for breach by the seller.

INTRODUCTION

The Sale of Goods Act 1893 (now superseded by the Sale of Goods Act 1979) codified the common law rules relating to the sale of goods. Although the 1893 Act incorporated most of the common law rules in statutory form, those rules which were not expressly codifed were preserved by the Act in so far as they were consistent with its express provisions.

DEFINITIONS

The Sale of Goods Act 1979, s. 2, defines two types of transactions which may arise on the sale of goods. A sale of goods is a contract by which the seller transfers his title to the goods to the buyer immediately whether payment of the purchase price also takes place immediately or not. This type of transaction is the more familiar to most individuals; it is exemplified by an individual going into a shop and selecting goods and paying for them in cash; the buyer takes delivery of the goods simultaneously and the ownership of the goods passes to him immediately on the completion of the transaction. The Sale of Goods Act also provides for another type of transaction in which the ownership of the goods does not pass to the buyer immediately the contract of sale is made but only at a later time on fulfilment of certain conditions as to the identification of goods with the contract. The Act calls this type of a transaction an agreement to sell. An example of such a contract is where a manufacturer agrees to make goods to the buyer's specification and to deliver them to the buyer for an agreed price; payment may be deferred until the goods have been delivered and checked by the buyer. There is a contract between the parties immediately, but the ownership of the goods only passes to the buyer when the manufacturing process is completed and (in most cases) the goods are delivered to the buyer.

What are goods?

The Sale of Goods Act 1979, s. 61, defines the term "goods" as including personal chattels, other then choses in action; consequently, although the holder of a bill of exchange or registered shares in a company may sell them a contract for their sale is not governed by the Sale of Goods Act 1979, but by the relevant rules of common law and equity (which are not dissimilar). The term "goods", however, does include industrial growing crops and things attached to or forming part of the land which are to be severed under or in consequence of the contract of sale (e.g. a crop of potatoes or wheat growing in a field).

The Sale of Goods Act 1979, s. 5, classifies the goods which may form the subject–matter of a contract for the sale of goods. Such goods may be already in existence and owned by the seller or supplier at the time the contract of sale is entered into; for example a particular motor car in a showroom or a particular item of jewellery. Existing goods may be either specific or unascertained. Specific goods are goods which are and can be identified and are agreed upon by the parties as being the subject–matter of the contract at the time the contract of sale is entered into. Curiously, however, goods may be specific even if they do not yet exist; for example, a ship or aircraft which is in course of construction under a contract for its sale. Here the ownership of the goods will pass to the buyer on or after the manufacturing process has been completed. The goods are nonetheless specific and it would be a breach of contract for the seller to sell the uncompleted ship to someone else. The Sale of Goods Act does not define unascertained goods, but they clearly include an unidentified part of specific goods; for example, where the seller agrees to sell 100 tons of wheat which at the time of sale forms a part of 500 tons in his granary. The goods which form the subject–matter of the contract are as yet unascertained, because the 100 tons sold under the contract have not been separated from the bulk and are therefore not yet identifiable.

Alternatively goods which may form the subject–matter of the contract may be future goods which are not identified by the contract of sale. This may be because they have yet to be manufactured by the seller or have yet to be acquired by him from someone else. Section 5(3) of the Act provides that where the contract relates to future goods (i.e. those not yet in existence or not yet owned by the seller or supplier), the contract entered into between the parties is an agreement to sell. For the purposes of passing ownership, future goods can never be specific goods, although they may form part of specific or existing goods. On the other hand, the fact that the form or quality of existing goods may change does not prevent them being specific. For example, in *Howell* v. *Coupland* (1876) a contract for the sale of potatoes to be grown on a particular piece of land was held to be a contract for the sale of specific goods on the ground that the potatoes grown on that land were automatically to be appropriated to the contract.

The price of goods

The Sale of Goods Act 1979, s. 8, provides that the price to be paid for goods under a contract of sale may be fixed under the contract by the parties reaching prior agreement, or may be determined in the course of dealings between the parties (e.g. where a retailer has a standing order with a supplier for the monthly delivery of a fixed quantity of goods at the supplier's current published prices). Alternatively the contract may provide that the price is to be fixed in a specified manner (e.g. by an independent valuation). If the parties have reached a binding agreement but the method of ascertaining the contract price remains undetermined, the purchaser must pay a reasonable price for the goods. In *May & Butcher* v. *R.* (1934) the House of Lords held that an agreement for the sale of goods at a price to be determined later was not a concluded contract; since the parties had not reached an agreement which was binding on them the court held it would not imply (under s. 8(2)) that the purchaser must pay a reasonable price. However, in *Hillas & Co Ltd* v. *Arcos* (1932) and *Foley* v. *Classique Coaches Ltd* (1934) it was held that in such circumstance the courts would imply that the parties had entered into an agreement to receive goods and to pay a reasonable price for them. In *Foley* v. *Classique Coaches Ltd* (1934) an agreement was entered into whereby the defendant agreed to purchase petrol from the plaintiff, the owner of a petrol station, at a price to be "agreed by the parties in writing from time to time". The court held that it was reasonable to imply a term into the agreement that the petrol supplied was to be of reasonable quality and that the purchaser would pay a reasonable price for deliveries; since according to the terms of the contract the price was to be determined by arbitration in the event of a dispute. In *Courtney & Fairbairn Ltd* v. *Tolaini Brothers Ltd* (1975) the plaintiff undertook to find someone who would agree to finance a property development scheme for the defendants, on the understanding that if a contract to provide finance was entered into between the defendants and a third party, the defendants would instruct their quantity surveyor to negotiate a fair and reasonable sum for him in return for the introduction. The court held the agreement was not a legally enforceable contract because the price was fundamental to the contract and the parties had not agreed to the price nor to a method of ascertaining the price which was not dependent on negotiations between them. Similarly, in *King's Motors (Oxford) Ltd* v. *Lax* (1970), the court held that the failure of the agreement to show how the consideration in return for an agreement to grant an option for a lease was to be determined was void. These cases can clearly be distinguished from *Hillas & Co Ltd* v. *Arcos* (1932) because in that case the parties had agreed to be bound by the decision of an arbitrator, whereas in *Courtney & Fairbairn Ltd* v. *Tolaini Brothers Ltd* (1975) the plaintiff had merely agreed to allow an independent party, namely the quantity surveyor, to enter into negotiations to arrive at a price which the plaintiff would nevertheless have been entitled to reject. The law therefore is that if the parties have agreed on a price, or have agreed to the method by which the price is to be ascertained, the courts will hold them bound since they have reached agreement.

Valuations

Where the parties decide, subject to the Sale of Goods Act 1979, s. 8, that the price is to be fixed by an independent valuation, then such a valuation will not be set aside merely because the valuer has been negligent (*see Arenson* v. *Arenson* (1973)). The courts will only set aside the valuation if fraud or bad faith can be shown on the part of the third party who carried out the valuation. If, however, the valuer has acted negligently, clearly he may be held personally liable to either party because of his breach of the duty of care which he owes to them, whether under the contract by which he is employed or under the general rules of tort. Section 9 provides that if the valuation to be made by a third party does not take place and the failure is not the fault of the buyer or seller, the agreement to sell the goods is avoided; but if a valuation has not been made because of the fault of one of the parties, the innocent party may bring an action for damages against him. For example, where the seller refuses to allow the valuer to enter his premises where the goods are stored to carry out the valuation, or refuses to provide the valuer with a sample of goods when the valuation is to be made by reference to a sample, the purchaser may bring an action for damages under s. 9(2). There is also the possibility in such situations that the courts may grant a mandatory injunction compelling the seller to allow the valuer to enter his premises or to supply him with a sample (*see Smith* v. *Peters* (1875)).

If the parties agree on an independent third party who is to carry out the valuation, and that third party fails to do so, then the contract is avoided (Sale of Goods Act 1979, s. 9(2)) but if the agreement does not name a third party, and merely provides that the goods are sold at a valuation, then the agreement is given effect as an agreement for sale at a reasonable price.

IMPLIED TERMS IN A CONTRACT OF SALE

In addition to any express terms incorporated by agreement in a contract for the sale of goods, the Sale of Goods Act 1979, will imply a number of terms in the contract which impose on the seller of goods certain obligations in relation to the goods in question and his title to them. The relevant provisions of the 1979 Act are ss. 12–15. Section 12 implies a condition on the part of the seller that he has a right to sell the goods and also to a warranty that the goods are free and will remain free from any encumbrance on the title not already disclosed to the buyer. Sections 13–15 deal with implied conditions relating to the quality and fitness for purpose for which the goods are bought. Section 13 implies a condition that the goods delivered will correspond to their description in the contract, and this applies regardless of whether the goods are existing or future goods. Section 14 implies a condition that the goods are of a merchantable quality when the seller carries on a business, and s. 15 implies certain conditions where goods are sold by sample. The sections imply a series of graduated duties on the seller.

The court may interpret an express term of the contract of sale either as a condition or warranty, and thus give the breach of an express term a meaning different from that intended by the parties, but the contract may expressly provide for a term to be treated in a particular way. The statutory terms implied in ss. 13–15 are only to be given effect in the manner provided by statute and there will therefore be more certainty in the way the courts interpret a breach of these provisions.

The seller's right to sell the goods

The Sale of Goods Act 1979, s. 12(1), implies a condition on the part of the seller that he has a right to sell the goods, or, in the case of an agreement to sell, that he will have a right to sell them at the time the property in the goods is to be transferred. Although the seller has the ability to pass the ownership of the goods, he may be in breach of s. 12(1) if his title can be impeached in any way, and this includes the right of a third party to prevent the seller from dealing with the goods in their original form. Thus in *Niblett* v. *Confectioner's Materials Co Ltd* (1921) it was held that the defendants who entered into a contract with the plaintiffs to sell to them 3,000 tins of preserved milk were in breach of s. 12(1). This was because a third party could bring an action to restrain them from selling tins of condensed milk which were their property on the grounds that the labels on the tins infringed a trade mark. The court held that the defendants could not transfer the full property in the goods since the buyer would be unable to resell them on the market bearing that trade mark. The defendants were therefore in breach of the implied condition under s. 12(1).

In addition to the normal remedies available against the seller (i.e. the right of the buyer to repudiate the contract and/or to claim damages) the buyer has an additional right under s. 12(1) to compel the seller to return the purchase price because the consideration for which it was paid has totally failed. To succeed in such a claim the buyer must show that he has not received that which he contracted to receive, namely the unencumbered ownership of the goods, including the right to enjoy the property and to deal with it without interference from a third party. Similarly, in *Karflex Ltd* v. *Poole* (1933) the plaintiffs sold a car to the defendant under a hire–purchase agreement. The defendant paid a deposit and took possession of the car but defaulted on the instalments. The plaintiffs brought legal proceedings against the defendant and then discovered that the person from whom they had bought the car was not in fact its owner. The plaintiffs paid the value of the car to the owner, and continued their action against the defendant. It was held that the action could not succeed because there had been a breach of an implied condition by them at the time the hire–purchase agreement was entered into. The defendant had entered into a contract under which the plaintiffs had undertaken to give him the option to purchase the car from them, but they could not at that time comply with this obligation because they themselves did not have ownership of the car when the contract was completed, and the buyer could repudiate it. Similarly, *in Rowland* v. *Divall* (1923) it was held that the seller is in breach of s. 12(1) if, when he enters into the contract, he has no right to sell the goods, the buyer can recover the full purchase price although he has used the goods. The period of time during which the buyer has had the use of the goods is irrelevant. In *Rowland* v. *Divall* he had used the car for approximately three months before it was discovered that the seller in fact had no right to sell the goods.

The wording of s. 12(1) makes it apparent that the seller cannot contract out of his obligation under that section, but it is possible for a seller expressly to agree to the sale of a limited title.

Warranty of freedom from encumbrances and of quiet possession

The Sale of Goods Act 1979, s. 12(2), provides that in a contract for the sale of goods there is an implied warranty that the goods to be sold are free, and will continue free, from any charge or encumbrance not already disclosed or known to the buyer before the contract for sale is entered into. Any charge or security created over the goods pursuant to the contract of sale must therefore be created with the view of passing title to the buyer. Thus, where the buyer has to raise a loan in order to finance the transaction and the goods are given as security by him, this will obviously be a valid encumbrance created by the buyer in consequence of the contract for sale, and not an encumbrance for which the seller is responsible. Section 12(1)(*b*), moreover, implies a warranty that the buyer will enjoy quiet possession of the goods, except in so far as the buyer's title may be impeached by the person in whose favour a charge or security has been created with his consent or in so far as he already has knowledge of the charge or security at the time of sale. Section 12(2) has been held to apply not only where a third party claims to enforce an encumbrance, right or charge over the goods, but also where the seller of the goods disturbs the possession of the buyer. In *Microbeads AC* v. *Vinhurst Road Markings Ltd* (1975), the defendants' claim that the plaintiffs were in breach of their implied warranty that the buyer should enjoy quiet possession was upheld. The court held that the words "shall have and enjoy" in s. 12(2) meant the right to enjoy the possession and use of the goods not merely at the time of sale but also at any time in the future. An injunction obtained against the defendants by a third party on the grounds that the defendants were in breach of the third party's right under a patent by using the goods, namely machinery purchased by them from the plaintiffs, amounted to a breach of s. 12(2) by the plaintiffs. Similarly in *Niblett* v. *Confectioner's Materials Co Ltd* (1921) the court held the defendants guilty of a breach of the implied warranty that the purchaser would enjoy quiet possession when an action by a third party to restrain the purchaser from reselling preserved milk succeeded on the ground that the milk was contained in tins improperly bearing the third party's trade mark. In *Lloyds and Scottish Finance* v. *Modern Cars & Caravans* (1966) it was held that a debtor who sells goods which have already been "seized" (although not physically removed from his possession) by the sheriff under a *fi fa* has a right to sell them even though subject to the sheriff's right to sell the goods in order to satisfy the judgment debt. The innocent purchaser who has to surrender the goods can bring an action against the seller for breach of s. 12(2).

Implied conditions that the goods correspond with their description

The Sale of Goods Act 1979, s. 13(1) and (2), provides that where the sale is by description, there is an implied condition on the part of the seller that the goods delivered correspond exactly to their description in the contract, and if the sale is by sample (as well as by description) the goods supplied must correspond with the sample, as well as with the description. However, the ordinary common law rules of contract apply in determining whether a sale is in fact by description, and the description of the goods must therefore form a part of the contractual terms and not merely be comprised in a representation during negotiations for the contract. The buyer will not have a remedy under s. 13 if the description of the goods is not incorporated into the contract. For example, in *Taylor* v. *Combined Buyers Ltd* (1924) the plaintiff purchased a car from the defendants which he selected from the defendants' stock, and subsequently brought an action for termination of the contract on the ground that the car he had purchased was not a new one as the defendants' sales representative had stated. The Supreme Court of New Zealand held that the statements made as to the quality and other attributes of the car were not a part of the contractual terms binding on the plaintiff. In the more recent cases, however, the view appears to have been taken that if the words of description are important, they will usually be held to be embodied in the contract of sale and to have a contractual effect. For example, in *Beale* v. *Taylor* (1967) a car bought by the plaintiff was described as a "Herald convertible... 1961" when in fact it was parts of two cars which had been welded together, and only one of the parts was a 1961 model. The Court of Appeal held that the words "Herald... 1961" constituted part of the contractual terms and the purchaser was entitled to repudiate the contract. In *Reardon Smith Line Ltd* v. *Australian Wheat Board* (1956), however, a case concerning a contract for the construction and delivery of a ship according to detailed specifications, it was held the words "No 354 at Osaka" used in the contract were not a part of the description and of no practical importance since the words merely referred to the yard number in Osaka where the ship was to be built.

The question whether a breach of a term relating to the description of the goods and forming a part of the contractual terms amounts to a breach of condition or warranty is unsettled. In the earlier cases the courts held that compliance with the Sale of Goods Act 1979, s. 13, must be strict. In *Arcas Ltd* v. *Ronaasen & Sons* (1933) the buyers were entitled to reject a quantity of staves which under the contract were required to be $\frac{1}{2}$ inch thick when those supplied by the sellers were $\frac{9}{16}$ inch thick. The staves supplied, although commercially within the contract specification, did not comply exactly with the contractual terms. Similarly, in *Re Moore & Co Ltd and Landauer & Co Ltd* (1921) the court held the method of packing the goods was a part of their description. When the seller agreed to supply a quantity of tinned pears to be packed in cases containing 30 tins each, but delivered some cases containing 24 tins, the buyer was held entitled to reject the goods even though the total number of tins supplied was correct. The description of the goods went beyond their physical appearance and included methods of packing which the sellers had failed to comply with so that they were in breach of the Sale of Goods Act 1979, s. 13.

Meaning of sale by description

A contract for the sale of goods is a sale by description if the buyer has not identified them at the time he enters into the contract, and it is unavoidably a sale by description where the contract is for the sale of unascertained or future goods. In *Varley* v. *Whipp* (1900) the plaintiffs entered into a contract for the sale of a particular reaping machine which had been described as "new the previous year". The purchaser eventually returned the machine on the ground that it did not correspond with the plaintiff's description, and since at the time the contract of sale was entered into he had not seen the goods, s. 13 implied a condition that the goods must correspond with their description. The court held that the plaintiff's action for the purchase price could not succeed because he was in breach of s. 13. Channell J held that a sale is always by description where the purchaser has not seen the goods but is relying on an identification made by description alone.

In some cases a contract for the sale of goods may be treated as a contract of sale by description where the purchaser has in fact seen the goods, for example where the goods are on display before the purchaser in a shop. In *Grant* v. *Australian Knitting Mills Ltd* (1936) the sale of a garment on display was held to be a sale by description.

The Sale of Goods Act 1979, s. 13, has a wider application than s. 14 and the former section will apply although the goods are not sold in the course of the seller's business. Thus, it will apply to a contract for the sale of goods where the parties act as private individuals. A car sold by its owner in consequence of a newspaper advertisement, where neither the seller nor buyer carries on the business of dealing with cars, is a sale by description; if the newspaper description of the car does not correspond with the actual car delivered, the seller is in breach of s. 13. The seller's obligation to conform with s. 13 is strict, but this duty is subject to the *de minimis* rule and the seller can avoid the effect of the section if the breach is immaterial. In *Steel & Bucks Ltd* v. *Bleecher Bik & Co Ltd* (1956), goods delivered under the contract of sale were held to be in accordance with their description where the contract provided that the quality must conform to those previously delivered; the fact that the goods contained some new chemical not present in the original bricks did not amount to a breach of s. 13 even though the chemical rendered the goods unfit for the purposes of the buyer.

Implied condition that the goods are merchantable

The Sale of Goods Act 1979, ss. 14(2) and 15(2)(c) imply into a contract for the sale of goods certain conditions as to the merchantable quality of the goods supplied. Section 14(2) provides that where the seller of goods sells them in the course of a business the goods must be of a merchantable quality unless the seller has drawn the buyer's attention to the defects in the goods which makes them unmerchantable before the contract of sale is entered into, or unless the buyer has examined the goods before entering into the contract of sale and a reasonable inspection should have revealed the defects, even though the buyer did not in fact discover them.

At common law it was held in *Thornett & Fehr* v. *Beers & Sons* (1919) that the implied condition of merchantability was excluded by the mere fact that the purchaser had an opportunity for an examination although the opportunity was not in fact taken. The facts of the *Thornett* case were that the buyer only examined from the outside some of the barrels of glue which he had agreed to buy, although the seller offered him an opportunity for a more complete examination. It was held that s. 14(2) (b) did not apply as regards defects which such an examination ought to have revealed. It therefore appears that the statutory wording is more generous to the buyer, and if a defect should reasonably have been discovered by a more thorough examination but the buyer did not examine at all, the seller is in breach of s. 14(2)(b).

Section 14(2) provides that the condition as to the merchantable quality of the goods will only apply if the seller is selling the goods in the course of business, or holds himself out as willing to supply such goods.

The Sale of Goods Act 1979, s. 14(5), provides that the implied condition that the goods are of a merchantable quality will still be effective even if the goods are sold by an agent (for the seller) in the course of the agents' business. However, the implied condition as to merchantability is excluded if the buyer is aware that the goods are not being sold in the course of the seller's business (e.g. because he carries on no business at all).

When are goods of a merchantable quality?

The common law test of merchantability was exemplified in *Kendall & Sons* v. *William Lillico & Sons Ltd* (1969), where the plaintiffs had bought from the defendants a quantity of compounded meals for feeding to pheasants and partridges. As a result of using the meal supplied, the plaintiffs lost much of their poultry. It was held that the defendants were in breach of the implied conditions that the goods were fit for the particular purpose under s. 14(1) (now s. 14(3)) and also were of a merchantable quality. In *Kendall* v. *Lillico* it was held that the goods are of a merchantable quality if they are in such a state that a buyer, fully acquainted with the facts and therefore having knowledge of any hidden defects in the goods, would purchase the goods without any abatement of the price and without attaching any special terms.

The statutory definition of merchantability is now contained in s. 14(6) of the 1979 Act which provides that goods are of a merchantable quality if they are reasonably fit for the purpose for which such goods are usually bought, having regard to the description of the goods, the price and any other relevant circumstances. The statutory test of merchantability comprises the same elements as laid down by the courts at common law, namely whether a reasonable business man would accept the goods in fulfilment of a contract in the terms the parties have agreed to. It appears that the courts will apply the same principles in giving effect to s. 14(6) as in interpreting the common law test of merchantability. It is therefore proposed to look at the factors which the courts will examine and the case law before the 1979 Act was enacted.

The courts have applied a more flexible standard of merchantability where the goods in question are second–hand. Thus in *Bartlett* v. *Sydney Marcus Ltd* (1965) the plaintiff bought a second–hand car from the defendants, who were dealers in second–hand cars. The plaintiff was notified that the clutch was defective and the defendants offered either to correct the defect or to sell the car at a reduced price. The plaintiff chose to purchase the car at the reduced price, but then brought an action against the defendant for breach of s. 14(2) when it was discovered that the defect in the clutch was more serious than anticipated. It was held that the goods were of a merchantable quality and it was said that the article may be merchantable in a particular case if it is of some use although not entirely fit for the purpose which the buyer intended. The goods may not be in a perfect condition but may nevertheless be of merchantable quality. The goods will be unmerchantable, however, if they are not of use for any purpose for which goods of that kind would normally be used. In *Kendall* v. *Lillico* (1969) it was held that goods will be of merchantable quality if they can be used for any of several purposes for which they are normally used.

The purchase price paid will also be taken into account in deciding whether the goods supplied are merchantable. If the price at which the goods supplied can be resold is substantially lower than the contract sale price, the court will more readily hold that the goods are not of merchantable quality. In *Brown & Sons Ltd* v. *Craiks Ltd* (1970) the buyers ordered a quantity of cloth from the sellers who thought that it was required for industrial purposes. The buyers, in fact, wanted it for the manufacture of dresses for which the cloth supplied was unsuitable. The buyers consequently resold the cloth at a lower price than they had paid and brought an action under what is now s. 14(3) of the Act. The claim was rejected on the ground that although the cloth was not fit for the purpose which the buyer had in mind, it was still suitable for industrial purposes, and was therefore acceptable for general use. The fact the buyers were only able to resell the cloth at a lower price did not necessarily mean that the cloth was unmerchantable. In *H. Beecham & Co Property Ltd* v. *Francis Howard & Co Property Ltd* (1921), however, the defendants bought timber for the manufacture of pianos from the plaintiffs, but the timber proved to be unsuitable because it was affected by dry rot which was not discoverable by an external examination. The sellers argued that the timber was of merchantable quality because it could be resold and used for the manufacture of boxes, but this defence was rejected. The court held that sellers' claim for the purchase price could not succeed because a businessman, knowing of the dry rot, would not have bought the timber without a substantial reduction of the price.

The mere fact that the goods are of an inferior quality is not necessarily an indication that they are unmerchantable. Thus if the goods are of the normal quality of goods of that kind and correspond to the description under which they are sold, they will not be unmerchantable merely because they are of an inferior quality. It was therefore held in *Wills & Co Ltd* v. *David Pty Ltd* (1956) that beetroot canned in vinegar (and therefore having a shorter life than beetroot canned in brine) was not for that reason alone of unmerchantable quality.

Where goods are sold under a contract of sale, and the parties are in two different countries or carry on business at some distance from each other so that the goods have to be transported, the question arises for what period of time must the goods remain merchantable after their transportation begins. In *Mash & Murrell* v. *Joseph I Emmanuel* (1962) the sellers sold potatoes c and f Liverpool. The potatoes, although in good condition when loaded, rotted during the journey. The court held that the sellers were liable under s. 14(2), since the goods must be in such a state that they could endure the normal journey and be in a merchantable condition on arrival. In *Cordova Land Corporation* v. *Victor Brothers Inc* (1966), however, it was held this case only applies to perishable goods.

Reliance of the buyer

The implied condition in s. 14(2) applies even where the buyer has not relied on the seller's skill and judgment. The reason for this rule is that normally the seller will himself be able to obtain an indemnity from the manufacturer. Where the seller makes goods to the specification of the buyer, however, it is sufficient if he uses all reasonable skill and care; if damage is caused to the buyer he cannot complain since he has merely received what he ordered (*see Hill* v. *Ashington Piggeries Ltd* (1972)).

Where only part of the goods supplied by the seller are of an unmerchantable quality the *de minimis* rule may apply (though this is never the case when the sale is to be financed by letter of credit), so that the purchaser cannot reject the whole consignment but may only recover damages for the part of the consignment which is unmerchantable. The *de minimis* rule, however, will not apply where a substantial part of the goods supplied are damaged or unmerchantable. In *Jackson* v. *Rotex Motor & Cycle Co Ltd* (1910), the buyer was held entitled to reject a consignment of motor car horns on the grounds of unmerchantability where about half of the horns supplied had been dented and scratched due to bad packing.

Implied condition that the goods are fit for a particular purpose

The new s. 14(3) of the Sale of Goods Act 1979, largely confirms the common law rule that if the seller sells goods in the course of a business and the buyer makes known either expressly or implicitly the purpose for which he requires them there is an implied condition that they are reasonably fit for that purpose. The onus is on the buyer to show that he has made known the purpose for which he buys the goods. The courts will then assume that the buyer relied on the skill and judgment of the seller if his business comprised the supply of goods of the same kind. Reliance will be assumed if the purchaser notifies the seller of the particular purpose for which the goods are required. In *Cammell Laird & Co Ltd* v. *Manganese Bronze & Brass Co Ltd* (1939) for example, the defendants entered into a contract to construct two propellers for the plaintiff's ships. The propellers were to be made to certain specifications but certain questions of detail were left in the hands of the defendants, including the thickness of the propellers. The propellers supplied caused considerable vibration and noise because of their thickness. The House of Lords held the defendants in breach of the old s. 14(1) (now s. 14(3)) on the grounds that there was a substantial area of expertise which had been left to the defendants' skill and judgment and they were in breach of the condition that the goods must be reasonably fit for the particular purpose for which they are supplied. Where, however, the buyer can be held to have relied only partially on the skill and judgment of the seller, in order for the purchaser to succeed under s. 14(3) the reliance must be such as to constitute a substantial and effective inducement which leads the buyer to purchase the goods, even though it need not necessarily be the sole inducement. In *Christopher Hill Ltd* v. *Ashington Piggeries Ltd* (1972) it was held that the plaintiffs, manufacturers of animal food stuffs, were not in breach of what is now s. 14(3) when they made a food compound for feeding mink and relied on a formula provided by the customer. The court held that the plaintiffs were not under an obligation to supply a food which would be suitable for mink, but merely to provide a food compound made in accordance with an agreed formula; the circumstances indicated that the defendants did not rely on the skill and judgment of the plaintiffs.

Section 14(3) provides that goods supplied must be fit for the particular purpose specified by the buyer. Thus where goods can only be used for one purpose (e.g. food for consumption), they must be fit for that particular purpose. In *Priest* v. *Last* (1903) it was consequently held that a hot water bottle was not fit for the particular purpose intended by the buyer when it burst on being filled with hot water. However, where goods would normally be fit for use for a particular purpose but the plaintiff suffers from a peculiar sensitivity not shared by the average buyer, the supplier of goods cannot be treated as having breached s. 14(3) if he is unaware of that plaintiff's condition (*see Griffiths* v. *Peter Conway Ltd*(1939)). Section 14(3) requires the seller to supply goods which are reasonably fit, not absolutely fit for all purposes. The seller is clearly not liable for latent defects which are not discoverable by any amount of care and diligence. In *Frost* v. *Aylesbury Diary Co Ltd*(1905), however, it was held that the defendants who were milk dealers were liable for breach of s. 14(1) under the 1893 Act, when the plaintiff's wife died as a result of consuming milk which was supplied by the defendants and which contained typhoid germs. The defendants had sufficient knowledge of the purpose for which the milk was supplied, and the defect, although not obvious, could have been discovered by investigation. Similarly, in *Vacwell Engineering Co Ltd* v. *BDH Chemicals* (1971) the defendants sold glass ampoules containing a chemical required by the buyers for use in certain manufacturing processes. The chemical was liable to cause an explosion if it came in contact with water although this was unknown to the plaintiffs. A violent explosion occurred when the chemical came in contact with water and the plaintiffs brought an action for breach of s. 14(1) of the 1893 Act. It was held that the goods were reasonably fit for the purpose for which they were sold because the defendants should have foreseen that the chemical might come in contact with water and cause a dangerous situation.

Implied conditions in sales by sample

The Sale of Goods Act 1979, s. 15, provides that a contract of sale is a contract for sale by sample where there is an express or implied term to that effect; there is such an implied term if the description of the goods has been agreed upon, wholly or partly, by reference to a sample or specimen of the goods produced by one of the parties. In a contract of sale by sample the quality of the goods supplied must correspond with the sample. In *E & S Rubin Ltd* v. *Faire Brothers Ltd* (1949) it was held that goods supplied do not correspond with a sample if any work has to be done on them so that they correspond to the sample.

Section 15(2)(*b*) provides that if goods are sold by sample the buyer must be given an opportunity to inspect the goods supplied and to ensure that they do conform with the sample. This means that the buyer is not treated as having accepted the goods until he has had an opportunity to inspect them and the title in the goods remains in the seller until the purchaser indicates his acceptance (*see Steels & Busks* v. *Bleecker Bikk & Co* (1936)).

Finally, s. 15(2)(*c*) provides that as regards matters which cannot be tested by inspection, the goods must be of merchantable quality; the seller is not liable, however, for defects in the goods which should have been discovered on a reasonable inspection of the sample.

Exclusion of implied conditions in consumer sale and other sales

The seller or supplier of goods under a contract of sale could, at common law, without restrictions exclude his liability to the buyer for defects in the goods. This right of exclusion has, however, been narrowed, and at present there are a number of statutory provisions which either prevent the seller from excluding his liability in total or restrict his rights.

THE UNFAIR CONTRACT TERMS ACT 1977

The Unfair Contract Terms Act 1977, s. 6(1), provides that the seller cannot exclude or restrict the effect of the Sale of Goods Act 1979, s. 12, regardless of whether the clause is reasonable, and any such attempted exclusion is void as against the seller. Although s. 12 provides that the seller undertakes that the buyer of goods will be entitled to the enjoyment of the goods without interference by a third party, it is possible for the seller to sell a limited interest in the goods, provided the buyer is aware that the seller is purporting to transfer only a limited title. The seller will be liable to the buyer for any encumbrance or charge on the goods of which the seller is aware but which he has failed to notify to the buyer.

Section 6(2) and (3) further provides that the seller cannot exclude his liability for breach of a contract under the Sale of Goods Act 1979, ss. 13–15, against a person who enters into the contract as a consumer; in the case of several persons entering into a contract, the position of each must be looked at individually. In *Rasbora Ltd* v. *JCL Marine Ltd* (1976) it was held that a private company may be treated as a consumer if it purchases goods for the use of its members. In the *Rasbora* case the sale of a boat which was destroyed because of a fire caused by electrical faults was held to be a consumer sale so the exclusion clause was void in so far as it excluded the implied conditions under the Sale of Goods Act.

Section 12 of the 1977 Act provides that a contract for the sale of goods is a consumer sale if one of the parties to the contract enters into it in the course of a business whilst the other party neither contracts in the course of a business nor holds himself out to be in business and the goods supplied are normally for private consumption.

It is possible, however, for a seller to exclude or limit his liability if the buyer enters into the contract otherwise than as a consumer, in so far as the exclusion clause or a clause limiting the seller's liability is reasonable. In a non–consumer sale the seller must show both that the exclusion clause is incorporated in the contractual terms and that it is reasonable.

The seller still has limited protection under the obligations imposed by the Sale of Goods Act 1979, ss. 13–15, under the wording of these provisions. It is possible for the seller to avoid liability under s. 14(2) by drawing the purchaser's attention to any defects in the goods. The implied term that the goods must be of a merchantable quality will thus be excluded to the extent that the defects have been pointed out to the buyer before the contract is made. The seller's conduct in drawing defects in the goods to the buyer's attention will itself exclude the implied condition under s. 14(2), and the exclusion does not have to be incorporated in the terms of the contract. Similarly, the seller may make it clear to the buyer before the contract is made that he should not rely on the seller's opinion as to the fitness of the goods for a particular purpose. The buyer cannot then rely on any implied undertaking by the seller under the Sale of Goods Act 1979, s. 14(3).

THE PASSING OF TITLE TO GOODS UNDER THE CONTRACT OF SALE

The common law rules as to whether the ownership or property in the goods passed to the buyer under a contract of sale were, with some modification, incorporated in the Sale of Goods Act 1893, and these rules remain unaltered in the present Sale of Goods Act 1979. At common law the ownership of the goods passed to the buyer when the contract of sale was made if the goods were specific or identified at that time; in any other case ownership passed when the goods were subsequently delivered to the buyer. Whether the purchase price had been paid for or whether the seller had agreed to allow the buyer credit was irrelevant, and ownership was retained by the seller if payment had not been made only in these cases where the contract of sale expressly so provided.

The common law rules were embodied in the Sale of Goods Act 1893, now the Sale of Goods Act 1979. The 1979 Act provides that the ownership of goods sold or contracted to be sold passes to the buyer when the parties intend; and when the contract is not explicit on this matter, according to *Kursell* v. *Timber Operators and Contractors* (1927), it must be determined having regard to the terms of the contract, the conduct of the parties and the circumstances of the transaction. Certain presumptions as to the intentions of the parties are set out in the Act, but the fact that the price remains unpaid or that the seller has agreed to give credit will not affect these presumptions. Where, however, the buyer is required to do something before ownership can pass to him, then the seller remains the owner of the goods; for example, an express reservation of ownership in the goods by the seller until they are fully paid for is effective under English law.

The passing of ownership of specific goods

The time at which ownership passes to the buyer depends on whether the goods are specific or unascertained. The Sale of Goods Act 1979 provides that the ownership of unascertained goods cannot pass to the buyer until they are ascertained. The title to specific goods, on the other hand, can pass immediately the contract of sale is made. Subject to these points, the actual time when ownership passes under a particular contract depends on the intention of the parties as expressed in the contract, or if not expressed, as deduced by the court from the terms of the contract, the conduct of the parties and the circumstances of the case. In ascertaining the intention of the parties, s. 18 of the Act establishes a number of presumptions which are applied in the absence of any other indication of the intention of the parties. These presumptions are embodied in five mutually exclusive rules.

Rule 1 in s. 18 provides that where there is an unconditional contract for the sale of specific goods in a deliverable state, the property in the goods passes to the buyer when the contract is made, and it is immaterial whether the time of payment or delivery (or both) are postponed. Under s. 18, rule 1 there has to be an unconditional contract, and although there has in the past been some uncertainty as to when a contract of sale is unconditional, it is accepted generally that it is conditional only if it expressly prescribes a condition which has to be fulfilled by the buyer before title in the goods passes to him (e.g. paying the price or discharging all his outstanding indebtedness to the seller). Secondly, the rule relates only to "specific goods", which are defined by s. 61 of the Act as those goods which are identified and agreed upon at the time the contract of sale is entered into. In *Kursell* v. *Timber Operators and Contractors* (1927), the plaintiffs sold to the defendants those trees growing on an estate which conformed to certain minimum measurements, and the buyers were to cut and remove such trees as and when they attained the prescribed measurements, but in any case within 15 years. Subsequently the forest was expropriated under a government order. The Court of Appeal held that the property in the trees had not passed to the defendants because the goods were not sufficiently identified by the contract to enable them to be ascertained when the contract of sale was made. In *Joseph Reid Property Ltd* v. *Schultz* (1949), however, it was held that when a contract was entered for the sale of all the millable or marketable timber growing on a certain site, the ownership had passed to the buyer. Finally s. 18, rule 1 requires that the goods should be in deliverable state, and in this connection s. 61(5) provides that goods are in a deliverable state when they are in such a condition that the buyer would be bound to take delivery of them in performance of the contract. The buyer can always reject goods which do not satisfy the terms of the contract when tendered for delivery, but it does not seem that for the purpose of determining when ownership passes that all goods have to be in a deliverable state if the departure from the contract requirements is so small that the seller is entitled to recover the price, subject only to an allowance for the cost of remedying the defects. It is possible for the parties to exclude the operation of rule 1 by showing a contrary intention; for example, by stipulating that ownership shall pass to the buyer even though the goods are not yet in a deliverable state (e.g. a ship or aircraft under construction).

Section 18, rule 2, deals with other cases of contracts for the sale of specific goods. Rule 2 provides that where there is a contract for the sale of specific goods and the seller is bound to do something to the goods in order to put them in a deliverable state, property does not pass to the buyer until that has been done and the buyer has been notified. For example, title to the goods will not pass to the purchaser if he acquires goods which have to be altered before they can be delivered, and until those alterations have been made and the buyer notified of that fact, the seller retains ownership of the goods.

Rule 3 deals with the sale of specific goods which are in a deliverable state, but they have to be weighed, measured or tested by the seller or require some other act to be performed by the seller before the purchase price can be ascertained. In this situation, where the amount of the price is dependent on a further act being done by the seller, the ownership of the goods does not pass to the buyer until it has been done and the buyer is notified to that effect.

Finally, in the case of specific goods, rule 4 of s. 18 deals with a different type of transaction, namely, where goods are delivered to the buyer on sale or approval terms or on sale–or–return terms. In such cases there is initially no contract of sale, and one comes into existence only when the buyer shows an intention to purchase the goods at the stipulated price. The ownership of the goods therefore passes to the buyer when he either signifies his approval or acceptance of the goods or does an act inconsistent with the seller's title. Thus, in *Kirkham* v. *Attenborough* (1897) and *London Jewellers Ltd* v. *Attenborough* (1934) title to the goods was held to pass to a bona fide pledgee who acquired the goods, in both cases, from the true owner on a sale–or–return basis. Once the pledgor dealt with the goods in a manner inconsistent with the title of the true owner and an innocent third party's rights were involved, title was held to pass so that the true owner had no right to recover the property from a bona fide pledgee. If goods are delivered on sale–or–return terms and the buyer does not signify his approval or acceptance to the seller, but retains the goods until after the goods should have been returned to the seller if the buyer did not wish to buy them, the buyer is taken to have accepted the goods and the ownership passes to him.

The passing of property in unascertained goods

The term "unascertained goods" may carry one of three possible meanings, namely that the goods have yet to be manufactured or grown by the seller, or that the goods are purely generic goods (e.g. 100 tons of high tensile steel), or that the goods are an unidentified portion of a specified whole (e.g. 50 tons weight of 100 tons of oil stored at a certain place). Although the Act does not distinguish between these three kinds of unascertained goods the rules as to the passing of property and risk necessarily differs in the three cases. The Sale of Goods Act 1979, s. 16, lays down the principle that where there is a contract for the sale of unascertained goods, the ownership of the goods cannot pass to the buyer unless and until the goods are ascertained. Section 18, rule 5, then provides that, unless a contrary intention is shown, where there is a contract for the sale of unascertained or future goods by description, and goods of that description in a deliverable state are appropriated unconditionally to the contract, either by the buyer or the seller, with the assent of the other of them, the ownership of the goods passes to the buyer. In *D. F. Mount Ltd* v. *Jay & Jay Provisions Ltd* (1960) goods were appropriated under the contract by the seller and the buyer's assent was deemed to have been given by the buyer re–selling the goods. Ownership cannot pass until the goods are in a deliverable state; therefore if the seller delivers the goods intended for the buyer to a carrier still mixed with other goods, ownership cannot pass to the buyer. Furthermore, ownership cannot pass until identifiable goods have been appropriated under the contract. Thus in *Healey* v. *Howlett & Sons* (1917) it was held that the ownership of a quantity of mackerel had not passed to the buyer, because although the seller had given the railway company which was to transport a consignment of mackerel instructions to earmark twenty boxes of mackerel for the buyer, that number of boxes had not been separated from the consignment and so had not been appropriated to the contract. Moreover, where unascertained goods can only be appropriated to a contract after they have been weighed, measured or tested in order to ascertain the price, the ownership of the goods does not pass to the buyer until this has been done. Thus in *National Coal Board* v. *Gamble* (1959) coal had been appropriated by the NCB to the contract to supply the defendant with a certain quantity by being loaded on to the buyer's lorry, but it was held that the appropriation was not unconditional until the coal was weighed so as to ascertain the total price payable and the weight–ticket had been accepted by the buyer.

Where the contract of sale is of an unidentified part of a larger whole, there can be no appropriation of the amount sold and ownership of it cannot pass by implication until there is a physical severance of the part sold. In *Wait & James* v. *Midland Bank* (1926), however, it was held that ownership could still pass to the buyer under the terms of the contract in this situation although there had been no unconditional appropriation of the part sold. In that case the goods sold had become ascertained by other means. The contract was for the sale of a quantity of wheat comprised in a particular cargo lying in a certain warehouse. The buyers were given delivery orders, which were accepted by the warehouse–keepers who stored the whole cargo and the buyers pledged the quantity of wheat they had purchased to a bank. The sellers subsequently sold and delivered the remainder of the cargo to other persons. It was held that the ownership of the wheat purchased by the original buyers had passed to them, and the pledge to the bank was consequently valid.

For the ownership of unascertained goods to pass to the buyer, not only must the goods be identified and appropriated to the contract by the seller or buyer but the other party must assent to the appropriation. Usually it is the seller who makes the appropriation by setting aside or despatching particular goods out of a larger stock in fulfilment of his contractual obligations, and the buyer's assent to the appropriation is shown by him taking delivery of the goods, whether he accepts them as conforming to the contract or not. The courts have been reluctant to hold that anything less than taking delivery amounts to an assent on the part of the buyer in the absence of any other express signification of his assent. Thus in *Carlos Federspiel & Co SA* v. *Charles Twiggs & Co Ltd* (1957) it was held that the buyer had not assented to an appropriation by the seller of the correct number of goods out of the seller's stock by the seller packing them and marking the packages with the buyer's name and arranging for the carriage of the goods to the buyer by sea and notifying the buyer that all these things had been done, when the buyer had not affirmatively indicated his assent but had merely not notified the seller of any objection. It is therefore clear that the buyer does not impliedly assent to an appropriation by receiving a notice of appropriation from the seller, however detailed it may be, nor by a carrier taking possession of the goods in order to deliver them to the buyer unless the carrier is expressly appointed by the buyer to be his agent to give his assent (which is unusual). On the other hand, express terms of the contract may make the seller the buyer's agent to assent to the appropriation which he makes as seller, and this will be so if the contract expressly provides that when he has appropriated particular goods to the contract, the seller is to hold them as agent or bailee for the buyer.

RETENTION OF TITLE CLAUSES

A seller may prevent the ownership of goods passing to a buyer under the rules dealt with above by providing in the contract of sale that the seller shall retain the ownership or disposal of the goods until they are paid for, or by expressly reserving the ownership or disposal to himself when he appropriates goods to the contract.

The simplest form of reservation of title clause provides that the ownership of the goods comprised in the contract of sale will be reserved to or retained by the seller until the buyer has paid the full purchase price, or alternatively that ownership of the goods will not pass to the buyer until payment of the purchase price has been made in full. There are various extensions or modifications to this clause which may be classified as follows:

(*a*) A provision that the ownership of the goods comprised in the contract will be retained by the seller until the price of the goods supplied under that contract and also the price of all other goods previously sold by the seller (or by the seller and companies in the same group) to the buyer (or to the buyer and companies in the same group as the buyer) have been paid in full. This kind of provision is called the "current account clause."

(*b*) A provision that the buyer will be obliged to provide in all contracts under which he re–sells the goods that the sub–purchasers under such contracts will not acquire ownership of the goods until the price payable to the original seller for the goods (with or without other amounts owing under a current account clause) has been fully paid. This type of retention of title clause places a contractual obligation on the buyer to include a further retention of title clause in the contracts under which he re–sells the goods to sub–purchasers, and this obligation may be perpetuated by the contract with the sub–purchasers requiring them to impose a similar obligation on the persons to whom they re–sell the goods.

(*c*) A provision that the buyer may re–sell the goods before ownership has passed to him, but the proceeds of re–sale will belong to the seller and will be held by the buyer as his agent or trustee until the price for the goods owing to the original seller (with or without other amounts owing to the seller under a current account clause) has been fully paid.

(*d*) A provision that the buyer may use the goods supplied by the seller in any manufacturing process so as to produce other goods (e.g. the fabrication of metal products) or in any manufacturing or other process which combines the goods sold with other goods so as to result in a composition product (e.g. the alloying of metals), but that the ownership of the resulting product will be retained by or vest in the seller until the price of the goods supplied by him (with or without other amounts owing to the seller under a current account clause) has been fully paid.

Effectiveness of retention clauses against third persons

The transfer of the possession of goods and the transfer of the ownership of the goods are two distinct and separate legal acts. Because of this it is possible for the ownership of the goods to remain in the original seller whilst the buyer takes possession of the goods and possibly re-sells them to a sub-purchaser. A situation may therefore arise where the buyer has bought goods subject to a retention of title clause and has obtained possession of the goods or the documents of title to them, so giving the appearance to third persons of being the owner of those goods. However, title to the goods can still be passed by the buyer to an innocent sub-purchaser under the Sale of Goods Act 1979, s. 25(1), if he acquires the goods in good faith and for value unaware of the condition for the passing of ownership or the retention of ownership by the seller. In order for s. 25(1) to apply, however, there must be a contract of sale between the seller and the buyer for a bona fide sub-purchaser to acquire ownership of the goods by purchasing them without knowledge of the seller's title. The fact that the contract is conditional or that it reserves ownership to the seller does not prevent it being a contract of sale for this purpose: *Lee* v. *Butler* (1893). But if the purchaser has merely an option to buy the goods (as under a hire-purchase contract) and the option has not yet been exercised or become exercisable (e.g. because the hire rental under a hire purchase agreement has not yet been paid in full), there is no present existing contract of sale and a sub-purchaser is not protected (*see Helby* v. *Matthews* (1895)).

A question which has become of particular concern and importance is what is the position of a secured creditor of the buyer of goods subject to a retention of title clause. Usually this is a bank which makes a loan or advance on the security of goods or the proceeds of sale of goods which have been sold by the original seller subject to a reservation in the ownership of the goods to the seller. The Sale of Goods Act 1979, s. 25(1), only protects a bona fide sub-purchaser or mortgagee or pledgee of the goods, but against other persons the unpaid seller's ownership of the goods can still be asserted. A situation of this nature arose in *Aluminium Industrie Vaassen BV* v. *Romalpa Aluminium Ltd* (1976) where the plaintiffs, a Dutch company which manufactured aluminium foil in Holland, sold quantities of foil to the defendants, an English company. The contract of sale incorporated an extended reservation of title clause which provided (*a*) that the ownership in the foil would only be transferred to the defendants when they had paid in full the amount owing for all foil delivered by the plaintiffs, and (*b*) that until payment was made, the defendants were under an obligation to store the goods in such a way as not to impair the plaintiff's title and to keep the goods separate from other goods in the defendants' possession. The clause further provided that if the foil was mixed with other goods in the course of a manufacturing process, the ownership of the resulting products was to vest in the plaintiffs until the defendants' indebtedness to the plaintiffs was discharged. The defendants were given a power to re-sell the goods supplied or goods manufactured with them, subject to the condition that until they had fully discharged their outstanding indebtedness to the plaintiffs they were to assign to the plaintiffs on demand any claims they had against the sub-purchasers and were to hold their rights against sub-purchasers and any payments received from them for the plaintiffs' benefit. The defendant company subsequently ran into financial difficulties and a receiver was appointed by debenture-holders at a time when the company already owed £122,000 to the plaintiffs for aluminium foil supplied by them. It was conceded by the receiver that approximately £35,152 held in a separate bank account by the defendant company immediately before the appointment of the receiver represented the proceeds of sale of foil sold by the defendants to sub-purchasers, but he contended that this money was subject to the debenture holders' security in priority to the plaintiffs' claim. The plaintiffs contended they were entitled to that sum in priority to the secured and unsecured creditors of the defendant company, because by the terms of the contract of sale with the defendants the proceeds of re-sale were held on their behalf and were therefore their property. The Court of Appeal held that the effect of the retention of title clause was that the ownership of the foil remained in the plaintiffs, but the clause conferred on the defendant company a power to sell the foil and imposed an obligation on them to account to the plaintiffs for the proceeds of sale, unless the defendant company's indebtedness to the plaintiffs had already been discharged. Secondly, so far as the sub-purchasers were concerned, the defendant company sold the foil to them as principals; but as between the plaintiffs and the defendant company, it sold the foil as agents for the plaintiffs and were therefore subject to the equitable fiduciary duty of an agent to treat the proceeds of re-sale as the plaintiffs' property. Finally, because in equity the proceeds belonged to the plaintiffs, they were entitled to trace them into the hands of the debenture holders' receiver and to recover them in priority to the secured and unsecured creditors.

Combinations of the goods sold with other goods

The *Romalpa* case was followed by the decision of Rubin J (sitting as a High Court Judge) in *Borden (UK) Ltd* v. *Scottish Timber Products Ltd* (1979), where the plaintiff supplied resin to the defendant on the condition that ownership would pass to the defendant only when the price of the goods was paid in full. The resin was to the plaintiff's knowledge to be used by the defendant company for the manufacture of chipboard, which was normally sold by the defendant before the plaintiffs were paid the price of the resin incorporated in it. The plaintiffs brought an action to trace their ownership of the resin into the proceeds of sale of the chipboard, despite the fact that the retention of title clause, unlike that in the *Romalpa* case, did not expressly extend to the proceeds of sale. The judge held the plaintiffs were entitled to trace the proceeds of the chipboard, ruling that unless the contract of sale expressly so provides, the supplier of raw materials who has reserved the ownership of them until payment is made to him does not become a co-owner of the resulting manufactured goods except where the raw materials form an "outstandingly large part of the elements required for the manufacturing process". Accordingly, the plaintiff did not acquire a proprietary title to the chipboard since the resin was not its main constituent. The judge held, however, that the defendant received the resin on delivery as a bailee for the plaintiff, and because of this a fiduciary relationship was created between them. Following the *Romalpa* case it was established law that the purchaser received the goods in question as a bailee, the seller's right to trace his claim into the proceeds of sale of the goods arose under the rule in *Re Hallett*. The right to trace would not exist, however, if there was implied into the contract not only a power for the defendant to use the resin in the manufacturing process, but also a further power to hold the resulting manufactured goods or the proceeds of selling them for its own account. The judge inferred a licence for the defendant to use the resin in manufacture before payment from the fact that the plaintiff gave the defendant one month's credit, but he refused to imply any further power to sell the manufactured goods on its own account since that would destroy the plaintiff's security completely. Consequently, the plaintiff was entitled to trace its resin into the chipboard manufactured with it and into the proceeds of sale of the chipboard, and it had a charge in equity on both the chipboard and the proceeds of its sale for the unpaid price of the resin.

On appeal by Scottish Timber Products, the Court of Appeal reversed the decision of Rubin J in *Borden (UK) Ltd* v. *Scottish Timber Products Ltd* (1979) and held that Borden was not entitled to trace its claim for the amounts owing into the resin it supplied and hence into the chipboard which incorporated it and ultimately into the proceeds of re–sale of the chipboard.

The court rejected the contention that Scottish Timber held the resin as a bailee for Borden, and consequently there was no fiduciary relationship between the parties. Borden had given Scottish Timber implied permission to use the resin in its manufacturing processes for its own benefit, thus destroying the separate existence of the resin. Bridge LJ further ruled that even if the beneficial ownership in the resin remained in the seller (Borden), the court would not go further and hold that the beneficial ownership of either the resin or the product in which it was embodied remained in Borden after it had been used in its manufacturing process. Scottish Timber therefore held the resin for its own purposes and not as the bailee for Borden, and consequently no tracing rights arose.

The second ground on which the court of appeal relied in reversing Rubin J's judgment was that the ownership of the resin incorporated in the chipboard vested in Scottish Timber at the latest when the resin was mixed with the other constitutents. The *Romalpa* case could not be applied by analogy, because in that case the aluminium foil remained unmixed, and if goods of a homogeneous character remain unmixed with other goods the tracing rights of the seller into the proceeds of re–sale remain unaffected. If, however, heterogeneous goods are mixed in the manufacturing process, the original goods supplied by the seller lose their separate character and the resulting composite goods are a conpletely new product owned by the manufacturer. As

Scottish Timber had used the resin for its own benefit, the property in the finished product was vested in it.

PASSING OF RISK

The Sale of Goods Act 1979, s. 20(1), raises the presumption that risk generally passes to the buyer with the ownership of the goods sold unless otherwise agreed. Once the ownership has passed, therefore, the goods are at the buyer's risk although he may not yet have taken delivery of the goods. Where, however, the parties have agreed that one of them should bear the risk, contrary to the presumption raised in s. 20(1), effect is given to that agreement. The position is therefore relatively clear where goods are in the possession of one of the parties. There may, however, be difficulties if goods are to be shipped under a cif or an fob contract where the risk is intended to pass to the buyer at the latest by the date on which they are put on board a ship.

In the case of *Sterns Ltd* v. *Vickers Ltd* (1923), the court decided that the risk in the goods passed to the purchaser before property had been transferred to him. In that case the defendants sold 120,000 gallons of spirit, which was stored in tanks containing 200,000 gallons belonging to a third party. The plaintiffs obtained a delivery order which the third party accepted but the buyers decided to leave the spirit in the tank for collection at their own convenience. The spirit deteriorated between the time of sale and the time when the plaintiffs eventually took delivery of the 120,000 gallons. The Court of Appeal held that although property had not passed to the buyers because the goods had not actually been appropriated to them, the risk of them being damaged, destroyed or deteriorating had passed and the buyers had to suffer the loss. The case, however, can be distinguished from *Healey* v. *Howlett & Sons* (1917) in which it was held that the risk in twenty boxes of fish which the buyer had agreed to purchase remained in the seller because the twenty boxes formed an unidentified part of a total of 190 boxes, none of which had been allocated to the purchaser. In this case, however, there had been no acknowledgment of the right of the buyer to delivery of the 20 boxes by a third person who held the 190 boxes.

In certain circumstances the ownership of goods may pass to the buyer before the risk; for example, where the seller agrees to dispatch specific goods at his own risk to the buyer. The Sale of Goods Act 1979, s. 33, provides, however, that the buyer must take the risk of the goods deteriorating if the risk is normally incidental to the course of transit.

The rules relating to the passing of risk are concerned with accidental loss, destruction or deterioration of the goods. If delivery of the goods is delayed or the goods are lost or damaged through the fault of one of the parties, s. 20 provides that the party at fault must bear the risk. In *Demby Hamilton & Co Ltd* v. *Barden* (1949) the court held the buyer liable for the loss when he failed within a reasonable time to take delivery of apple juice which he had agreed to purchase from the seller. Under s. 20, the party at fault is not liable for all the risks and damage sustained by the goods, but only such risks as materialise while he is guilty of delay in making or taking delivery.

Avoidance of contract for sale of specific goods which have ceased to exist

The Sale of Goods Act 1979, s. 6, provides that where the contract is for the sale of specific goods and those goods, unknown to the seller at the time the contract of sale is entered into, have perished, the contract is void. The application of s. 6 assumes that the goods were in existence and gives statutory force to the decision in *Couturier* v. *Hastie* (1856) in which case the defendant sold a cargo of corn shipped to him by a third party in Salonika; but unknown to the defendant because the cargo had started to deteriorate it had already been lawfully sold by the master of the ship at the time the defendant entered into the contract of sale. It was held that the defendant was not liable since the contract was void for mistake. Similarly in *Barrow, Lane Ballard Ltd* v. *Phillip Phillips & Co Ltd* (1929) the plaintiffs entered into a contract to sell to the defendants 700 bags of nuts which were stored in a warehouse. In fact, unknown to the plaintiffs, some of the bags had been stolen at the time the contract of sale was entered into and further bags disappeared before the buyers obtained delivery. It was held that under s. 6 the contract was void.

The section applies to a contract for the sale of specific goods; these are defined by s. 62 as goods "identified and agreed upon at the time the contract is made."

SALE BY A NON-OWNER OF GOODS

Where a seller of goods who has no right or only a limited right to deal in the goods sells them, the question which arises is which of two innocent parties should suffer. If, for example, a thief steals goods and sells them to a third party who purchases them in good faith and for value, the question is whether the true owner of the goods or the innocent third party who gives value for the goods should suffer the loss. Alternatively where an agent has been given authority to receive offers on certain goods and in fact actually sells those goods to an innocent third party the same question arises.

The Sale of Goods Act 1979, s. 21(1), provides that generally the buyer acquires no better title to the goods than the seller himself had, unless the true owner of the goods is estopped from denying the seller's authority to sell them, as he will be if he holds out the seller as his agent for this purpose. The fact that the true owner knows that the seller has re-sold the goods raises no estoppel against him. In *Mordaunt Brothers* v. *British Oil and Coke Mills Ltd* (1910) the defendants sold oil to the purchaser who re-sold part of it to the sub-purchasers, who received the delivery orders in respect of the part of the oil they had agreed to sub-purchase. The plaintiffs paid for the oil and sent the delivery orders to the defendants who accepted them. The defendants delivered oil to the plaintiffs as and when they received payment from the original purchaser. Subsequently he fell into arrears with the payments and the defendants refused to deliver further consignments of oil to the plaintiffs. It was held that the defendants had not consented to re-sale of the oil (under s. 47) since they clearly did not intend to renounce their rights against the original purchaser for non-payment, and the mere fact the defendants were aware of the sub-sale did not necessarily indicate consent. On the other hand in *D. F. Mount Ltd* v. *Jay & Jay Provisions Ltd* (1960) the defendants, who were owners of 500 cartons of tinned peaches, sold 250 cartons to a purchaser on the understanding that the defendants would be paid only when the purchaser had resold them to a third party. The defendants claimed a lien on the goods when they did not receive payment for them from the purchaser, but it was held on the facts that they had consented to the re-sale and therefore had no rights to a lien.

There are a number of exceptions to the rule that a buyer who acquires goods from a person who is not their owner or who does not sell them with the authority of the true owner acquires no title or no better title than the seller himself has. The exceptions to the rule are as follows:

(a) Where the true owner is precluded either by express words or by his conduct from denying the seller's authority to sell. In such a situation the seller represents either by word or conduct that the person selling the goods had authority to deal with the goods as the true owner. In *Henderson & Co* v. *Williams* (1895) a fraudulent person, F, induced the true owner to sell to him certain goods held by the defendants in a warehouse. The true owner instructed the defendants to transfer the goods in their books to F, who sold the goods to the plaintiffs. The plaintiffs made enquiries from the defendants, who supplied them with a written statement that they held the goods to the order of F. The true owner failed to receive payment from F, and he instructed the defendants not to deliver the goods to the plaintiffs. The court held that both the true owner and the defendants were estopped from denying the plaintiffs' rights to the goods, the true owners because they had instructed the warehouseman to hold them to the order of F, and the plaintiffs because they had relied on this fact in buying them from F.

Similarly in *Eastern Distributors Ltd* v. *Goldring* (1957) it was held that a person may be prevented from claiming the goods if by his conduct he has represented to an innocent third party that anyone dealing with the goods has the attributes of the true owner. In this case M signed and delivered forms to C in pursuance of a plan to deceive a finance company; the plan enabled C to represent to the finance company that he had M's authority to sell a car belonging to him to a buyer who was financed by the company. It was held that the estoppel would operate to pass a good title to the plaintiff company under the hire-purchase arrangements made with the buyer.

(b) Estoppel by negligence may be established as a defence where the owner has by his negligence allowed a third party to represent himself as the true owner of the goods or as having the true owner's authority to sell them. However, estoppel by negligence can only be raised if the owner of the goods is under a duty of care to see that the property does not get lost or stolen. In

Lickbarrow v. *Mason* (1787) the court said that where one of two innocent persons must suffer by the acts of a third party, it is the person who is responsible for allowing the situation to arise who must sustain the loss. However, in *Central Newbury Car Auctions Ltd* v. *Unity Finance Ltd* (1957) a fraudulent person offered to buy two cars on hire–purchase terms, leaving with the plaintiffs in part–exchange a Hillman car which, unknown to the plaintiffs, was also on hire–purchase. The fraudulent person was allowed to drive away with the car and was given possession of the registration book. The finance company refused the hire–purchase proposal and the car was subsequently discovered in the possession of the defendants who had purchased it in good faith. The court held that the plaintiffs were entitled to recover the car and said that merely because the fraudulent person was in possession of the documents of title to the car did not confer ownership on him. Similarly in *Mercantile Credit Co Ltd* v. *Hamblin* (1965) an innocent third party was held not to be estopped from denying fraud on the part of a car dealer who purported to enter into a hire–purchase transaction for a car of which she was herself the owner and which she had left with the car dealer as security for a loan made to her. The court said she owed a duty of care but had satisfied that by taking the car to an apparently honest dealer.

Factors Act 1889, s. 2

The doctrine of estoppel operates to protect a third party who buys goods from a factor (i.e. a person whose business consists of buying and selling goods for others) in the ordinary course of business if the goods had been entrusted to the factor by the true owner; the common law did not protect a pledgee. The Factors Act 1889, s. 2 (now incorporated in the Sale of Goods Act 1979, s. 26), however, provides that where a mercantile agent in the customary course of his business as an agent receives goods with authority either to sell the goods or to consign the goods for the purpose of sale, or to buy goods or to raise money on them as security for the sale, and he sells those goods to an innocent third party, the sale is valid.

The mercantile agent must have possession of the goods with the consent of the owner. In *Pearson* v. *Rose & Young* (1951) the merchantile agent had obtained possession of the car registration book by a trick from the true owner, but it was held that this did not mean that the agent did not have the owner's consent to sell the car: when he did so he was acting in the ordinary course of his business and had obtained possession of the car with the owner's consent so that the defendant acquired a valid title.

A purchaser from a mercantile agent will not obtain a valid title from the mercantile agent unless the agent receives the goods from the owner in the course of his business as a mercantile agent, even though he may not actually receive them for sale; for example, he may receive them for the purpose of display or to receive offers. Section 2(2) also provides that where the mercantile agent receives the goods with the consent of the owner, the subsequent withdrawal of his authority by the owner will not affect the title of an innocent purchaser who bought the goods without notice of the withdrawal of consent.

A purchaser of goods from the mercantile agent can only claim the protection of s. 2 if he can show that the agent acted in the ordinary course of business. In *Oppenheimer* v. *Attenborough* (1908) it was held that a sale by a mercantile agent at a place other than his business premises is generally not in the ordinary course of business, and the words "acting in the ordinary course of business" mean acting in such a way as a mercantile agent would normally act in the ordinary course of business; having regard to the hours of business and the place of business. The purchaser must have acted in good faith and without notice that the goods were sold without the consent of the true owner.

Special powers of sale

The Sale of Goods Act 1979, s. 21(2)(*b*), provides that any contract of sale entered into under a common law or statutory power of sale whereby a third party who is not the true owner of the goods is entitled to sell them is a valid power and the purchaser acquires a valid title; for example, a sheriff or a bailiff has a power to seize and sell goods under a writ of execution, and a warehouse keeper has a lien for unpaid rent or storage charges over the goods he stores for the owner so that he can sell the goods to satisfy the amounts owed to him. When litigation is pending, the courts also have a jurisdiction to order the sale of goods which for any just and sufficient reason it may be desirable to have sold at once because of their perishable nature.

Sale in market overt

The Sale of Goods Act 1979, s. 22, provides that where a purchaser acquires goods in market overt in accordance with the customs and usage of that market, the purchaser acquires a good title provided he buys them in good faith and without notice of any defect in the title of the seller. The goods purchased in the market place must be of the kind normally dealt with in that market. In *Bishopsgate Motor Finance Corporation Ltd* v. *Transport Brakes Ltd* (1949) evidence was given that cars were sold regularly in Maidstone market and it was an accepted practice of the market that if at the auction the car did not reach its reserve price, the owner could sell it by private negotiation. In this case, after it failed to reach a reserve price, a car was sold by private agreement by a person with a limited title, and the true owners subsequently sought to recover the car from the innocent third party. The court held that the car was sold in market overt in accordance with the customs of the market place and the burden of proof was therefore on the true owner to show that the sale had not complied with the rules of the market. The true owner had failed to show this and therefore the sale was not set aside. In *Reid* v. *Commissioner of Metropolitan Police* (1973) it was held that a sale in a market overt in the early morning but during market hours did not constitute a sale which would defeat the title of the true owner since the sale was not between the hours of sunrise and sunset and not an open sale in that the goods were not on display when purchased.

Sale under a voidable title

The Sale of Goods Act 1979, s. 23, provides that where the seller of goods has a voidable title to the goods but his title has not been avoided at the time of the sale to an innocent third party who buys in good faith and without notice of the defect, that third party acquires a valid title. In general the true owner can only rescind the contract by communicating with the person responsible for the fraud, but in *Car & Universal Finance Ltd* v. *Caldwell* (1965) it was held that the owner of the goods could avoid a contract by showing an intention to do so and taking all reasonable steps open to him, for example, notifying the police and AA, when he could not communicate with the fraudulent party.

Protection of sub-purchasers

The Sale of Goods Act 1979, ss. 21 *et seq.*, create a number of exceptions to the general rule that a person who has no title or only a limited title to goods (e.g. an agent with a limited authority who acts beyond the scope of his authority, i.e. by selling the goods) cannot confer on a third party a valid title to the goods which is effective against the true owner of the goods. In this section it is not proposed to deal with all those exceptions, but only with the particular case of dispositions made by the seller or buyer of goods in favour of a third party.

The Sale of Goods Act 1979, s. 24 (originally the Factors Act 1889, s. 8), provides that where a person who has sold or agreed to sell goods but continues in possession of them or of documents of title relating to them, delivers or transfers those goods or documents of title under a further sale or pledge to any person who takes them in good faith and without notice of the previous sale, the disposition has the same effect as if the person making the transfer were expressly authorised by the owner of the goods to make the sale or pledge.

The Privy Council held in *Pacific Motor Auctions Property Ltd* v. *Motor Credits (Hire Finance) Ltd* (1965) the sub–purchaser under such a sale acquires a valid title from the seller if he continues to have physical possession of them, regardless of whether he held the goods in his capacity as seller or in a more limited capacity (e.g. as agent or bailee for the buyer). Consequently provided the seller had continuous possession of the goods after selling or agreeing to sell them to the buyer, the sub–purchaser acquires a valid title which defeats the original buyer's title. The facts of the *Pacific Motor* case were that M Ltd bought a number of cars from a car dealer for the purpose of entering into hire–purchase agreements to Motordom's customers. The dealer continued in possession of the cars as bailees for M Ltd with its authority to deliver to its customers. M Ltd later revoked the dealer's authority to deliver the cars or to dispose of them, but the dealer nevertheless sold a number of cars to Pacific Motor Auctions which bought and took delivery of them in good faith. M Ltd brought an action claiming the return of the cars and damages. The Privy Council held that the action by M Ltd failed, because Pacific Motors had acquired a good title under s. 28(1) of the New South Wales Sales of Goods Act 1923–53 (which corresponds to the English Sale of Goods Act 1979, s. 24(1)). The dealer who held the cars as bailee for M Ltd had continued to possess the cars after selling them to M Ltd although in an entirely different capacity from that of seller. A seller is therefore to be treated as being in continuing possession of the goods for the purpose of s. 24(1) provided he has not actually parted with possession of the goods, and is therefore able to pass a good title to a third party who purchases and takes delivery of the goods after the sale to the first buyer. The Privy Council applied the same rule in *Mitchell* v. *Jones* (1905) where the seller sold and delivered a horse to the buyer, but later borrowed it back for use and then wrongfully sold it again to a third party. In this case, the second purchaser was not protected and did not acquire a title which would defeat the first buyer's title. This was because the seller's possession of the goods had not been continuous from the time of the original sale, but had been broken by a period during which the buyer had been in possession. Once this happens there is no longer any room for s. 24 to operate in favour of a third party who buys the goods from the seller. These cases have been followed by the Court of Appeal in *Worcester Works Finance Ltd* v. *Cooden Engineering Co Ltd* (1972). In that case the defendants sold a car to Griffiths, a car dealer, and received a cheque in payment. Griffiths took delivery of the car and sold it to the plaintiffs for cash and then hired it to Millerick, a customer of Griffiths, under a hire–purchase agreement. Millerick never took possession of the car, and Griffiths paid the hire–purchase instalments to the plaintiffs in order to conceal his fraud, but he subsequently stopped these payments. His cheque in favour of the defendants for the original purchase price was dishonoured and so, with his consent, they retook possession of the car and agreed that the sale to Griffiths should be cancelled. The plaintiffs, on discovering what had happened, claimed the car from the defendants, but the defendants claimed they had a good title under the Sale of Goods Act 1979, s. 24, because, although Griffiths had sold the car to the plaintiffs, he had remained in possession of it and the defendants re-taking the car with his consent amounted to a resale to them. Consequently, because they took back the car in good faith for value and without notice of the sale to the plaintiffs, they claimed to be protected as purchasers under s. 24. The Court of Appeal held that the defendants' contention succeeded, and they had a good title to the goods since they re-took the car for value and without notice of the re–sale. Moreover, Griffiths had continued in possession of the car throughout although in a different capacity from that of seller to the plaintiffs; but that was held to be immaterial in view of the continuity of the possession. The earlier cases of *Staffs Motor Guarantee Ltd* v. *British Wagon Co Ltd* (1934) and *Eastern Distributors Ltd* v. *Goldring* (1957), which had decided the contrary were considered no longer to be good law. In those cases it had been held that the statutory words "continues in possession" in s. 24 meant that the seller must continue in possession as seller, and not as a bailee or in any other capacity, so that if the person who had sold goods continued in possession merely as a bailee for the first buyer a second purchaser was no longer protected by s. 24(1).

Section 24 only protects the second purchaser from a seller who remains in possession of the goods or documents of title to the goods if the goods or the documents of title to them are delivered to the second purchaser. Thus if the seller sells goods to A and retains possession of them, and then proceeds to sell them to B, still retaining possession, B will not be protected despite his good faith and A may recover the goods. B, however, will be able to defeat A's title to the goods if B takes delivery of documents of title to the goods from A; for this purpose documents of title include any documents issued by a third party by means of which the right to possession or ownership of goods is proved in commercial practice. They therefore include bills of lading, air waybills, railway consignment notes, warehouse warrants, delivery orders and similar instruments.

The Sale of Goods Act 1979, s. 25(1) (originally the Factors Act 1889, s. 9), deals with the converse position where a person who has bought or agreed to buy certain goods obtains the possession of the goods or the documents of title to them with the consent of the seller and sells, and then pledges or disposes of those goods or documents of title to a person who receives them in good faith and without notice of any lien or other right of the original seller. Such a person obtains a good title to the goods as though the delivery or transfer of the goods or documents of title to him were made with the consent of the owner. Section 14(1) applies where a buyer has acquired the ownership of the goods before the sale to the second purchaser, whereas s. 25(1) applies whether or not the property has passed to the first buyer. In part, s. 25 has been dealt with above in connection with retention of title agreements. The following additional points should also be noticed.

The protection given by s. 25(1) to a third party who acquires goods from a buyer who himself holds them subject to a lien or other interest of the seller, is available if the goods were in the possession of the buyer with the consent of the seller. It is therefore immaterial how the buyer obtained the goods, provided that he did so with the consent of the seller; moreover it is immaterial that the seller has revoked his consent. In *Car and Universal Finance Co* v. *Caldwell* (1965) it was therefore held that if a seller is induced to sell goods by the buyer's fraud, he may rescind the sale in an appropriate case by simply publishing his intention to rescind and without communicating with the fraudulent buyer. The reasoning is effective as between seller and buyer, but a third person who purchases the goods from the buyer would nevertheless be able to rely on the Sale of Goods Act 1979, s. 25(1), if he takes delivery from the buyer and acts in good faith.

Where the buyer has obtained the documents of title to the goods with the consent of the seller, the seller may still have a lien or right of stoppage in transit over the goods if they have not been paid for. The Sale of Goods Act 1979, s. 47 (originally the Factors Act 1889, s. 10), provides that where the documents of title to goods have lawfully been transferred to any person who buys or otherwise acquires them, and he then transfers the documents to a third party who takes them in good faith and gives valuable consideration for them, then if the transfer was upon a sale, the seller's lien or right of stoppage is defeated, and if the transfer was by way of a pledge or other disposition for value, the unpaid seller's lien or right of stoppage in transit can only be exercised subject to the rights of the transferee. The third party must take the goods in good faith and without notice of any lien or other right of the original seller in respect of the goods. In *Cahn & Mayer* v. *Pockett's Bristol Channel Steam Packet Co* (1899) the sellers forwarded to the buyer a bill of lading for copper shipped on the defendants' ship. The buyer who was insolvent transferred the bill of lading to the plaintiffs in return for payment of the purchase price for the copper under a contract previously entered between them. The plaintiffs took the bills of lading in good faith and without notice of the rights of the original sellers to the copper. The sellers exercised their right of stoppage in transit and the plaintiffs brought an action against the defendants for non–delivery. The Court of Appeal held that the buyer, having obtained possession of the bills of lading with the consent of the sellers, transferred a good title to the plaintiffs who took in good faith and the sellers had no right of stoppage.

The significance of the Sale of Goods Act 1979, ss. 24 and 25(1), in connection with contracts for the sale of goods which reserve the ownership of the goods to the seller until the purchase price has been paid or some other condition has been fulfilled, is that so long as that has not happened the seller or buyer who is in possession of the goods or of the documents of title to them can pass the ownership of them to a third party free from the rights of the other party to the contract of sale provided the third party takes delivery of the goods or documents of title in ignorance of those rights. In *Lee* v. *Butler* (1893) L had delivered to him certain furniture under a hire–purchase agreement, but before making a final payment he sold and delivered the furniture to the defendant, who took it in good faith and without notice of the plaintiff's rights. The court held that where L had possession of the goods with the consent of the true owner and he wrongfully sold and delivered the goods to an innocent third party, that third party acquired a valid title, even against the true owner, and the sale was effective as though it had been with his consent. This case was distinguished in *Helby* v. *Matthews* (1895) where a clause in the contract of sale expressly stated that ownership in the goods should remain in the plaintiff until full payment had been made. The court therefore held that a third party to whom the goods were pawned could not retain them as against the true owner and that the title to the goods did not pass to him. The only exception to this is where a purchaser is in possession of goods under a conditional sale agreement by which he acquires the goods for use as a consumer and not commercially on terms that the purchase price is to be paid by instalments, with the consequence that the contract is a consumer credit agreement subject to the Consumer Credit Act 1974. This Act and the topic of consumer credit constitute a separate subject in themselves and are not dealt with in this book.

OBLIGATIONS OF A SELLER

Duty to deliver the goods

The Sale of Goods Act 1979, s. 27, provides that it is the duty of the seller to deliver the goods and of the buyer to pay and to accept delivery of the goods in accordance with the terms of the contract. The word delivery is defined in s. 61 as the "voluntary transfer of possession", but in law delivery may be interpreted as one of a number of possible situations:

(*a*) the seller may physically transfer the goods themselves to the buyer or his agent; or

(*b*) the seller may transfer possession of the goods to the buyer or his agent by transferring the means of control over the goods (i.e. by handing over the keys to a warehouse where the goods are stored); or

(*c*) by a third party who is in possession of the goods attorning to the buyer that he holds the goods on his behalf; or

(*d*) the goods may be delivered by the delivery of documents (i.e. by the delivery of a bill of lading or dock warrant); or

(*e*) the parties may agree that the seller holds the goods as an agent of the buyer.

Section 29 lays down certain rules relating to the obligation to deliver the goods. The parties may by an express or implied agreement decide whether it is for the seller to send or deliver these to the buyer's place of business, or for the buyer to arrange and take delivery from the seller. In the absence of any agreement the place of delivery is the seller's place of business or his residence, and it is for the buyer to arrange to take delivery.

The time of delivery

Whether the terms in a contract of sale which relate to the time of performance are of the essence depends on the contract itself. However, the courts have held that in commercial contracts of sale the time for the delivery of the goods is prima facie of the essence. If the goods must be delivered on or by a particular date, then failure to deliver on that date or by that date or within a reasonable time thereafter is a breach of condition and will entitle the buyer to repudiate the contract. Where no time is fixed for delivery the seller must deliver the goods within a reasonable time. Since a failure on the part of the seller to deliver the goods on time is a breach of condition the buyer may reject the goods when they are delivered even though he has not suffered any damage. In *Bowes* v. *Shand* (1877) the sellers agreed to ship a quantity of rice during March and/or April. A consignment of rice was shipped in February and the rest in March. The court held that although the buyer did not suffer any loss or damage, he was entitled to reject the goods because the clause relating to the time of delivery was of the essence of the contract. Although time is of the essence of the contract with respect to delivery, the buyer can waive the condition; if he does so the waiver will be binding on him whether he has received fresh consideration or not for the variation of the contractual terms. He can, however, later give notice fixing a reasonable time for delivery and thus making time again of the essence of the contract. If performance is not completed by that time he will have a right to terminate the contract. In *Rickards Ltd* v. *Oppenhaim* (1950) the plaintiffs agreed to supply a Rolls Royce chassis for the defendant to be ready at the latest by 20th March 1948. The plaintiffs failed to deliver the chassis by that date but the defendant continued to press for delivery. In June 1948 the defendant wrote to the plaintiffs informing them that he would not accept delivery after 25th July. The plaintiffs failed to deliver the chassis by that date too, and the court held that the defendant was entitled to reject the chassis when it was finally delivered as he had given reasonable notice that delivery must be by a certain date.

If it is clear that the party who has been granted additional time to complete his part of the bargain will be unable to perform his contractual obligations within a reasonable time it may be unnecessary to give notice of intention to repudiate the contract.

Payment and delivery are concurrent conditions

Unless the parties agree to the contract the delivery of the goods must be concurrent with the payment of the price. The seller does not actually have to tender delivery of the goods before bringing an action for payment of the purchase price or for damages when it is apparent that the buyer would have refused to accept the goods. It was originally thought that the seller must show that he was ready and willing to comply with his part of the bargain, but in *British & Bennington Ltd* v. *NW Cachar Tea Co* (1923) it was held that where the buyers had wrongfully repudiated a contract for the sale of goods, the sellers were not bound to prove that they were ready and willing at the date of the repudiation to deliver the goods in order to be able to sue for the price or for damages for non–acceptance of the goods. The facts of the case were that the appellants agreed to buy a tea crop from the respondents but the delivery date in London had not been agreed upon. The ships carrying the consignment of tea were diverted to ports outside London, and the parties agreed that delivery would be accepted there. The buyers subsequently repudiated the contract, and it was held that they were liable in damages to the seller for wrongful repudiation. The sellers did not have to show that they themselves were in a position to fulfil their part of the bargain. However, where it is obvious that the seller will be unable to deliver the goods and the buyer wrongfully repudiates the contract that is likely to reduce his damages.

Delivery of more or less than the contract quantity

The seller must deliver the quantity of goods agreed by the parties under the contract of sale and if the seller delivers to the buyer a smaller quantity of goods than agreed under the contract, the buyer may reject the goods delivered or if the buyer accepts the goods actually delivered he must pay the contractual rate, Sale of Goods Act 1979, s. 30(1). The buyer is not obliged to accept delivery in instalments unless otherwise agreed in the contract (*see* s. 31(1)). In *Behrend & Co Ltd* v. *Produce Brokers Co Ltd* (1920) the sellers agreed to sell a quantity of cotton seed to arrive on board the "Port Inglis" in London. The ship discharged a part of the cargo in London and left for Hull. It returned fourteen days later and discharged the rest of the cargo. It was held that the buyers were entitled to reject the later delivery of the cotton whilst retaining the earlier consignment delivered to them. Presumably the buyers could have rejected the earlier consignment too on the ground that the seller had not delivered the quantity contracted for sale.

The seller must not deliver a greater quantity of goods than that agreed in the contract of sale, and if he does the buyer can reject the whole quantity or an amount equivalent to any excess supplied over the amount called for by the contract.

Section 30(4) provides that if the seller delivers the goods which he contracted to sell, but they are mixed with other goods not comprised in the contract of sale the buyer may accept those goods he agreed to purchase under the contract and reject the rest, or he may reject the whole consignment delivered. Thus in *Re Moore & Co Ltd and Landauer & Co* (1921) the buyers agreed to buy 300 tins of canned fruit packed in cases of 30 tins. When the goods were delivered it was found that, although the correct quantity had been delivered, about half the cases delivered contained only 24 tins. It was held that the purchasers were entitled to reject the whole consignment because, although the value of the tins actually delivered was the same as the tins the plaintiffs had agreed to purchase, there was a breach of s. 13 (*see also* s. 3 above).

REMEDIES OF THE UNPAID SELLER

In addition to personal remedies available to the seller for breach of contract (i.e. an action for the price of the goods sold or an action for damages for non–acceptance of the goods), the seller has certain other rights of action; for example, the seller has a lien over the goods, or a right of stoppage in transit and a right to re–sell the goods. It is proposed to look briefly at the rights of the seller under the contract of sale. A seller may have one of the following alternatives open to him:

(*a*) an action to recover the price of the goods where the property has passed and the buyer has accepted the goods; or

(*b*) an action (under the Sale of Goods Act 1979, s. 50(1)) for the price and for damages if the buyer refuses to accept the goods; or

(*c*) an action (under the Act of 1979, s. 49(1)) for the price or for damages where the property has passed and the buyer refuses to accept the goods.

Under s. 49(2) of the Act, however, the seller may sue for the price although the property has not passed; for example, where the price is payable on a certain date irrespective of whether the seller has delivered the goods. If the price is payable before delivery the seller can sue for the price immediately it becomes due.

Where property in the goods has not passed, the seller's normal remedy is to bring an action against the buyer for damages for non–acceptance of the goods. Section 50(2) provides (subject to the obligation on the seller to mitigate his loss) that the measure of damages is the "estimated loss directly and naturally resulting in the ordinary course of events" from the buyer's breach.

Where there is an available market in the goods, the damages will be assessed by ascertaining the difference between the contract price and the market price at the time when the goods should have been accepted. In *Campbell Mostyn (Provisions) Ltd* v. *Barnett Trading Co* (1954) the seller re-sold the goods after a breach and obtained more than the market price at the date of the breach. It was held that the seller was nevertheless entitled to recover the difference between the contract and market price and did not have to account for the higher price at which he had in fact sold the goods.

The seller's rights and remedies against the goods

In addition to the seller's right to bring an action for damages for non-payment or for non-acceptance of the goods, he has certain rights whereby he can look on the goods as security and exercise remedies in respect of the goods themselves. The Sale of Goods Act 1979, s. 39, provides an unpaid seller of goods with the three following remedies against the goods:

(*a*) a lien on the goods or the right to retain them for the price while he has possession of them;

(*b*) where the buyer becomes insolvent, a right of stoppage in transit after he has parted with the possession of the goods and they are in the possession of a carrier who is transporting them to the buyer; and

(*c*) a limited right of re-sale.

The remedies granted by s. 39 can be exercised only by an unpaid seller of goods. An unpaid seller is one who sells the goods as owner, or any other person who is in the position of the seller (i.e. an agent) who has not received or been tendered the full price for the goods or who has received a negotiable instrument which had been dishonoured.

Unpaid seller's lien

The seller's lien is a right to retain the goods until the whole of the price has been paid or tendered. If property to the goods has passed to the seller the lien does not give the seller any property in the goods but merely a right to retain them until the price outstanding has been paid or tendered. The lien in favour of the seller only arises if the three following conditions have been satisfied:

(*a*) The seller must be an unpaid seller. The buyer can only claim a discharge of a lien if the whole of the price has been paid or tendered. If the price is to be paid in instalments, the unpaid seller can claim a lien on those parts of the goods which correspond to the amounts outstanding from the buyer.

(*b*) The sale must not be a credit sale. If the seller sells goods on credit he cannot exercise his right of the unpaid sellers lien because the Act assumes that the buyer is entitled to the delivery of the goods before the payment becomes due. The seller therefore has no right of a lien if he sells goods on credit, but s. 41(1) creates two exceptions to the rule:

(*i*) where the goods have been sold on credit and the term for which credit was granted has expired, or

(*ii*) where the buyer has become insolvent.

(*c*) The seller must have possession of the goods.

The seller will lose his lien:

(*a*) if the purchaser pays or tenders the purchase price of the goods;

(*b*) when the seller delivers the goods to a carrier or bailee with the intention that they should be conveyed to the purchaser;

(*c*) when the buyer or his agent lawfully obtains possession of the goods;

(*d*) when the seller waives his lien over the goods.

Unpaid seller's right of stoppage in transit

The Sale of Goods Act 1979, s. 44, provides that an unpaid seller who has parted with the possession of the goods has a right to stop them in transit and to regain possession of them. The seller may resume possession of the goods while they are in transit (but not when the goods have actually been delivered to the buyer or his agent) and may then retain them until the purchase price is paid or tendered. A seller can exercise a right of stoppage in transit if the following conditions are satisfied:

(*a*) the seller must be unpaid; and

(*b*) the buyer must be insolvent; and

(*c*) the goods must be in transit.

The goods are in transit when they have passed out of the possession of the seller into the possession of a carrier but have not yet been delivered to the purchaser or an agent authorised to receive delivery. The seller will lose his right of stoppage when the goods are no longer in transit; for example, when they have actually been delivered to the buyer or if the carrier has attorned the goods to the buyer. The right of stoppage in transit may be exercised over some part of the goods where some of the goods have been delivered.

The right of stoppage may be lost by sub–dealings with the goods by the buyer. If, for example, the buyer mortgages or charges the goods, the seller can still exercise his right of stoppage notwithstanding that the goods have been pledged, but his rights will be subject to the rights of the secured creditor.

Position between the vendor and the carrier

If the carrier to whom a notice of stoppage has been delivered wrongfully delivers the goods to the buyer, he is liable for conversion to the vendor. The carrier, however, has a lien on the goods for the freight due, and this will take priority over the seller's right of stoppage; the carrier can refuse to redeliver the goods to the seller unless the seller discharges the amount of the freight.

Unpaid seller's right of resale

The seller has a power of re–sale:

(*a*) if he still has property in the goods;

(*b*) if the property in the goods has passed but the seller still has possession of the goods; or

(*c*) if the property has passed but the seller has exercised his right of lien or stoppage in transit.

The 1979 Act, s. 48(2), provides that where an unpaid seller has exercised his lien over the goods or his right of stoppage in transit, he may re-sell the goods and the buyer will acquire a good title as against the original purchaser.

REMEDIES OF BUYER FOR BREACH BY SELLER

Claim for damages

The buyer's action for breach of contract may take one of two forms:

(*a*) an action for damages for non-delivery; or

(*b*) an action for breach of warranty or condition.

The Sale of Goods Act 1979, s. 51, lays down the main rules for the assessment of damages, and provides that the seller is liable for all the loss naturally flowing from the seller's failure to deliver the goods. If there is a market for the goods the damages are to be assessed by reference to the market price of the goods at the time when they ought to have been delivered. The effect is that the buyer is placed in the position he would have been in had the goods been delivered under the contract. If the market price is lower than the contract price, the buyer is only entitled to nominal damages.

If the seller repudiates the contract and notifies the buyer that he will not deliver the goods when delivery becomes due, the market price for the goods when the delivery should have been made (not the prevailing price when notice of repudiation was given) must be taken into account in assessing damages. However, the buyer must mitigate his loss if this is possible, and if the price for the goods is increasing at the time of repudiation he must purchase substituted goods immediately on the market if he can.

Where the market price rule does not apply

In exceptional cases it may be impossible for the buyer to purchase goods on the market. In such a case the damages would have to be assessed by some other method; for example, the buyer may be able to claim damages on the loss of a sub-sale known to the seller, or he may be able to claim special damages for loss he may suffer due to the special circumstances in which the contract was made. The buyer may be able to claim the loss actually suffered as a result of not being able to supply the goods under the contract of re-sale if the goods in question have been re-sold and the contract of sale with the seller itself anticipated a resale of the goods. Moreover, if the original buyer is sued by the sub-buyer and has to pay damages to him, the buyer is entitled to claim from the seller the total sum he has to pay in compensation provided the buyer has acted reasonably in defending the action.

Damages for breach of a term of the contract

Where the seller actually delivers the goods but there is a breach of condition or warranty on his part, the buyer is entitled to recover damages. For example, where the seller delivers goods which do not correspond to the contract description or goods which are not of the quality required by the contract, the buyer is prima facie entitled to the difference between the value of the goods actually delivered and the value of the goods which should have been delivered. If the goods are delivered late the buyer is entitled to the difference in the value of goods on the date they should have been delivered and their value on the date they were actually delivered, but he may alternatively recover the additional price he has paid for substituted goods on the open market to fulfil contracts he has made with sub–purchasers, if the seller was aware of them.

Conversion

The buyer is entitled to bring an action in conversion if the property in the goods has passed to him and the seller either refuses to deliver the goods or renders himself unable to deliver them (e.g. by selling them to another person). The measure of damages is the value of the goods when the seller refused to deliver them or renders himself unable to do so.

Specific performance

The buyer can ask the courts to enforce the contract by an order of specific performance, but since this is an equitable remedy it is necessary for the buyer to show that damages would be an insufficient remedy. Normally only a contract for goods for which the buyer cannot obtain a satisfactory substitute by buying on the overt market would be specifically enforced by the courts.

Rescission of termination of contract for breach by a buyer or seller

A party to a contract will be in breach of contract if either before or at the time performance becomes due he refuses to perform his part of the bargain. The other party to the contract can treat the contract as terminated when notice of refusal to perform the contract is given, or when the time for performance has arrived and the terms of the contract remain unfulfilled.

PROBLEMS

1. What are the rules relating to the price of goods under the Sale of Goods Act 1979, s. 8?

2. What terms as to title are implied under the Sales of Goods Act 1979, s. 12?

3. Explain the scope of the implied condition that the goods must correspond to their description under a contract of sale.

4. What factors will be taken into account in order to determine whether the goods are of merchantable quality under the Sale of goods Act 1979, s. 14(2)?

5. When must goods be fit for the particular purpose for which they are sold?

6. To what extent will the Unfair Contract Terms Act 1977 apply to declare an exclusion clause invalid?

7. When does title to the goods pass under the Sale of Goods Act 1979 if the goods are (a) specific and (b) unascertained?

8. What are the types of retention of title clauses used in a contract for the sale of goods? To what extent will retention of title clause be effective against a third party?

9. When does risk in the goods pass under the Sale of Goods Act 1979?

10. The general rule is that a buyer who acquires goods from a person who is not the owner, or who sells them without the true owner's authority, acquires no title or no better title than the seller himself has. What are the exceptions to this rule?

11. What are the obligations of the seller under a contract of sale under the Sale of Goods Act 1979?

12. What are the remedies of an unpaid seller of goods?

13. What remedies does a buyer have for breach of a contract for the sale of goods by the seller?

CHAPTER FIVE

The Law of International Trade

OBJECTIVES

It is proposed in this chapter to deal with the law relating to the international sale of goods. In particular the chapter deals with:

(a) special terms and types of contracts in connection with the international sales contract and responsibilities of the parties;

(b) finance of international trade with particular emphasis on letters of credit, including;

(i) the varieties of letters;

(ii) transfer of a benefit of credit;

(iii) the relationship between the debtor and beneficiary;

(iv) the effect of a failure to fulfil the obligations by the buyer under the contract of sale;

(v) the debtors continuing liability for the debt;

(vi) the relationship between the beneficiary and the issuing and confirming banks;

(vii) tender of documents;

(viii) rejection of documents on extraneous grounds;

(ix) security interests under a letter of credit;

(c) the carriage of goods by sea, air, rail and road:

(i) payment in freight;

(ii) carriage covered by bills of lading;

(iii) the Carriage of Goods by Sea Act 1971;

(iv) liability of the shipowner for loss or damage to goods;

(v) excepted perils under the 1971 Act;

(vi) container transport.

CONTRACTS FOR INTERNATIONAL SALES

The parties to a contract for the international sale of goods will find that their contract involves the application of specialist terminology and conditions, in addition to being governed by the law of the relevant country relating to contracts for sale. In order to avoid the problems relating to interpretation of these specialist terms, the parties may use standard form contracts where appropriate (e.g. the International Chambers of Commerce or Incoterms or the Standard Contract Terms of one of the London trade associations) or they may expressly incorporate the Uniform Law on International Sales Act 1967. Any contract for the sale of goods abroad will contain terms used only in connection with international contracts (e.g. cif and fob contracts). The object of these terms is to enable the parties to contract on terms with an internationally understood meaning and in the case of cif contracts to deal with cargoes afloat and to transfer them freely by giving the buyer constructive possession of the goods by the delivery of shipping documents to him.

CIF CONTRACTS

A cif contract is an agreement to sell goods at an inclusive price, comprising the cost of the goods, the marine insurance premium for the value of the goods and the freight or the cost of transportation. A seller who ships goods in accordance with the requirements of a cif contract fulfils his obligations when he tenders the shipping documents required, and he can require payment on that tender although the goods are lost or damaged before delivery to the buyer. The buyer may be able to pursue any remedies he has against the carrier of the goods or the ship–owner, or the insurer but not the seller of the goods. A cif contract is therefore a contract for the sale of goods to be performed by the delivery of certain documents, and not for the goods themselves. A seller who fails to ship goods complying with their contractual description is therefore in breach of contract when the documents are delivered and again when non–conforming goods are tendered to the buyer.

Seller's obligations

The obligations of a seller under a cif contract are:

(a) to deliver goods complying with the contractual description;

(b) to procure a contract of carriage by sea under which the goods will be delivered to the agreed destination;

(c) to procure a clean bill of lading issued by the master of the carrying vessel or by the carriers evidencing a contract of carriage by sea to the agreed place of delivery;

(d) to arrange for insurance of the goods on the terms current in the trade, in addition to covering any agreed risks; and

(e) to tender the bills of lading and the insurance policy to the buyer together with an invoice debiting the buyer with the agreed inclusive price, or, if the price is not inclusive of insurance and freight, the agreed price and any forwarding agent's commission, freight and insurance premium.

The seller must deliver to the buyer a billing of lading, invoice and insurance certificate and the delivery of these and any additional shipping documents is tantamount to the delivery of the goods. In return for the seller complying with these obligations, the buyer is obliged first to take–up the shipping documents and to tender the purchase price either simultaneously or as agreed under the contract of sale, and secondly to bear all risks of the goods being lost or damaged after they are delivered over the ship's rail, provided the seller has tendered the correct shipping documents.

The parties may vary expressly the terms of a cif contract to incorporate a trade practice or custom. However, the basic legal requirements of a cif contract must still be complied with: i.e. the seller must obtain and tender to the buyer the correct shipping documents. In *The Julia* (1949) the sellers reserved the right to tender a delivery order addressed to the master of the ship instead of a bill of lading. The delivery order, however, was made out in the name of the sellers' agent (thereby reserving the property in the good to the seller) and when war broke out the buyers reclaimed the purchase price they had paid because of the sellers' failure to deliver the goods. The court held that the contract between the parties did not comply with the requirements of a cif contract and did not give the buyers a direct claim against the ship which had carried the goods. There had been a total failure of consideration and the payment by the buyer was therefore an advance payment for an executory contract which the seller had not performed. The buyers were therefore entitled to recover the purchase price. In *Holland Colombo Trading Society Ltd* v. *Segu Mohamend Khaya Alawdeen* (1954) the court held that the contract of sale did not comply with the nature of a cif contract because the seller was not obliged to tender the shipping documents.

Refusal of buyer to accept the documents

In a cif contract the buyer or his agent has two distinct rights of rejection: the first is the right to reject non–conforming documents on them being tendered to him; the second is the right to reject the goods themselves if they are defective or do not comply with the terms of the contract. However, the right to reject the documents is lost when the buyer or his agent takes up non–conforming shipping documents without objection. The documents are inaccurate when taken together they disclose a defect.

Where it is not apparent from a reasonable examination that the documents are defective, however, the buyer retains this right to claim damages for breach of condition due to non–conforming documents being tendered. In *Kwei Tek Chao* v. *British Traders & Shippers Ltd* (1954) the buyers, having accepted the shipping documents and subsequently disposed of the goods, discovered that the bill of lading gave a false date for the loading of the goods. The court held that the buyers were entitled to damages for the non–delivery of goods conforming to the contract although they had accepted the shipping documents, and the fact that they had disposed of the goods did not deprive them of their right to sue, but merely of their right to reject the goods.

Secondly, the buyer can reject the goods when on an inspection of the goods delivered he discovers that they do not conform to the description under the contract of sale.

Passing of property and risk in the goods under a cif contract

The seller's responsibility for the goods terminates when he delivers them in accordance with the terms of the contract over the rail of the ship which is to carry them at the port of shipment. The buyer then bears the risk for the loss or destruction of the goods, although the seller may still be responsible for payment of the freight. In a cif contract title to the goods is conditionally transferred to the buyer on delivery of the bill of lading, but the buyer retains his right to reject the goods if they prove to be defective on inspection. In *Clemens Horst Co* v. *Biddell Bros* (1912) the buyers, relying on the Sale of Goods Act 1979, s. 34(2), refused to pay for the goods until they had been delivered and they had had a reasonable chance to accept the goods. The court held the buyers in breach of contract because under the cif contract the buyer was bound to pay for the goods in exchange for the documents.

Port of shipment and destination

A cif contract which stipulates the time and place of shipment contains conditions the breach of which entitle the buyer to reject the shipping documents. Where a cif contract provides for shipment from a specified port and does not permit the transhipment of goods, the buyer is entitled to a bill of lading which evidences continuous carriage from the specified port to the port of destination.

Loss of goods

By the nature of cif contracts, if goods are lost in transit, the seller is still entitled to receive payment if he tenders the proper shipping documents; this applies even if the seller is aware at the time he tenders the documents that the goods have in fact been lost. The buyer's remedy for loss caused in transit is against the carrier or shipowner, or against the insurer of the goods in transit.

Assessment of damages

The damages recoverable for the breach of a contract for the sale of goods are the loss directly and naturally resulting in the ordinary course of events from the breach. Where there is an available market for the goods the measure of damages is the difference between the contract price and the higher market price for the goods at the time of breach. In cif contracts the date for ascertaining the measure of damages is the date on which the documents should have been tendered if the seller had shipped at the agreed time.

VARIANTS OF cif CONTRACTS

c and f contracts

This means cost and freight contracts. The seller has to arrange for the delivery of the goods to the ship which is to carry them to a specified port at his expense, but the goods are at the buyer's risk once the goods are placed on board the ship. The seller does not arrange the marine insurance, which is the buyer's concern.

fob contracts

The characteristic of fob (or free on board) contracts is that the seller must at his own expense deliver the goods to a named ship or a ship nominated by the buyer for transportation to the buyer. All charges incurred up to and including the delivery of goods over the ship's rail are borne by the seller (i.e. all handling and transportation charges arising in connection with delivering the goods over the ship's rail). The buyer, however, will nominate the ship by which the goods are to be carried and he must secure the necessary shipping space in the designated or a substitute vessel. All charges incurred after the seller has delivered the goods to the ship are borne by the buyer (i.e. unloading charges at the destination).

The parties can vary the obligations imposed on them without the contract losing its character as an fob contract. In *Carlos Federspeil & Co* v. *S A Charles Twigg & Co* (1957) the court held that the contract between the parties was still an fob contract although the seller had agreed to pay the freight and the marine premium as agent of the buyer on the understanding that the buyer would reimburse the seller for this expense. In *N V Handel My J. Smiths Import – Export* v. *English Exporters* (1957) the court held that the contract between the parties was an fob contract even though the seller had agreed to secure the necessary shipping space as agent for the buyer.

Responsibilities of the parties
The Institute of Export provides that under an fob contract the parties have the following obligations. The seller has to make available at the port of loading and to ship free on board goods under the contract of sale, to pay all handling and transport charges, to complete any customs declarations and to meet all charges arising in connection with the goods up to the time of their passing over the ship's rail. The buyer, on the other hand, has to advise the seller in good time on what ship and at which port the seller has to load the goods, secure shipping space in the designated vessel, obtain any necessary export licence, designate an effective ship in time to enable the seller to deliver within the period agreed in the contract, make any customs declarations and pay any charges arising from the up–keep and conservance of waterways used by the ship in her passage out of port.

The goods
By virtue of the Sale of Goods Act 1979, s. 13, the goods must correspond with any description under which they are sold, but this description may relate not only to the actual goods but also their packing and shipment. Thus where herrings were sold fob London to an Australian buyer it was held that the seller was in breach of the implied term that the goods must be fit for any known purpose when, due to inadequate packing, the herrings deteriorated.

The port of loading
The contract of sale will usually state this precisely (e.g. fob Hull) but may give alternatives (e.g. Grimsby, Liverpool or Immingham). In a multi–port contract the choice of port will normally be the buyer's and he has a corresponding duty to notify the seller of his choice of port in good time. Once the buyer has nominated the port and informed the seller of his choice, then neither party can fulfil the contract by delivering the goods or loading them at a different port. In *Turnbull Pty & Co* v. *Mundas Trading (Australasia) Pty Ltd* (1954) the sellers alleged that they could not deliver the goods at the nominated port (Sydney) and asked to be allowed to deliver the goods at Melbourne. The buyers refused and in an action for non–delivery of the goods at Sydney the

sellers were held liable. Their breach was not excused by the buyer's failure to nominate a ship for Sydney since the seller's insistence that they could not deliver there made the nomination pointless. Conversely, the buyer cannot claim delivery elsewhere than at the port agreed in the contract.

The nomination of the ship

The buyer's duty to nominate a ship is a condition precedent to the seller's duty to load the goods; if the buyer fails to nominate an effective ship, the seller's remedy is in damages. In *Colley* v. *Overseas Exporters* (1921) the buyers successively nominated five ships, all of which failed to arrive at the nominated port. The seller who had delivered the goods at Liverpool claimed the purchase price as compensation. The court held that the sellers were only entitled to damages for the delay, including the costs of storing the goods.

The buyer can substitute the ship nominated by him provided that the substituted ship will be available for loading within the period of shipment.

Delivery

Once the buyer has nominated an effective ship, the seller is under a duty to deliver the goods by putting them on board the ship within the stipulated time. In *All Russian Co-operative Society Ltd* v. *Benjamin Smith & Sons* (1923) delivery under an fob contract was to be made in January. A consignment of the cargo was brought alongside the ship fifteen minutes before the end of the working day on 31st January. It was held that the seller had not delivered the goods within the contract period.

The goods are at the buyer's risk until they are loaded. In *J J Cunningham Ltd* v. *R. A. Munro & Co Ltd* (1922) the buyers agreed to purchase bran under a contract fob Rotterdam, shipment October, arranged for loading on 28th October. The seller delivered the bran for shipment on 14th October but the buyers were entitled to reject the bran when it heated and loading on board the ship was refused, since the goods were held at the seller's risk until delivery alongside the ship for loading.

The passing of property and risk

The time at which the property passes under an fob contract is when the goods cross the ship's rail. This is usually also the time of delivery. In *Pyrene Co Ltd* v. *Scindia Navigation Co Ltd* (1954) a fire tender, the subject of an fob contract, was held to have been the property of the seller at the time it was damaged when it fell back into a lighter from a crane before it had passed over the ship's rail. Under an fob contract, property is said to pass when the seller has performed the last act required by him, i.e. loading the goods on board. However, this is subject to any specific agreement between the parties.

Under the Sale of Goods Act 1979, s. 20, the risk of loss or damage to the goods passes with the property. Under an fob contract risk usually passes to the buyer on shipment and this will not be affected by the fact that the property does not necessarily pass at the same time; e.g. if goods are sold subject to a reservation of title clause.

Multi–port fob clause
A contract may provide that the goods can be delivered at one of several different ports. The buyer's duty to nominate a ship includes a duty to elect the actual port of shipment and to notify the seller of that port.

Duty to procure an export licence
The duty to procure an export licence is usually imposed on the seller. Where there is no express agreement to that effect, the courts will imply such a term since, if export restrictions are in force in the seller's country, he is the only party competent to apply for a licence.

VARIANTS OF fob CONTRACTS

for contracts
The seller is responsible under "free on rail" (for) contracts for all charges incurred until the goods are delivered to the appropriate railway undertaking for transportation to the buyer.

fot contracts
Under free on truck (lorry) (fot) the seller is responsible for all charges incurred in delivering the goods to the carrier and loading them on the truck or lorry which is to carry them.

fas contracts
The clause "free alongside ship" embodies certain elements which are not to be found in a sale on the home market. The seller's responsibility and risk in respect of the goods is discharged when they are placed alongside the ship which is to carry them so that they can be lifted and stowed on board. The actual loading of the goods over the ship's rail is the buyer's responsibility. Where the ship is berthed alongside a wharf or quay, the goods have to be placed ashore near her anchorage. Where a ship cannot enter port, the seller has to provide and pay for lighters which will take the consignment alongside the ship.

FINANCE OF INTERNATIONAL TRADE

There are several methods of financing a transaction for the sale of goods but most of these require the purchaser to pay the purchase price in advance. These methods require the buyer to pay for the goods before the seller has actually shipped them or before the buyer has received delivery.

(*a*) The buyer may send cash or a bankers' draft with his order to the seller, but the buyer will stand out of his money from the time of remittance until the goods arrive and are sold, and if the seller's commercial integrity is dubious the buyer will have parted with his money before he has any assurance of the existence or suitability of the goods.

(b) The sellery may ship the goods and rely on the buyer's promise to remit the purchase price when the goods arrive, but the seller will now lack security for the buyer's promise to perform his obligations.

(c) The seller may draw a bill of exchange on the purchaser for the purchase price, attaching the bill of lading, policy of insurance and invoice. These documents are then forwarded to a bank in the buyer's country with instructions not to part with them until the bill is accepted or paid. However, the problem still remains that during this period the buyer's financial position may have deteriorated and he may be unable to honour the bill.

(d) A method commonly used in the export trade and which ensures that the seller receives prompt payment is for the seller's bank to advance the price, or part of it, to him in return for a pledge of the relevant shipping documents. The seller's bank will discount a bill of exchange drawn by the seller on the buyer of his bank, and hold the documents of title to the goods as security until the bill is accepted or paid. The draft and documents are presented to the buyer or his bank, which either pays the amount of the bill (documents are then marked D/D) or accepts the draft if it is drawn on the bank (in which case they are marked D/A). Where the documents are marked D/D the buyer or his bank may refuse to pay the bill and if documents are marked D/A, the difficulty arises if the buyer and not a reliable bank accepts the bills. The shipping documents will be surrendered to the buyer in return for acceptance, and if the buyer becomes insolvent before the date for payment of the bill, the seller's bank can only look to the buyer personally for payment.

(e) A guarantee may be given to the seller by the purchaser's bank or the seller may insure the credit risk; this may be expensive for the seller since the bank will charge a commission and the insurer a premium depending on the degree of the risk of the buyer not paying for the goods.

(f) The buyer's bank may issue a letter of credit promising either to pay the seller the amount of his invoice or to accept or purchase a bill of exchange for that amount payable at a specified date.

It is of the essence of a banker's commercial credit that there is an antecedent underlying contract for the sale of goods in which it is agreed that the purchase price will be paid by means of a banker's letter of credit. The duty of arranging payment by this method rests on the buyer, who makes an application in writing for this purpose to the issuing bank. This application is at the same time a mandate, a request and an indemnity undertaking. It requests the bank to issue or open a letter of credit and sets out the conditions under which the bank is to pay the beneficiary or honour his bills of exchange. In the letter of application the applicant undertakes to reimburse the bank for all payments made by it under the letter of credit, and this forms the basis of the contract between the issuing bank and the applicant for the credit. Once the bank is satisfied that the letter of application is in order and the conditions in it are practicable, it issues the letter of credit in favour of the beneficiary. It may be sent directly to him, or it may be sent to the bank's agents in the beneficiary's country. The letter of credit may be in any form, but it should contain an undertaking by the issuing bank to pay the amount for which it is issued or to accept or purchase bills of exchange drawn by the beneficiary for that amount provided the conditions set out in the letter are fulfilled (e.g. presentation of shipping documents).

There have been attempts to standardise the conditions on which banks are prepared to issue and to act on commercial credits. The Uniform Customs and Practice for Commercial Documentary Credits were formulated in 1933 by the International Chamber of Commerce and were virtually universally applied. The general provision and definitions at the beginning of the Uniform Customs state that these provisions and definitions and the following articles apply to all documentary credits and are binding upon all parties unless otherwise expressly stated. For the purposes of these provisions, a documentary credit means any arrangement, however named or described, whereby a bank (the issuing bank), acting at the request and in accordance with the instructions of a customer (the applicant for the credit), agrees to make a payment to or to the order of a third party (the beneficiary), or is to pay, accept or negotiate bills of exchange (drafts) drawn by the beneficiary, or authorises such payments to be made or drafts to be paid, accepted or negotiated by another bank against stipulated documents provided that the terms and conditions of the credit are complied with.

The letter of credit is issued by the issuing bank to a third person who is named by the customer and with whom the customer has commercial dealings, in order to carry through a particular transaction.

LETTERS OF CREDIT

General and special credits

A general letter of credit is one addressed by the issuing bank to the world generally, requesting that advances be made to a named person (the bank customer) by anyone to whom it is shown. In *Re Agra and Masterman's Bank, ex parte Asiatic Banking Corporation* (1867) it was held that a general letter of credit constitutes a continuing offer which is capable of acceptance by anyone who acts in reliance upon it. In that case a bank issued to D T & Co, a letter addressed to them and expressed as follows:

"No. 394. You are hereby authorised to draw upon this bank to the extent of £15,000 and we undertake duly to honour such drafts on presentation...."

D T & Co drew bills under this letter to the extent of £6,000 in favour of the appellant for valuable consideration and the appellants duly indorsed particulars of the bills on the letter of credit. The bank was afterwards ordered to be wound up, and D T & Co were indebted to the bank to an amount exceeding that due on the bills. The court held that the letter of credit constituted a contract to the benefit of all persons taking and paying for the bills on the faith of it, and that the appellant was entitled to prove for the amount payable under the bills even though the bank had not accepted them.

A special letter of credit is one which is not addressed to the world generally, but instead to some specified person or persons, and only a person to whom the letter is addressed can acquire rights under it.

Clean (or open) and documentary credits

In a clean or open letter of credit, the issuing bank undertakes to accept or negotiate drafts drawn by the beneficiary without any shipping or other documents being delivered to it. A bank issuing such a letter of credit lacks the security given by the possession of documents of title and for this reason the bank will normally require the customer to lodge sufficient security to cover any bills which may be drawn under the credit.

A documentary credit is one in which the person or bank issuing it undertakes to honour bills drawn under the credit only if they have attached to them certain specified documents, such as bills of lading, insurance policies and invoices which the bank or person can hold as security for the advances made.

Revolving credit

A revolving credit is one the amount of which remains constant for a specified period, so that whenever during that period it is drawn upon it becomes automatically available again for the full amount of the credit.

Anticipatory credits

This term refers not to letters of credit themselves, but to advances made on the strength of them. These advances are made by bankers abroad to enable suppliers or agents for purchasers to acquire raw materials or produce. The advances are made to the beneficiary of the letter of credit and the letter expressly provides that the goods for which anticipatory advances are made or the products into which they are incorporated are to be shipped and the relevant shipping documents delivered to the issuing bank.

Negotiation credits

The issuing bank undertakes to purchase bills of exchange drawn by the creditor on the debtor. The bills are rarely accepted by the debtor before presentation to the issuing bank, and when the bank has paid the face value or the discounted value of the bills to the holder of the bill, it reimburses itself by debiting the debtor's account as its customer, and not by relying on its rights as an indorsee of the bills.

Confirmed and unconformed credits

An exporter may require that a commercial credit in his favour should be issued by a bank in his own country, or that a credit issued by a foreign bank in the purchaser's country should be confirmed or guaranteed by a bank in the exporter's country. The issuing bank in the purchaser's country will in such a case employ a second bank in the exporter's country not only to advise the exporter of the issue of the credit but also to undertake to pay the amount of the credit or to accept or negotiate bills drawn under it, whether or not the issuing bank places with it funds to make payment. Where the intermediary bank accepts a direct obligation toward the exporter to honour the credit, it is a confirmed irrevocable credit; otherwise it is unconfirmed and the advising bank is not liable to the exporter. There can be no confirmation of a revocable credit.

Revocable or irrevocable credits

The main feature of a revocable credit is that the issuing bank reserves to itself the right to modify or cancel the credit, and a person acting in reliance on a credit of this nature is deemed to have notice that the credit may be withdrawn at any time. However, if an intermediary bank acts on the credit before notice of cancellation is given to it, then that bank is entitled to be reimbursed for its expenditure.

By the Uniform Customs and Practice, art. 3, an irrevocable credit constitutes a definite undertaking by the issuing bank to make payment if the terms of the credit are complied with. In such a case the issuing and confirming banks, if the credit is confirmed, cannot withdraw their undertaking to honour it once the credit has been communicated to the beneficiary.

Transferable credits

In addition to the types of credit here dealt with, certain other types of credit were devised the purpose of which was to enable the beneficiary of the credit to transfer or assign the benefit to a third party.

Technical terms

It is proposed to deal merely with the technical terms associated with commercial credits and the names assigned to the parties in a commercial credit transaction.

The bank which issues a commercial credit is known as the "opening bank" or the "issuing bank", the latter term being derived from the fact that the notification of the credit to the creditor is by a letter of credit issued to him by the bank.

The person in whose favour a credit is opened is known as "the beneficiary" and he alone can require the issuing bank to pay the amount of the credit or to accept bills drawn under it, but his rights under the contract can be assigned by a written instrument.

The issuing bank often employs another bank to notify the issue of the credit to the beneficiary. The bank so employed is known as the "advising bank", and it acts as an agent for the issuing bank, which is therefore responsible for its acts or omissions under the ordinary rules of agency law. The advising bank is not a party to the credit itself, and so is not obliged to honour the credit if the issuing bank fails to do so, nor in the case of revocable credit is it liable to the beneficiary if the issuing bank cancels the credit. Where, however, the advising bank "confirms" a credit issued by another bank, it becomes responsible for the performance of the issuing bank's obligation to the beneficiary in addition to the issuing bank. In this situation the confirming bank accepts the bills drawn by the beneficiary, usually on its own account, or on behalf of the issuing bank if the beneficiary requests this to be done. The confirming bank then passes the shipping documents to the issuing bank so that it or its customer (at whose request the credit was opened) will be in possession of the documents by the time the goods covered by the credit arrive in the customer's country. Often the presentation of the bills to the confirming bank for payment is anticipated by it purchasing them at their face value less interest to maturity when the beneficiary presents the bills drawn by him for acceptance by the confirming bank. In such a case the confirming bank either passes the bills unaccepted to the issuing bank for acceptance by it, or, if the confirming bank both accepts and discounts the bills presented to it by the beneficiary, it retains them and debits the issuing bank with their amount on maturity. However, a bank which has not confirmed a credit does not become a confirming bank merely because the credit provides that bills drawn under it may be negotiated to that bank, and the bank in fact purchases them at their face or discounted value. Instead it becomes a holder of the bills itself with the usual right of recourse against the drawer and payee if the issuing bank dishonours them, and also a right to claim from the issuing bank under the letter of credit if the benefit of it is assigned to the negotiating bank.

Transfers of the benefit of credits

Only the person who is expressly named in the letter of credit as the beneficiary of it can draw bills under it, and it is he alone who can require the issuing bank to accept or negotiate those bills, unless the credit otherwise provides. A beneficiary cannot therefore authorise another person to draw on the credit unless the letter of credit expressly permits him to do this.

A letter of credit, is therefore, clearly not in law a negotiable or even an assignable instrument, but it may be made transferable by its terms as a matter of contract.

However, art. 47 of the Uniform Customs allows the rights of the beneficiary under the credit, as with any other contract, to be assigned at law by a written instrument which is notified to the issuing bank, and in equity by an agreement to assign it for value. The assignment of rights at law does not have to be in any particular form, provided it is in writing and is signed by the beneficiary. The assignee can then present bills drawn by the beneficiary under the credit and require the issuing bank to accept or negotiate them.

Where the letter of credit expressly authorises the beneficiary to transfer the benefit of a letter of credit the credit is said to be "transferable" or "assignable". By art. 46 of the Uniform Customs the rights and benefits of a credit expressed to be transferable may be transferred to a third person or in fractions to several persons. Transferable credits are mostly used where the seller of goods is not the manufacturer or supplier, but is a dealer or exporter who arranges with a manufacturer or supplier to supply goods to the ultimate purchasers at a higher price than the dealer or exporter pays for them, thus enabling the latter to obtain a dealing profit. The ultimate purchaser procures a transferable credit in favour of the dealer or exporter and the latter then instructs the issuing bank to issue a credit in favour of the manufacturer or supplier for an amount less than the original credit and expiring a few days earlier than the original credit. In order to enable the beneficiary of the original credit to conceal the profit he is making by employing a manufacturer or supplier, the agreement for the transfer of the credit often enables him to substitute his own invoice for the goods supplied for the invoice of the manufacturer or supplier, and to draw bills on the issuing bank in favour of the manufacturer or supplier for such part of that invoice price as he wishes and in his own favour for the balance.

Where the credit is transferred to a third party, there is a novation because in fact there is a change in the parties to the contract for the credit. However, the transfer of the credit does not amount to a novation of the underlying contract for the sale of goods. The buyer agrees to the substitution of a third party as the beneficiary of the credit but he does not agree to the substitution of the third party as the seller of the goods comprised in the underlying contract of sale, and if there is a breach of that contract by the third party failing to deliver the contract goods, it is the seller and not the third party whom the buyer must sue for the breach.

The same purpose of making a credit available to a third person is achieved by a back–to–back credit arrangement. This type of credit arrangement is usually used to finance a string of contracts for the sale of the same goods through several intermediaries, as well as the type of transaction for which a transferable credit is normally used, namely to finance the acquisition of goods from sub-contractors. Under a back–to–back arrangement the obligations of the issuing bank to the beneficiary are used as security for the issue by the beneficiary's bank of a second credit in favour of a third party. For example, if A sells goods to B, and B sells the same goods to C, and C to D, D's bank may open a credit in favour of C, which he uses as a security to induce his own bank to open a credit in favour of B, and B in turn may use this credit as a security for his own bank to open a credit in favour of A.

The relationship between the debtor and the beneficiary of a letter of credit

The underlying contract

A commercial credit is used to finance a contract for the sale of goods under which the purchaser is obliged to make payment to the creditor by means of a documentary letter of credit. The rights and obligations of the buyer and seller are determined by the terms of the underlying contract for the sale of goods, and the contract is in no way affected by the terms of the credit procured by the debtor. Once the commercial credit has been issued, this contract between the buyer and the issuing bank exists independently of the contract of sale of goods between the buyer and the seller. The bank is therefore not concerned with any disputes that arise between the parties to the underlying contract concerning non–delivery or the quality or quantity of goods delivered. In *Hamzeh Malas* v. *British Imex Industries Ltd* (1958) the court held that a bank cannot refuse to accept or purchase a bill of exchange drawn by the beneficiary of a credit merely because the beneficiary has broken the underlying contract, even if the buyer is entitled to reject the goods delivered or proposed to be delivered to him because they are not of the contract description or quality. The bank cannot refuse to accept the beneficiary's draft even if the bank's customer has rescinded the underlying contract or has terminated it because of a fundamental breach by the beneficiary (*see Fray* v. *Sherbourne* (1920)) provided the documents presented to the bank are in proper order and fulfil any conditions under the letter of credit.

If the underlying contract of sale requires the provision by the buyer of a letter of credit, then the opening of the letter of credit is a condition precedent to the performance by the seller of his part of the contract. The credit must be issued by the bank named in the underlying contract, (if any), and it must be opened and notified by the bank or its agent to the creditor within the time agreed. If the underlying contract calls for a confirmed commercial credit; the debtor must also ensure that the confirmation is given to the creditor within the same time limit. In *Dix* v. *Grainger* (1922) the plaintiff was an export merchant who brought an action against the defendant claiming damages for an alleged breach of a contract under which the plaintiff agreed to buy blankets from the defendant. It was a term of the underlying contract that an irrevocable letter of credit should be opened, and on failure to open the credit there was a fundamental breach by the plaintiff which excused the seller from performing his part of the contract (*see also Garcia* v. *Page & Co* (1936) and *Trans Trust SPRL* v. *Danubian Trading Co Ltd* (1952)).

The time for opening the credit

If the underlying contract does not specify the bank which is to open or confirm the credit, the kind of credit to be opened or the time within which it must be opened and notified to the creditor, the court will have to construe the terms of the contract, and, if necessary, imply terms as to the intention of the parties in order to determine the extent of their obligations. In *Knotz* v. *Fairclough, Dodd and Jones Ltd* (1952) the underlying contract did not expressly require the seller to send a provisional invoice to the buyer so as to enable him to procure the opening of a credit for the amount set out therein, but the court implied a duty on the seller to do this since it was obviously the parties' intention. If the sales contract contains a stipulation that the credit is required to be opened within a certain time, the seller is discharged if it is not notified to him within that time. In the absence of such a stipulation, the buyer has a reasonable time within which to provide the credit. In *Garcia* v. *Page & Co* (1936) a contract of sale was entered into by an English company to supply certain goods to a buyer in Spain. It was a term of the contract that the buyer should open a "confirmed credit in London immediately" in favour of the seller. There was a delay in providing the credit and the seller notified the buyer that if the credit was not received in London by 24th August, it would cancel the contract. The credit was opened in Spain by 24th August, but the seller did not receive notification until 27th August. The seller purported to repudiate the contract of sale and the court held that a confirmed credit had to be opened immediately after the contract of sale was entered into, that is, within such a time as the buyer needed as a person of reasonable diligence to get the credit established. The buyer had failed to do this and the seller was consequently entitled to repudiate the contract of sale.

In certain contracts, however, there may be no express stipulation as to the time within which the buyer must open the credit; in such cases the buyer has a reasonable time within which to obtain the opening of the credit. Alternatively the contract may stipulate that it is to be opened within a reasonable time. In case of a dispute the court would have to decide, in both instances, what is a reasonable time and whether the buyer, in fact was given a reasonable time to open the credit. In *Kronman & Co* v. *Steinberger* (1922) the contract of sale required a credit to be opened in favour of the defendant and the plaintiff gave instructions for this to be done, but due to a mistake the credit was opened in dollars instead of in sterling. This was rectified, but the defendant purported to cancel the contract. The court held that the plaintiff was entitled to a reasonable time in which to open the credit and therefore the defendant was wrong in declining to send the goods.

By way of contrast, in *Baltimex Ltd* v. *Metallo Chemical Refining Co Ltd* (1955), the court said it will take into account any special facts of which the seller was aware as likely to cause delay in opening the credit, in order to determine whether a reasonable time had elapsed without the buyer opening the requisite credit. In *Etablissements Chainbaux* v. *Harbormaster Ltd* (1955), there was a delay in opening the letter of credit because of an exceptionally long delay in obtaining exchange control permission from the French Government; during this time an extension of the time for opening the credit was granted by the sellers, but they later purported to repudiate the contract before the extension period had expired and without giving advance notice to the buyers. In an action by the buyers for alleged wrongful repudiation of the contract of sale it was held that the plaintiffs had failed to procure the opening of a credit in time and were liable for breach of the underlying contract, even though the failure to comply was not attributable to any personal fault on their part.

If, however, the debtor's failure to procure the opening of the credit is due to the creditor's acts or omissions, the debtor is not in breach of the underlying contract. In *Knotz* v. *Fairclough, Dodd & Jones Ltd* (1952) the contract was for the sale of goods, the quantity being between a stated maximum and minimum. The seller failed to provide the buyer with an invoice so that the credit could not be opened; as a direct consequence of this the buyer failed to open the credit. The court held that the seller could not treat the underlying contract as terminated for that reason and the buyer was in breach of it.

If the contract provides for shipment of the goods by the seller at any time during a stated period, in the absence of an express stipulation, the buyer must open the credit and make it available to the seller at the beginning of the shipment period. In *Pavia & Co* v. *Thurmann–Nielsen* (1952), the contract provided for the sale of certain goods to be shipped from Brazil in February and/or March and/or April at the seller's option c i f Genoa. The buyers were repeatedly pressed by the sellers to provide the credit facilities but these did not become available until 22nd April. The buyers were held liable for failure to provide the credit as provided by the contract. In a confirmed credit it was said the credit must be made available to the seller at the beginning of the shipment period since the seller is entitled to be assured that he will get paid on shipment (*see Ian Stach Ltd* v. *Baker Bosley Ltd* (1958).).

The identity of the issuing bank

The underlying contract often does not specify the bank which is to open the credit, or the banks which are respectively to open and confirm it. If a letter of credit is required to be issued by an English bank, the institution which opens the credit must be a recognised bank or a licensed institution within the terms of the Banking Act 1979, and the seller would be entitled to reject a credit issued by any other institution or organisation.

The requirement of an irrevocable credit

If the contract of sale calls for a particular form of credit and such a credit is not opened, the seller is under no liability. It was held in *Giddens* v. *Anglo–African Produce Co Ltd* (1923), that if the underlying contract merely requires payment to be made by a "bankers credit" or "confirmed banker's credit", it is not sufficient for the debtor to procure the opening of a revocable credit, since the whole purpose of financing the transaction by a credit is to assure the creditor that he will be paid by a reliable institution which commits itself irrevocably to do so. The Uniform Commercial Code, art. 2–323(3), provides that the debtor's obligation is to open an irrevocable credit unless the underlying contract of sale permits him to open a revocable credit. If the buyer in error provides a form of credit different from that stipulated in the contract, he is entitled to rectify the error provided that the seller does not alter his position in reliance on the credit supplied. In *Kronman & Co* v. *Steinberger* (1922) a credit was opened, by mistake, in dollars instead of sterling. The mistake was rectified within the time for opening the credit, but the sellers sought to take advantage of the mistake and cancel the contract. The court held that they were not entitled to do so since they had not taken steps in pursuance of the credit originally provided. Consequently, if the buyer replaces a revocable credit by an irrevocable one within the time permitted by the underlying contract, he fulfils his obligations to the seller.

The requirement of a confirmed credit

If by the terms of the underlying contract of sale the credit to be opened is to be a confirmed credit, it is not sufficient for the buyer to tender an irrevocable credit issued by the bank. So if the credit is to be "confirmed" it must contain undertakings to honour the beneficiary's bills by at least two banks. In *Panoutsos* v. *Raymond Hadley Corporation of New York* (1917) a contract for the sale and shipment of a cargo of flour provided that each shipment should be deemed to be a separate contract and that payment should be by "a confirmed banker's credit." The buyer opened a banker's credit which was not in fact confirmed. The seller, with notice of the fact, made some shipments and received payment by means of the credit and also obtained from the buyer an extension of time for the shipment of the goods. The seller afterwards purported to cancel the contract on the ground that the credit was not in accordance with the contract. The court held that the seller was entitled to insist on strict compliance with the terms of the contract of sale and to require a "confirmed credit" to be made available, but he had waived this requirement by his conduct. The purpose for which a seller normally requires a confirmed credit is that he thereby acquires an undertaking by a bank in his own country, of whose standing he has little doubt, that he will be paid if the issuing bank fails to do so.

Waiver by the seller

Where the buyer is in breach of a term inserted in the credit, the seller may waive strict compliance. This, however, does not mean that the seller can never avail himself of the condition in future, but he must give reasonable notice to the buyer of his intention to insist upon its future performance. If the buyer then fails to comply with the condition within a reasonable time, he is in default and the seller is entitled to cancel the contract without the buyer being entitled to damages. According to *Rickards* v. *Oppenhaim* (1950), however, the seller may be entitled to give peremptory notice.

The seller may waive strict compliance with the terms of the letter of credit either expressly or impliedly. In *Panoutsos* v. *Raymond Hadley Corporation of New York* (1917) the seller, with knowledge of the fact that a confirmed credit had not been opened as required by the terms of the sale contract, shipped part of the goods under the contract. He later purported to cancel the sale contract without notice on the basis that the buyers had failed to open a confirmed credit. The court held that the seller, by his conduct, in continuing the shipments and actually drawing on the credit, must be held to have waived strict compliance and that he was not entitled to cancel the contract without giving the buyers reasonable notice of his intention to do so, if a confirmed credit was not made available for payment of balance of the price and future shipments. The seller was therefore himself liable for damages. A waiver may also be inferred from inaction on the part of the seller but this question raises some difficulties.

Damages

If the buyer fails to fulfil his obligations under the underlying contract in respect of the opening, confirmation or notification of a banker's credit, he is liable to the creditor in damages for the consequential loss suffered by the seller, who may also treat the contract as terminated.

The measure of damages awarded by the court for breach of the underlying contract will normally be the same as for any other breach of contract. The test in assessing the measure of damages is that laid down in *Hadley* v. *Baxendale* (1854) (as explained in *Victoria Laundry* v. *Newman Industries Ltd* (1949)), i.e. the loss suffered by the creditor must be a direct and ordinary consequence of the buyer's breach of contract. If under the underlying contract is for the sale of goods, the loss will usually be the difference between the contract price of the goods and the lower market price of similar goods on the last date by which the credit should have been opened, or on the later date when the creditor treats the contract as repudiated because of the buyer's breach. In *Ian Stach Ltd* v. *Baker Bosley Ltd* (1958) it was held that prima facie the measure of damages is the loss of profit on the transaction, but on the facts of the case, because the seller had not treated the breach as terminating the contract until a later date, the amount of damages awarded was the difference between the contract price and the market price at the time the seller accepted the buyer's repudiation. The normal measure of damages is therefore the seller's loss of his bargain, but the circumstances in which the underlying contract was made may indicate that a different measure of damages is appropriate.

The debtor's continuing liability for the debt
Once the debtor has procured the opening and notification of a commercial credit in accordance with the underlying contract of sale, the issuing bank becomes liable to the creditor to accept and pay his drafts. A question of importance is whether the seller, by requiring payment by means of a commercial credit, agrees to release the buyer from liability for payment under the contract of sale once the credit is issued. This is important where the issuing bank becomes insolvent before it accepts or negotiates the seller's bills of exchange or before it pays bills it has accepted under the credit. In *Saffron* v. *Société Miniere Cafrika* (1958) it was held that, on the facts of the case, the provision of the letter of credit did not constitute absolute payment. The facts were that the seller contracted to sell certain chrome ore to the buyer, and the contract of sale provided for "payment by opening a letter of credit with the Banque de l'Indochine—80 per cent on shipment, 20 per cent on delivery." It was assumed by the parties that an irrevocable, unconfirmed letter of credit would satisfy the condition. The seller delivered the goods to the buyer, but payment was not made by the bank under the letter of credit. The seller then brought an action against the buyer for the price. The court held that the stipulation for payment by means of a letter of credit did not go beyond requiring the establishment of such a letter as a primary, but not the exclusive, method of payment; the seller was therefore entitled to recover the price from the buyer on the bank's default. An undertaking to provide a revocable credit cannot be an undertaking that the buyer will be discharged from his liability to

pay, since a revocable credit by its nature provides no protection against cancellation.

Similarly in *E D & F Man Ltd* v. *Nigerian Sweets and Confectionery Co Ltd* (1977) and in *Alan & Co Ltd* v. *L Nasr Export and Import Co Ltd* (1972) it was said that a letter of credit, when issued and accepted by the seller, operates merely as conditional payment; it does not operate to discharge the liability of the buyer, but the seller cannot look to the buyer personally for payment until the issuing bank has refused payment. In *Alan & Co Ltd* v. *L Nasr Export and Import Co Ltd* Lord Denning MR went on to say that if the letter of credit is honoured by the bank when the documents are presented to it, the debt is discharged and the buyer absolved from liability.

The relationship between the beneficiary and the issuing and confirming banks

Binding effect of the terms of the credit

The contractual obligations between the creditor and the issuing and confirming banks arise from the terms of the letter of credit. The issuing and confirming banks are therefore under a duty to the beneficiary to honour the credit, i.e. to accept or negotiate bills presented to it by the beneficiary, either on demand if the credit is an open one, or, if the credit is a documentary letter of credit, on fulfilment of the conditions set out in that letter of credit. The duty to honour the credit is unilateral and so the bank is bound to honour the credit if it is strictly complied with. There is no duty or obligation on the beneficiary to fulfil the terms of the credit, but if he wishes to benefit under it he must conform to the terms of the credit as a condition precedent to insisting on performance of the bank's obligations.

There are numerous cases in which the courts have held that only strict compliance with the terms of credit will suffice to activate the duty of the banks to accept or negotiate bills under it. The courts have refused to apply the *de minimis* rule to letters of credit as between the issuing or confirming bank and the beneficiary. Consequently it was held in *Moralice (London) Ltd* v. *E D & F Man Ltd* (1954) that a tender of documents for 499,100 kilos of sugar under a credit calling for 500 metric tons was bad. Furthermore, the issuing bank need not accept substantial compliance even if the seller offers an indemnity.

There must be strict compliance with the terms of the letter of credit if the beneficiary is to have a claim on the bank for two reasons:

(*a*) If the issuing bank is to be entitled to reimbursement by its customer for the sum paid to the beneficiary under the credit, the documents it accepts must conform strictly to the terms of his instructions reflected in the letter of credit.

(*b*) The documents must be in proper order so that if the goods or other subject–matter financed by the credit are non-existent, destroyed, lost or damaged, the bank and its customer will have documents on which they could rely to found claims against the responsible parties (e.g. the carrier who has issued the bill of lading or air waybill). It is the terms and conditions of the credit alone which govern the rights of the beneficiary and it is not possible to look at the underlying contract to modify the terms of the credit.

Tender of documents

The letter of credit specifies the documents which the creditor is required to present under the credit. The documents required under an international sales contract are governed by the technical rules relating to c i f and f o b contracts. In the former instance the seller is required to present to the buyer or his bank a clean bill of lading, an invoice and a marine insurance policy. The documents must be presented within the period specified in the credit, and the bank which has issued the credit is entitled to insist that the documents presented correspond exactly to the requirements of the credit. If they do not, the bank can refuse to take up the documents presented to it although the goods actually shipped are of the description and quality required to fulfil the underlying contract of sale.

The bill of lading tendered by the seller under a letter of credit must conform to the description of the goods as represented in the terms of the credit. In *Bank Melli Iran* v. *Barclays Bank D C O Ltd* (1951) the plaintiffs, a Persian bank, authorised the defendants to issue a letter of credit for $30,000 representing the value of "100 new Chevrolet trucks" against the presentation of a delivery order, insurance policy invoice and a United States Government certificate that the trucks were new. The defendants issued a letter of credit in accordance with the buyer's instructions, and the invoice tendered and accepted by the defendants referred to the trucks as "in new condition". However, the document accepted by the defendants as complying with the required United States Government certificate that the trucks were new, described them as "100 new, good Chevrolet . . . . . . trucks." The delivery order described the trucks as "new goods". The court held that the documents tendered and accepted by the defendants were defective, and consequently the defendants were not entitled to debit the plaintiffs with the amount paid against the document tendered.

In *Rayner & Co* v. *Hambros Bank Ltd* (1943) a bank received instructions from a customer to open a confirmed credit in favour of the plaintiffs covering a cargo of "coromandel groundnuts". The bank opened the credit and notified the plaintiffs that it was available against an invoice and bills of lading for "coromandel groundnuts". The plaintiffs presented bills of lading for "machine–shelled groundnut kernels" accompanied by an invoice for "coromandel groundnuts". The bank refused payment, and the plaintiffs sued for breach of the undertaking in the letter of credit. The judge said that a person who ships in reliance on a letter of credit must do so in exact compliance with its terms.

Furthermore, in dealing with the question of whether the defendant bank was under any obligation or duty to acquaint itself with trade names, the court said the bank is not obliged or deemed to be acquainted with customs of a trade or specific trade names and therefore the description in the letter of credit and so the bank was justified in rejecting the documents.

In the *Bank Melli* case the bank issuing the letters of credit was entitled to reject the documents because 100 new, good trucks are not the equivalent of a 100 new trucks, but clearly indicates second–hand or used trucks; similarly, coromandel groundnuts are not to the knowledge of the bank equivalent to machine–shelled groundnut kernels, although in the trade they would be recognised as equivalent.

Where, in addition to the bill of lading, other documents are to be presented under a credit it is sufficient if the description of the quality of the goods is contained in one of these documents, provided there is no need that the bill of lading should itself contain this description in order to fulfil its function as an undertaking by the carrier to deliver goods of the description in question. In *Guaranty Trust Company* v. *Van den Berghs Ltd* (1926) an action was brought for a declaration that the defendants were bound to reimburse the plaintiffs for sums of money paid under a letter of credit issued by the plaintiffs at the request of the defendants, covering a cargo of Manila coconut oil. The defendants pleaded that the documents accepted by the plaintiffs were not in order in that the bill of lading described the goods as "coconut oil" and not "Manila coconut oil". They were, however, so described in a certificate of origin accompanying the bill of lading, as there was no specific requirement that the bills of lading should include this description. The court held that assuming the documents required the goods to be described as Manila coconut oil, the certificate of origin made it clear that the goods were of that nature and there was therefore sufficient compliance by the bank with the customer's instructions.

A full description of the goods obtained from a collective examination of the documents is therefore sufficient, unless the letter of credit expressly requires each document to give a full description of the goods. If the goods are described in the buyer's instructions to the bank by reference to weight or quantity and are consequently so described in the letter of credit, then the bill of lading must contain a corresponding statement of weight or quantity. This is so that the buyer will have an effective claim against the carrier for not delivering goods as described in the bill of lading. In *London and Foreign Trading Corporation* v. *British and North European Bank* (1921) the question was whether the bank had been negligent in accepting documents relating to a cargo of maize meal shipped to the UK. The letter of credit required the bill of lading to be made out to the consignor's order endorsed in blank, and dated not later than October 1920. The plaintiffs contended that the bank paid on an insufficient bill of lading, which stated that 5895 bags of maize were shipped (this was in accordance with the contract) but there was no reference to the weight of the bags, as required. The defendants contended they were entitled to rely on the statement in the invoice as to the weight of each bag, but this was rejected and judgment was given for the plaintiffs. The authority given to the bank was limited, i.e. to pay against a bill of lading showing the quantity of the goods shipped. In *Midland Bank* v. *Seymour* (1955) the defendant required the plaintiff, a London bank, to open a letter of request in favour of a Hong Kong company from whom they were buying duck feathers. The credit was to be available by drafts at ninety days' sight against delivery of an invoice, a weight account, a certificate of origin and a bill of lading evidencing shipment from

Hong Kong to Hamburg. The following description of the goods was given in the letter of request by the defendant: "Hong Kong duck feathers 85 per cent clean, quantity, 12 bales each, weighing about 190 lbs, and price 5 shillings per lb." A confirmed irrevocable credit was issued by the plaintiff bank and it made payment against the tendered shipping documents. The invoice contained a full description of the goods, but the bill of lading described them simply as "12 bales Hong Kong duck feathers". The bill of lading contained made no reference to the weight of each bale nor to the "85 per cent clean" stipulation. The defendant alleged that the plaintiff bank had not complied with his mandate and refused to reimburse the bank. It was held that it was sufficient if the set of documents contained all the particulars called for in the letter of request and the defendant was obliged to reimburse the bank. Only two alternatives were open: first, that each document must contain all the particulars; or, secondly, that all the documents between them must contain all the particulars, subject to the qualification that each document must contain enough of the particulars to make it a valid document for its own purposes. If a complete description of the goods shipped can be obtained from the full set of documents that corresponds to the description in the letter of credit, the bank is entitled to be reimbursed for payments made under the letter of credit. Although the documents must be read together as demanded by the letter of credit, each document must be effectual in itself, that is, each document taken alone must be sufficiently detailed to fulfil the functions of that particular document.

Bills of lading, insurance policy and invoice

The beneficiary under a commercial credit issued by a bank to finance an import or export sale is normally required to present to that issuing bank a full set of clean, "on board" (or shipped) bills of lading for the goods endorsed in blank, an insurance policy or certificate and the beneficiary's invoice for the price of the goods, freight and insurance. If the goods are to be transported by land or air, the credit will require an appropriate bill of lading or air waybill and an insurance policy covering the carriage by land or air.

The duty of the beneficiary is to tender documents to which no reasonable exception can be taken under the rules governing c i f contracts and under the Uniform Customs, if these are incorporated. Bills of lading are usually issued in sets of three and the letter of credit may require the beneficiary to present a "full set" of bills of lading.

However, in the absence of such an express term in the credit, it was held in *Sanders* v. *Maclean & Co* (1883) that the beneficiary need only tender one copy of a bill issued in a set and the issuing or confirming bank may only refuse to take up the documents if it can show that another copy of the set has been indorsed to another person. A bill of lading can be used by the issuing bank to collect the goods at the port of arrival only if it is made out to the bank's order (which is unlikely) or to the beneficiary's order and is indorsed by him in blank.

The general law requires a bill of lading to be signed on behalf of the carrier and be an "on board" bill, i.e. one acknowledging that the goods have actually been loaded on the ship which is to transport them. A "received for shipment" or a forwarding agent's bill of lading will not be accepted under a credit requiring a "shipped" or "on board" bill of lading, for these merely indicate that the goods have been received for shipment but are not actually on board. In *Diamond Alkali Export Corporation* v. *Bourgeois* (1921), goods were to be shipped from America c i f Gothenburg. The sellers tendered an invoice and a bill of lading which stated the goods to have been "received in apparent good order and condition from ... to be transported by the S.S. Anglia", and a certificate of insurance in place of the policy. The court held the buyers were entitled to reject the documents; the bill of lading did not acknowledge actual shipment of the goods and the insurance document was not good tender of a marine policy under the ordinary rules governing c i f contracts.

An issuing or confirming bank is not concerned with any general conditions in the bill of lading which are not required to be fulfilled by the letter of credit but with which the seller may have to comply under the underlying contract of sale or which may affect the rights of the buyer against the carrier. In *British Imex Industries Ltd* v. *Midland Bank Ltd* (1958), a bill of lading contained a clause providing that in the case of a cargo of iron and steel sheets and bars the ship–owner would not be responsible unless every piece was distinctly marked and secured. The issuing bank rejected the documents on the ground that there was no acknowledgment in the bill of lading that the terms of the additional clause had been complied with. The beneficiary under the credit brought an action for the amount due. The court held that a clean bill of lading was called for and had been provided in conformity with the letter of credit, and the bank was wrong in rejecting the documents. The court said that even if the bank was concerned with the clause in question, its effect and conformity, the question of the sufficiency of the marking of the cargo would strictly be irrelevant to the underlying contract of sale and so the bank was not required to call for proof that the condition as to marking had been fulfilled. It would be otherwise, however, if the letter of credit expressly required evidence of conformity.

Finally, bills of lading must specify the port of shipment and arrival, and the bill must be a through bill of lading covering the whole of the voyage between those ports. If part of the journey is to be by road or air the bill must also cover this portion of the journey. The same applies to an air waybill. The Uniform Customs, art. 23, now provides that if the letter of credit expressly permits the tender of a combined transport document for the transportation of goods partly by land, partly by sea or partly by air, the issuing bank may accept any form of transportation document (whether a bill of lading, air waybill or road or rail consignment note or a combination of these) provided it covers the whole journey. The policy of insurance must cover all the risks expressly required to be covered in the letter of credit. Where the credit calls for an insurance certificate which refers to the terms of an open policy under which the certificate has been issued but does not set out the terms the documents presented are insufficient, and the bank will be entitled to reject them. In

Donald M Scott & Co v. *Barclays Bank Ltd* (1923) the issuing bank opened a letter of credit the terms of which were that it would honour the seller's drafts for the amount of the purchase price, provided the drafts were accompanied by an approved insurance policy covering the shipment of the goods. The seller presented a draft for acceptance accompanied by a certificate of insurance which neither contained nor indicated any means of ascertaining the full terms of the insurance cover. The draft was dishonoured and the seller brought an action against the bank. It was held that the certificate was not an "approved insurance policy" within the terms of the letter of credit, and the bank was justified in refusing to accept the documents. The court followed the rule laid down by Bailhache J in *Wilson & Co* v. *Belgian Grain Co* (1920), where it was held that the tender of a cover note was insufficient when the buyer requires an insurance policy. Similarly, a certificate of insurance is not an insurance policy and does not purport to be one; it is a certificate that a policy has been issued which covers the goods mentioned in the certificate and it incorporates the terms of the policy, but it does not enumerate those terms of the policy or summarise the material terms, so that in order to discover those terms one has to examine the original policy (*see Diamond Alkali Export Corporation* v. *Bourgeois* (1921).

An insurance policy or certificate must cover all the risks specified in the letter of credit, or all the risks which are usually insured against in the trade in question. If the policy contains exclusion clauses limiting or excluding the insurer's liability, and these are inconsistent with the terms of the credit or other usages in the trade, the issuing or confirming bank can reject the documents tendered by the beneficiary.

Additionally, the beneficiary is required to tender an invoice stating the total price of the goods, and any adjustment which may have to be made should be effected by means of a refund claim on the buyer, refunded to him by the seller, and not by way of an addition to or a deduction from the price specified in the credit.

The letter of credit may sometimes require the beneficiary to present other documents, apart from a bill of lading, insurance policy and invoice, such as consular invoices, certificates of weight, quantity or analysis, or expert's certificates. The beneficiary, once again, must comply strictly with these requirements. Consequently, in *Equitable Trust Co of New York* v. *Dawson Partners Ltd* (1926) it was held that the tender of a certificate of quality by one expert was insufficient when the letter of credit required a certificate by experts in the plural, thus calling for at least two.

Rejection of documents on extraneous grounds

It is now proposed to deal with the point whether the bank can refuse to honour the credit on any other grounds unconnected with the terms of the credit, such as forgery of the documents presented or fraud on the part of the beneficiary. When the credit issued by the bank is conditional on the presentation of shipping documents, it requires the presentation of genuine documents under which a real consignment of goods or their value may be collected from the carrier or the insurer. Forged documents confer no such rights and are worthless pieces of paper which the bank may reject (*see Établissement Esefkn International Anstalt* v. *Central Bank of Nigeria* (1979)). The bank is required to accept the documents tendered only if all of them are genuine and it may reject the documents even if all except one of the documents is genuine and although the bank will have no occasion to rely on it. Where, therefore, a forged bill of lading and a valid insurance policy are tendered and the goods are lost under circumstances which give the buyer the right to rely on the policy, the bank is entitled to reject the documents tendered because the bill of lading is a forgery. A document is a forgery not only if it bears a forged signature but if it purports to be a different kind of document from what it really is. In *Kwei Tek Chao* v. *British Traders and Shippers Ltd* (1954), bills of lading on which the date had been falsified by showing the date of shipment as 31st October 1951, the last date by which shipment could be made under the letter of credit, instead of 3rd November 1951, when shipment actually took place were presented to the issuing bank, together with other documents which were genuine. The bank accepted the documents in ignorance of the falsity of the stated shipment date and it was subsequently discovered when the goods were delivered to the buyers that the bills of lading were false. The buyers brought an action against the sellers for the repayment of the price, claiming that it was a condition of the contract of sale that only genuine bills of lading should be presented. The court held that the bill of lading was a forgery because it showed the goods in question as having been loaded on the ship within the time specified in the credit, whereas in fact the loading had taken place afterwards. A bill of lading which bears a false shipment date deliberately entered on it is a forgery because it relates to a voyage which purports to have commenced on that date when in fact there was no such voyage.

If the seller knows that the documents are forgeries when he presents them and deliberately induces the bank to accept this draft, he will be liable to the bank in damages for fraud. In *Szteyn* v. *J Henry Schroder Banking Corporation* (1941), the defendant issued an irrevocable letter of credit to a seller in India for the price of a consignment of bristles. The seller loaded fifty cases on board the ship and procured the clean bills of lading and other documents from the shipping company. The documents described the goods in terms which complied with the letter of credit, but the cases in fact contained worthless rubbish. The seller then presented the draft and documents to the issuing bank for payment. The plaintiffs, the buyers, on discovering the true state of affairs brought an action against the issuing bank and the beneficiary to restrain the issuing bank from paying the draft. The court held the plaintiffs were entitled to succeed and could restrain the issuing bank from honouring the credit where it was known that the documents presented were a forgery. The court accepted this as one exception where it would look behind the documents to restrain the bank from fulfilling its obligations.

In *The American Accord* (1981), the Court of Appeal held that where the beneficiary of the credit relies on a third party to prepare a document, and unknown to the beneficiary that document contains a forgery (e.g. a wrong date inserted on the bill of lading by the carrier's agent), the beneficiary cannot argue that the forgery is that of a third party, and if the bank rejects the documents with the knowledge of forgery, it will not be liable for dishonour under the credit.

Measure of damages for dishonour of a commercial credit
If the issuing or confirming bank wrongfully refuses to accept the documents tendered under a letter of credit the seller may sue either for the amount payable under the credit if the tendered documents are still available, or alternatively for the same amount as the seller could recover from the buyer for breach of the underlying contract of sale, provided this does not exceed the amount of the credit.

In *Belgian Grain and Produce Co* v. *Cox & Co* (1919) and *Larios* v. *Gurety* (1873) it was held that the beneficiary may sue the bank for the actual amount payable to them under the credit without showing that he has suffered loss by the bank refusing payment. However, the beneficiary can only bring an action of this nature if he still has the shipping documents required under the letter of credit and is prepared to deliver them to the bank.

Instead of suing the issuing bank for the amount of the credit, the beneficiary under the credit may sue it to recover the same amount as would be recoverable from the buyer for breach of the underlying contract of sale. These damages will normally be the difference between the amount payable under the credit and the lower market value of the goods covered by the credit, or, if the bank repudiates the credit before the goods are shipped, the difference between the purchase price of the goods as set out in the letter of credit and the lower market value of the goods in the country from which they were to be shipped.

The relationship between the buyer and the issuing and confirming banks

As a result of the issuing bank's undertaking to open a letter of credit, there arises a direct contractual relationship between the issuing bank and the buyer (the applicant for the issue of the letter of credit) by which the obligations of the parties are determined. The issuing bank opens the credit in accordance with the instructions given to it by the buyer, and the bank's obligations are confined to honouring the drafts of the beneficiary when presented provided the shipping documents called for by the letter of credit are presented and the conditions to be inserted in the letter of credit comply with the buyer's instructions. Although the obligation of the issuing bank is simply to honour the letter of credit, it imposes both a positive and a negative duty on the issuing bank, and breach of either of these obligations will render it liable to the buyer. The issuing bank is liable to the buyer as follows:

(*a*) if it fails to issue the credit in accordance with his instructions and to honour drafts presented by the beneficiary if the shipping documents accompanying the drafts comply with the conditions of the letter of credit; and (*b*) if it honours drafts presented by the beneficiary when the documents do not in fact comply with the credit.

In addition to the bank losing its right to reimbursement if it exceeds its mandate, the issuing bank is under a contractual duty to the buyer to obey his instructions and carry them out carefully.

If the documents taken up by the issuing bank do not correspond to those required under the credit, the bank fails to conform to its mandate and it may also be guilty of negligence, but if the disparity is not obvious the bank is liable only if a competent banker exercising reasonable care would not have accepted the documents tendered.

The liability of the issuing bank may be extended to the acts of a third party if it employs the third party as its agent to fulfil the whole or part of its functions under the credit. This arises where, for example, the issuing bank employs another bank to advise or confirm the credit. In *Equitable Trust Co* v. *Dawson Partners Ltd* (1926), the court held that where a confirming bank took up shipping documents which did not conform to the buyer's instructions as a result of an error in the transmission of the instructions by the confirming bank to one of its own branches, the issuing bank was responsible to the buyer but it was entitled to be reimbursed by the confirming bank for the amount for which it was liable.

Finally, the law imposes on the issuing bank a duty to pass on to its customer any information which it may acquire concerning the standing of the beneficiary and which may affect the relationship between the buyer and the seller. In *Midland Bank* v. *Seymour* (1955), the plaintiff bank agreed at the request of the defendant to open a letter of credit in favour of a firm in Hong Kong with which the defendant buyer was dealing. The issuing bank made routine inquiries as to the financial standing of the Hong Kong firm; the replies were satisfactory, and it passed the information to the defendant. The issuing bank later received information which cast doubts on the financial standing of the Hong Kong firm, the beneficiary under the credit. The bank failed to pass this information to the defendant, and would have been held liable for its failure to do so if the defendant could have prevented his loss by forestalling payment under the credit because of the Hong Kong firm's fraud. However, as the defendant was unable to prove such a fraud he only recovered nominal damages.

The Uniform Customs and Practices on Bankers' Commercial Credits codify the duties of an issuing bank towards an applicant for a credit, and impose a lighter duty on the banks than that imposed by the common law. As these provisions form the basis of the contract between the buyer and a United Kingdom bank which issues a commercial credit and are incorporated in the buyer's instructions by reference, they override the rules of common law where the two conflict. By art. 7 of the Uniform Customs banks are required to examine all documents with reasonable care, and if the issuing bank takes up documents which appear on their face to be in accordance with the terms and conditions of the credit, by virtue of art. 8(*b*) the applicant must reimburse the bank. The issuing bank assumes no liability "for the form, sufficiency, accuracy, genuineness, falsification or legal effect of any documents," (see art. 9), nor for the consequences of delay and/or loss in transit of any messages, letters or documents (art. 10), and issuing banks "utilising the services of another bank for the purpose of giving effect to the instructions of the applicant" are not liable for the acts or omissions of the other bank employed, who are deemed to act, not for the issuing bank, but as agent for the applicant for the credit (art. 12).

If the issuing bank conforms to the letter of credit and fulfils its duties under it, the buyer is under a duty to put the issuing bank in funds to meet the seller's drafts before they become due. In Reynolds v. Doyle (1840) the court held that a customer of a bank at whose request the credit is issued is under a duty to pay it the amount for which it has accepted bills of exchange a reasonable time before the bills fall due for payment. This is to ensure that the issuing bank has funds sufficient to meet the bill when it is required to pay it.

The customer is not required to put the bank in funds when the credit is actually issued, but the issuing bank can expressly stipulate that its customer must pay it the amount payable by it to the beneficiary of the credit before or at the time the credit is issued, so that the bank does not at any time risk its own funds commiting itself to pay the beneficiary without the buyer having put it in funds. If the customer already has at the bank an account on which there is a credit balance, the bank usually requires that it be given power to debit the amount of the credit when the letter of credit is issued. Where, however, the customer does not have a balance sufficient to cover the amount of the credit, or where the credit is issued at the request of a bank, it may agree to advance the amount of the credit. The issuing bank will then rely on its right to be reimbursed the amount it pays under the credit together with its expenses and charges, and it may rely on any security interest it has over the shipping documents or in the goods they represent to recover the amount which the buyer owes it.

The obligation of the applicant to put the bank in funds is the counterpart of the bank's obligation to honour the credit. If the bank repudiates its obligation, either expressly or by implication, as a result of ceasing to pay its debtor, or going into liquidation, or having a receiver appointed, the applicant's obligation to provide it with funds is terminated. Any sums paid by the buyer specifically for the purposes of the credit can be recovered, or, if sums standing to the credit of the buyer's account are not specifically appropriated to the credit, the buyer can recover the balance of his account as an ordinary creditor.

Finally, the bank's right to reimbursement is dependent on it having conformed strictly to the instructions given to it in the application for the opening of the credit. If it exceeds its mandate in any respect, however slight, its right to be reimbursed is lost. Alternatively, if the applicant has put the bank in funds prior to the seller's drafts being presented, and the issuing bank departs from its mandate, the applicant is entitled to the return of his money. An issuing bank will exceed the mandate if it accepts or purchases a bill of exchange drawn by the seller without insisting on the beneficiary delivering the documents required by the applicant's instructions.

If a bank takes up shipping documents and accepts or pays bills of exchange under a credit containing conditions not relating to the contents of the shipping documents, it is liable if it is negligent in failing to make adequate inquiries before deciding that the conditions have been fulfilled, and would lose its right to be reimbursed in any case. The Uniform Customs, art. 8, protects the bank by providing that "payment, acceptance or negotiation against documents which appear on their face to be in accordance with the terms and conditions of a party . . . binds the party giving the authorisation to take up the documents and reimburse the bank"; furthermore, the banks assume no liability or responsibility for the conditions stipulated in the document (art. 9). The effect of these provisions is that the bank, despite the Unfair Contract Terms Act 1977, s. 3, only loses its right to be reimbursed if it is negligent.

The relationship between the buyer and the confirming bank

If a commercial credit issued by one bank is confirmed by another so as to make it liable to the beneficiary, there is a contractual relationship between the issuing and confirming banks, but no such relationship between the applicant for the credit and the confirming bank. Consequently, if the confirming bank exceeds its mandate by accepting or paying drafts when the conditions of the credit are not fulfilled, it is not liable in damages to the applicant for breach of contract. In *Orr and Barker* v. *Union Bank of Scotland* (1854) it was held that the applicant could not sue the confirming bank when it had paid on a forged draft and subsequently refused to honour a genuine draft presented by the beneficiary. In *Equitable Trust Co* v. *Dawson Partners Ltd* (1926) the court held that there is no agency relationship between the buyer as principal and the confirming bank as his agent, so that an issuing bank cannot escape liability at common law by arguing that the error committed by the confirming bank in accepting documents was committed by it as agent of the buyer. The confirming bank acted as an agent of the issuing bank and so the issuing bank was liable as its principal to the buyer. Because the buyer is not responsible for any errors committed by the confirming bank, it follows that the buyer cannot claim against the confirming bank for any default which operates to the buyer's detriment. If, therefore, the confirming bank acts negligently it is not liable to the buyer, since the confirming bank owes the buyer no duty of care (*see Calico Printers' Association* v. *Barclays Bank* (1930)).

The relationship between the issuing and confirming banks

The seller may make it a term of the contract of sale that the letter of credit is to be issued not by a foreign bank in the buyer's country, but by a bank in his own country on whose solvency the seller is more inclined to rely. The buyer can request that his bank, or a bank in his own country, make arrangements with the nominated bank so that that bank will open the credit in favour of the seller. The terms of this arrangement are a matter of private negotiation between the banks. Alternatively, the issuing bank may issue the credit itself and procure the bank in the seller's country to confirm it.

The relationship between the issuing bank and the intermediary banker whether it issues, confirms or advises the credit, is that of principal and agent, so that when the intermediary bank has fully complied with the mandate it has a right to be reimbursed by the buyer's bank; if it has suffered any loss by reason of its complying with the mandate, it is likewise entitled to be indemnified by the buyer's bank. If the intermediary bank has accepted bills payable a fixed period after sight or on a specified date, it is entitled to be reimbursed on paying the bills, whether or not there is any dispute between the buyer and seller, provided that the documents it has taken up are in conformity with the terms of its instructions. In *Bank Melli Iran* v. *Barclays Bank DCO Ltd* (1951), the Court of Appeal held that an issuing bank waives its right to reject documents taken up by the intermediary bank if it delays in exercising that right for an unreasonable length of time from the time the documents are tendered to it, or from the time it has knowledge that the documents taken up by the intermediary bank do not conform to the conditions in the credit.

A further consequence of the confirming bank being in the position of an agent for the issuing bank is that a confirming bank is not entitled, on its own behalf and for its own benefit, to discount drafts drawn by the seller on the issuing bank. It would be guilty of a breach of duty in making a profit out of the transaction which it has entered into as an agent, and would be accountable for the amount of the discount to the issuing bank.

Security interests under letters of credit

The function of a letter of credit is normally to finance the sale of goods, and the bank which advances money to pay for the goods will either expressly or impliedly have a security over the shipping documents, and in certain cases the goods themselves, to safeguard its right to the reimbursement of its advance by the customer at whose instance it issued the credit. The bank will have a right to retain the possession of the shipping documents, and, ultimately, if the buyer fails to reimburse it, to sell the goods. Furthermore, by express agreement the bank may have a pledge over the goods or an equitable charge over them created by a letter of hypothecation or a letter of trust signed by its customer. The method used by the bank to secure its right to reimbursement will govern the nature and extent of its interest in the shipping documents and the goods they represent and the remedies it may exercise, whilst leaving the ownership of the goods vested in its customer.

The banker's lien

An issuing or confirming bank is entitled to hold the shipping documents which it receives from the beneficiary as security for the amount it has paid or committed itself to pay under the bills of exchange which it pays or accepts. The banker's lien arises by operation of law in consequence of the instructions given to the issuing bank to open the credit and the lien is independent of any other security the bank may take by express agreement. The ordinary right of the bank under its lien is a right merely to retain possession of the shipping documents, but in the case of such documents the lien carries with it the right to sell the goods represented by them; as such it approximates more closely to a pledge than to a common law lien.

The pledge

An applicant for a letter of credit may create different forms of security over the shipping documents and the goods in favour of the issuing or confirming bank. The pledge arises only by the express agreement of the parties and its effect is determined by agreement. The third party holds the goods for the account of the pledgee by attorning to the pledgee (i.e. acknowledging that the third party holds the goods on behalf of the pledgee) and the latter in such a case has constructive possession. Where, however, the goods are represented by documents, the mere delivery of the documents to the pledgee does not generally vest possession of the goods themselves in him unless the person who has custody of them is notified of the arrangements and agrees to hold the goods on behalf of the pledgee. In the absence of such an agreement the pledge of the goods is incomplete and ineffective.

CARRIAGE OF GOODS

The transportation of goods overseas requires expert knowledge, and the seller may either use the services of a forwarding agent, loading broker or forwarding department of a shipping company, or have his own shipping department if the quantity of export transactions he is involved in warrants it.

CARRIAGE BY SEA

Where a seller in this country is obliged to arrange for the carriage of goods to the port of destination, he will enter into a contract of carriage with a shipowner by which the latter undertakes to carry the goods from a port in the UK to the foreign port of destination. If the quantity of goods to be exported justifies it, the seller may charter a complete ship, in which case the terms of the contract of carriage are embodied in a charterparty. Where, however, the goods form only part of the ship's cargo, the seller will simply reserve space in the ship for the carriage of the cargo. The terms of the contract of carriage are evidenced by a bill of lading, which is an acknowledgment by the shipowner that goods have been delivered to him for the purpose of carriage. The remuneration received by the shipowner is known as freight.

The seller (shipper) will normally instruct a forwarding agent to obtain space for a cargo, and the agent is under a duty to ascertain the date and place of sailing, obtain space for the carriage of goods and prepare a bill of lading for signature on behalf of the shipping company. The forwarding agent will send the bill of lading to the loading broker who act as an agent of the shipowner;

the loading broker's duty is to obtain cargoes for carriage and to arrange for the goods to be brought alongside and pay any customs duties. The loading broker advertises the date of sailings and circulates a sailing card to the customer. He will supervise the loading and stowage of the cargoes and usually he will sign the bill of lading on behalf of the shipowner and hand it to the shipper (seller) in exchange for the shipper paying the freight (freight pre–paid). The sailing card will contain the last dates when goods are to be received by the ship for loading. When the goods are delivered to the shipowner the shipper will receive a mate's receipt.

The essential feature of the modern method of container transport is that several cargoes are combined and carried in a single container; the goods are not handled separately for sea or inland transport. In container transport, the shipper, having made arrangements with a forwarding agent or directly with the office of a container shipping line, will send goods to the nearest container loading depot where the shipping line has facilities for combining and containerising cargoes.

When the goods are loaded on board the ship they are inspected by tally clerks who keep a record of their date of loading, identification marks, individual number of packages, their weight and measurement and a description of any defects or the condition of the goods. When the loading is completed, the ship's officer in charge of the loading signs the mate's receipt. This document should not contain any qualifications as to the goods, but if it is qualified as to the description or quality of the goods it is known as claused or foul. The qualification on the mate's receipt is later incorporated in the bill of lading.

Shutting out goods

When the goods of a shipper are shut out by the shipowner because the ship is full even though the goods were sent to the appointed place of loading before the closing date, two situations must be distinguished. First, if in reliance on the sailing card, the owner of the goods sends them to the docks without an agreement with the shipowner to reserve space for the goods, the shipper cannot claim damages from the shipowner because no contract has been concluded. The notification on the sailing card is merely an invitation to make an offer, and the tender of the goods for loading is merely an offer which the shipowner can accept or reject. Secondly, where the shipowner has booked freight space in advance, there in a breach of the contract of affreighment, and an action will lie against the shipowner.

Freight

Freight is payable to the carrier for the safe carriage and delivery of goods, but if goods are lost then nothing is payable. If the cargo arrives in a damaged condition the shipowner is entitled to the freight unless the damage is so serious that the goods have totally lost their merchantable character. Freight is not payable until the goods arrive at the port of destination unless otherwise agreed (e.g. freight to be pre-paid when the goods are loaded or accepted for loading). The freight payable under bills of lading is calculated by weight measurement or on an *ad valorem* basis. The shipowner is entitled to elect the method of calculation most favourable to himself.

The contract of sale may expressly provide who bears the ultimate responsibility for the payment of freight, but in the absence of an express provision the following rules apply namely;

(*a*) the shipper is primarily liable for payment of the freight because it is he who enters into the contract with the shipowner;

(*b*) the shipowner may demand payment of freight from the buyer if he is named in the bill of lading as the consignee or the bill of lading is indorsed to him and he has acquired the property in the goods, or if he expressly or implicitly undertakes with the shipowner to pay the freight;

(*c*) a seller who exercises his right of stoppage in transit is liable to pay the freight to the shipowner.

The parties can by agreement modify the rule that the shipowner is not entitled to claim freight before the cargo has arrived at the port of destination and this right is not restricted by the Carriage of Goods by Sea Act 1971. Thus the parties may agree that freight is to be payable in advance, and in such a case the freight is payable at the latest when the ship finally sails. The shipowner may, however, have to return the advance freight if the ship never earned the freight (e.g. if it failed to sail, or if the goods were lost before advance freight became payable, or if the goods are lost by an event other than an excepted peril).

Dead freight

Where the shipper fails to load the cargo or the full cargo he has agreed to deliver on board a ship, he is in breach of the contract of carriage and is liable to pay the agreed freight as damages, known as dead freight.

Lump sum freight

In order for the shipowner to earn lump sum freight the ship must complete the voyage or the cargo must be forwarded by some other means. In the absence of an agreement to the contrary, the whole lump sum freight is payable if only part of the loaded cargo is delivered by the shipowner at the port of destination and the remainder is lost. The shipowner cannot claim freight if the whole of the cargo is lost.

Back freight

The shipper is liable to pay back freight where the goods shipped are carried, on his instructions, to a place other than the port of destination. Where, for example, the seller exercises his right of stoppage in transit, and instructs the shipowner to deliver the goods to a port other than the port of destination named in the bill of lading, he is liable for any additional freight.

Pro-rata freight

Pro-rata freight is payable where the parties to the contract of carriage enter into a new contract to the effect that the goods will be delivered at an intermediate port and not the port of destination in the bill of lading. A payment proportionate to the part of the voyage will be made in such a case.

The shipowner's lien

The shipowner has a lien at common law over the seller's goods for the freight payable and for any expenses incurred by the shipowner in preserving the goods. The shipowner's lien is lost when goods are delivered to the buyer or his agent. If goods are placed in a warehouse at the port of arrival, the shipowner can preserve his lien by giving the warehouse–keeper express notice of the lien.

Carriage covered by bills of lading

A bill of lading in law has three distinct functions:

(*a*) it is a formal receipt by the shipowner which acknowledges that goods of the specified quantity and condition have been shipped to a stated destination in the named ship;

(*b*) it is evidence of the contract of carriage; and

(*c*) it is a document of title to the goods in question.

A shipper is protected from the unreasonable limitation of liability by shipowners by the Carriage of Goods by Sea Act 1971. The Act contains rules relating to bills of lading imposing on the carrier certain minimum responsibilities which cannot be avoided or diminished by express provisions in the contract (e.g. the duty to exercise due diligence, to provide a seaworthy ship and to issue a bill of lading in a particular form). These rules apply to all goods exported from Great Britain and Northern Ireland with the exception of livestock and deck cargo. Where there is no statement on the face of the bill of lading that cargo is in fact to be carried on deck the carriage is subject to the rules under the 1971 Act. Where the bill of lading allows the shipowner liberty to carry cargo on deck he is under an obligation to stow it diligently (*see* Sched., art. III, r. 2).

The Carriage of Goods by Sea Act 1971

The Carriage of Goods by Sea Act 1971 applies to the carriage of goods from a UK port where the carriage is evidenced by an outward bill of lading to another country and to bills of lading issued in certain other countries, or under which shipment is made from certain other countries, or if the bill of lading provides that it is governed by the rules or by the law of such a country. A bill of lading to which the 1971 Act applies must contain an express statement that it is to have effect subject to the rules contained in the Act.

Liability of shipowner for loss of or damage to the goods

The liability of the shipowner for goods exported from the UK is governed by the Carriage of Goods by Sea Act 1971, which applies to all outward shipments under bills of lading, except a few minor cases where the parties may be able to contract out of the Act. The rules may expressly be adopted for journeys where the Act does not apply either by statutory provision or by express agreement; the liability of the shipowner is determined by the contract as evidenced in a bill of lading, which may contain exemptions for loss or damage. In the absence of express contractual provision the rules of the common law will apply to contracts of carriage by sea which do not fall within the 1971 Act.

By common law the shipowner implicitly undertakes the liability of a common carrier, i.e. to carry the goods at his own absolute risk, accept where the goods are lost or damaged by Act of God, by the Queen's enemies, by an inherent defect in the goods themselves or by the shipper's default.

The Carriage of Goods by Sea Act 1971, Sched., art. III, para. 1, provides in respect of the goods entrusted to him that the carrier is bound before and at the beginning of the voyage to exercise due diligence:

(a) to make the ship seaworthy. In *Riverplate Meat Co Pty Ltd* v. *Lancashire Co Ltd* (1961) a carrier was held not to have discharged his duty of due care when cargo was damaged because water entered the cargo hold on account of negligent work done by a fitter employed to repair the ship. If due diligence has not been exercised to make the ship seaworthy, the carrier will be liable for loss or damage resulting from unseaworthiness although the primary cause of the loss was one for which the carrier would not be liable under the rules.

(b) properly to man, equip and supply the ship;

(c) to make the holds, refrigerating and cool chambers, and all other parts of the ship in which the goods are carried, fit and safe for their reception, carriage and preservation.

Moreover the carrier is under an obligation properly and carefully to load, handle, stow, carry, keep, care for and discharge the goods carried by him (*see* Sched., art. III, para. 2).

The shipowner is only liable under the 1971 Act if he acts negligently, whereas the common law (where applicable) imposes an absolute liability on the shipowner for the safety of the cargo. Under the 1971 Act, however, the shipowner cannot contract out of his duty to exercise due care and diligence and to ensure that the ship is seaworthy. Further, the shipowner is liable if servants and agents employed by him fail to act with due diligence or load and stow the cargo with proper care. In *Minister of Food* v. *Lamport and Holt Line Ltd* (1952) the shipowners were held liable to the owners of a cargo of maize for damage caused by bad stowage. In that case the shipowner's servants had stowed tallow shipped in casks in the hold above which maize was stored. During the voyage some of the casks were broken and the tallow, which became heated, began to leak and penetrated the hold in which the maize was stowed, causing damage to it. Similarly, in *Pyrene Co Ltd* v. *Scindia Navigation Co Ltd (The Chyebaisa)* (1954) the shipowners were held not to be liable in negligence when in an intermediate port the cover plate of a storm valve in a hold was stolen by stevedores during an unloading operation and sea-water damaged the cargo in the hold. The court held the shipowners had supervised both the loading and unloading of cargo with care and were not liable for the acts of the stevedores.

The 1971 Act does not define the scope of the carriers involvement to load the cargo, but the cargo must be loaded "properly and carefully" (*see* Sched., art. III, para. 2). In *Pyrene Co Ltd* v. *Scindia Navigation Co Ltd* (1954) the shipowners were held responsible under an f o b contract for the whole of the loading operation and not only for the part following the crossing of the rail. The duty of the carrier properly and carefully to discharge the goods carried usually ends when the goods are delivered from the ship's tackle to the person entitled to receive them in the same order and condition as on shipment. Where the goods are discharged into a lighter, the shipowner continues to be liable if the goods loaded into the lighter are damaged.

Excepted perils

The Carriage of Goods by Sea Act 1971, contains a list of excepted perils; if loss or damage caused to the cargo is due to one of these events, the carrier will not be subjected to any liability. The excepted perils contained in Sched., art. IV include riots and civil commotions, insufficiency or inadequacy of packing or identification markings, acts of war or an Act of God. The burden of proof is on the shipowner who seeks to avoid liability because the cargo is lost or damaged due to an excepted peril.

A shipper can himself insure against the possibility of loss or damage caused by one of the excepted perils (e.g. a shipper can cover himself for any loss caused by strikes, riots or civil commotion).

Deviation

An unpermitted deviation is a breach of contract and neither the exceptions nor the limitation of liability can be relied on. The rules, however, allow deviation in three cases namely, to save life at sea; to save property at sea; and where deviation is reasonable.

Maximum limits of shipowner's liabilities

The Carriage of Goods by Sea Act 1971, Sched., art. IV, places a maximum liability of £100 per package or unit on the shipowner for loss or damage caused to the goods unless the nature and value of the goods has been declared by the shipper before shipment and inserted in the bill of lading. The money value mentioned is to be taken in gold. The maximum limits mentioned are not absolute, and the liability of the shipowner may be increased by agreement of the parties by declaration of the value of the goods. In such a case the shipper may claim damages in excess of the maximum limits imposed by statute. The shipowner can limit his liability, and protection is given by the Carriage of Goods by Sea Act not only against the party to the contract of carriage but under an f o b contract also against the seller who loads the goods on board the nominated ship if goods are damaged by the negligence of the shipowner's servants before they cross the ship's rail. The maximum liability of the shipowner is calculated by package or unit.

Claim for loss of or damage to goods

If goods delivered at the port of destination are damaged or only part of the consignment is delivered, then notice of the loss or damage must be given in writing to the carrier or his agent at the port of discharge at the time or before the goods are removed by the person entitled to delivery or his agent. If the defect is not obvious or apparent until after the buyer or his agent has taken delivery, then notice of the defect must be given to the shipowner within three days. A failure to give notice within the specified time is prima facie evidence that the condition of the goods delivered corresponds to that in the bill of lading. Moreover, the carrier will be discharged from all liability in respect of loss or damage caused to the goods unless the action is brought within one year after delivery of the goods or date of delivery. The Maritime Law Association Agreement 1950 has extended this one-year period to two years, subject to the cargo-owner giving notice of his claim to the carrier within the first year.

Container transport

The methods of container transport have made it possible to carry goods in the same article of transport from the inland place of dispatch to the final destination. The transportation of the goods is treated as a single-movement operation although by different means of transport. Where goods are to be carried from door to door, all container bills are "received for shipment" bills instead of "shipped" bills since the carriage begins when the goods are delivered by the consignor to the place where they are containerised; this is often an inland establishment from which the containerised goods are carried by rail to the port of shipment.

CARRIAGE BY AIR

The law relating to the carriage of goods by air has reached considerable international uniformity and the present law is contained in the Carriage by Air Act 1961 which gives effect to the Warsaw Convention of 1929 and the Hague Protocol of 1955. The Carriage by Air Act 1961, itself, is supplemented by the Carriage by Air (Supplementary Provisions) Act 1962, which gives effect to the Guadalajara Convention which applies to both the original and amended Warsaw Conventions.

There are three separate set of rules, any one of which may apply to the carriage of goods by air depending on whether the parties are resident in a country which is a party to the Conventions and whether or not the parties are resident in different countries.

The basic system of liability is that the carrier of goods by air is automatically liable for the loss, destruction, damage or delay to the cargo if it occurs during the carriage of the cargo by air. The carrier cannot contract out of his liability, but he can rely on the limitations placed on the amount of his liability even if the actual damage is greater. The maximum for which an air carrier may be made liable is the present value of 250 gold francs per kilogram or the value declared by the shipper if it is greater.

The carriage of goods by air comprises the whole period during which the cargo is in the hands of the carrier, whether at an airport, on board an aircraft, or in any other place if goods are handled anywhere other than at an airport. In the case of transhipment of an air cargo, any damage caused to the goods is presumed to have occurred during the air carriage unless the contrary can be proved.

Carrier's defences

The carrier is not liable if he can prove that both he and his agents or servants took all necessary steps to avoid damage to the goods.

If the carrier can show that damage was caused or contributed to by the negligence of the injured party, then the carrier's liability may be proportionally reduced by the contributory negligence. A carrier can expressly incorporate into the contract terms which are contrary to the statute law; thus the carrier can restrict or exclude his liability.

It is no longer simple to determine which of the Conventions (as given statutory effect) apply but the carriage of cargo for reward by aircraft or the gratuitous carriage by an aircraft is governed as follows:

(a) The original Warsaw Convention applies when the parties to the contract, the places of departure and destination are located either in two countries both of which are parties to the original Warsaw Convention, or where the places of departure and destination are in the same country but with a stopping place outside that country. The Convention therefore applies to all international carriage if the countries involved are members. Thus in *Corocraft Ltd* v. *Pan American Airway Inc* (1969) a contract was made in New York for the carriage of diamonds from New York to London; they were stolen in London by the carrier's servant. The consignee sued in London for non-delivery and it was held that the Warsaw Convention applied because England was a party to the Convention.

(b) The amended Convention applies where the agreement between the parties, the places of departure and destination are located either in two countries both of which are parties to the amended Convention, or in the same country but with an agreed stopping place in a country not party to the Convention.

A problem can arise where the place of departure is in a country which is party to only the original Convention (e.g. USA) whilst the place of destination is in a country which is party to both the original and amended Convention (i.e. UK). In such a case only the obligations contained in the original Convention bind both the states and apply to a contract for air carriage between them.

(c) Where the carriage of cargo is governed neither by the original nor the amended Convention (e.g. air carriage to or from Turkey) and there is no agreed stopping place in another state, then whatever the country of departure, the contract or agreement for carriage is governed by neither of the two Conventions. An action in the English courts would be governed by the ordinary rules governing the carriage of goods at common law.

The Convention does not apply in the following cases:

(*a*) if the place of departure and destination are not *both* in Convention countries and there is no agreed stopping place in a Convention country;

(*b*) if the place of departure and destination are in the same Convention country and there is no agreed stopping place in *another* Convention country.

Carriage governed by the original Warsaw Convention

The document of carriage where the carriage of cargo is governed by the original Warsaw Convention is an air consignment note. An irregularity or the absence or loss of the air consignment note does not affect the validity of the contract between the parties or the operation of the Convention rules. The air consignment note is not a document of title. There must be three original parts to each air consignment note and these must be delivered to the carrier with the goods. The first part is for the carrier and is signed by the consignor; the second part is for the consignee and must be signed by the consignor; it accompanies the goods; the third part is signed by the carrier and returned to the consignor after the goods have been accepted for carriage. The consignor must also furnish any further information or documents necessary for customs before the goods can be delivered to the consignee. The consignor is liable to the carrier for any damage arising out of the absence or irregularity of these documents, including the air consignment note.

If the carrier accepts goods without an air consignment note or if it does not contain certain provisions (i.e. the place and date of issue of the air consignment bill, the places of departure and destination, any agreed stopping places, the name and address of consignor and consignee, the nature of goods, the number of packages and their description and a statement that the carriage is subject to the rules relating to liability established by the Convention) the carrier cannot rely on the limitations on his liability for loss or damage prescribed by the Convention.

The air consignment note is prima facie evidence of the conclusion of a contract, the receipt of the goods and the conditions of the goods.

Special rights of the consignor and consignee

The consignor has the following special rights, unless these are expressly varied by a provision in the air consignment note:

(*a*) the right to dispose of the goods prior to their delivery to the consignee. This right is subject to the production of the consignor's copy of the air consignment note to the carrier and the payment of all expenses;

(*b*) the right to enforce any rights in his own name.

On the other hand the consignee has the right to require the carrier to hand over goods and the second copy of the air consignment note on arrival at the destination on the payment of any charges. He, too, can enforce any rights in his own name.

The consignee can exercise his rights if the carrier admits the loss of the goods or if they have not arrived within seven days after the date by which they should have arrived.

Carriage governed by the amended Warsaw Convention

The document of carriage is called an air waybill, the American equivalent of the European expression "air consignment note". The provisions applicable to the air consignment note apply to an air waybill. When cargo is accepted without an air waybill or if notice is not given on the air waybill that the Warsaw Convention may apply and may limit the carriers liability, the carrier cannot protect himself under the limitation of liability clauses of the Convention unless the carriage is performed in unusual circumstances.

A consignor can instruct the carrier to stop the goods in transit on any landing, to deliver the goods to someone else at the destination or intermediate landing place, or to return the goods to the airport of departure. The consignor, however, must indemnify the carrier for any costs he has to incur because of a change in the original instructions.

Liability of the carrier

The carrier is responsible for loss or damage to the cargo during the carriage by air, but he will escape liability if he can show that all necessary steps were taken to avoid damage. A complaint about damage to the cargo must be made within 14 days of receipt, and claims for delay must be notified within 21 days of the cargo becoming available.

CARRIAGE BY ROAD

The Carriage of Goods by Road Act 1965, regulates the transport of goods abroad by road. The Act gives effect to the provisions in the 1956 Geneva Convention for the International Carriage of Goods by Road. The Convention applies when goods are carried from one state for delivery in another, and at least one of the states is a party to the Convention. The Convention and the Act only apply if the goods were damaged whilst being transported by road, but if the goods were carried for a part of the journey by sea, rail or air and it can be shown that damage could only have occurred while they were being carried otherwise than by road, the carrier's liability is not determined in accordance with the rules of the Carriage of Goods by Road Act 1965, but by whatever other rules would apply at that stage of the journey. In *Thermo Engineers Ltd* v. *Ferrymasters Ltd* (1981) it was shown that damage to the goods occurred during its journey by sea, and the plaintiffs, who had contracted to carry the goods by road from the port of arrival to their final destination, were consequently not held liable.

The Convention does not apply to postal deliveries. When goods are carried by road a consignment note is usually issued confirming the contract of carriage, but the Convention applies even if no note has been issued. A consignment note is not a document of title to goods. Three copies of the note are usually issued and the note must include details of the sender, carrier, consignee, number of packages, quantity and packing and a statement that the Convention is to apply to that particular contract. The consignment is prima facie evidence of the contract of carriage and of the receipt of the goods by the carrier. It is presumed that the goods received were in apparent good condition at the time of the receipt unless otherwise stated.

A consignor can instruct the carrier to stop the goods, to change their place of delivery or to deliver them to a person other than the consignee.

Liability of the carrier

A carrier can only escape liability for loss, delay or damage to the goods if he can show that the occurrence of the event causing the loss was due to the act of the claimant, or to an inherent vice of the goods, or to circumstances which the carrier could not avoid. If goods are not delivered at the agreed time, or within a reasonable time if no delivery date is specified, the consignor/consignee may claim compensation for the delay. If goods are not delivered within 30 days of the agreed time or within 60 days from the time of their receipt by the carrier, they may be treated as lost for the purpose of claims by the consignor or consignee.

The limitation period for claims is one year, or three years if the loss is due to the carrier's wilful misconduct. The carrier must be given notice of any apparent loss or damage on delivery, or in writing within 7 days after delivery if the loss or damage was not apparent at that time.

The parties cannot contract out of the statutory rules embodying the Convention.

CARRIAGE BY RAIL

The international transportation of goods by rail is regulated by the Berne Convention. The Convention must be expressly incorporated in the contract of carriage if it is to have the force of law in the UK. The contract of carriage must be for the carriage of goods between one Convention country and another. The terms of carriage are set out in the consignment note and full details of the goods and consignee should be given. The consignment note is not a document of title. The consignor has a right of disposal in transit, but not if the consignee has received the consignment note.

An action against the carrier must be brought within one year, or, where fraud or misconduct is alleged, within two years.

PROBLEMS

1. What are the obligations and responsibilities of the parties to a contract of sale where goods are sold c i f or f o b?

2. Explain the requirements of the different types of letters of credit, particularly confirmed and unconfirmed credits.

3. Explain the relationship between the debtor and the beneficiary under the underlying contract of sale when the sale is financed by means of a letter of credit. How are damages assessed against a buyer who fails to fulfil his obligations under the underlying contract of sale?

4. What documents are required to be tendered under a letter of credit? What is meant by the term "a clean bill of lading"?

5. Can a bank reject documents presented under a letter of credit on any grounds unconnected with the terms of the credit, such as forgery or fraud?

6. (a) Explain the relationship between the buyer and the confirming bank which has issued a letter of credit at his request.

(b) What is the relationship between the buyer and the confirming bank under such a letter of credit?

7. When does the Carriage of Goods by Sea Act 1971 apply and what is the liability of the shipowner for loss of or damage to the goods carried?

8. What defences does a carrier under an agreement to carry goods by air have if the goods are lost or damaged in transit?

CHAPTER SIX

Consumer Protection and Consumer Credit

OBJECTIVES

The purpose of the law governing consumer protection is to impose requirements on suppliers of goods and services to consumers (as distinct from commercial customers) in addition to those normally implied in contractual relationships so as to safeguard consumers' interests in respect of matters where they are particularly vulnerable. These additional requirements are mandatory and cannot be contracted out of. It is proposed in this chapter to examine the main enactments for consumer protection. In particular the chapter deals with:

(*a*) the main legislation relating to advertising;
(*b*) the main legislation relating to unfair trade practices;
(*c*) the main legislation relating to consumer credit.

THE TRADE DESCRIPTIONS ACTS

The main objective of the Trade Descriptions Acts 1968—1972, is to protect consumers by making it a criminal offence for traders or manufacturers to make misleading statements in connection with offers or advertisements to supply goods or services. Criminal liability depends on the proof of *mens rea* (i.e. an intention to do the act complained of).

False statements as to goods

The Trade Descriptions Act 1968, s.1, provides that a person who in the ordinary course of his trade or business makes a false trade description in respect of any goods, or supplies or offers to supply goods to which a false description relates is guilty of an offence. An offence is committed under the Act only if the false statement relating to goods (including ships, aircraft, and crops grown on land) is made in the course of the trader's trade or business. A misleading statement made in the course of a private transaction is therefore not an offence under the Trade Descriptions Acts.

The offence can be committed in relation only to the supply of goods. In *Wycombe Marsh Garages Ltd* v. *Fowler* (1972) a conviction on the ground that a misleading statement had been made when a car was tested for the purposes of M.O.T., was quashed on the grounds that the statement did not relate to the supply of goods but to the supply of services.

The offence must involve statements made with the intention to induce the customer to enter into a transaction for the supply of goods. It is insufficient that the statement is made when the customer returns the goods for some reason. In *Wickers Motors (Gloucester) Ltd* v. *Hall* (1972) the defendants sold a car which was in an unroadworthy condition. When the purchaser subsequently complained about the car he was told by the defendants' employee that "there was nothing wrong with the car". The defendants were charged with making a false trade description contrary to the Trade Descriptions Act 1968. It was held that no offence had in fact been committed for the statement about the condition of the car had been made a considerable time after the completion of the contract for sale.

The offence can, however, be committed by the trader either as prospective seller or as prospective buyer. In *Fletcher* v. *Bugden* (1974) a car dealer stated in the course of negotiations with a private individual for the sale of a car that it was only fit for scrap. The dealer acquired the car for a minimal amount, and after repairs sold it at a large profit. It was held that he had committed an offence under section 1 of the Trade Descriptions Act 1968.

Where a false trade description is made in connection with the supply of goods, the 1968 Act s.1, creates two separate offences which involve strict liability:

(*a*) *Applying a false description to goods.* The 1968 Act, s.4, provides that a person applies a trade description to goods if he affixes or annexes it to or incorporates it with the goods themselves or anything with which the goods are supplied, or if he places the goods in or with anything to which the trade description is affixed or attached or uses the trade description in a manner likely to be interpreted as referring to the goods. The Trade Descriptions Act 1968, s.4, imposes liability for both oral and written statements. It is not necessary for the person making the statement to be a party to the contract for the supply of goods. In *Flecher* v. *Sledmore* (1973) the defendant was a dealer in cars and he sold a car to another dealer X, but it was agreed between the parties that the car would remain on the defendant's premises for repair. The plaintiff inspected the car with a view to purchasing it whilst it was on the defendant's premises and was told by the defendant that the engine was in a satisfactory condition. The plaintiff bought the car from the defendant and subsequently brought an action under the Trade Descriptions Act on the ground that the engine was defective. The action succeeded and the defendant was held guilty of making a false trade description in respect of the car.

(*b*) *Supplying goods to which a false trade description has been applied.* The offence may also be committed by supplying goods or offering to supply goods in respect of which a false trade description is made. An offence is committed by merely holding oneself out to supply goods in respect of which a false trade description has been made. Thus it is sufficient if the goods are in a stockroom awaiting delivery. A retailer may commit an offence in supplying goods in respect of which another person (e.g. the manufacturer) has made a false description, for example in an advertisement.

The Trade Descriptions Act 1968 contains an exhaustive list of matters which are considered as part of a trade description. Section 2(1) of the Act provides that a trade description is an indication by whatever means of certain matters in respect of any goods or part of goods, namely the quantity, size or gauge, the manufactures, production or reconditioning process applied to the goods, the composition, fitness for purpose, strength, performance behaviour or accuracy and any other physical characteristics. Additionally, the trade description will apply to any tests and the results therein in respect of the fitness, place and date of manufacture, production, processing or reconditioning and the name of the person responsible for those tests and any other history including previous owners.

The Trade Descriptions Act 1968 does not make every inaccurate statement an offence, and s.3(1) provides that the statement must be "false to a material degree". In *R* v. *Ford Motor Co Ltd* (1974) a car manufactured by the Ford motor company was damaged whilst in the care of forwarding agents. It was repaired and supplied to a car dealer as a "new car". The court held that the damage was sufficiently limited for the car still to be a "new car" after repairs.

Exclusion clauses

The question which arises under the Trade Descriptions Act is whether a disclaimer of liability is sufficient to negative the trade description. Thus it has been held that a dealer who wishes to exclude his liability on a false odometer on motor vehicles must take positive steps to do so. It is not enough that the dealer might have remarked during the course of negotiations that he disclaims liability for the mileage shown on the odometer.

Other offences in connection with the supply of goods

Definition and markings

The government may assign a definite meaning to certain expressions used in relation to goods and where a certain meaning is assigned to words, they are deemed to have that meaning when used in a trade description.

The Department of Trade and Industry has power to require that certain goods shall be marked or accompanied by any information as to their origin or contents, or to regulate or prohibit the supply of goods.

False or misleading pricing

The Trade Descriptions Act 1968, s.11 created two new offences in relation to false or misleading indications as to the price of goods. The offences may be committed although the defendant was unaware of the falsity of the statement. The two offences are:

(*a*) *False comparisons.* If a supplier of goods falsely indicates or represents that the price at which the goods are being offered is equal to, or less than, either a price recommended by the manufacturer or the price at which the goods were previously offered by him, the supplier is guilty of an offence. An indication that goods were previously offered at a higher price or at a particular price is treated as indicating that they were so offered within the previous six months and were so offered continuously for a period of not less than twenty–eight days.

(b) *Misleading pricing.* A person who gives an indication, by whatever means, that the goods are being offered at a price less than that at which they are in fact being offered commits an offence (e.g. by omitting VAT from the advertised price without stating that it is to be added). In *Doble* v. *David Grieg Ltd* (1972), the defendants displayed in their self–service store bottles of fruit juice marked 5s 9d. The manufacturer's labels on the bottles said that a 4d deposit was refundable on the return of bottles but a notice was displayed at the store's cash desk stating that it would not accept the return of empty bottles and that no deposit was charged on the purchase of the fruit juice. It was held that an offence was committed since the price of 5s 9d could be inclusive or exclusive of the 4d deposit, the notice at the cash desk being irrelevant.

False claims as to approval.
In relation to the supply of goods and services it is an offence to give a false indication of a royal award or approval having been conferred.

False statements as to services
The Trade Descriptions Act 1968, s.14(1), provides that it is an offence for any person in the course of trade to make a false statement on the following matters:

(a) the provision of any services, accommodation or facilities in the course of any trade or business;

(b) the nature of any services, accommodation or facilities provided in the course of any trade or business;

(c) the time at which and the manner in which any services are provided;

(d) the location or amenities of any accommodation provided; and

(e) the time and manner in which or the persons by whom any services, accommodation or facilities are provided.

Where a statement within s. 14(1) is made in a brochure, an offence will be committed every time it is communicated to a different reader. In *R* v. *Thomson Holidays* (1974), the defendants advertised holidays in Greece through brochures which misrepresented the hotel amenities available. The court held that a false statement had been made within the Trade Descriptions Act and every time the brochure was communicated to someone else an offence was committed.

The offences under s.14 are similar to the offences under s.1 in that an offence is committed under the former if the statements are false to a material degree and they are made in the course of a trade or business. Liability may be avoided only if the exclusion of responsibility is considered adequate.

The offence created by s.14 is directed towards "statements" or anything "likely to be taken for such a statement" (e.g. conduct intended to convey a certain impression would be sufficient). The falsity must relate to matters of fact or an existing fact (e.g. holiday brochures which state the hotel is complete and conforms to certain specified standards).

The Act applies to services, accommodation and facilities and empowers the

Government to give definite meanings to these terms.

Offences under the Acts

The representor's state of mind

It is an offence for a person to make a statement which he knows to be false or to make a false statement recklessly. A statement made regardless of whether it is true or false will be deemed to have been made recklessly. Under s.14 the statement may be made "recklessly" regardless of whether there is any dishonest intent on the part of the person who makes it. In *MFI Warehouses* v. *Nattrass* (1973), the defendant advertised the sale by mail order of louvre doors on 14 days' free approval. The advertisement also offered folding door gear on approval. The defendant intended that the gear should only be supplied with the doors, and did not appreciate that the advertisement could be read as a willingness to supply the gear separately. The defendant's unwillingness to supply door gear alone was held to be a reckless breach of s.14.

Sanctions

A person guilty of an offence under the Act may be fined, but a sentence of imprisonment may be imposed after a conviction on indictment. Where a company is responsible for a breach of the Trade Descriptions Act 1968, a director, manager or secretary of the company may be held personally responsible for the offences if the offence was committed with the consent, connivance or neglect of an officer of the company. However, such persons can only be found personally liable if the company itself has been found guilty of an offence.

Defences

The 1968 Act, s.24, sets out two defences:

(*a*) that the commission of the offence was due to a mistake, or to reliance on information supplied to the defendant, or to the default of another person, or some accident beyond the defendant's control. Moreover, the defendant must show that he took reasonable precautions and exercised due diligence to avoid the commission of the offence by him or his employee. In *Tesco Supermarkets Ltd* v. *Nattrass* (1971), a company owning chain stores had established a system of supervision over its employees in order to avoid the commission of an offence under the Trade Descriptions Acts. However, a store manager failed to check the work of his staff, with the result that certain goods advertised to be sold at a special price were not available, and an offence was therefore committed under s.11(2). However, Tesco Ltd was acquitted of the offence because it was committed through the default of an employee, and the company had established a satisfactory system of control in order to avoid such offences being committed although the system was ineffective on this particular occasion;

(*b*) Where a person has merely supplied goods to which another applied a false trade description, then, provided the person supplying the goods can show that he could not with reasonable diligence have ascertained that the goods did not conform to the description applied to them, he will not be liable for an offence.

Innocent publication

The 1968 Act, s.25, provides a special defence for owners of news media. It is a defence for such a person to show that he received the advertisement for publication in the ordinary course of his business, and did not know or have any reason to suspect that its publication would amount to an offence under the Act.

Enforcement

It is the duty of local authorities to enforce the Trade Descriptions Acts within their area, under the direction and supervision of the Director–General of Fair Trading.

THE FAIR TRADING ACT 1973

The objectives of the Fair Trading Act 1973 are to promote increased economic efficiency through the wide powers given to the Office of Fair Trading to deal with monopolies, mergers and restrictive practices and the protection of consumers against unfair trading practices. If the Director–General of Fair Trading considers an activity to be detrimental or not in the best interests of consumers, he may either initiate a process culminating in a statutory order to regulate that conduct, or, if the activity is already governed by law, he may obtain an injunction to prevent further breaches of the law.

A consumer transaction for the purposes of this legislation is one where the supplier supplies goods or services in the course of a business and the person to whom they are supplied receives them otherwise than in the course of a business carried on by him.

Orders against unfair trade practices

The Fair Trading Act 1973, Part II, applies to "consumer trade practices," that is any practice which is carried on in connection with the supply of goods to consumers or in connection with the supply of services for consumers and which relate to:

(*a*) the terms or conditions on which the goods or services are to be supplied;

(*b*) the method by which those terms or conditions are communicated to the consumer;

(*c*) the promotion of the method of salesmanship employed in dealing with consumers;

(*d*) the method of packing used; and

(*e*) the method of payment to be employed.

The practices over which the Office of Fair Trading is given power under the Fair Trading Act 1973, Part II, are exhaustive and certain services are expressly excluded (e.g. legal or medical services and goods or services supplied by the nationalised industries). Where there is a consumer trade practice, the Director-General of Fair Trading or the Minister for Consumer Protection may refer the practice to the Consumer Protection Advisory Committee (CPAC) to determine whether the practice exists and if so whether it adversely affects the interests of consumers in the UK. The role of the CPAC is merely to investigate the practices referred to it and advise on that practice; unless a reference is made to the CPAC under s.17 of the Act, there is no means by which remedial action may be taken on the CPAC report. The section is limited to consumer trade practices which adversely affect the economic interests of UK consumers within s.14 and which also appear to the Director-General to mislead consumers as to their rights and obligations under the consumer transactions, or subject the consumer to undue pressure to enter into a consumer transaction whose terms are adverse or inequitable.

Reports by the CPAC
A report of the CPAC must be made to the Secretary of State, generally within three months of the reference setting out the full terms of the practices in question and the Committee's conclusions.

Statutory orders in pursuance of CPAC reports
The Secretary of State is under a general duty to lay reports of the CPAC before Parliament and a draft order giving effect to the proposals in the report may be laid before Parliament.

Persistent breaches of the law
The Director-General of Fair Trading may exercise his powers under the Fair Trading Act 1973, Part III, where it appears to him that a person carrying on a business had persisted in a course of conduct which is detrimental to the interests of consumers in the UK and which is also unfair to consumers in that it contravenes one or more enactments which impose duties, prohibitions or restrictions enforceable by criminal proceedings, or things are done or omitted to be done in the course of the business in question in breach of contract or in breach of a duty owed to any person by virtue of any enactment or rule of law and enforceable by civil proceedings.

If these conditions are satisfied, the Director-General will first attempt to obtain a written undertaking from the owner of the business concerned that he will cease the practice; if such an attempt fails or such undertakings are broken, he may apply for a court order.

THE CONSUMER CREDIT ACT 1974

The Consumer Credit Act 1974 affects regulated agreements, namely consumer credit agreement and consumer hire agreements other than exempted agreements.

By virtue of the Consumer Credit Act 1974, s.8, a consumer credit agreement is an agreement between an individual (the debtor) and any person (the creditor) by which the creditor provides the debtor with credit not exceeding £5,000. Section 9 provides that the term "credit" includes a cash loan and any other financial accommodation. The £5,000 limit denotes the amount of credit extended, and not the amount which the debtor has to repay. The amount of deposit, interest and credit charges paid under the agreement after it is entered into do not therefore form part of the credit extended. The definition of consumer credit agreement does not include a consumer hire agreement, but it does include credit sale and conditional sale agreements, bank loans, credit card agreements, and hire–purchase agreements.

A consumer hire agreement is an agreement made by a person, usually the owner of the goods, with an individual for the bailment or hiring of goods to the hirer. The agreement must be intended to subsist for more than three months, and it must not require the hirer to make payments which exceed £5,000. The agreement must, moreover, not be a hire–purchase agreement.

Definitions

The Consumer Credit Act 1974, defines certain concepts:

(*a*) *Restricted-use/unrestricted-use credit.* Section 11 provides the test whether the debtor may use the credit for any purpose he wishes (e.g. bank loans or overdraft facilities) or whether the credit is available to him only for use in connection with a specific transaction (e.g. hire–purchase agreements, credit sales and conditional sale agreements).

(*b*) *Debtor-creditor/debtor-creditor-supplier agreement.* The essence of the consumer credit agreement depends on how the credit is to be supplied. The credit may be supplied by the supplier of the goods or somebody connected with him, or by an entirely independent third party. A connection between the creditor and supplier of goods may arise if there is a pre–existing arrangement between the creditor and supplier for the supply of finance by the creditor for transactions negotiated by the supplier, or where the transaction between the consumer and supplier is entered into in contemplation of the creditor agreeing to provide credit for carrying out the transaction (*see* the Act of 1974, s.187).

The Act then defines two distinct types of agreements:

(*i*) *Debtor-creditor agreement.* This is a relationship entered into between the person who is both the creditor and supplier of the goods and the person who obtains the goods using money or credit provided by a finance company or other creditor under a pre–existing or contemplated agreement between himself and the supplier, or if the agreement is a regulated–use credit agreement relating only to existing indebtedness of the debtors (whether to the creditor or to another person), or the agreement is an unrestricted use credit agreement which is not made by the creditor under a pre–existing or contemplated arrangement between himself and the supplier of the goods in the knowledge that the credit is to be used to finance a transaction between the debtor and the supplier.

(*ii*) *Debtor–creditor–supplier agreement.* This is an arrangement to supply goods and credit as a joint venture participated in by a separate supplier and a separate creditor. A debtor–creditor–supplier agreement must fall into one of the three following categories:

(1) a regulated–use credit agreement to finance a transaction between the debtor and the creditor whether forming part of the agreement or not;

(2) a regulated–use credit agreement to finance a transaction between the debtor and the supplier and made by the creditor under a pre–existing or contemplated arrangement between himself and the supplier;

(3) an unrestricted–use credit agreement which is made by the creditor under a pre–existing or contemplated arrangement between himself and the supplier in the knowledge that the credit is to be used to finance a transaction between the debtor and the supplier.

(*c*) *Credit token agreements.* Such an agreement is a regulated agreement for the provision of credit in connection with the use of a credit–token (i.e. any document which is given to an individual by a person carrying on a consumer credit business and which enables the individual to obtain cash, goods or services from the person issuing the document or from a third party).

(*d*) *Linked transactions.* There may be a number of incidental agreements to the regulated consumer credit or consumer hire agreement (e.g. for insurance of the goods). The Consumer Credit Act 1974, s.19, defines what may amount to linked transactions, and the Act may also affect these transactions.

Exempt agreements

Subject to one exception exempt agreements are not regulated by the Act. The effect of the exemption is that the court has power to re–open an exempt consumer credit agreement only if it is an extortionate credit bargain. The following are exempt agreements:

(*a*) consumer credit agreements secured on land;

(*b*) land mortgage agreements entered into with an insurance company, a friendly society, a trade union, an employers' association, or a charity;

(*c*) a fixed sum debtor–creditor–supplier agreement under which the debtor is to repay the credit in no more than four instalments;

(*d*) a debtor–creditor–supplier agreement financing the purchase of land where the number of payments to be made by the debtor does not exceed four;

(*e*) a running account debtor–creditor–supplier agreement where the debtor is required to pay the whole of each periodical account by a single payment;

(*f*) a debtor–creditor agreement where the cost of credit is less than a certain minimum; and

(*g*) a consumer credit agreement providing credit to be used by the debtor in connection with overseas trade.

Small agreements

The Consumer Credit Act 1974, s.17, provides that a regulated agreement which does not exceed a specified financial limit (£30) is a small agreement. A fixed–sum credit agreement is a small agreement provided the "credit" does not exceed £30. A hire–purchase or conditional sale agreement does not fall within the definition of a small agreements. It is not possible artificially to contrive to make several small agreements in place of one larger one; the agreements will be treated as a single agreement embodying them all.

Non–commercial agreement
Under the Consumer Credit Act 1974, s.189(1), a non–commercial agreement is a "consumer credit agreement or a consumer hire agreement not made by the creditor or owner of goods in the course of a business carried on by him"—in other words, a private agreement.

Formation of a consumer credit agreement (hire–purchase, conditional sale and credit sale agreements)

Offer, acceptance and revocation
The customer will normally make an offer to the finance company by filling in a form and leaving it with the supplier of the goods. That offer will usually be accepted by the finance company posting its acceptance to the customer directly. In such a case the contract will be made when the acceptance is posted but at any time before the letter of acceptance is posted by the finance company or the offeror is notified in any other way of the finance company's acceptance of his application for a credit, the offeror can revoke his offer. For a revocation to be effective it must actually be notified to the finance company. Therefore a customer's letter of revocation will only be effective if it arrives at the offices of the finance company before the company posts its letter of acceptance. A dealer in goods is the agent of the finance company for the purposes of receiving a revocation; i.e. when the customer notifies the dealer that he wishes to revoke his offer to the finance company it has the same effect as if notification of the revocation had been given to the finance company provided he does so before the finance company posts its letter of acceptance. The position at common law was dealt with in *Financings* v. *Stimson* (1962), where a customer completed a hire–purchase proposal form and he was allowed to drive away the car he wished to acquire. The dealer forwarded the hire–purchase proposal forms to the finance company but the customer subsequently changed his mind and returned the car to the dealer. Shortly afterwards the car was stolen from the dealer's premises and recovered in a damaged state. The following day the finance company purported to accept the customer's offer and sent him a copy of the agreement. It was held that there was no binding contract for two reasons. Firstly, by returning the car to the dealer and notifying him that he did not want the car the customer had re-voked his offer to the finance company. Communication of the revocation to the dealer was sufficient, as the latter was the finance company's agent for the purposes of receiving a revocation. Secondly, the customer's offer to the finance company must be taken to have been conditional upon the goods being in substantially the same state at the time of acceptance as they were at the time

of the original offer. There was therefore no contract and the customer was under no liability to the finance company.

The Consumer Credit Act 1974, s.57, now provides in case of all regulated hire–purchase and conditional sale agreements (other than non–commercial agreements) and all regulated credit sale agreements (other than non–commercial agreements or small agreements) that:

(*a*) a withdrawal of an offer takes effect on posting;

(*b*) the dealer is an agent of the creditor for the purpose of receiving notice; and

(*c*) the withdrawal of either party from a prospective agreement takes effect as if the agreement

      (*i*) had been actually made; and

      (*ii*) had been a cancellable one; and

      (*iii*) had been cancelled by the debtor under s.69.

Thus the debtor will be in the same position as he would be in after cancelling a cancellable agreement. Consequently s.57 has the effect of strengthening his position after he withdraws from a prospective agreement.

A withdrawal from a prospective agreement means that there is no agreement and therefore no obligations arise under the agreement. If the customer has taken delivery of any goods, he will be bound to return them, and if he has made any payments he will be entitled to recover them. Where s.57 applies, however, the effect of treating it as a cancelled agreement is that the customer has in addition a lien over the goods to compel repayment of any deposit. This entitles him to retain possession of the goods until he is repaid.

Other regulated agreements

Under other kinds of credit agreement the seller and the creditor may be two different people. In such cases the customer therefore will make two separate agreements.

Usually the credit agreement will be made first so that the debtor has funds or credit facilities to make the purchase. Consequently, someone who has a Barclaycard will have made his credit agreement when he accepted his card by signing it or first using it. When he later uses the card to purchase goods he will not be making a new credit agreement but using the credit facilities available under a credit agreement made earlier. In such cases two people are deemed to be the agent of the creditor or owner of the goods supplied, namely the debtor's or hirer's representative in the course of negotiations, and the negotiator in antecedent negotiations.

Customer's representative

The Consumer Credit Act 1974 uses the words "any person who, in the course of a business carried on by him, acts or acted on behalf of the debtor or hirer in any negotiations for the agreement". This includes a person who runs a business with a view to arranging loans or other forms of credit for the customer. Such persons do not grant credit themselves, but negotiate on behalf of the customer with a prospective creditor. Such a person is deemed for three purposes to be the agent of the creditor, namely;

(*a*) receiving notice of withdrawal of his offer (*see* the 1974 Act s.57);

(*b*) receiving notice of cancellation (*see ibid.,* s.69);

(*c*) receiving notice that the customer intends to rescind his regulated agreement (*see ibid.,* s.102).

Negotiator in antecedent negotiations

A negotiator in antecedent negotiations is deemed to be an agent of the creditor or owner of the goods supplied. There are three types of persons who fall within the definition of a negotiator in antecedent negotiation:

(*a*) the creditor or owner of the goods supplied;

(*b*) the dealer in cases of hire–purchase, conditional sale or credit sale agreements; and

(*c*) the dealer in the case of any other debtor–creditor–supplier agreement.

Offer and acceptance

To discover whether and when an acceptance takes place the communications between the parties have to be examined. In the case of a hire–purchase agreement the finance company will require the customer to make an offer by filling in a proposal form containing the terms of the prospective agreement. The agreement (contract) will be made if and when the finance company communicates to the customer its acceptance of his offer.

Formalities

The Consumer Credit Act 1974, ss.55 and 60–65 deal with the formalities which must be complied with in the making of a regulated agreement. The aim of these provisions is to ensure;

(*a*) that the debtor is fully aware of the nature and cost of the transactions he is about to enter into (including the cost of the credit); and

(*b*) that the debtor's written agreement gives him a clear account of his rights and obligations.

Agreement subject to the formalities requirements

These provisions apply to regulated agreements only and do not apply to any non-commercial agreements or to any agreement which fulfils all of the following conditions:

(*a*) it is a small agreement; or

(*b*) it is a restricted use agreement; or

(*c*) it is a debtor–creditor agreement.

A regulated hire–purchase or conditional sale agreement will always be subject to the formalities unless it is a non–commercial agreement. The reason why non–commercial agreements are not subject to the formality requirements is that those requirements are intended to protect the consumer against the financially powerful creditor; it is possible, however, for two private individuals to enter into what is a regulated consumer agreement.

Pre-contract disclosure

Section 55 of the Act requires certain specified information to be disclosed in a particular manner to the debtor or hirer before the agreement is made. The information required to be given in the case of a fixed sum credit agreement includes the amount of the total charge for credit, i.e. the cost to the debtor of having the credit and the true annual rate of the total charge for the credit which the debtor will have to pay, expressed as a percentage rate per annum.

This information is required to be disclosed in writing (e.g. by letter) before the agreement is made. The idea underlying this is that the debtor must have in advance sufficient information for him to calculate and compare the cost of one possible source of credit with another and also with the reduced cost of paying cash for whatever he is buying.

Form and content

The regulated agreement must comply with provisions laid down in s.60 of the 1974 Act. These provisions require the agreement to be written in legible print or typescript of a certain minimum size. As to the contents of the agreements the regulations require that the agreement clearly shows such things as:

(*a*) the names of the parties to the agreement and their addresses;

(*b*) the amounts of all payments due under the agreement and when and to whom they are payable;

(*c*) the total charge for credit (i.e. its cost to debtor);

(*d*) the true annual rate of the total charge for credit expressed as a percentage per annum; and

(*e*) the debtor's right to pay off his debt earlier than agreed.

Additionally every copy of the agreement must embody all the terms of the agreement (1974 Act, s.61) and s.64(1) requires it to contain certain details of the debtor's rights (if any) to cancel the agreement.

Signatures

By s.61 of the 1974 Act the agreement must be contained in a document which is signed by the debtor or hirer and by or on behalf of the creditor. Thus the debtor must sign it in person; it is not sufficient if he signs it while still in blank or incomplete. When it is presented to him or sent for his signature, it must include all the terms of the agreement (other than implied terms) and it must be legible.

Copies

Sections 62 and 63 provide for the debtor or hirer to receive copies of the agreement. Depending on the circumstances, the hirer must be given one or two copies of the agreement; whatever the circumstances he should always be given one copy when he signs the agreement. If the agreement is sent to him for his signature then a copy should be sent to him at the same time. If the agreement is presented to him personally for signature, then the copy should be handed to him immediately after he has signed.

A further (second) copy is required by s.63 to be given to the debtor or hirer if the agreement was not actually made on the occasion when he signed it. This type of situation arises where an agreement is not made until both sides accept it. When a customer signs a finance company's standard form of agreement (e.g. for hire–purchase) that is no more than a proposal (i.e. an offer) by the customer. There is no agreement and therefore no contract until the finance company accepts the proposal. The finance company will sign the form and send a copy of it back to the customer. That will constitute acceptance of the customer's offer and an agreement will therefore be made (i.e. when a fully signed agreement is posted or given back to the debtor). An agreement will not be made when the hirer signs the form. This will normally be so where the customer signs a finance company's hire–purchase proposal form at the dealers' place of business.

Where a second copy is required it must, in the case of a cancellable agreement, be sent by post; any second copy of an agreement which is required must be given to the hirer within seven days following the making of the agreement. The seven–day period begins to run when the agreement is made (i.e. when the customer's proposal is accepted) not when the customer signs the agreement because in that case a second copy would not be necessary. Where posting is the means of acceptance a duly signed copy must reach the customer within the required time (i.e. within seven days of the making of the agreement).

In addition to the two copies already mentioned, the customer is entitled under ss.77–79 to require further copies to be supplied during the currency of the agreement. Where a statutory copy of the agreement is given or posted and that copy of the agreement refers to other documents, copies of those other documents should also be provided.

Special formalities for cancellable agreements

Section 64 lays down additional formalities for cancellable agreements by requiring that every copy of the agreement given to the debtor or hirer under ss.62 or 63 must contain a notice telling him of his right to cancel the agreement and giving the name and address of a person to whom notice of cancellation may be given. In the case of an agreement where a second copy need not be sent under s.63, a notice must generally be sent by post to him. The time limit is the same as for sending a second copy under s.63. The notice must give the hirer details of his right of cancellation.

Effect of non-compliance with the requirements

Any agreement which does not comply with the formal requirements is "improperly executed". The debtor or hirer will not in any way be penalised for this, and he can if he wishes enforce the agreement even if it was never signed or never put in writing.

The creditor or owner of the goods supplied may find it either impossible or difficult to enforce an improperly executed agreement. The 1974 Act, s.127, provides that he will be unable to enforce the contract if the following three requirements are not complied with:

(*a*) the debtor or hirer must sign the agreement or a document containing terms required by regulation to be included in the agreement;

(*b*) in the case of a cancellable agreement, the requirements of s.64 must be complied with;

(*c*) in the case of a cancellable agreement, the creditor must serve the copy or copies required and also serve (at some time before commencing proceedings) a copy of the fully signed agreement.

The creditor or owner, even if he does not come within one of above three cases, may find it difficult to enforce an improperly executed agreement, but he can enforce an improperly executed agreement subject to the following three restrictions:

(*a*) he can enforce it only by action in court (*see* s.65);

(*b*) without an order of the court he cannot re–take possession of the goods or land associated with the agreement because that would constitute enforcement of the improperly executed agreement;

(*c*) he cannot enforce any security except to the extent that the court will allow him to enforce the regulated agreement (*see* s.113).

In granting any order enforcing the agreement the court has power:

(*a*) to reduce or extinguish any sum payable by the debtor or hirer (*see* s.127);

(*b*) to exclude from the contract any term not contained in the signed agreement;

(*c*) to impose any conditions;

(*d*) to suspend the operation of an enforcement order or any part of it;

(*e*) to amend the agreement as it considers just (*see* s.137).

Before the court makes any order enforcing the agreement the creditor or owner will have to convince the court that despite the non–compliance it is nevertheless just and fair that the order should be made.

Cancellation; cancellable agreements

The cancellation provisions are aimed at transactions negotiated by door–to–door salesmen and particularly credit agreements entered into under what may be considered to be pressure by such salesmen. The debtor has a short period in which to cancel the agreement even after the contract has been concluded.

Section 67 provides that certain regulated agreements can be cancelled by the debtor or hirer. A regulated agreement is cancellable if the following two conditions are satisfied:

(*a*) The antecedent negotiations must have included representations made in the presence of the customer by or on behalf of the seller. This requirement will be satisfied where the agreement is made after the prospective customer has spoken face to face either with the dealer or the owner of goods. However, it would not be satisfied if the agreement was made by the customer through the post. The person making the oral representations must make them in the presence of the customer;

(*b*) the customer must have signed the agreement at a place other than the business premises of the seller (e.g. where the purchaser signs the agreement at his own business premises or at his house).

There are two categories of regulated agreement which are excluded from the cancellation provisions:

(*a*) an agreement involving a land mortgage or bridging loan; and

(*b*) an agreement not subject to the formalities requirements.

Who bears the costs of returning the goods?

If the customer rejects goods for breach of a condition then he is under no obligation to pay for their carriage, but is entitled to wait for them to be collected. The position is the same if he cancels the agreement under the cancellation provisions of the 1974 Act. However, if he cancels outside these provisions (e.g. under an express term of the contract) the contract may require him to bear the costs.

Notice of cancellation

The debtor or hirer must serve a notice indicating his intention to withdraw from the transaction. The notice of cancellation must be served on the creditor or owner of the goods (or his agent), the person specified in the agreement as being the person to whom such notice may be sent and the dealer or any person who in the course of a business acted on behalf of the customer in negotiating the agreement. The notice must be given within a time limit.

Time limit

After the debtor or hirer has signed the agreement the debtor can serve a notice of cancellation at any time after he signs and before the end of a period of five clear days. The five clear day period does not begin until the day after he receives his second copy of the agreement. The 1974 Act, s.69(7), provides that if a notice of cancellation is posted within the last of these five clear days it will still be effective although it does not arrive until later or never reaches its destination.

Where a second copy of the agreement does not have to be sent under s.63, the five day period begins on the day after the debtor or hirer receives the notice informing him of his rights of cancellation.

Where a second copy does not have to be sent and notice of cancellation is similarly not required, the cooling-off period lasts until the end of the fourteenth day after the debtor has signed the agreement.

Effect of notice

Once notice has been given the parties are freed from any further commitment in the agreement or in any transaction if the agreement or linked transactions are avoided. The notice of cancellation operates as a withdrawal of that offer. If the agreement has been made it is cancelled. The debtor or hirer must return any goods and he can obtain a refund of any payment he has already made.

The debtor or hirer is under no obligation to make any payment under the agreement or under any linked agreement, but money paid as a fee or commission to a credit broker can be recovered only to the extent it exceeds £1.

If the debtor has traded in other goods in part exchange, he is entitled to their return in substantially the same condition within 10 days of serving his notice of cancellation. If they are not so returned he is entitled to an equivalent sum called a part exchange allowance as if he had paid it as cash under the agreement. The choice of whether to return the part exchanged goods or to repay the part exchange allowance is that of the person who took the goods in part exchange.

The debtor can enforce his rights upon cancellation by taking action in the courts. He also has a lien over any goods of which he has possession under the terms of a cancelled agreement.

Subject to a lien, s.72 imposes a duty on the debtor to take reasonable care of the goods. Unless he is holding goods to compel repayment of sums due to him, he must hand them over, provided he is requested to do so in writing signed by or on behalf of the supplier or owner of them. He is entitled to wait for them to be collected and is not obliged to arrange transportation. If within 21 days after notice of cancellation the hirer is still in possession of the goods and has received no written demand for their return, he no longer has any obligation even to take reasonable care of them. The section does not apply to perishable goods.

After cancellation the supplier should be in the same position as if the agreement had never been made, but he may be out of pocket where the debtor has received services (i.e. free service of a car under the agreement) and he cannot return them.

The finance of hire–purchase transactions

A hire purchase contract may be financed by one of two following methods:

(*a*) the supplier makes a cash sale of the goods to the finance company which then enters into a hire–purchase contract with the consumer; or

(*b*) the supplier enters into an instalment contract with the consumer, and subsequently assigns the benefit of the contract to a finance company in return for payment of the outstanding price less a certain percentage of the purchase price in consideration of the supplier receiving payment.

Relationship between the finance company and the hirer
The relationship between the finance company and the hirer is one of contract.

Relationship between the dealer and the finance company
At common law it was held that the dealer is an agent of the finance company for certain purposes including the purposes of receiving offers for goods on hire-purchase terms, delivery of the goods, and receiving notice of revocation

of an offer; but it was also held that, prima facie, the dealer, not the finance company, was agent for the purposes of receiving payment. In *Branwhite* v. *Worcester Works Finance Ltd* (1969) it was held that, although the dealer is not an agent of the finance company for the purposes of receiving a deposit, because the finance company receives the benefit of the deposit, it is liable to return the amount to the customer on the hire purchase agreement being cancelled. The Consumer Credit Act 1974, ss.56 and 69, also provide that a retailer is constituted an agent for two other purposes, namely in relation to any representations made during the course of negotiations (whether they form a part of the terms of the contract or not), and for the purposes of receiving notice of cancellation of the agreement during the cooling-off period.

Relationship between retailer and hirer
The debtor will prima facie have no right of action against the retailer under a hire purchase contract. However, the debtor may have a cause of action if, for example, the retailer expressly warrants the quality of the goods supplied. This may be construed as a collateral contract between the hirer and the retailer. Alternatively, if the goods purchased are second-hand the retailer may be liable in negligence (e.g. where the retailer sells a second-hand car which is in a dangerous condition).

The remedies of the creditor
The creditor's three main remedies are to sue the debtor either for the arrears of instalments due under the agreement, or for damages generally for breach of contract, or to recover possession of the goods.

Action for instalment or damages: agreement not regulated by the Consumer Credit Act 1974
The owner of goods cannot sue for instalments until they fall due, although it is common for hire-purchase agreements to provide that if the debtor fails to pay any instalment on the due date, the whole amount unpaid under the agreement will become due and payable immediately.

Where however the debtor refuses to accept delivery of the goods, the creditor's only remedy is to claim damages for non-acceptance. In such cases damages are assessed on the same principles as under a contract of sale. The courts have laid down two special rules in the case of hire purchase agreements.

(*a*) If the debtor repudiates the contract, either expressly or by committing breaches which go to the root of the contract, the creditor is entitled to accept the repudiation and sue for damages. The damages will be the total amount payable under the contract subject to certain deductions. The deductions are an amount equivalent to the resale value of the goods if and when they are repossessed, and account must also be taken of the fact that the finance company will receive payments in a lump sum, instead of instalments spread out over the period of hire; therefore a proportion of the interest should be deducted to reflect the accelerated payment (*see Yeoman Credit Ltd* v. *Waragowski* (1961).

(*b*) If the debtor's breach does not amount to a repudiation of the contract, the damages recoverable are prima facie the instalments in arrear up to the date of commencement of the action, or, if the goods have been repossessed, up to the date of the repossession (*see Financings Ltd* v. *Baldock* (1963).

Remedies under regulated agreements

The 1974 Act does not give the creditor any absolute right to claim instalments or damages from the buyer. Section 129 of the Act gives the court power to make a "time order" giving the debtor additional time to pay.

Seizure of goods

A contract for hire–purchase normally entitles the creditor to retake possession of the goods where, for example, there is a breach of the agreement by the debtor (e.g. a failure to pay the instalments) as well as where there is no such breach (e.g. on the death of the debtor or any other person levying execution against him). The right to retake possession of the goods is modified by the Consumer Credit Act 1974.

In the case of an unregulated agreement, the right to retake possession of the goods is subject to the agreement itself, but in the case of a regulated agreement the 1974 Act imposes certain restrictions on the creditor's right to recover possession. Section 87 of the Act provides that a creditor cannot terminate the agreement or retake possession of the goods unless he has first served a default notice on the debtor, giving him at least seven days in which to remedy the breach. The default notice must comply with the strict statutory requirements. In *Eshum* v. *Moorgate Mercantile Ltd* (1971) the defendant, a hire–purchase company, was held not to have served a proper notice of default which would give it the right to repudiate the contract of hire when, from the nature of the notice, the date of termination was uncertain; further, the notice did not specify the consequences of default but merely stated that the company would assume the hirer did not wish to continue with the contract.

The Consumer Credit Act 1974, s.90, also provides that where one–third of the total price has been paid by the debtor, the creditor can no longer take possession of the goods without a court order unless the agreement is terminated by the debtor himself. If the creditor retakes possession of the goods in contravention of this section, the Act provides that the debtor is released from all liability under the agreement and is entitled to recover from the creditor any sums already paid under it.

Finally, s.92 of the Act provides that the creditor is not entitled without an order of the court to enter the debtor's premises to retake possession of any goods let under a hire–purchase agreement. This applies whether or not one–third of the purchase price has been paid.

In an action to recover possession of the goods the court has a wide discretion to make an order. Thus the court may make an order for the immediate delivery of the goods to the creditor, or it may make an order for delivery but postpone its operation and give the debtor the opportunity to pay the balance due by such instalments as the court considers reasonable. Alternatively the court may apportion the goods, ordering a part to be returned to the creditor and transferring title to him in the remainder.

Minimum payments and forfeiture clauses

The 1974 Act has two sets of provisions dealing with minimum payments and forfeiture clauses. The first set are general and apply to all credit arrangements and the second apply solely to regulated agreements.

(a) *General provisions.* The general provisions apply to all credit agreements and not merely to regulated agreements, and do so irrespective of the amount of the credit, but do not apply to agreements entered into by companies or other corporations as debtors since they are designed only to protect individuals.

A credit bargain is "extortionate", according to s.138, and liable to be set aside or re–opened (under s.139) if it requires the debtor to make payments which are grossly exorbitant, or if the agreement otherwise contravenes the ordinary principles of fair trading. In determining whether a credit bargain is extortionate the court will have regard to a number of factors; e.g. interest rates and the experience and business capacity of the borrower, and the degree to which he was under financial pressure at the time of making the bargain. The degree of risk undertaken by the creditor is also an important factor.

If the court holds that the agreement is extortionate it may re–open the transaction, and may then alter the rights and duties of the parties. The court may set aside or reduce any obligation imposed on the debtor, or it may require the creditor to repay any sums paid by the debtor. These provisions also cover the minimum payments and forfeiture clauses.

(b) *Regulated agreements.* Under s.99 of the Act, the debtor is entitled to terminate the agreement at any time before the final payment falls due; in this event the Act provides for a minimum payments clause. The debtor is prima facie liable to pay an amount to bring the total payments up to one–half of the total price, but if it is shown that the creditor's loss is less than this amount, then that is the debtor's maximum liability.

So far as the forfeiture provisions are concerned, the debtor's protection lies in the provision that the creditor cannot retake possession of the goods without a court order when one–third of the price has been paid.

The remedies of the debtor

(a) *Rejection of the goods.* The debtor has a right to reject the goods for breach of condition by the creditor. The rights of the parties are then governed by the general principles of contract law.

(b) *Damages.* The proper measure of damages would appear to be the difference between the value of the goods as warranted and the lesser value of the goods actually delivered. In *Charterhouse Credit Co Ltd* v. *Tolly* (1963) it was held that the measure of damages recoverable by the debtor is a sum equal to the cost of hiring similar goods on similar terms, less a deduction for the use he has already had for the use of the goods.

(*c*) *Termination under s.99.* In a regulated hire–purchase agreement the debtor is entitled to terminate the agreement at any time before the final payment falls due simply by giving notice to the creditor. In a conditional sale agreement in which the price is payable by instalments the buyer is similarly entitled to determine the agreement, and may do so even after the property has passed to him, provided he has not yet resold the goods to a third party. A cooling–off period of five days is allowed after service of a copy if the agreement has not been signed at the premises of the creditor.

Rebate for early payment

The Consumer Credit Act 1974 entitles the debtor to pay off the whole amount due under a hire–purchase or other credit agreement at any time. The debtor must be notified of his right to pay off the debt before the conclusion of the credit period and he must be given an appropriate rebate for the accelerated payment.

PROBLEMS

1. The Trade Descriptions Acts 1968 and 1972 were enacted to protect consumers against manufacturers and traders using misleading statements in connection with offers or advertisements to supply goods or services. What are the requirements that must be satisfied if a consumer is to succeed in an action under these Acts?

2. What is the purpose of the Unfair Contract Terms Act 1977?

3. What are the powers of the Director-General of Fair Trading and the Consumer Protection Advisory Committee under the Fair Trading Act 1973?

4. What is meant by (*a*) a consumer credit agreement; (*b*) a restricted-use/unrestricted-use credit; (*c*) a debtor-creditor/debtor-creditor-supplier agreement?

5. What formalities must be complied with under the Consumer Credit Act 1974, ss.55 and 65, in order to make a regulated agreement enforceable?

6. What are the rules relating to the cancellation of a regulated agreement?

7. Explain the relationship between the finance company and the hirer, and the dealer and the finance company in connection with a hire–purchase transaction.

8. What are the remedies available to the owner of goods if the hirer of them fails to comply with the terms of a hire–purchase agreement he has entered into with the owner?

9. What remedies are open to the hirer for the failure of the owner of goods let to the hirer under a hire–purchase agreement?

PART THREE

Ancillary Transactions

CHAPTER SEVEN

Banking Law

OBJECTIVES

It is proposed in this chapter to examine the law which governs banks and banking transactions. In particular the chapter deals with:

(a) the institutions which carry on the business of banking;

(b) the banker-customer relationship, including:

(i) the appropriation and consolidation of bank accounts;

(ii) duties of a bank owed to its customers;

(iii) the duty of a bank to a third party who is not a customer of the bank;

(iv) duties of the customer to a bank;

(v) termination of a banker-customer relationship;

(c) bills of exchange, including:

(i) definition;

(ii) indorsements;

(iii) inchoate instruments;

(iv) holder in due course;

(v) defects of title to the instrument;

(vi) liability and estoppel; and

(vii) discharge of a bill.

(d) cheques, including:

(i) the special rules relating to cheques;

(ii) the liability of the paying and collecting banks;

(iii) the protection of the paying and collecting banks; and

(iv) recovery of amounts incorrectly paid.

THE DEFINITION AND AUTHORISATION OF BANKS

Common law

The courts have attempted to define the word "bank" or "banking institution" in a series of cases, culminating with *United Dominions Trust* v. *Kirwood* (1966). In that case UDT brought an action against one of the directors of the defendant company when bills of exchange drawn by UDT on the defendant company and indorsed by the director to guarantee payment were dishonoured. The defendant alleged that UDT was a firm of moneylenders who had not obtained a statutory licence under the Moneylenders Acts 1900–1927, and therefore could not recover the amount of the loan. The plaintiffs, however, claimed they were bankers, and hence exempt from the need to obtain a statutory licence. The court held that the plaintiffs must be bona fide bankers in order to be exempt from the Moneylenders Acts, namely their banking business must be a real, genuine business enterprise and not a mere facade for moneylending. The lender's motive in making a particular loan is irrelevant, except where the genuine nature of the banking business is in doubt.

In the *Kirkwood case,* it was said that three essential characteristics were found in bankers today:

(*a*) they accept money from and collect cheques for their customers and place them to their credit;

(*b*) they honour cheques or orders drawn on them by their customers when presented for payment and debit their customers' accounts accordingly; and

(*c*) they keep current accounts or something of that nature in their books in which the credits and debits as between themselves and their customers are entered.

The Court of Appeal further held that banking need not be the only activity of a company for it to qualify as a bank, but it must be a substantial and independent activity.

It is partly in order to regulate the conduct of these institutions which combine banking activities with other non–banking activities that the Banking Act 1979 has been enacted and the concept of licensed institutions been introduced. The Act does not purport to define the term "bank"; it merely enumerates the requirements an institution in the business of banking must satisfy.

The Banking Act 1979

The Banking Act 1979 gives the Bank of England statutory powers of supervision over financial institutions of a generally more extensive nature than those in the Bank of England Act 1946. The 1979 Act empowers the Bank to grant recognition to banking institutions; it also controls advertisements inviting deposits, the use of banking names and descriptions and provides for the setting–up of the Deposit Protection Scheme. The Act implements the provisions of the first EEC directive (*see* the Official Journal of the European Communities (1977), L332/30) on the co–ordination of the laws, regulations and administration relating to credit institutions.

Authorisation of deposit–taking

The Act provides that, subject to the provisions contained in it, no person or institution may accept a deposit in the course of carrying on a deposit–taking business; this is defined by the Act of 1979, s.1(1) and (2), as taking deposits from the public for the purpose of lending onwards to other persons, or carrying on any other business activity financed wholly or partly out of the capital or interest earned on the deposits. A concern is not a deposit-taking institution if it does not hold itself out as willing to accept deposits in the course of its regular business.

The institutions authorised to accept deposits which fall within the provisions of the Act include the Bank of England, a recognised bank, a licensed institution and any body specified under Sched. 1 to the Act, i.e. the National Savings Bank, the Post Office, and the building societies.

The definition of "deposit" in the Act is similar to that laid down by the courts, namely a sum of money which will be repaid with or without interest either on demand or at the time agreed upon between the parties, the whole transaction between them being governed by either an express or implied contract.

An institution may gain recognition as a bank by an application (under the Act of 1979, s.3(1)) for that purpose. Recognition as a bank will not be granted by the Bank of England unless the institution fulfils certain conditions laid down in Sched. 2 to the Act; namely the institution must have net assets equal to at least £5 million or £250,000 if it provides a specialised banking service (see the Act of 1979, Sched. 2, para. 5), and it must have enjoyed for a reasonable period of time a high reputation and standing in the financial community. Under the 1979 Act, Sched. 2, para. 6(1), the institution has to maintain such a scale of net assets as the Bank of England thinks proper with regard to the scale of its operations. Where an institution is not yet carrying on a deposit–taking business, or does carry on that business but has not yet acquired the necessary standing for recognition as a bank, the 1979 Act, Sched. 2, para. 6(2), provides that it is taken to have fulfilled the requirements of the Act if it is a subsidiary of another institution with appropriate standing.

The institution recognised as a bank must provide either a wide range of banking services or a highly specialised banking service. For it to provide a wide range of banking facilities Sched. 2, para. 2(2), provides that it must provide at least the following:

(*a*) current and deposit account facilities in sterling or some foreign currency;

(*b*) finance in the form of overdrafts or loan facilities;

(*c*) foreign exchange services for domestic or foreign customers;

(*d*) finance through bills of exchange and promissory notes; and

(*e*) financial advice for members of the public and corporate bodies.

If the bank provides highly specialised services, it need only provide those listed under (*a*) and (*b*) above, and one or more of those listed under (*c*) to (*e*).

A financial institution other than a recognised bank will not be granted a full licence by the Bank of England to carry out a deposit–taking business, unless certain other conditions in the Banking Act 1979, Sched. 2, are fulfilled. In addition, any institution seeking a licence will have to conduct its business in a prudent manner and maintain net assets of such an amount and nature as the Bank of England considers appropriate in order to safeguard the interest of depositors.

The grant of recognition as a bank or a full licence for any other financial institution can be surrendered by the institution or revoked by the Bank of England (see the 1979 Act s.7(1)) on certain grounds; the procedure for revocation is laid down in the Act. The Bank of England may revoke the full licence held by a financial institution and instead grant a conditional licence giving the institution authority to carry on a deposit–taking business subject to compliance with conditions set out in the licence. The Bank may, if it thinks desirable and necessary for the protection of depositors give directions to an institution holding a conditional licence (i.e. prohibit the institution from dealing with or disposing of the assets in a manner specified), prohibit it from entering into certain transaction or class of transactions, prohibit it from soliciting deposits either generally or from persons who are not already depositors and also require it to take certain steps or pursue a particular course of action.

The terms of the Banking Act 1979, ss.14–15, place upon banks and licensed institutions certain duties, namely to give notice in writing to the Bank of England of any change in the control, management or directorships of the institution. Each bank and licensed institution must keep a copy of its most recent audited accounts at each place where it carries on business and the copy must be available for inspection by the public during normal business hours.

The Bank of England may require (under the Act of 1979, s.16) a bank or licensed institution to furnish such information as the Bank requires about the nature and conduct of its business and its future development. The Bank may also require a bank or licensed institution to produce for examination by the bank such of its books and papers as the Bank requires; where the Bank thinks desirable it is given power to take extracts of any such books or papers, and in the interests of depositors the Bank may appoint competent persons to investigate and report on the state and conduct of a recognised bank or licensed institution (*see* the Act of 1979, s.17).

The Deposit Protection Scheme

The 1979 Act, s.21, established a Deposit Protection Board, which manages a fund known as the Deposit Protection Scheme. It levies contributions from recognised banks and licensed institutions and any sums constituting the fund are placed by the Board in an account with the Bank of England which then invests such sums in treasury bills. All recognised banks and licensed financial institutions must contribute to the fund, unless particularly excluded (*see* the 1979 Act, s.23). The contribution of each institution is ascertained by the institution's "deposit base", and is charged at a percentage of that base figure determined by the Board. The initial total of the contributions levied was above £5 million and will not exceed £6 million. If at the end of any financial year the total contributions from all contributory institutions is less than £3 million, ss.24–25 provide that the Board may with the approval of the Treasury levy further contributions. If at any time a recognised bank or licensed institution becomes insolvent, the Board will compensate each depositor who holds a deposit with that institution an amount equal to three–quarters of his protected deposit. The Board may decline payment to a person who, in its opinion, has caused or profited in any way from the institution's financial difficulties (*see* the 1979 Act, s.28(1)–(2)).

Advertisements and banking names

The Treasury is empowered, by ss.34 and 35, in consultation with the Bank of

England by statutory instrument to regulate the issue, form and content of advertisements inviting the public to make deposits. These include every form of advertising including the display of notices, circulars, films or publications. If the Bank of England considers an advertisement inviting deposits is misleading, it may give the institution concerned a direction in writing requiring the advertisement to be modified, prohibited or withdrawn.

Banking names and descriptions

The 1979 Act, s.36, lays down that only certain institutions namely, a recognised bank, the Bank of England, a Trustee Savings Bank. the Central Trustees Saving Bank and the Post Office may use a name and indicate that it is a bank or banker or is carrying on a banking business.

THE BANKER AND CUSTOMER RELATIONSHIP

The customer of a bank

A customer of a bank is one who has applied to it to open a current or deposit account in his name and whose application has been accepted. It is unnecessary that an account should have been opened for a minimum length of time or that it should have been operated by the customer having conducted a minimum number of transactions. Once the account has been opened it does not matter that the customer is overdrawn, for that does not render him any less a customer. In *Commissioners of Taxation* v. *English, Scottish and Australian Bank* (1920), the appellants brought an action against the respondent bank claiming damages for conversion of a cheque. The court gave judgment in favour of the bank and held the word "customer" signifies a relationship in which duration is not of the essence; once the bank has undertaken to honour cheques drawn on the account, the account holder is a customer of the bank regardless of the length of time since the time when the account was opened.

It is unnecessary for the customer to have drawn on his account or for him to be in a position actually to draw on the account in order that he should be a customer. In *Ladbroke* v. *Todd* (1914), it was held that the mere fact that an account had been opened for him by the bank is sufficient. However, a person does not become a customer of a bank unless he opens an account personally or instructs another person to do so. If an account is opened in a person's name by someone who impersonates him or who falsely represents himself as having authority to open an account on his behalf, there is no contract with the person in whose name the account is opened. In *Robinson* v. *Midland Bank* (1925) the defendant bank opened an account in the plaintiff's name. Unknown to the bank, the person who opened the account had used a false name and the cheque paid into the account had been obtained by blackmail. The court held that since the blackmailer had acted without the plaintiff's authority and used his name fictiously, there was no contract between the bank and the person in whose name the account was opened and he could not claim the proceeds of the cheque as a customer of the bank.

The relationship of banker and customer only arises when an account is opened with the bank; but the bank may in some circumstances owe fiduciary duties before the party becomes a customer. In *Woods* v. *Martins Bank Limited* (1959), the plaintiff invested money in a company after receiving advice from the defendant bank manager in the course of negotiations for opening an account. The court held that the plaintiff was a potential customer, and the bank was aware of the relevant facts which would influence the plaintiff's decisions to invest. It therefore owed a duty to advise the plaintiff with reasonable care when giving investment advice of the kind which the bank undertook.

There are three basic reasons why it is necessary to define the customer of a bank:

(*a*) the rights and liabilities between the bank and customer are based on contract, and any breach of such a contract gives the injured party a right to sue for damages;

(*b*) the contents of the terms to be implied in the contract by the courts have to be established in order to ascertain the rights and obligations of a customer; and

(*c*) generally a bank does not owe duties to third parties who are not its customers.

Anyone may become a customer of a bank provided he is not under a legal incapacity. A bank may refuse without any reason to accept any person as a customer, but the relationship once entered into subsists at the will of the parties and may be terminated at any time, though in the case of the bank it is under a duty to give a reasonable length of notice.

A bank which uses another bank to clear cheques for it is a customer of the bank which acts as an agent in clearing the cheque.

THE LEGAL CHARACTER OF A BANK ACCOUNT

The legal relationship of a banker and customer is one of contract and this forms the basis of all transactions between them, together with any special contracts that may arise by express or implied intention of the parties. The contract between the parties will govern their obligations; for example, the duty of the bank to repay the credit balance on the customer's account, or conversely the obligation of the customer to repay to the bank if he is overdrawn is that of a debtor and a creditor. In the latter case the situation is the same as where the bank lends money to a customer. The rights of the parties are enforced by bringing an action for debt and not for unliquidated damages for breach of contract. In the case of *Foley* v. *Hill* (1848), where the plaintiff sought to recover the credit balance held by the bank in his favour by an action for account, it was argued that the relationship of a banker with his customer was, by analogy, that of an agent and principal. The House of Lords, in rejecting this argument, held that the relationship between a bank and its customer is one of debtor and creditor and that money paid into a bank ceases to be the money of the account–holder. It is then the property of the bank, which is bound to return the equivalent sum by paying him when a demand is made. The money paid into the bank is under the absolute discretion of the bank and not to be available for use only for specified purposes, as in the case of payment made by a principal to his agent. It is then the money of the bank which is free to deal with it as its own, to make and retain any resulting profit and pay to the account–holder only the rate of interest (if any) agreed on by the parties. The bank is not guilty of a breach of trust in employing the money in any manner it chooses, and it is not accountable to the account–holder for any specific part of the totality of its customers generally. The bank is only answerable for the amount of the credit balance and must repay the account–holder an equivalent sum. In *Joachimson* v. *Swiss Bank Corporation* (1921) a firm of three partners was dissolved by the death of one of the German partners. The other German partner became an enemy alien due to the outbreak of the war and the English partner commenced an action to recover the credit balance of the account but this was done without either partner having made a demand for repayment. The court held that where money is standing to the credit of a customer on a current account at a bank, a previous demand is necessary before an action can be maintained against the bank for the balance. Once an amount has been credited to an account the new balance is treated as one entire debt and a demand has to be made for repayment.

The money which is paid into the bank account becomes the property of the bank and so if the bank pays a cheque on which the signature of its customer as drawer has been forged, it is the bank who can sue the person to whom payment has been made for the recovery of the money paid under a mistake of fact or in damage for the tort of deceit. Similarly, if a bank collects the amount of such a cheque, the money paid to it becomes its property and not that of the customer whose account is credited. If the account–holder is at the time the true owner of the bill or cheque which is used to obtain payment, he can sue the person who has wrongfully obtained payment, or, subject to the statutory defences available to a collecting bank, he can bring an action against the collecting bank for conversion of the bill or cheque, and the damages he will recover will equal the face value of the cheque or bill. In *Arnold* v.*Cheque Bank Ltd* (1876), the plaintiffs, in order to transmit £1,000 to W & Co, purchased from S & Co a draft for that amount drawn by S & Co on Smith, Payne & Co in London, payable to the order of the plaintiffs on demand. The plaintiffs indorsed the draft specially to W & Co or order, and sent it in a letter addressed "W & Co" which was placed in a letter-box in their office to be posted. The letter was stolen by a clerk employed by the plaintiffs, who forged an indorsement on the draft. The defendants presented the draft and obtained payment. The clerk withdrew the amount and absconded. The plaintiffs' action for the proceeds, in an action for money had and received, succeeded. The court held that in neither an action for conversion nor an action for money had and received does the plaintiff assert any title to the money collected; he claims a title only to the cheque or bill by means of which the collection has been made and brings a personal action for damages for the amount of the cheque.

The customer with a credit balance can recover the debt owed to him by making a demand for repayment to the bank. The customer has six years from the time of the demand in which to bring an action for the bulance (*see* the Limitation Act 1980, s.5).

APPROPRIATION AND CONSOLIDATION IN RELATION TO A BANK ACCOUNT

A banker is not obliged to let his customer overdraw on a current account unless there is an express agreement between the bank and its customer, or an agreement can be implied from conduct as where a customer without previous agreement draws a cheque which, if honoured by the bank, overdraws the customer's account, or is implied from the bank's previous conduct in paying overdrawn cheques. Advances made by the bank are repayable on demand unless otherwise agreed; if there is an agreement not to require repayment on demand but no time is fixed for repayment the bank can insist on repayment on giving reasonable notice. The question which arises is whether a bank has any rights to recover a debit balance from a customer who has overdrawn his account without resorting to an action in the courts if the customer subsequently deposits money on account. The creditor can appropriate any payment made by him to whichever of the outstanding debts he chooses, but he can only appropriate in this way if the payer does not indicate which of his debts is to be satisfied. The right of appropriation is important where some of the debts owed to the creditor are secured and others are not, or if the limitation period has expired in relation to some but not all of them.

In the case of a current account it is usually implicit that amounts paid to the credit of the account are not appropriated by either party in satisfaction of any specific debit items and where the customer wishes to appropriate a payment the transaction should be made through a separate account. However, a customer can appropriate amounts paid into an account: e.g. where a customer whose account is overdrawn informs the bank he has issued two cheques in favour of A and B and pays into his account a sum sufficient only to meet one cheque, and gives instructions to the bank to honour a cheque in favour of C. The bank must act in accordance with the customer's instructions to honour that cheque and the customer can sue for damages if the bank fails.

In the absence of instructions from the customer, items credited to a current account are deemed to satisfy the earlier debts before later ones, so that debit and credit items are set off against each other chronologically and the balance on the current account reflects the difference between the total of the credit and debit items to date. In *Devaynes* v. *Noble (Clayton's Case)* (1816), a partner in a banking firm died in 1809. Clayton had a credit balance in his account and subsequently drew against this balance and also paid in items to the account.

At the subsequent bankruptcy of the surviving partners Clayton had a credit balance which he sought to recover from the dead partner's estate on the basis that his drawings against the account since the deceased partner's death should be primarily debits against payment into the account since that time, so leaving a larger balance recoverable from the deceased partner's estate. The court held that the bank did not break the account on the death of the partner and so the account was to be treated as a continuous one and the credit balance of the deceased partner's death had been exhausted by later drawings and consequently nothing was recoverable from the deceased partner's estate.

The case has practical consequences and the rule can work against the bank, as well as in its favour. In *Deeley* v. *Lloyds Bank Ltd* (1912), the bank had advanced money against a second mortgage and the borrower made a further mortgage in favour of Mrs Deeley of which the bank had been given notice. The bank did not break the account with its customer and on his becoming bankrupt the bank sold the property for a sum sufficient to discharge the first two mortgages in favour of bank. Mrs Deeley claimed an account against the bank. The House of Lords held that notice of the third mortgage prevented the bank from claiming priority for subsequent advances and subsequent payments into the credit of the account discharged the debit balance at the date when notice of the third mortgage was given. Mrs Deeley's mortgage accordingly had priority over any fresh advances made by the bank after notice of the third mortgage had been given. In such a case the bank could have preserved its position by breaking the account and opening a separate account for all subsequent advances which would not then have discharged the earlier debit balance.

Again, in *Royal Bank of Scotland* v. *Christie* (1841), a partner in a trading firm mortgaged his own land to secure advances made to the firm by its bank. At the date of the partner's death the firm had overdrawn on its current account but on the death of the partner the account was continued unbroken. The surviving partners paid into the account amounts which exceeded the debit balance at the deceased partner's death, and then withdrew an even larger sum. The court held that the rule in *Clayton's case* required payments made into the account by the surviving partners to be credited first against the earlier debit items in the account (that being the amount of the overdraft at the partner's death), and since those payments exceeded the overdraft the mortgage was discharged.

The rule in *Clayton's case* is further exemplified in *Re Yeovil Glove Company Ltd* (1965), where a company had created a mortgage over the whole of its assets by way of a floating charge to secure its existing and future indebtedness to the bank. The company went into liquidation within twelve months with the consequence that the floating charge given to the bank was void except as security "for cash paid to the company at the time of, or subsequently to the creation of, and in consideration for, the charge". The Court of Appeal held that the floating charge was a valid security for advances made by the bank after it was created, but not for earlier advances (which were, of course, an existing debt of the company); because the company had paid amounts into its current account since the creation of the floating charge, however, those amounts went towards satisfying its existing indebtedness under *Clayton's case* and the advances made since the date of the floating charge therefore were still owing and were secured by the charge.

There are certain situations, however, where the rule in *Clayton's case* will not apply. In the case of *The Mecca* (1897) it was held the rule does not apply when, instead of a current account between the parties, there are a number of separate transactions, or when it appears from the circumstances that the creditor intended to preserve the right of appropriation. Similarly, it does not apply where a trustee has mixed trust money with his own by paying both into the same banking account.

Consolidation

Where the customer has two or more accounts in the same name, some of which are in credit, the bank will have the right to combine these accounts to produce an overall balance. The rules relating to set–off between a bank and its customer are essentially those applicable to a debtor and creditor. In *Garnett* v. *McKewan* (1872), the court ruled that a customer is not entitled to expect his cheques to be honoured at one branch of a bank where he has a credit balance, if at the same time he has a debt balance at another branch of the same bank and there is no duty on the part of the bank to keep the accounts separate. The facts of the case were that the plaintiff, having an account at one branch of the defendant bank which showed a credit balance, drew cheques for that full amount on that branch. At the same time he was indebted to the bank on an account held at another branch. This reduced his overall balance to a few shillings. The bank was held entitled to dishonour the cheque drawn by the customer on presentation as there was no agreement between the parties not to combine. In *Buckingham and Company* v. *London and Midland Bank Ltd* (1895) the court held a bank liable for wrongful dishonour of a cheque when a bank combined a loan account and a current account without notice of its intention to do so, with the result that the credit balance on the current account was insufficient to meet the cheque. The bank cannot combine or close a loan account without reasonable notice to the customer, and the debit balance on the loan account cannot be made immediately payable. A failure on the part of the bank to give the required notice renders the bank liable for wrongful dishonour because the credit balance on the loan account is still available. In *Halesowen Pressworks and Assemblies Ltd* v. *Westminster Bank Ltd* (1972) it was settled that, in the absence of express or implied agreement to the contrary, the banker has the right to combine accounts of a customer and it can be exercised without notice to the customer. Both the debit and credit items, however, must be immediately payable on demand (*see Garnett* v. *McKewan* (1872)). In the *Halesowen* case it was held that a bank was entitled to combine an active current account with a deposit account because the banker–customer relationship was terminated by the winding up of the company; notice was unnecessary because the bank did not combine the two accounts until after the winding up order had been made and notice could serve no purpose. This is an exception to the normal rule that a current account and deposit account cannot be set–off since in the ordinary case the deposit account is not immediately due and owing.

A bank does not have any right to consolidate if it has knowledge at the time of the fiduciary nature of the account which is in credit. The bank cannot combine a private account of a customer which is overdrawn with that of a credit balance held on trust by the customer. In *Re Cross, ex.p Kingston* (1871) the court held a bank is not entitled to a set–off if an account is plainly headed in such terms that a banker cannot fail to know it to be a trust account. In this case a solicitor had a private drawing account and as county treasurer for the county police force he also had an account in his own name designated "Police account" and the bank had knowledge that it was not the solicitor's personal account. The solicitor absconded, leaving his private account overdrawn and the police account in credit. The court held that a bank can refuse to open a trust account when so requested by a customer, but it cannot later claim the right to consolidate if it does open an account which it knows is fiduciary in character. If the bank can prove that it had no knowledge of the true facts, it can consolidate (*see Union Bank of Australia v. Murray–Aynsley* (1898)). A bank cannot further exercise its right to set–off so as to retain amounts which are immediately payable to the customer as security for future indebtedness. In *Jeffreys v. Agra and Masterman's Bank* (1886), a customer of a bank was indebted to it for advances and handed to it certain receipts from another bank representing deposits lodged with that other bank. The court held that the bank to which the customer was indebted could only set–off such sums as were due and payable immediately, and it could not retain the balance as security for amounts which the customer might owe to it in the future if it exercised a right of recourse against him.

The right of consolidation is discretionary on the part of the bank, but in certain circumstances the express or implied terms of the advance will give the bank an automatic right of set–off.

The Companies Act 1948 provides where a bank advances money to a company which subsequently goes into liquidation, for the purposes of paying remuneration to its employees the bank can claim to be a preferential creditor for the full amount of the advance, if the advance is made to enable a company to pay wages and salaries of its employees who at the time of the liquidation have not been fully paid.

Where a third party pays into the account of a company a sum which is known to the bank to be used specifically for the purposes of paying wages, the bank cannot claim to set–off this amount against the debit balance on another account of the company if the company goes into liquidation before disposing of the credit balance at its disposal. In *Barclays Bank Ltd v. Quistclose Investments Co* (1970), X Ltd advanced a sum to Rolls Razor Ltd shortly before its bankruptcy on the understanding it would be used solely to pay a dividend; before the dividend was paid Rolls Razor Ltd went into voluntary liquidation. The court held that the money paid into the bank was held with the knowledge of the bank for a specific purpose, and, the purpose having failed, the bank could not claim a set–off; it therefore held the credit balance on trust in favour of the respondents.

THE DUTIES OF THE BANK TOWARDS ITS CUSTOMER

A number of duties are implied on the part of the bank and come into existence when the banker–customer relationship is established. All of these duties are recognised by the courts, and their scope and extent has been established by judicial decisions. The duties implied on the part of the bank are discussed in the four following sections.

The duty to conform to the customer's mandate

The bank has a duty to conform to the customer's mandate and obey his instructions in making payments out of his account. The paying bank is under a binding obligation to honour cheques drawn on it by its customer, if they are regular and unambiguous in form, and if the customer has sufficient funds available in his account, or the bank has agreed to allow the customer to overdraw on his account. In *Morzetti* v. *Williams* (1830) it was held that a banker is bound by law to pay a cheque drawn by a customer, within a reasonable time after he has received sufficient funds belonging to the customer, and the customer may maintain an action in tort against the bank for refusing payment of a cheque in such circumstances. In this case the plaintiff drew on his current account (which was in credit) in favour of a third party and the bank wrongfully refused to honour the cheque. The court held the plaintiff could maintain an action against the defendant bank although he had not suffered actual loss. In *Whitaker* v. *The Governor and Company of the Bank of England* (1835) it was held the bank is not under a duty to honour instruments presented after the usual hours of business and can refuse to honour the customer's mandate although he has a credit balance. If overdraft facilities are available to the customer, the bank is estopped from dishonouring the cheque provided that it is within the overdraft limit.

Another aspect of this duty is that a bank is under a duty not to make payment out of the customer's account which does not conform to the customer's mandate, so that the bank cannot debit the customer's account if it does make a payment outside the limits of his mandate. A bank acts outside the customer's mandate where it pays a bill of exchange or cheque bearing a forged signature, or pays a bill or cheque bearing a forged indorsement. In *Greenwood* v. *Martins Bank Ltd* (1933) the court held that a bank has no authority to debit his customer's account when the customer's signature to a cheque or a mandate has been forged; because the plaintiff in that case failed to inform the bank of previous forgeries of his cheques of which he was aware, however, he was estopped from enforcing any claim against the bank by his own breach of duty. The bank also fails to conform to the customer's mandate if it pays a cheque which is signed by an agent for the customer in excess of the powers conferred. In *Liggett (Liverpool) Ltd* v. *Barclays Bank Ltd* (1928) it was held that the bank exceeded its mandate when paying a cheque drawn on a company's account when it was signed by only one of its directors, contrary to express instructions given to honour cheques only if signed by two directors. However, because the payment went towards discharging a legal liability of the company, the bank was entitled to debit the customer's account on equitable grounds.

If the bank fails to pay a cheque or fails to make a payment within the customer's mandate at a time when the credit balance or overdraft facilities are sufficient, the customer is entitled to sue the bank for breach of contract. In *Gibbons* v. *Westminster Bank Ltd* (1939) an action was brought for breach of contract against the defendant bank which wrongfully dishonoured a cheque on the ground that the plaintiff had insufficient funds standing to his credit, when in fact he had paid into his account amounts sufficient to meet the cheque. The court awarded nominal damages on the ground that a person who is not a trader is not entitled to recover substantial damages for the wrongful dishonour of a cheque unless actual damage is both alleged and proved.

Where a private customer cannot recover general damages for loss of reputation by bringing an action for breach of contract, general damages may be recoverable by bringing an action for defamation if any reason given by the bank for wrongly dishonouring the cheque appears to reasonable people to convey a defamatory meaning when the cheque is returned to the collecting bank. In *Davidson* v. *Barclays Bank Ltd* (1940) the court held the bank could plead qualified privilege when, by mistake, it dishonoured a cheque of the customer and marked it "not sufficient". The occasion of making the communication must be privileged, so that a bank can only justify dishonouring a cheque if the actual circumstances entitle it to do so. The court held that for the bank to communicate that the plaintiff could not meet a cheque for a small amount would seriously affect his credit standing, and it could not justify dishonouring the cheque by pleading that if the facts had been as it mistakenly supposed (i.e. an earlier cheque had not been countermanded) the dishonour would have been justified. Similarly, in *Baker* v. *Australia and New Zealand Bank Ltd* (1958) the court held that by marking the cheque "present again" the defendant bank had published words concerning the plaintiff which were reasonably capable of a defamatory meaning in that they conveyed the imputation that the plaintiff had insufficient funds standing to his credit on the original presentation of the cheque. In *Jayson* v. *Midland Bank Ltd* (1968) it was held that the words "refer to drawer" were capable of a defamatory meaning, but because the plaintiff had an insufficient credit balance to meet the cheque the bank was justified in dishonouring the cheque and stating on it the reason for dishonour. However, in *Frost* v. *London Joint Stock Bank Ltd* (1906) the defendant bank returned a cheque drawn by the plaintiff without stating a reason for dishonour but marked the cheque with the words "reason not stated". The court held the words were not ordinarily defamatory and the plaintiff had failed to prove they would naturally be understood by reasonable persons as conveying a defamatory meaning. The expression would not automatically indicate a defamatory meaning, since it is equally capable of some other innocent meaning.

Where a cheque is wrongfully dishonoured by a bank, the customer may recover special damages if he can show that loss was suffered, and that it was foreseeable (generally damages are only awarded with a view to compensating the plaintiff for foreseeable loss). Alternatively, the customer whose cheque is wrongfully dishonoured may have a cause of action for libel, but only if the reason inserted by the bank for dishonouring the cheque conveys a defamatory meaning.

The bank has a duty to obey the customer's mandate; therefore if it receives in sufficient time instructions not to pay a cheque, it will be liable if the cheque is paid. The bank cannot debit the customer's account with the amount of the cheque. However, the customer's instructions must be clear and unambiguous, so where a customer in countermanding a cheque gives the wrong cheque number by mistake, the bank can pay the cheque intended to be counter-manded and debit the customer's account (*see Westminster Bank Ltd* v. *Hilton* (1926)). If the customer's instructions are open to ambiguity and capable of interpretation in one of several ways, the bank is not liable if it adopts a reasonable interpretation even if it one not intended by the customer. For a countermand to be effective it must come to the knowledge of the bank and moreover, in *Curtice* v. *London City and Midland Bank* (1908), it was said this means to the knowledge of the manager of the branch where the customer's account is kept.

For the purposes of countermanding a cheque the countermand is effective only when communicated to the branch where the customer holds his account. Thus in *Burnett* v. *Westminster Bank Ltd* (1968) a customer using a cheque form issued by one branch of a bank drew a cheque on another branch (where he had a second account) by altering the name of the branch printed on that form. He later countermanded the cheque but the countermand was given by the customer to the branch substituted by him on the cheque form. The court held the countermand was effective although the cheque had been presented to the branch whose name was originally imprinted on it as a result of the mechanical operation of the clearing. If the bank is to impose an obligation on the customer not to alter cheque forms, this should be done by an express clause, either in the main body of the written contract (if any) or by a written clause at the front of the cheque book. It has been held that where a bank receives from a customer a cheque drawn on another bank not carrying on business in the same town, it is sufficient for the bank to present it either on the day it receives the cheque from its customer or on the following day (*see Hare* v. *Henty* (1861)). A bank is not under any duty to credit its customer's account with the amount of cheques or other instruments handed to it for collection until it has actually received payment, but where a bank voluntarily credits the customer's account with the amounts of uncleared effects and does not reserve the right to debit the customer if the instrument is returned unpaid, the customer has an immediate right to draw on the uncleared amount.

In *Capital and Counties Bank Ltd* v. *Gordon* (1902) it was held that where a bank credits the customer's account with the amount of instruments which had not yet been cleared, the bank received payment of the instruments subsequently as holder of them on its own account and consequently where the customer is allowed to draw the amount of such instruments the bank cannot later debit the customer's account with an equivalent amount if the instruments are dishonoured.

The duty to render an account

A duty is imposed on a bank to render accounts to its customers periodically or on demand; failure to do so gives the customers the right to demand payment of the balance of his account and then to sue the bank for debt.

The question is whether the customer can rely on the credit balance of his account as shown on statements supplied by the bank, especially where the credit balance is increased whether by amounts being credited which have not actually been paid into the customer's account or by amounts which should have been debited not having been deducted from the credit balance. In *Holland* v. *Manchester and Liverpool District Banking Co Ltd* (1909) the court held that where the customer acts in good faith on a wrong entry made in a pass-book and alters his position by relying on it, the bank is estopped from claiming that the error be rectified. The plaintiff had an account with the defendant bank and the pass-book showed a balance of £70, when the actual credit balance was £60. The plaintiff, relying on the pass-book, drew cheques on his account for £67 and the defendant bank dishonoured the cheques on presentation for payment. The court held that a bank is normally entitled to have the wrong entry corrected, but once the customer has acted on the entry in good faith the bank is not entitled to have the error corrected if the customer would suffer damage as a result. Similarly, in *Skyring* v. *Greenwood* (1825), where the plaintiff maintained a higher standard of living than he would otherwise have done as a result of relying on the credit balance shown on his account, the court held that he had accommodated his style of living to what he supposed his true income to be, and it would be prejudicial to him if the bank, having given him the credit and the opportunity to rely on the mistake, was entitled to demand repayment. The customer's belief in the accuracy of the statement is essential, so that if the customer is aware of the mistake by the bank it is not estopped from adjusting the error. In *British and North European Bank Ltd* v. *Zalzstein* (1927) the defendant had two accounts with the plaintiff bank; he was overdrawn to the extent of £900 in excess of the agreed limit, and to conceal the fact the bank manager transferred £2,000 from another account to the credit of the defendant's account. The defendant, being unaware of the credit entries until his account was later debited with the amount alleged, that the bank had no authrotity to debit his account. The court held that where the customer is unaware of the error, or where the bank wrongly credits the customer's account but corrects the error before the customer becomes aware of the credit entry, the bank is entitled to debit the account with that amount, and the customer had no claim against the bank. In *United Overseas Bank Ltd* v. *Jiwani* (1977) the customer alleged that he had acted in the belief that an incorrect balance was in fact correct and the bank should not be allowed to debit the amount wrongly credited. In that case the plaintiff bank wrongly credited its customer's account twice under the belief that it had received two separate transfers of money to be credited to his account and the bank sought to rectify the account by deducting the amount wrongly credited. The court held that if the plaintiff bank was to be estopped from claiming the balance wrongfully credited, the customer had to show that the bank was under a duty to give him accurate information about the state of his account, that in breach of that duty it gave him inaccurate information, that the inaccurate information about the credit balance on his account misled him and caused him to believe that the bank was his debtor for a larger sum than was actually the case, and finally, because of his mistaken belief, he changed his position so that it would be inequitable to require him to repay the money wrongly credited. The court held the bank was not estopped from debiting the customer's account because he could not show that he entered into the transaction to purchase a hotel in reliance on the statement of account. He would have entered into the transaction in any event, and he was not influenced by the excess credit balance shown on his account which a reasonable man would have realised to be a mistake made by the bank.

The duty of secrecy

The bank owes a duty of secrecy in respect of the customer's affairs and the customer can obtain an injunction to prevent it from disclosing information. Where disclosure has already been made, the only remedy available to the customer is to sue for damages for breach of contract. In *Tournier* v. *National Provincial and Union Bank of England* (1924) the court said that it is an implied term of the contract that the bank undertakes a qualified obligation not to disclose information concerning the affairs of the customer without his consent. The bank's customer was overdrawn and agreed to reduce his overdraft by weekly instalments; on his failure to maintain the instalments, the bank manager phoned the customer's employers and disclosed to them that he was overdrawn due to unpaid gambling debts. Consequently, the customer lost his employment. In an action against the bank, the court held that a bank is under a legal duty not to reveal information about the customer to third parties without his consent. The obligation of secrecy extends beyond the state of the account and whether there is a credit or debit balance. It extends to all transactions that go through the account and to any securities given in respect of the account; furthermore, the duty may extend beyond the operative period of the bank account. The court outlined four occasions on which a bank may disclose information about its customer, without being held liable for wrongful disclosure:

(*a*) where it discloses information under compulsion by the law; for example, the Bankers' Books Evidence Act 1879, s. 7, provides that any party to a legal proceeding may apply to the court for an order allowing him to inspect and take copies of any entries in a banker's books for the purposes of the litigation. This provision has been held to apply to criminal proceedings (*see Williams* v. *Summerfield* (1972));

(*b*) where it is under a public duty to disclose it; for example, where non-disclosure would result in danger to the state or the public, or alternatively where frauds or crimes would be perpetrated;

(*c*) where it does so with the express or implied consent of the customer; for example, where he gives a banker's reference. The extent to which a bank is entitled to disclose information on such occasions is a question of fact in each case; and

(*d*) where there is litigation between the customer and the bank, or if a bank brings an action against someone other than the customer; for example, against a guarantor.

The bank's duty of skill and care

A bank owes to the customer a duty to exercise proper skill and care in carrying out any business it agrees to transact. A bank must undertake certain minimum services, but there is no limit on the extent of its duties, which will therefore depend on any express undertakings between the bank and customer. The standard of skill and care which bank officials must exhibit when acting on behalf of the bank is that reasonably expected from officials of that standing and competence. Where a bank holds out an employee as having special skill, he must also display competence in that particular field; therefore where a bank receives dividends on behalf of a customer it is bound to discharge that duty with reasonable care and cannot be expected to have knowledge of tax repercussions, as this would place an unreasonable burden on the banks.

Where, however, a bank gives advice on investment, this may be considered to be within the scope of a bank's business so that if the bank is negligent or gives improper advice, it is liable to the customer. In *Woods* v. *Martins Bank Ltd* (1959) the plaintiff brought an action when, after relying on the advice of the bank manager, he made a large investment in a company which in fact was in financial difficulties. The court held the bank liable for negligence after considering the bank's advertisements and booklets, from which it concluded that giving investment advice to the plaintiff was within the scope of the bank's advertised business, and the plaintiff was a customer at the time the advice was given although an account was not opened until later. The precise circumstances in which a bank owes a duty of care is difficult to determine, but if the bank represents to its customer that it will undertake certain business activity (for example, by advertising generally) or if the bank undertakes certain transactions specifically on the customer's behalf, the duty to take reasonable and proper care attaches. If a bank's knowledge is based on its personal pecuniary interests, the banker can give advice so long as full disclosure of the facts known by it is made to the customer. Where, however, a bank has received information in confidence, then it is under a duty to refuse advice to its customer, and not to reveal the confidential information but if it does give advice it will be liable if it fails to exercise reasonable care and skill. The duty to advise does not mean that the bank commits a breach of that duty if by the exercise of some extraordinary skill and care it might have discovered something which it did not discover and which might have affected the advice given by it. So the measure and skill required of the bank depends on the extent of the facts known to it; but if a bank, with knowledge of the complexity of the matter, undertakes to give advice but entrusts the task to inexperienced officials, it will be liable for the loss which the customer suffers.

THE DUTIES OF THE BANK TOWARDS A THIRD PARTY

The banker–customer relationship is based on contract and so generally the duties of the bank are owed only to the other contracting party, i.e. its customer. A bank, therefore, does not owe any duties to a third party who is not a party to the contract, and its obligations extend only to those customers with whom it has a directly binding relationship. If under these circumstances a third party who is not a customer suffers loss due to an action or omission of the bank in dealing with its customer, the bank is not liable to him. In *Auchteroni and Co* v. *Midland Bank Ltd* (1928) the defendant bank was instructed by its customer to pay a bill of exchange which the customer had accepted in favour of the plaintiffs; when the bill was presented by the plaintiffs' clerk for payment over the counter, the bank paid the clerk in cash; the clerk then absconded with the amount. It was shown in the course of evidence that it was normal for bills for substantial amounts payable at a bank to be presented by the collecting bank to the bank acting as agent for the acceptor and for such bills not to be paid in cash to an individual. It was held that the defendant bank acted negligently, but it could only be guilty of a breach of contract to its own customer, and not to the payee of the bill. Consequently they could not recover the value of the bill as damages. However, a bank may owe a duty to a third party who acquires some proprietary interest in the credit balance of the account. In *Greenhalgh & Sons* v. *Union Bank of Manchester Ltd* (1924) a bank could not set off the proceeds of bills sent to it by its customer for collection when, to its knowledge and to that of the third party, the proceeds had been appropriated by the customer in favour of the plaintiff in order to pay a debt which the customer owed him.

DUTIES OF THE CUSTOMER

The duties of a bank towards its customer are firmly established and recognised, but the duties of a customer towards the bank are somewhat uncertain. Strictly speaking, the only duties which a customer owes to the bank, whether he has a current or deposit account are:

(*a*) to repay on demand any sums overdrawn on the current account; and

(*b*) to pay reasonable charges for the services of the bank if no charge has been agreed or the agreed charge if it has.

These duties may both be regulated by express agreement between the parties; for example, it may be agreed that the customer can overdraw up to a limited amount, and it may also be agreed that the bank will give reasonable notice before demanding repayment. The scale of charges for banking services, on the other hand, is usually available on inquiry to the customer and a customer who instructs the bank to undertake business is deemed to have agreed to pay the charge.

The customer additionally has certain duties imposed for his own self–protection; a breach of them results in the customer losing any right of action he would otherwise have against the bank. These duties are:

(*a*) to notify the bank when, and if, he discovers forgery of cheques drawn to his account; and

(*b*) to draw cheques in such a way as not to facilitate fraud or alteration.

The failure of the customer to notify a bank that he has discovered forgeries of cheques drawn on his account will prevent him from challenging the right of the bank to debit his account if the bank acts in good faith and without negligence in failing to detect the forgery. In *Greenwood* v. *Martins Bank Ltd* (1933) it was said that if a customer discovers that cheques purporting to have been signed by him have been forged, he must inform the bank immediately; failure to do so will estop the customer from challenging the right of the bank to debit the customer with the amount of the cheque, because failure to notify the bank of forgeries operates as an inducement to the bank to treat the cheques as genuine. Similarly in *Brown* v. *Westminster Bank Ltd* (1964) the plaintiff was estopped from setting up forgeries of her cheques against the bank when she had represented their genuineness to the bank. The bank had on several occasions drawn the attention of their customer, an old lady, to the number of cheques for small amounts passing through her account which had been drawn fraudulently by an employee and paid in cash. There was evidence available that the bank manager had visited the customer and made repeated requests to her to verify the number of cheques being drawn on her account. On each occasion the customer had either affirmed the cheques drawn on the account or said nothing.

The other duty imposed by the courts on the customer is to draw cheques on his account in a way which does not facilitate fraud or alteration. Failure to do this will entitle the bank to debit the customer's account with the amount of an altered cheque provided it acts in good faith and without negligence. The customer is bound to take any usual and reasonable precautions to prevent forgery. In *Young* v. *Grote* (1827) the plaintiff left with his wife for the purposes of his business a number of blank cheques signed by himself. The wife instructed one of the plaintiff's clerks to draw a cheque but the clerk did so in such a way as to enable him to make subsequent additions in the amount of the cheque; after showing it to the wife, he increased the amount by adding an extra figure between the "£" sign and the first number representing the sum to be withdrawn. He also subsequently filled in the amount in words so as to agree with the altered amount in figures. The court held the loss must fall on the plaintiff, because a customer who draws an incomplete cheque, leaving its completion to an agent, cannot object to the banker debiting him with the amount fraudulently entered in the cheque. In *London Joint Stock Bank Ltd* v. *Macmillan* (1918), there is also imposed on the customer a duty of care to ensure that when he signs the cheque, he does not leave spaces facilitating fraud. However, the courts have refused to extend the application of this principle and in *Slingsby* v. *District Bank Ltd* (1932) the banker was held not entitled to debit the customer's account when a cheque which was payable to 'John Prust and Co' with a blank between these words and "or Order" was fraudulently altered by the drawer's solicitor, who added the words "per Cumberbirch and Potts" after the payee's name. It was held that such an alteration was a form of fraud that could not reasonably be anticipated by the customer, and so he was not negligent in leaving the blank space in the cheque.

TERMINATION OF THE BANKER–CUSTOMER RELATIONSHIP

The contractual relationship between a bank and its customer is terminated either by one of the parties taking appropriate steps for that purpose or by the occurrence of certain events. The result of the termination is that the bank's mandate to act for the customer is withdrawn and the whole of the credit balance on the customer's account becomes payable immediately either to the customer himself or, in certain circumstances (e.g. bankruptcy or death), to persons to whom the title to the account is transmitted. On termination of the relationship the bank can recover any debit balance on the customer's account by suing him in debt; but where the advance is only repayable by the customer at a fixed future date, the termination of the banker–customer relationship does not of itself affect this agreement between the parties.

Termination by the customer or the bank

A customer may terminate his contract with the bank by demanding repayment of the balance of his current or deposit account, but if he has several such accounts the closing of one or more of them will not terminate the contract with the bank so long as at least one account remains open. A demand for repayment of a current account will normally take effect immediately, provided that it is made at the branch of the bank where the account is kept; if it is made at any other branch, the customer has to wait a reasonable time for the credit balance to be made available.

A bank may terminate its contractual relationship with its customer by giving him notice to that effect and tendering repayment of the credit balance. In *Joachimson* v. *Swiss Bank Corporation* (1921) it was said that the basis of the banker–customer relationship is that the bank cannot cease to do business with the customer unless it gives reasonable notice of its intention to close his account. The purpose of requiring reasonable notice is not only to allow cheques already drawn on the account to be presented for payment, but also to allow the customer to complete any pending transactions. In *Prosperity Ltd* v. *Lloyds Bank Ltd* (1923) the court held that a bank could close its customer's current account by giving reasonable notice, the length of notice depending in each case on the time the customer would require to rearrange his affairs and notify his business clients, if any.

Where a bank seeks to close a deposit account, notice is not required unless otherwise agreed, and so a bank may pay a deposit account at any time and if it adds interest for the length of a normal notice of withdrawal which its customer would have to give if he initiated the closure, the bank satisfies its obligations. The effect of an account being closed is that the relationship of banker and customer comes to an end and the duties on both parties are terminated, except the duty of the bank to maintain secrecy in relation to the customer' affairs (*see Tournier* v. *National Provincial Bank* (1924)).

Customer's death

The death of a customer terminates the contract between him and his bank because of the personal nature of the relationship. The credit balance on the customer's current or deposit account vests in his personal representatives, but they cannot sue the bank to recover the amount credited to his account until they have obtained a grant of probate or letters of administration. If the deceased customer's account is overdrawn, his personal representatives must discharge the debit balance out of his estate, but they are not personally liable to pay it. A bank's duty to pay cheques drawn by a deceased customer is terminated when the bank receives notice of his death, not by the fact of the death if it is unknown to the bank.

Customer's mental illness

If the customer of a bank suffers from a mental illness to such an extent that he cannot manage his own affairs properly, the banker–customer relationship is terminated in the same way as if the customer had died. The bank is likely to suspend the customer's account pending the appointment of a receiver by the court to administer the estate of the person who is mentally ill; any immediate business would be conducted through a new account in the name of a relative in the meantime. In honouring cheques drawn by a receiver appointed by the court the bank must have regard to the limitations of his powers. If a receiver is not appointed to administer the affairs of a customer suffering from mental illness, there is no one who is legally entitled to draw on the amount credited to his account and give a valid discharge. However, if the bank makes advances out of the customer's account at the request of relatives or custodians and the advance is used to pay for goods and services which are necessaries for the customer, the bank is entitled to debit the acount with the amount advanced.

Customer's bankruptcy

If a customer is adjuged bankrupt by the court, the contract between him and the bank is terminated, and all his assets vest in the trustee in bankruptcy appointed to administer his property. On the production of certificate of appointment issued by the Department of Trade and Industry, the trustee in bankruptcy is entitled to receive the balance standing to the credit of the customer's account. The rule is that where the customer of a bank becomes bankrupt, the title of his trustee in bankruptcy to his assets relates back to the date of the earliest act of bankruptcy proved to have been committed by him within three months before the presentation of the petition on which the adjudication is made. In such a situation the bank would have to account to the trustee in bankruptcy for all amounts paid out of its customer's account after that date although such payments were made in ignorance of the customer having committed an act of bankruptcy. However, banks are protected by the Bankruptcy Act 1914, ss.45 and 46, which provide that so far as the bank is concerned, it can honour cheques drawn by the customer in favour of himself, third persons or the bank itself up to the date when a receiving order is made against him, provided that it is unaware of a pending bankruptcy petition; if the bank makes such payments it will not be accountable to the trustee in bankruptcy for the amounts paid out of the customer's account.

Company customer's liquidation

If the customer of a bank is a company the court can make a compulsory winding-up order, or the shareholders of the company can resolve at a general meeting that it shall be voluntarily wound up because it cannot continue to carry on its business in view of its liabilities. On the commencement of its winding-up a company ceases to carry on business. Regardless of whether it is a compulsory or voluntary liquidation, the bank can honour cheques which are drawn on the company's account and which are presented after the winding-up order has been made or the winding-up resolution passed only if the cheque is signed by the liquidator, or if it is signed by one or more of the former directors and the liquidator authorises payment.

In the case of a compulsory winding-up the company's bank should not dispose of any part of the amount standing to the credit of the company's account, at the instance of the directors, after a winding-up petition has been presented, unless the court authorises such a disposition (*see* the Companies Act 1948, s.227). If the court's approval is not obtained at the time of payment the disposition is invalidated on the making of a winding-up order, and the liquidator is entitled to reclaim the amount paid out by the bank, unless the court approves the payment at that stage.

In *Re Gray's Inn Construction Ltd* (1980) the question which arose was whether certain transfers by a bank in favour of itself made out of a current account to reduce an overdraft which its customer (a company) held with it together with other payments made out of the same account in favour of third parties on the company's instructions were valid or could be validated under the discretionary power given to the court by the Companies Act 1948, s.227. The company was trading at a loss when a creditor presented a winding–up petition on 2nd August 1972. The petition was advertised on 10th August but did not come to the attention of the bank until 15th August, although the manager of the bank where the company held its account did not become aware of it until 17th August. A winding–up order was made in October. The bank had allowed the company to operate the sum account between 3rd August and October without distinguishing between pre–liquidation debts and debts incurred by the company after that time. The liquidator applied for a declaration that the payment of amounts received by the bank to the credit of the account after the presentation of the petition amounted to a disposition of the company's assets under s.227 of the 1948 Act. The court held that payments into the account and used by the bank to reduce the overdraft amounted to dispositions, and amounts paid in favour of third parties also constituted dispositions by the bank under s.227, and that the proper course would have been for the bank to discontinue further transfers to or from that account. The bank would then have had to prove as an unsecured creditor for the overdraft in the winding–up. However, the court said it would validate amounts paid into and out of the company's account before the winding–up petition was presented but that the bank would be treated as having been unaware of the petition before 15th August and therefore the pre–liquidation draft was reduced to £2,652. The bank would not be justified in appropriating amounts subsequently credited to the account towards the discharge of the overdrawn balance. The bank was therefore obliged to pay the liquidator the further amounts credited to the account and appropriated towards the repayment of the overdraft. The court further held that it would not validate payments made out of the current account by the bank for goods and services supplied before the commencement of the winding–up petition, but that these payments should primarily be recovered from the creditors to whom payment had been made. The bank's only liability in respect of these amounts would be for such amounts as could not be recovered from the creditors. In a voluntary liquidation there is no retrospective invalidation of transactions entered into by the directors or agents of the company on its behalf before the winding–up resolution is passed, and so cheques drawn on the company's bank account may be safely honoured if presented before the resolution is passed, even though the bank is aware that a meeting of the shareholders to pass such a resolution has been called.

Outbreak of war

The outbreak of war between the country where a bank is established (or where the branch at which the customer has his account is situated) and the country of which the customer is a national or a resident does not terminate the relationship of banker and customer. In *Arab Bank Ltd* v. *Barclays Bank* (1954) the court held that the right to payment of a credit balance held by a branch of an overseas bank exists until the branch suspends business or is wound up in accordance with English law although its head office may have terminated business in accordance with the laws of the country in which it is resident. The appellant bank which had its registered office in Jerusalem opened a current account with the Jerusalem branch of the respondent bank which had its registered office in England. In 1948 war broke out between the newly constituted state of Israel and the Arab states, and consequently performance of the contract became impossible. In 1950, the appellant bank sued the respondent bank for repayment of the amount standing to its credit as money had and received on the ground that the contract had been frustrated by war. The court held that the right to be paid the credit balance survived the outbreak of the war; it remained in existence subject to a suspension of payment.

Liquidation of bank

The relationship between a bank and its customer may be terminated by the bank being wound up or dissolved under the system of law governing it.

Alternatively, the relationship may be terminated by the banks ceasing to pay its customer's cheques or on a failure to repay the balances on their accounts in accordance with its contractual obligations, whether the bank is in liquidation or not (*see Re Farrows Bank Ltd* (1923)). The consequence of the banks being wound up or stopping payment is that the customer may no longer draw on his current account by cheque and he merely has an immediate claim for repayment of the credit balance. Conversely, the bank's mandate to honour the customer's cheques and to collect the amount of cheques or other instruments is terminated. If the bank does present such items for payment, it holds the proceeds at the disposal of its customer as his property and the customer may require the proceeds to be paid to him before the bank satisfies the claim of its general customers.

NEGOTIABLE INSTRUMENTS

A negotiable instrument is a freely transferable document embodying an obligation on the part of one person to pay money to another. The recipient will normally hold the document and will then receive payment when it is due. He may, however, wish to make the instrument payable to a third party and he may do this by transferring the document in such a way as to entitle the third party to claim the amount payable from the person originally obliged to pay it. The third party may in turn pass the document to a fourth and subsequent parties. If the third party or any of the subsequent parties gives value for the instrument and takes it without knowledge of any defects in title of his transferor to the document and the obligation it embodies, he can enforce that obligation without regard to any such defects; they do not affect him. The legal relationship between the person obliged to make the payment embodied in a negotiable instrument and the person first entitled in the instrument is governed by the rules of contract law, but his relationship with subsequent parties is governed by the special rules governing negotiable instruments.

Purposes served by negotiable instruments

Where an original debtor (A) owes money to another (B) but does not wish to pay cash, he may himself instruct a third party (C), who is his debtor, to make payment to B of the whole of part of the amount C owes to A. A may send a bill of exchange to B entitling B to call upon C to pay to B the whole or part of the sum originally owed by C to A. When C pays B, he discharges his debt to A to the extent of the payment made to B.

The person who drew up the document ordering C to pay B is known as "the drawer" of the bill; B, to whom the payment is to be made, is known as "the payee"; and C, to whom the instruction is given to make the payment to B, is known as "the drawee". C will usually be the banker with whom A has an account in credit and in that case the bill of exchange may take the form of a cheque.

The person holding a bill of exchange or cheque may wish to use it to make a payment to some other person. Thus B may wish to use the bill or cheque to make a payment to X, who then may want to use it to make a payment to Y. The steps taken to achieve this will depend on the instruments given by A to C. If A has not named B in the document, but directed C to pay whoever is "the bearer" of the document, then he has created a "bearer instrument" and mere delivery of it by B to X with the intent to pass ownership will be enough to give X a valid title. In turn X could similarly pass title to the instrument to Y by merely delivering it to him.

If, however, A's order to C reads "pay B or order" or simply "pay B", A has created an order instrument, and if B wishes to transfer it to X he must "indorse" the instrument by writing his signature on the back. If B merely writes his signature, this is known as an "indorsement in blank" and converts the instrument into a bearer instrument. Then X can pass title to the instrument to Y by mere delivery with intent to transfer ownership. If B, in addition to his signature on the back of the instrument, directs that payment shall be made to "X or order" or "to X", the indorsement is a "special indorsement" and if X in turn wishes to transfer the instrument to Y he must himself indorse it, either specially or in blank.

The document sent out by A may not merely direct C as to whom payment is to be made, but also state when payment is to be made. Thus C may be ordered to pay the bearer (or B or order) "on sight or demand" (i.e. as soon as the document is produced to him). These documents are called "sight" or "demand" bills of exchange. A cheque must always be payable on demand. Alternatively, A may order C to pay the amount only on a stated date or after the lapse of a specified time (e.g. 90 days from the date when A issued the bill to B, or 90 days after sight (i.e. after B presents the bill to C for his signature). In the case of these time bills, B may require an assurance that the amount represented by the document will be paid and may look for such an assurance some time before the date on which C is required to pay. In that case B will seek to obtain C's acceptance; this is an acknowledgment by C that he is liable to pay when the document matures (namely when the time for payment arrives).

In order to obtain C's acceptance, B is required to "present" the document to C for acceptance. C will usually accept the bill by writing the word "accepted" across the face of the document, together with his signature and return the instrument to B who will then "discount" the bill to a bank or a discount house. The bank or discounting house will then pay B an amount less than the face value of the instrument; the difference between the amount paid to B and the face value of the bill is the amount of interest and commission charged by the bank or discount house for discounting the bill before maturity. If the instrument is an order instrument, B will indorse the bill to the bank or discount house so that it may present the instrument to C for payment when it matures.

In addition to bills of exchange and cheques there is a third kind of negotiable instrument, the "promissory note". This is an instrument by which a person (the maker) promises that he will make a payment to another (the payee) or to the bearer of the instrument. In the case of promissory notes there are two original parties instead of the three in the case of a bill of exchange.

Bills of exchange and cheques
Definition
In considering whether a particular document is a bill of exchange, it is necessary to take into account the provisions in the Bills of Exchange Act 1882 relating to the capacity and authority of parties, consideration, negotiation and the duties and liabilities of a holder. A bill of exchange may be defined as an unconditional order in writing addressed by one person to another requiring that other person to pay the sum specified in the instrument to a named person or to bearer on a fixed or determinable date or on demand. A cheque is a bill of exchange drawn on a bank and payable on demand. Both bills and cheques must contain an unconditional order addressed to the drawee so that an instrument which requires, as a condition of payment, the signing of a receipt by the payee is not a cheque. In *Bavins & Sims* v. *London & South Western Bank* (1900) it was held that an instrument which required the drawee to obtain the payee's signature to an indorsed receipt was not an unconditional order, and therefore was not a cheque. If, however, the condition is merely a direction to the payee and not to the drawee bank to obtain a receipt, the instrument is unconditional and is a bill or cheque within the requirements of the law. In *Nathan* v. *Ogdens* (1905), a note at the foot of a cheque requiring that the payee should sign a receipt on the back of the cheque was held to be addressed to the payee alone, and not to the bank on which the cheque was drawn; therefore the instrument was a valid cheque. An instrument will be a valid bill or cheque although it indicates that a particular account of the drawer is to be debited (e.g. through the use of the words "number 1 account" or "business account" in the body of the cheque); this operates merely as a supplemental instruction to the drawee bank to debit the amount paid under the cheque to the account indicated.

A bill or cheque must be "an order", in that it must be expressed in imperative terms. In *Little* v. *Slackford* (1828) an instrument in the form "You will oblige your humble servant..." was held to be a mere request and not a demand on the drawee (*see also Ellison* v. *Collingridge* (1850)).

The instrument must be in writing to be a bill or cheque, and the Bills of Exchange Act 1882, s.2, provides that writing includes print, so that a bill or cheque prepared on a typewriter would be valid. A customer who writes a cheque by hand would probably facilitate fraud by drawing cheques in lead–pencil, and in such a case a bank would probably return it unpaid.

A bill or cheque must contain an order to make payment "addressed by one person to another" so that there must be one person as drawer and another as drawee: in the case of a cheque the drawee must be a bank. It is possible to have sole or joint drawees, but not drawees in the alternative.

To be a valid instrument, a bill or cheque must be signed by the person issuing it; thus the drawer or a person authorised by him must sign the bill or cheque and the instrument is not complete until the drawer has signed it. A cheque form which is otherwise complete is therefore not a valid cheque until the drawer or his agent signs it. By the Bills of Exchange Act 1882, s.91(1), it is possible for an agent or official of an organisation to be vested with the power to draw bills or cheques on behalf of the organisation. A cheque, unlike a bill, must always be payable on demand. A bill may be payable on demand or at a determinable time in the future. As with bills of exchange, cheques can in practice be post–dated or ante–dated; although post–dated cheques are not payable on demand immediately they are treated as valid by the courts. A post–dated cheque is one which bears a date of issue which is later than the date of its actual issue, and such a cheque will not be paid by the drawee bank until the date on which it is expressed to be issued; the drawee bank's only concern is to see that the post–dated cheque is not paid before the date on the cheque. In *Whistler* v. *Forster* (1863) it was held that a holder for value can recover from the drawer on a post–dated bill or cheque payable to "AB or order", and the instrument is to be taken to have been drawn according to the date appearing on the face of it. In *Austin* v. *Bunyard* (1865) the plaintiff received an indorsed cheque from the payee but without knowledge that when it was drawn it was post–dated. He was held entitled to recover against the defendant, the drawer, the amount of the post–dated cheque, which was a valid instrument.

A bill or cheque may be drawn for any sum of money, but it must be for a certain sum, which normally is expressed both in words and figures. In *Cohn* v. *Boulken* (1920) a cheque drawn for 7,680 francs was held to be for a certain sum of money although it was required to be paid according to the rate of exchange prevailing when that cheque was presented. In *Barlow* v. *Broadhurst* (1820) an instrument drawn "Pay B after deducting what he owes me" was held not to be a bill since without looking beyond the wording of the instrument it was not possible to ascertain the amount which was to be paid to the payee. Where there is a discrepancy between the words and figures in a bill or cheque, under the Bills of Exchange Act 1882, s.9(2), the sum denoted by the words is payable unless the sum in figures is smaller. In practice, the banks usually return cheques unpaid if there is a discrepancy between the amount in words and in figures. Finally, a cheque must be payable to a specified person or his order or bearer. An instrument drawn "pay cash or order" is therefore not a cheque (*see Orbit Mining and Trading Co* v. *Westminster Bank* (1963).

FICTITIOUS OR NON-EXISTING PAYEES

Where the payee of a bill is a fictitious or non–existing person, the bill may be treated as payable to bearer. Any holder of the bill who could recover if the bill were drawn payable to bearer can recover on it if it is made payable to a fictitious or non–existing person. It will be impossible for any holder of it to be a holder in due course unless the bill is treated as a bearer instrument.

The effect of the Bills of Exchange Act 1882, s.7(3) was discussed in *Bank of England* v. *Vagliano Brothers* (1891). The plaintiffs in that case were a firm of merchants in London who banked with the Bank of England and who were in the habit of accepting bills which were drawn payable at the Bank. Among the firm's foreign correspondents was one Vucina, who in the course of business habitually drew bills on Vagliano in favour of Petridi & Co, a firm in Constantinople. A clerk of Vagliano forged a series of bills which were purported to be drawn by Vucina on Vagliano in favour of Petridi & Co; in order to obtain Vagliano's acceptance of the forged bills he also forged corresponding letters of advice purporting to come from Vucina. When Vagliano had accepted the forged bills, they were misappropriated by the clerk and indorsed by him with a forgery of Petridi & Co's signature. The clerk presented the bills on maturity to the Bank of England. The Bank, having been advised of the acceptance of the bills by Vagliano, paid them over the counter to the fraudulent clerk and then debited Vagliano's account. When the fraud was discovered, Vagliano brought an action to determine whether the Bank was entitled to debit their account with the amounts paid out. The bank argued, first, that Vagliano were estopped from denying the validity of the bill and, secondly, that the bank was protected by Bills of Exchange Act 1882, s.7(3).

The House of Lords held that the intention of the forger could not affect the existence of the payee and since the payees were real they could not be fictitious. There was a real firm of Petridi & Co in existence, and since it was held as a fact that the bill was payable to an existing person it could not be made in favour of a fictitious payee. The majority in the House of Lords held that the fictitious character of the payee is determined by reference to the forger's state of mind; if he did not intend the payee (although an existing person) to receive payment (as here) the payee must be fictitious.

The *Bank of England* v. *Vagliano* case left certain matters in doubt:

(*a*) whether the intention of other parties to the bill should be taken into account in determining the character of the payee; and

(*b*) whether the character of the payee as real or fictitious should be linked with the presence or absence of a real transaction in carrying out which the bill was issued.

In *Clutton* v. *Attenborough* (1897) it was held that a cheque drawn to the order of a fictitious or non-existing person may be treated as payable to bearer within the Bills of Exchange Act 1882, s.7(3), although the drawer believes and intends the cheque to be payable to the order of a real person. In that case a clerk in the appellants' accounts department by fraudulently representing to them that work had been done on their account by a person called B, induced them to draw cheques payable to the order of B. The cheques, when signed by the appellants, were handed by them to their accounts department for transmission to the payees. The clerk then obtained possession of the cheques, indorsed them with B's name and negotiated them to the respondents who gave value and took the cheques in good faith. The cheques were paid to the respondents by the appellants' bankers, and when the appellants subsequently discovered the fraud, they brought an action against the respondents to recover the amount of the cheques as money paid under a mistake of fact. The House of Lords said that, although the cheques were drawn in favour of a person named B, and there might be a person of that name, the payee of the cheques was nevertheless fictitious because the name B had been provided by a person who wished to commit a fraud on the appellants and since they knew no-one of that name they could not have intended the payee to be a real identifiable person. The cheque was held payable to a fictitious payee and was therefore payable to bearer under s.7(3) so that the appellants could not recover the amount which the respondents had collected.

The case is distinguishable from *Vinden* v. *Hughes* (1905), where a cashier filled in a number of cheque forms with the names of customers of his employers as payees and obtained the employers' signature as drawer, forged the signatures of the payees by way of an indorsement and discounted the cheques to an innocent third party who obtained payment from the drawers' bankers. It was held that, on the facts of the case, the payees could not be regarded as fictitious or non-existing because, at the time the cheques were drawn, the drawers intended identifiable persons, namely certain of their customers, to be the payees in the belief that the drawers owed the sums of money represented by the cheques to those persons. In *North & South Wales Bank Ltd* v. *Macbeth* (1908), White fraudulently induced Macbeth to draw a cheque in favour of Kerr "or order". Kerr was an existing person known to Macbeth, and Macbeth, although misled by White as to the use to which he would put the cheque, fully intended that Kerr should receive the money. White, in obtaining the cheque, forged Kerr's indorsement and paid the cheque into his account with the appellant bank. On discovering the fraud, Macbeth brought an action against the bank to recover the money collected by it on the ground that the bank was guilty of conversion by collecting a cheque to which its customers had no title. The House of Lords held that the subsection did not apply because the drawer of the cheque, Macbeth, intended that a real person known to Macbeth, namely Kerr, should receive the amount of the cheque and so it could not be said that the payee of the cheque was fictitious.

Partial indorsements

The Bills of Exchange Act 1882, s.32(2), provides that, if an indorsement is to operate as a negotiation of the instrument, it must be an indorsement of the entire bill. A partial indorsement or an indorsement which purports to transfer only a part of the amount payable under the bill is not effective.

Thus if A is the holder of a bill for £100 and he purports to indorse £50 of it to X, retaining £50 for himself, or if A purports to indorse the bill as to £50 to Y and as to £50 to Z, the indorsements do not amount to a valid negotiation of the bill, and X, Y and Z will, if they give value, acquire only equitable interests in the bill as assignees and so will take subject to any defects of title affecting A. They will have no title to the instrument as holders, and so the acceptor or prior parties may safely pay the whole amount of the bill to A.

Transfer without indorsement

Where the holder of a bill payable to his order transfers it for value without indorsing it, the transfer passes to the transferee such title as the transferor had in the bill. In *Whistler* v. *Forster* (1863) A fraudulently obtained a cheque payable to his own order from B, and he handed it to C in satisfaction of a bona fide debt, but without indorsing the cheque. The court held that C could not acquire the right to sue B upon the instrument by obtaining A's indorsement to it after he had received notice of his fraud, because anyone who receives an indorsed bill of exchange (though for value) acquires no better title under it than the person from whom he receives it. However, by s.31(4) of the 1882 Act, the transferee also acquires the right to have the indorsement of the transferor added to the bill or cheque, and on a subsequent indorsement the transfer takes effect as a negotiation from the time when the indorsement is given. Where a bill has been indorsed in blank, it is converted by the holder into a specially indorsed bill by writing above the indorser's signature a direction to pay the bill to or to the order of himself or some other person (*see* the Bills of Exchange Act 1882, s.34(4). Thus, if a bill is payable to A, who indorses it in blank and negotiates it to B, B may write above A's signature the word "Pay B" or "Pay B or order". In either case the effect will be the same as if A had written those words himself, and the bill will have become specially indorsed in favour of B.

If the transferor's bankruptcy commences before the transfer of the instrument and the transferee is aware of an available act of bankruptcy when he takes the bill, he obtains no title to the instrument. If, however, the transferee was unaware of an act of bankruptcy the trustee in bankruptcy may be ordered to indorse the bill.

INCHOATE INSTRUMENTS

An inchoate instrument is a bill of exchange, cheque or a promissory note which contains one or more but not all of the necessary elements to constitute it a bill, cheque or a promissory note. Consequently where an acceptance is written on an instrument in the form of a bill which does not contain the name of a drawer or payee and is addressed to no named drawee, the instrument is as yet neither a bill nor a note. It may, however, be completed in accordance with the conditions of the Bills of Exchange Act 1882 s.20, and if the instrument then purports to be addressed to the person who has signed as acceptor, it is valid as a bill (see *Haseldine* v. *Winstanley* (1936)).

The holder of a bill is entitled by s.20 to fill any omissions in the case of inchoate and blank instruments. There are, however, a number of requirements which have to be satisfied in order to take advantage of s.20. In the case of a blank or inchoate instrument, it is essential that the drawer has either actually delivered the instrument to another person with authority to complete it, or that his agent or servant has been given the instrument for that purpose. In *Baxendale* v. *Bennett* (1878) the defendant gave H his blank acceptance and authorised H to fill in his name as drawer and the name of anyone who would discount the bill as payee. H was unable to discount the defendant's acceptance and returned the blank acceptance to the defendant. The defendant put the instrument into the drawer of a writing table at his chambers and it was either lost or stolen. The instrument came into the possession of C, who filled in his own name as payee without the defendant's authority and discounted it to the plaintiff. The plaintiff, who claimed to be a holder in due course, brought an action against the defendant. The defendant was held not liable on the bill on the grounds that he had given limited authority to H to complete the bill and the subsequent completion was not in accordance with the authority given by him.

A bill which is incomplete at the time of issue is to be treated, when completed in accordance with the s.20, as though it had never been incomplete. The instructions of the drawer or acceptor must be complied within a reasonable time. In *Griffiths* v. *Dalton* (1940) it was held that a year was an unreasonable time for filling up a blank signed cheque. If the person who exceeds his authority in completing the instrument negotiates it, the holder will be protected under s.20(2) if it was completed before it was negotiated to him and he is a holder in due course. Section 20 is supplemented by ss.12 and 15 which enable the holder of a bill which is issued or negotiated undated to insert the true date of issue or negotiation. If the holder acts in good faith but inserts the wrong date by mistake the instrument is not invalidated to a holder in due course.

THE HOLDER IN DUE COURSE

The essence of negotiability is that a transferee of a bill of exchange is capable of taking free of equities if he gives value and acts in good faith, so that the transfer of the instrument vests in him an absolutely valid title.

The liability of a party to a bill is contractual, and the position of the holder is therefore dependent on whether he or his predecessor in title has given consideration for the instrument. A holder who has not given value for the bill cannot claim therefore against any person who became a party to the bill without receiving consideration unless consideration has been given by an intermediate party. However, every party is presumed to have received consideration so that the burden of proof to the contrary rests on him. A holder who has not given value himself will have the benefit of the fact that a previous holder has given valuable consideration. For example, B draws a bill payable to himself upon A, who accepts it gratuitously; C gives B value for B indorsing the bill to him, and C further indorses the bill to D by way of a gift. D can sue A on the bill although he gave nothing for the bill and A received nothing for his signature, and this applies even though D knew that A had accepted the bill gratuitously. D can also sue B who received value from C, but D cannot sue C, as C did not become a party prior to the giving of value for the bill by himself.

A holder for value has complete title to the bill, and his title can only be impeached by proof of a defect in his title, namely that the issue or transfer of the bill was void or voidable. For example, if the issue or any transfer of the bill had been obtained by fraud, a holder for value obtains no benefit from the mere fact that he has himself given value for the bill or that he takes through one who has given value. To take free from the defect of title the holder for value must also be a holder in due course.

The holder in due course is unaffected by any defect in the title of any previous holder or by any omission on the part of any previous holder to carry out the steps necessary to preserve the rights of recourse of a holder against prior parties. A holder who derives title through a holder in due course has, generally, the rights of a holder in due course, but this is not the case if he was a party to any fraud or illegality affecting the bill before it came into the hands of a holder in due course through whom he derived the title.

The Bills of Exchange Act 1882, s.29(1), provides that the holder in due course must take the bill complete and regular on the face of it. He is deemed to satisfy these requirements if he became the holder of it before it became overdue and without notice that it had been previously dishonoured, if such was the fact, if he took the bill in good faith and for value, and without notice of any defect in the title of the person who negotiated it.

Capacity to be a holder in due course

To be a holder in due course the holder of the bill must have taken the bill in such circumstances as to constitute him a holder under s.2 of the 1882 Act. For example, a person in possession of an unindorsed bill payable to the order of someone else is not a holder, although he may have given value for the bill, and he cannot sue on the bill in his own name. The original payee of a bill cannot be a holder in due course although he is a holder and can be a holder for value. In *Jones* v. *Waring and Gillow* (1926) an action was brought by the drawer of a cheque for recovery of money paid under a mistake of fact. A was induced by the fraud of X to believe that the cheque was a deposit to B, the payee, in order to secure the delivery of certain cars. B obtained payment of the cheque in the mistaken belief that it was given in payment of a debt owed to him by X, and in consequence B restored to X certain goods let to him on hire purchase which B had seized on X's default under the agreement between them. On discovering his mistake A tried to recover the money from B who pleaded that he was a holder in due course of a cheque and therefore had an unimpeachable title to the cheque and the proceeds which he could not be called upon to repay. The House of Lords held that the expression "holder in due course" cannot include the original payee of the cheque.

The completeness and regularity of the bill

A holder of a bill may be a holder in due course only if the bill is complete and regular on the face of it (and this includes the back) when he takes it. If the bill itself conveys a warning of possible defects because of its formal irregularity the holder, however honest, can acquire no better title than his transferor. Consequently the holder takes at his own risk a blank acceptance or a bill in which essential features have been omitted or a bill which has been torn and the pieces pasted together if the condition of the instrument shows that a prior holder may have cancelled it. The effect of s.29(1) was discussed in *Arab Bank Ltd* v. *Ross* (1952) where the plaintiff bank sued as holders in due course of two promissory notes made by the defendant in favour of "Faithi and Faysal Nabulsy Company" and which had been indorsed on the reverse "Faithi and Faysal Nabulsy". The court held that the indorsements were sufficient to pass title to the bank, but it had not become a holder in due course because the indorsement was irregular in form, in that it did not set out the name of the indorser, the company, in full.

The question which arises, however, is whether a person who signs the back of the bill with an intention other than that of transferring title to the bill makes himself liable as an indorser, for example, whether a director of a company who signs the back of a bill of exchange drawn on the company as a guarantor can be made personally liable as indorser of the bill.

In *Macdonald & Co* v. *Nash & Co* (1924) N had agreed to finance a purchase of goods by A from M, and had indorsed certain bills drawn by M on A payable to the order of M; A handed the bills so indorsed to M in exchange for delivery orders for goods but the bills handed to M were incomplete by reason of the absence of an indorsement by M above the indorsement of N. The bills were dishonoured, and an action was brought by M against N as indorser. The House of Lords held that a bill to the drawer's order which had been indorsed by a third party before any indorsement by the drawer in his capacity as payee was a bill of exchange, although the chain of indorsements was incomplete and could be completed by the drawer's afterwards indorsing his signature at any time, including a time after N had indorsed the bill to make himself liable on it to the drawer.

In the *MacDonald* case the "backer" signed the bill in order to guarantee its payments. However, it is clear from s.56 that it is the act of signing which makes the backer liable on the bill and not his motive in doing so, whether he did so as surety, indorser or guarantor.

The order in which indorsements are placed on the back of the instrument does not constitute a material irregularity and the intention of the parties is taken into account in judging the liability which they intended to incur.

Overdue bills and notice of dishonour

A holder in due course must have taken the bill he holds before it became overdue and without notice of any prior dishonour which had taken place.

When a bill is overdue it can be negotiated within the limits of the Bills of Exchange Act 1882, namely, it remains transferable, but it cannot be negotiated so as to confer a title on a subsequent holder free from the defects affecting it when it became due. On the other hand, where a party takes a bill which has previously been dishonoured by non–acceptance with knowledge of that fact, he cannot be a holder in due course, but if A takes a bill payable on demand before it has been in circulation for an unreasonable time, although it has in fact been presented for payment and dishonoured, he can still be a holder in due course if he took the bill without notice of the dishonour and gave valid consideration.

The necessity for value and good faith

A holder in due course must himself have given value or have derived his title through a prior holder in due course. For example, if A gives value for a bill with notice of a defect in the prior title and indorses the bill to B, who takes it gratuitously but without knowledge of the defect, B cannot be a holder in due course. The conditions for holding in due course cannot be split up among successive holders and value and good faith must proceed from the same person to constitute a holder in due course. However, once this has happened, the benefits of a holder being a holder in due course are enjoyed by subsequent holders of the bill and they therefore take free from defects which do not affect him.

In order to be a holder in due course, it is essential that the holder should act in good faith. The Bills of Exchange Act 1882, s.90, provides that a thing is done in good faith where it is in fact done honestly, whether it be done negligently or not. It is a question of the state of mind of the person who takes the instrument at the time he takes it. A party who has not taken the bill in good faith, whether he gave value or not, will not therefore be able to retain it and will obtain no better title than the person who negotiates it.

A person who buys a bill from another whom he realises is not its true owner cannot be a holder in due course and, similarly, a person who wilfully shuts his eyes to the existence of a defect of title which is apparent cannot be such a holder. In *Jones* v. *Gordon* (1877) a London agent of a firm drew bills on the firm for £1,727. The firm accepted the bills. At the time both the drawer and acceptors were insolvent and contemplating bankruptcy, and the transaction had been concocted in order to defraud the creditors of the acceptors. The drawer offered the bills to the plaintiff who, before purchasing them, kept them for a while to make inquiries. He ascertained that the acceptors were in financial difficulties, but that they had some assets and might be able to pay something, but he did not inquire into the degree of insolvency of the drawer. He accordingly gave only £200 for the bills. The acceptors afterwards became bankrupt. It was held that the plaintiff knew sufficient about the acceptors' condition to put him on his guard, that he was fixed with notice of the fraudulent purpose of accepting the bills and could not prove for the whole amount of the bills, but only for the £200 which he paid for them. It is not sufficient to establish negligence or carelessness, however serious, on the part of the holder of a bill to deprive him of the status of a holder in due course. It is necessary that he should have appreciated from the circumstance that the title of his transfer was suspect and have failed to satisfy himself by inquiry that his suspicions were groundless. In *Raphael* v. *Bank of England* (1855) bank notes had been stolen and a circular giving notice of the theft together with a list of the stolen notes was sent to bankers and money–changers, including V & Co. One of the notes was changed by a clerk of V & Co, who swore that he could not recall that the note of the number corresponded to one numbered in the circular at the time he changed the note. The court held that the note was therefore taken bona fide and that negligence did not invalidate the title of a person taking a negotiable instrument in good faith and for value.

The title of the holder in due course

If a person's title to a bill is defective, the transferee will obtain no better title to it than the transferor himself unless the transferee is a holder in due course. The true owner of the bill of exchange can therefore enforce his rights, notwithstanding any ineffective transfer of title to it by other persons. If someone forges an indorsement of a bill to a person who believes the indorsement to be genuine, the indorsement is a nullity and the true owner may recover the bill and enforce it himself. Similarly, if an indorser is induced to indorse a bill by mistake the negotiation of the bill is void, and the indorsee obtains no title to the bill despite his good faith.

Defects of title from which the holder in due course take free

A holder in due course, in addition to having all the rights and powers of a holder, is provided by the Bills of Exchange Act 1882, s.38(2), with certain additional protection; namely the holder in due course takes free from any defect of title of the prior party, in addition to taking free from personal defences available to the parties among themselves. He can therefore enforce payment against all the parties liable on the bill. Section 29(2) specifies that the defects of title from which the holder in due course takes free are when the person who negotiates the bill obtains it by fraud, duress or illegal consideration or force and fear or other unlawful means. Under s.38(2) the holder in due course takes free from defences like set–off and counterclaim. The list of defects in s.29(2) is not exhaustive and the holder in due course will take a good title despite any other defects.

The Act provides that every holder is prima facie deemed to be a holder in due course, but if it is proved or admitted that the acceptance, issue or negotiation of a bill was affected by fraud, duress or force and fear, the burden of proof is shifted and the person who sues on the bill must prove that value has been given in good faith for the bill subsequent to the fraud or illegality.

It is now proposed to examine the defences available to a debtor when he is sued by a person claiming title to the instruments under one or more successive transfers and the extent to which the holder in due course is in a stronger position than someone whose title can be impeached.

Forgery

Under the ordinary rules of assignment, the forgery of any instrument creating the chose in action is a valid defence against even an innocent assignee. The Bills of Exchange Act 1882, s.24, provides that forgery is a defence to a person sued on a bill, cheque or promissory note even as against a person who is a bona fide holder for value or a holder in due course. The section deals with forged or unauthorised signatures and lays down the principle that a forged signature is a nullity whether the forgery be of the drawer, acceptor or indorser.

There are two kinds of forgery:

(a) where the signature of the drawer is forged at the inception of the bill. An instrument drawn, whether to bearer or to order, on which the drawer's signature is forged is not a bill at all and is a complete nullity;

(b) a bill may be valid at its inception, but the holder's title to it will be invalid if an indorsement is forged on it.

In the first case, it is clearly settled that an instrument on which the drawer's signature is forged is not a bill of exchange and no–one may sue him on it. An instrument sham in its inception may, however, by the addition of a genuine signature become a negotiable instrument by estoppel. Section 54 estops the acceptor from denying the genuineness of the drawer's signature and s.55(2)(b) estops an indorser from denying the genuineness of the drawer's, acceptor's or any previous indorser's signature in each case as against a "holder in due course".

In the second case the Bills of Exchange Act 1882, s.55 applies. This states that an indorser of a bill is precluded by his indorsement from denying to a holder in due course the genuineness of his signature and the signatures of any previous indorsers. The person who would otherwise be a holder in due course normally cannot recover the proceeds of the bill from the person whose signature was forged, or from a party to the bill prior to the forged indorsement, and any payment made by that party can be recovered as paid under a mistake of fact, subject to the defence of estoppel by payment. The rights available to a holder in due course are limited to rights of recourse against indorsers subsequent to the forged signature. However, an acceptor is liable on his acceptance to a holder claiming through a forged instrument:

(a) where, at the time of the acceptance, the acceptor knew of the forgery and intended that the bill should be put into circulation by a forged indorsement (*Beeman* v. *Duck* (1843)); and (*b*) where the payee is a fictitious or non–existing person and consequently the holder does not need to take title through the indorsement, since by s.7(3) of the Act the instrument is payable to bearer.

The person whose signature has been forged may represent the forged signature to be his own and thus by inducing subsequent holders for value to take the instrument he is estopped from setting up the fact that it is a counterfeit and may become liable on it. In *Leach* v. *Buchanan* (1802) a holder who had doubts as to the signature on a negotiable instrument asked the party whether it was his signature and received a positive answer. The holder then negotiated the bill, and the transferee assumed the signature to be genuine. It was held that the transferee could recover on the bill from the party in question on the ground that by his statement he had given credibility to the bill and induced others to take it, which they would not have done if he had denied that the signature on it was his own.

Even mere non–disclosure of the forgery may result in an estoppel where there is a duty of disclosure to the person who raises the estoppel, as in the instance of a customer in relation to his banker (*Greenwood* v. *Martins Bank* (1933)).

A bill may be forged in other ways than by the forgery of the signature of a party to the bill. For example, if a material alteration, such as raising the amount of the bill is made to an existing bill, its subsequent issue or negotiation involves altering a forged document. However, such a forgery does not necessarily invalidate the bill completely and, if the forgery is not apparent, a subsequent holder in due course may, under s.64(1), enforce the instrument in its original form.

Void and illegal consideration
The illegality of the consideration under the transaction which gave rise to the doubt in question may be raised as a defence by the debtor against an innocent assignee of the debt.

In the case of a holder for value of a bill of exchange, the position is similar; it is of no consequence whether the consideration which moves from him is illegal or merely void, for in neither case has he given value in the eyes of the law and so cannot recover on the bill. However, on transfer by such a person, the position is different in the following two cases:

(*a*) where B obtains a bill from A for an illegal consideration and transfers it to C, who gives value, C cannot recover from A if he knows of the manner in which B obtained the instrument, but he can recover from A if he was unaware of the illegality. In *Woolf* v. *Hamilton* (1898) a cheque given by the defendant in payment of bets on horse races lost by him was indorsed by the payee to the plaintiff for value with notice of the consideration for which it was given. The court held the plaintiff could not maintain an action on the cheque as it must be deemed to have been given for an illegal consideration by the Gaming Act 1845. The court added, however, that the illegality of the wagering consideration would have been immaterial if the plaintiff had been a bona fide holder without notice of the consideration; as a holder in due course he would have been able to sue both the issuer and other parties to the cheque;

(*b*) if B obtains a bill from A for a consideration which is not illegal but merely void, and B transfers the bill to C for value, C, by giving value himself, cures the want of value between A and B, and C can recover from A even if he knew that the consideration given by B was void. In *Lilley* v. *Rankin* (1886) the defendant gave a cheque to X in payment of a gaming loss and X indorsed the cheque to the plaintiff for value who had knowledge of the circumstances. It was held that the plaintiff could recover on the cheque as the consideration was merely void by virtue of the Gaming Act 1845 and not illegal as a wagering loss would have been.

The Bills of Exchange Act 1882, s.29, provides that, if illegal consideration has been given for a bill, it does not affect the title of a subsequent holder in due course. In *Bank für Gemeinwirtschaft* v. *City of London Garages ltd* (1971) the first defendant, City of London Garages Ltd, had accepted accommodation bills drawn by the second defendant in its own favour so that the bills could be discounted by brokers or discount houses after being backed by the second defendant and by the Central Bank of India Ltd, with whom the second defendant had a current account. The discounting facilities were arranged by Patel, the London Manager of the Central Bank but, on his advice, the proceeds of discounting the bills were never used for their intended purpose, namely to purchase securities. At the end of 1968 it became difficult to discount bills backed by the Central Bank on the London market and so Patel arranged for further bills drawn by the second defendant and accepted by the first defendant to be denominated in Deutschmarks and to be discounted in Germany by L. Behrens and Sohne, a private bank in Hamburg. In order to meet the bills discounted in London which were now maturing, Behrens induced the Internationale Genossenschaft bank, a German bank owned by co–operative societies, to rediscount the bills and in June and December 1969 they were twice renewed and on the second occasion replaced by further six month bills maturing in June 1970. In May 1970, Patel absconded with most of the money standing to the credit of the second defendant's account with the Central Bank of India. When the bills drawn in December 1969 matured in 1970 they were dishonoured on presentation at Behren's offices in Hamburg. After the first and second defendants and the Central Bank of India had been notified of the dishonour, writs were issued against all of them. The plaintiff, Bank für Gemeinwirtschaft, had received the bills for collection from the Internationale Genossenschaft bank, and they had been indorsed for this purpose, but it was the Internationale itself whose status as holder in due course was relevant. The Court of Appeal treated the illegality as constituting at the most a purely collateral matter as between the first and second defendants and the Central Bank of India and not as affecting the issue of the bills in question; such a collateral illegality therefore affected the title of a subsequent holder for value of the bills only if he knew that the Exchange Control Act 1947, had been breached. The result of the *City of London Garages* case is therefore a limited one. If a bill or other negotiable instrument is validly issued, the fact that its negotiation is illegal does not affect the title of a subsequent holder in due course. However, if the issue of the instrument is illegal (e.g. an issue of a bill, cheque or promissory note by an adult in repayment of a loan contracted by him during his minority (contrary to the Betting and Loans Contracts Act 1892, s.5)), the instrument is completely void, and the only claims which a subsequent holder in due course may enforce are those which result from prior parties being estopped from denying the validity of the instrument under the Bills of Exchange Act 1882, s.55.

Mistake

A party to an instrument, whether it is negotiable or not, may escape liability on it if he can show that the document he signed was clearly different from that which he intended to sign or, alternatively, that he made a fundamental mistake when he entered into the contract.

The Bills of Exchange Act 1882, s.29, provides that the title of a person who negotiates a bill of exchange is defective if at the time he obtained the issue or acceptance of the bill he did so by fraud, duress, force and fear or other unlawful means or if he obtained the negotiation of it to himself under such circumstances as amount to fraud. An innocent holder in due course has no protection against mistake if he sues a person who was induced by the mistake to sign the document. However, the courts have not dealt with the situation where there is a mistaken indorsement and the question is whether a holder in due course can sue any parties prior to the mistaken indorsement who in fact were in no way connected with the mistake.

A final problem that may arise is where a person signs a bill of exchange but makes a mistake which invalidates the transaction under which the bill is issued or accepted. In *Ayres* v. *Moore* (1939) F, the secretary of a company, was indebted to the plaintiff, A, for personal loans and he persuaded the defendant, M, who was the chairman of the company, to accept certain bills payable to A by representing that the bills were in repayment of advances made by A to F for the purposes of the company. F then handed the accepted bills to A in repayment of the personal loans. It was held that M could avoid liability on the bill for mistake only if his mistake was as to the nature of the document or as to the existence of a legal liability imposed on him in satisfaction of which he accepted the bill.

Minors

The Bills of Exchange Act 1882, s.22(1), makes no exception to general contract law relating to a person's capacity to bind himself by a contract. The section merely provides that the capacity to incur liability under a bill is co–extensive with the capacity to contract. A minor may therefore sue on a bill (*see Warwick* v. *Bruce* (1813)) but he cannot be made liable on a bill or other negotiable instrument as drawer, acceptor or indorser, even though the plaintiff is a holder in due course, and even though the transaction is one on which the minor could have been sued, namely the supply of necessaries. In *Re Soltykoff,* (1891), P was an indorsee of some bills of exchange which had been accepted by Prince Soltykoff when he was a minor. The bills had been drawn in payment for necessaries. It was held that if a minor accepted a bill of exchange he could not be made liable upon it under any circumstances. However, the person who supplied a minor with the necessaries can sue on that contract for the value of what he has supplied.

A holder in due course has no special additional remedy against a minor who is party to a bill, but is in the same position as any other holder for value. The Bills of Exchange Act 1882, s.22(2), provides that, where a bill is drawn or indorsed by a minor, a holder in due course is entitled to enforce it against any other party.

Where, however, an instrument is drawn after the minor has attained his majority in satisfaction of a promise which arose during his minority, the question of liability, if any, involves two different statutes, the Infants Relief Act 1874 and the Betting and Loans (Infants) Act 1892.

The Infants Relief Act 1874, s.2, provides that no action can be brought against a minor after he attains his majority under any contract entered into whilst in his minority, regardless of whether a new contract is entered after he attains his majority. In *Smith* v. *King* (1892) this was interpreted as stating that a former minor is liable to a holder of a bill or other negotiable instrument issued in payment of a debt contracted during minority unless the holder has notice of the purpose for which the instrument was issued. In that case D, during minority, became indebted with two other persons to a firm of brokers who brought an action against them after D attained his majority. The action was compromised on the basis that D should accept two bills for £50, and one of the bills was indorsed by the brokeres to P, who had acted as a solicitor in the action and thus took with notice. It was held that the transaction was a mere promise made by D after full age to pay a debt incurred during minority and s.2 prevented the solicitor's recovering against anyone on the bill. In *Belfast Banking Co* v. *Doherty* (1879) W lent money to D, a minor, and in return D, during his minority, accepted a bill drawn by W. It was held that a holder in due course of the bill could recover on the instrument and the court restricted the application of s.2 to the original parties and holders of the bill with notice of the purpose for which it was accepted.

The Betting and Loans (Infants) Act 1892, s.4, provides that an instrument made after an infant attains his majority is absolutely void in the hands of any holder, even a holder in due course, if the original contract in respect of which it was given during his infancy was void. In *Hutley* v. *Peacock* (1913) it was held that the plaintiff, a holder in due course, was not able to sue on a cheque which had been issued before the drawer attained his majority but was post–dated for acceptance after he did so. The cheque was drawn in payment for commission on a loan and the Betting and Loans (Infants) Act 1892, s.5, Appendix, states that, for the purpose of s.4, commission and interest are considered part of the loan.

Fraud, duress and misrepresentation

The holder in due course of a bill of exchange or other negotiable instrument is not affected by a misrepresentation or fraud relating to the issue, acceptance or negotiation of a bill of exchange.

Corporate incapacity

The Corporate Bodies Contracts Act 1960 allows corporations to contract in the same form as individuals, so that contracts entered into by a corporation are no longer required to be under seal. This was already the case for companies registered under the Companies Act 1948, s.33 of which enacts that a company can be bound by a contract on a bill of exchange by the signature of any person acting under its authority.

A holder in due course is now absolutely prevented from suing a corporation which is party to a bill only if it is a statutory corporation other than a company registered under the Companies Act 1948, and is acting ultra vires, but, as in the case of minors, the fact that a bill has been drawn or indorsed by a corporation does not affect the liability of other parties to the holder.

Defects of which the holder in due course does not take free

There are certain defects of title which will affect the title of a holder in due course. It is not the whole title of a holder in due course which is invalid, other than in case of forgery, but his right to sue one or more parties to the instrument. The title of a holder in due course will be affected in the following circumstances:

(*a*) a party who expressly negatives liability by signing *sans recours* (without recourse to him personally) for defect in title cannot be sued, although title can be traced through him, e.g. a company director who signs a bill of exchange *sans recours* as guarantor that the company will pay on the bill;

(*b*) a person whose signature has been forged or is unauthorised incurs no liability, even to a holder in due course, unless that person is precluded from alleging forgery or want of authority (Bills of Exchange Act 1882, s.24);

(*c*) a holder in due course cannot sue a person who can plead the defence of *non est factum* (i.e. that he did not realise the nature of the document he was signing) but it seems that a title can be obtained through such an invalid signature (*Ayres* v. *Moore* (1939));

(*d*) where an overdue bill is negotiated, it can only be negotiated subject to any defect of title affecting it at its maturity, so no person can give or acquire a better title than that of the person from whom he took it;

(*e*) where a bill that is not overdue is dishonoured before the date on which it becomes due, any person who takes it with notice of the dishonour takes it subject to the defect of title and therefore not in good faith. However, if the holder takes without notice of any defect or the fact of dishonour he will be a holder in due course and takes free from the defect;

(*f*) a former holder in due course is not protected against defects arising after he negotiates the bill if he later re-acquires it after maturity even in ignorance of the defect, but he is protected against defects which arose before he first acquired the bill;

(*g*) a holder in due course is not protected against failure to give notice of dishonour by non–payment of a demand bill by the Bills of Exchange Act 1882, s.48(1);

(*h*) a former holder in due course is not protected against failure to give notice of dishonour at common law or under the Bills of Exchange Act 1882.

Other defects

Other defects which relate to the incapacity or the immunity from suit of the party whom the holder seeks to make liable on the bill are as follows:

(*a*) minors and statutory corporations contracting ultra vires incur no liability on negotiable instruments, although title to such instruments can be traced through their signatures and acts in negotiating the instrument;

(*b*) sovereign and diplomatic immunity of foreign ambassadors and corporations prevent a holder in due course from suing them as parties to the instrument unless the immunity is waived, or the case falls within one of the statutory qualifications. Again, the fact that a sovereign power or a person or body which enjoys sovereign or diplomatic immunity cannot be sued on the instrument does not prevent a holder deriving a title to it through them and his title is in no way impaired by the immunity of a prior party.

Estoppel and bills of exchange

The rules of estoppel prevent parties responsible for the issue, acceptance or negotiation of a bill from denying to a holder in due course his title to the bill. The estoppels operate by each successive party to the bill being assumed to have passed it to the subsequent holder in the normal and valid form. On this assumption each party is precluded from denying the regularity and validity of the bill, the validity and effectiveness of all signatures on it prior to his own and the capacity of the next person to take the bill and negotiate it further.

Liability and estoppels of the acceptor

The Bills of Exchange Act 1882, s.54(1), provides that the acceptor undertakes to pay the amount of the bill on maturity.

Where, therefore, the bill has been altered so as to increase its amount after it has been accepted, the acceptor will only be liable to pay the original amount, and he is under no obligation to see that the bill is in such a state so as to preclude possible alterations. In *Schofield* v. *Londesborough* (1896) the defendant accepted a bill for £500 but the amount was completed in such a manner that it was possible to alter the amount. The drawer, altered the amount to £3,500 and indorsed it to a holder in due course. It was held that the defendant, as acceptor, was not liable for more than £500 and was under no duty to take precautions to protect a possible holder.

The acceptor cannot deny the genuineness of the drawer's signature and the courts have consistently held that in an action against the acceptor of a bill of exchange, the authenticity of the drawer's signature need not be proved.

In *Beeman* v. *Duck* (1843) a bill of exchange, purporting to be drawn by B & W an existing firm, payable to their order and to be indorsed by them was accepted by the drawee with that indorsement on it. The court held that of the drawer and payee, a drawee who accepts the bill in ignorance of the forgery is estopped from denying the validity of the drawer's signature, but not the forged indorsement of the payee, although in the same handwriting.

Similarly, in an action by a bona fide indorsee against the acceptor of a bill of exchange payable to the drawer's order, the defendant is estopped from pleading that the drawer indorser was an undischarged bankrupt.

Liability and estoppels of the drawer

The Bills of Exchange Act 1882, s.55(1), deals with the liability of the drawer. It provides that the drawer in drawing the bill undertakes that, on due presentation, it shall be accepted and paid, but that if it is dishonoured he will compensate the holder or any indorser compelled to pay the amount.

Furthermore, an indorsement by the drawer does not give him a new character as indorser, or divest him of any liability to which, as drawer of the bill, he would have been subject, and he remains the ultimate debtor.

Liability and estoppels of an indorser

The indorser of a bill undertakes that on due presentation it will be accepted and paid and if the bill is dishonoured he will compensate the holder provided the proper steps required on dishonour are taken. An indorser therefore guarantees the acceptance and payment of the bill and also guarantees to parties subsequent to himself that he will reimburse them if the holder enforces his right of recourse against them.

DISHONOUR AND NOTICE OF DISHONOUR

A bill of exchange may be dishonoured either by non–acceptance (Bills of Exchange Act 1882, s.43(2)) or by a failure to make payment on maturity. A bill may be dishonoured when it is properly presented for acceptance and acceptance is either refused or cannot be obtained or when presentment for acceptance is excused and the bill is not in fact accepted. The bill will be treated as dishonoured for non–acceptance if the drawee becomes bankrupt, dies, is a fictitious person, does not have the capacity to draw a bill or fails to accept within a reasonable time.

The holder will have an immediate right of recourse against the drawer and indorsers of the bill and is discharged from his obligation to present the bill for payment on maturity. If the drawee gives a qualified acceptance, the holder may elect whether or not to treat the bill as dishonoured.

A bill is dishonoured by non–payment either when the instrument is presented for payment and payment is refused or when the time for payment has passed and the instrument is still unpaid. The holder of the bill again has an immediate right of recourse against the drawer and indorsers.

If the instrument has passed through the hands of a number of indorsers, the holder may elect to sue any or all of them jointly. Alternatively, the holder may elect to sue the indorser who transferred the bill to him. That indorser may then sue any indorsers prior to him until the chain of indorsers flows back to the original indorser and the drawer and he can then sue the acceptor. Moreover, an indorser who has been held liable to the holder can sue any one or more of the indorsers prior to him, or sue all of them jointly.

When a bill has been dishonoured for non–acceptance or non–payment the holder must, in order to protect his cause of action, give notice of the dishonour to the drawer and indorsers if they are not to be discharged from their liability. The drawer and indorsers are discharged from liability not only on the bill but also for the consideration received.

The Bills of Exchange Act 1882, s.48, provides that the drawers and indorsers will remain liable although there has been a failure by the holder to give notice, firstly, where a holder in due course takes a bill after the transferor has failed to give notice without notice of this failure and, secondly, where a bill has been dishonoured by non–acceptance and notice of the dishonour has been given, the holder need not give notice of a subsequent dishonour by non–payment unless in the interval the bill has been accepted.

The notice of dishonour is not required to be formal or in a specific form of words. The notice may be given either in writing or personally and in any terms which identify the bill and indicate whether it has been dishonoured for non–acceptance or non–payment. Thus, merely returning the bill to the drawer or indorser is sufficient. Notice of dishonour must, however, be given within a reasonable time. If the parties live in the "same place", notice must reach the holder or indorser the day after the dishonour of the bill or, if they live in different places, notice must be sent off on the day following the dishonour. The rules relating to notice of dishonour provide that the notice must be given by or on behalf of the holder or by an indorser or on his behalf. An indorser can rely on the notice given by the holder but in order to ensure that he will be indemnified, any indorser who may be held liable can give notice to the drawer and prior indorsers. However, notice given by the holder will be effective for all subsequent holders and any prior indorsers entitled to sue the holder. The same rules apply to an indorser who gives notice of the dishonour.

The obligation to give notice of dishonour is dispensed with if it is actually impossible or the right to be notified has been waived. Section 50(2) dispenses with the notice if, after the exercise of reasonable diligence, notice cannot be given.

Noting and protest

When a foreign bill is dishonoured, notice of dishonour must be given, as in the case of an inland bill (i.e. a bill which is drawn and payable within the United Kingdom on a person resident there), but the bill must also be protested in order to preserve the holder's right of recourse against the drawer and indorsers. The holder must employ a notary who will represent the bill to the drawee or acceptor. The notary will note that the bill was represented and note the answer given when he presents the bill and date and initial the bill. After the instrument has been noted it will be "protested". This will take the form of a document which contains a copy of the bill which is signed by the notary after he has set out the demand made (i.e. acceptance or payment of the bill) and the answer given by the drawee or acceptor.

An inland bill does not have to be noted or protested to preserve any right of recourse.

Acceptance and payment for honour

A person who is not a party to the bill may either accept or pay a dishonoured bill to save the "honour" of those involved in the default. An acceptance for honour will be valid if the bill has been protested for dishonour and is not overdue. In addition, the holder must consent to the bill's being accepted for honour and the acceptance must be written on the bill and indicate that it is an acceptance for honour (Bills of Exchange Act 1882, s.65).

An acceptor for honour is liable to the holder and to all persons who have become parties to the bill after the party for whose honour it was accepted. The acceptor for honour undertakes to pay the bill in accordance with the terms of the acceptance if the drawee, on proper presentment, fails to pay and the bill has been protested for non–payment. The acceptor for honour must be aware of these facts at the time the bill is properly presented to him for payment (Bills of Exchange Act 1882, s.66).

A cheque is a negotiable instrument but unlike a bill it does not have to be presented for acceptance. Consequently, the provisions of the 1882 Act relating to acceptances do not apply.

Discharge of a bill

In order to discharge the parties from liability, holders must be paid the amount on the bill at or after maturity. A transfer of the bill to the acceptor before maturity does not operate as a discharge of the bill, because there cannot be payment by anticipation. Consequently, if the holder of a bill obtains payment from the acceptor before maturity, the bill is not discharged, since payment of the bill before it becomes due is not payment in accordance with its terms. To discharge a bill on or after its maturity the payment must be made to the holder or some authorised person on his behalf. It must have been made in good faith and without notice of any defect in the holder's title. Finally, the payment must be made by or on behalf of the drawer or acceptor; payment by another will not serve to discharge the bill and relieve the other parties from liability, unless the bill is an accommodation bill under the 1882 Act s.59(3).

A bill may be discharged by the acceptor's becoming the holder of it (Bills of Exchange Act 1882, s.61) at or after its maturity. Thus, if the holder of a bill indorses it before maturity to an acceptor who retains the bill until maturity, the bill is discharged but, if the acceptor becomes the holder through a person with a defective title, he will not have acquired the bill in his own right within the meaning of the section unless he is a holder in due course.

A bill of exchange may be discharged by renunciation (Bills of Exchange Act 1882, s.62(1)) whether or not consideration is given for the renunciation. However, renunciation must be "at or after maturity" and renunciation before maturity will not discharge a bill. The renunciation must be of the holder's rights against the acceptor in order to discharge prior parties from liability. A record of a mere intention to renounce is insufficient.

A bill may be discharged by cancellation provided the cancellation is apparent; some unmistakable method should, therefore, be employed. The cancellation must be intentional; accidental destruction is insufficient.

Finally, a bill may be discharged by deliberate alteration of a material part of the bill. In *Hong Kong and Shanghai Banking Corp* v. *J. Lo Lee Shi* (1928) it was held that accidental alteration was insufficient to discharge the parties from their liability under the bill.

SPECIAL RULES RELATING TO CHEQUES

Crossings

A crossing is an instruction to a bank to pay a cheque either to any bank collecting it, if the crossing is general, or to the bank named in the crossing, if it is special (Bills of Exchange Act 1882, ss.76–79). A crossed cheque should not be paid by the paying bank in cash across the counter. The relationship of the bank with its customer is governed by the contract between the parties, but a crossed cheque may also be used by the customer–drawer as a means of instructing the collecting bank as to how the cheque should be presented. The purpose of crossings is to minimise the risk of loss if the cheque is lost or stolen. The paying bank will refuse to pay such cheques over the counter and a thief or person finding a crossed cheque must either have a bank account or arrange for someone with a bank account to receive payment so that proceeds fraudulently collected on crossed cheques can be traced. If the cheque is specially crossed, he must have an account at the bank named in the crossing.

The forms of crossings are set out in the Bills of Exchange Act 1882, s.76, and they are divided into two main types:

(*a*) a general crossing, consisting of two transverse lines across the face of the cheque. This merely requires that the cheque should be presented for payment by a bank;

(*b*) "special" crossing consisting of transverse lines between which the name of a specified bank is written. In this case that bank alone can receive payment. The crossings, whether general or special, should appear on the face of the cheque and it would seem that a crossing on the back of the instrument giving a slight impression on the face of the cheque is not sufficient, since the crossing must be visible on the front of the cheque.

Section 77 provides that the drawer of the cheque may cross it specially or generally, or if the cheque is uncrossed the holder may cross it either generally or specially, or convert a general into a special crossing or add the words "not negotiable" to a special or general crossing. When a cheque is crossed specially, the banker to whom it is crossed may again cross it specially to another banker for collection; this will occur where the first banker is employing the second as his agent for the purposes of collecting the proceeds.

The 1882 Act provides that a crossing is a material part of the cheque and it is unlawful, except as authorised by the Act, to add or alter the crossing but the drawer of a crossed cheque, especially when using cheque forms printed with a crossing, may open the crossing by writing words such as "open cheque" or "pay cash" over the crossing and adding his signature. If the bank pays the amount of the cheque to someone other than the true owner of it on the strength of such an "opening", it may debit the drawer's account unless it later appears that the crossing was opened by a person other than the drawer. The Committee of London Clearing Bankers, in 1912, resolved that such cheques are not to be paid in cash, unless the full signature of the drawer is added to the opening, and even then payment is only to be made to the drawer or his known agent. Where the drawee bank disregards a crossing, i.e. payment is made over the counter or, in the case of a special crossing, it is made to someone other than the named banker, the paying bank is liable in conversion to the true owner of the cheque and is also guilty of a breach of duty to its customer.

Not negotiable crossing

The "not negotiable crossing" is provided for in the Bills of Exchange Act 1882. The effect of the words is not to deprive the cheque of its transferability, but it does deprive the instrument of its negotiability, so that no–one can subsequently become a holder in due course. In *Great Western Railway Company* v. *London & County Banking Co,* one Higgins obtained cheques drawn in his favour and crossed "not negotiable" from the respondent bank by fraud and indorsed them to the appellant company. It was held that the appellant company could not be a holder in due course of the cheque. The words "not negotiable' do not prevent the cheque's being transferred, but mean that the holder of the cheque cannot have and is not capable of giving a better title to the cheque than that of the holder from whom he obtained it.

The words "not negotiable" have no effect unless combined with a general or special crossing, and a cheque bearing these words without a crossing is not a crossed cheque. The words do not have to appear in the transverse lines, so long as they appear on the face of the cheque.

"Account payee" crossing

The words "account payee" or "account payee only" are not strictly speaking crossings at all, but merely a memorandum of instruction to the collecting bank that the proceeds of the cheque are not to be collected for any account other than that of the named payee without a full inquiry. The words do not prevent the transfer of a cheque but if the collecting bank recieves payment to the credit of anyone other than its customer without making sure that the payee consents, the bank is liable for negligence and loses the protection of the Cheques Act 1957, s. 4, but, if the bank makes reasonable inquiry, it is protected by s. 4 if the cheque is wrongly collected.

Crossing by a collecting bank
If the collecting bank is the holder of a cheque it may exercise the powers of crossing cheques, i.e. by converting a general into a special crossing or crossing an open cheque generally. A bank which uses another bank as its agent to collect cheques on its behalf may put a second crossing on the cheque.

THE LIABILITY OF PAYING AND COLLECTING BANKS IN CONVERSION

A bank which pays, collects or transmits a cheque bearing a forged or unauthorised indorsement is guilty of conversion and is liable to the true owner for the amount of the cheque. This liability still exists, but is now subject to the statutory defences available to the bank. A conversion is a wrongful interference with goods (including documents) by taking, using or destroying them inconsistently with the owner's right to possession. (Conversion is now a statutory tort under the Torts (Interference with Goods Act 1977).) There must be some act which amounts to a denial of the owner's rights or the exercise of some dominion over the subject matter which is inconsistent with that right.

A bill, note, cheque or the paper on which it is written is "goods" within the definition of goods coming within the action of conversion. The damages awarded will be equivalent to the face value of the instrument. In cases involving the payment of money by a bank, the bank's liability for conversion of the instrument is independent of its right to debit its customer's account with the amount paid, so the bank may be liable in conversion to the true owner of the instrument and also disentitled to debit its own customer's account, in which case it stands to bear double loss.

The person to whom the right of action in conversion is available is the "true owner" of the instrument but there is no definition of the term. It would appear to mean the holder of the instrument whose title cannot be proved to be defective, but who in turn can defeat another person's title. Except for suing for money had and received as an alternative to conversion, there is no alternative form of action available to the true owner. The essential feature of the plaintiff's case in an action for conversion is that at the relevant time he was entitled to the subject–matter. Consequently, in *Smith* v. *Union Bank of London* (1875) where a cheque which had become payable to bearer by indorsement by the payee was stolen and negotiated to a holder in due course on whose behalf the defendant bank collected the cheque, it was held that the holder in due course, not the person from whom the cheque was stolen, was the true owner at the time of the defendant bank's alleged conversion and so the bank was not liable to the plaintiff. In order to bring an action in conversion, the plaintiff must be entitled to immediate possession of the chattel at the date of the conversion.

The protection of the paying bank

A cheque is a mandate of the customer to its bank, which is under a duty, if certain conditions are satisfied, to obey the drawer's instructions and pay the cheque to the holder who presents it or to his bank. If the cheque is payable to bearer, the bank can debit its customer with the amount of the cheque if it pays in good faith any person who presents the cheque, whether in fact he is entitled to the payment or not. If such a payment is made in due course it amounts to a valid discharge and the paying bank is protected by the Bills of Exchange Act 1882, ss. 60 and 80 and the Cheques Act 1957, s.1, if it pays a cheque to someone who has no title to it. Nevertheless, if the bank pays the cheque inconsistently with the drawer's order, for example, contrary to a crossing, it is still unable to debit the drawer's account and it may be liable to the true owner of the cheque.

Protection under the Bills of Exchange Act 1882, s.60

By s.60, the paying bank is protected if it pays a cheque in good faith and in the ordinary course of business to a person other than the true owner of it where the defect in the title of the person who receives payment is the forgery of an indorsement on the cheque. The section applies to both crossed and uncrossed cheques and, apparently, even though the paying bank has been negligent in making the payment, provided that it has acted in good faith and in the ordinary course of its business. The effect of s.60, therefore, is that if a bank pays a cheque on the assumption that all indorsements on it are valid, but one or more indorsements are in fact forgeries, the bank is put in the same position as if the indorsements had been valid, provided that it acts in good faith and in the ordinary course of business. It is important to note that the protection given by the section is confined to "forged or unauthorised indorsements"; irregular but genuine indorsements do not fall within the section.

A bank which pays in obviously suspicious circumstances will lose the protection of s.60 if it pays the instrument without a proper inquiry, because payment will not be in the ordinary course of business. The question of what is in the ordinary course of business is a question of fact to be determined in the light of custom in the banking community. In *Auchteroni & Co v. Midland Bank Ltd* (1828) a bill paid over the counter for £876.9s was held to have been paid in the course of business, but it was suggested that a different course might have been adopted if an office boy or tramp had presented a cheque for a large amount. In *Baines v. National Provincial Bank Ltd* (1927) a cheque paid five minutes after closing time was within the ordinary course of business because the time limits during which the bank is open to do business with the public are for its own convenience.

Where the indorsement of cheques is required by a paying bank (since the Cheques Act 1957 this does not include cheques paid in for the credit of the account of the payee) the cheque must be indorsed by or under the authority of the proper person if the paying bank is to be protected under s.60. If an irregularity in the indorsement is disregarded or overlooked by the paying bank it will have difficulty in relying on the section.

There is a duty on the part of the bank to know the signatures of its customers in their capacity as drawers of cheques, but a bank is not taken to know whether other persons' signatures on the cheque are genuine and the deception of a bank by a forgery of such other signatures does not necessarily involve breach of duty or negligence; thus the bank can debit the customer's account with the amount of the cheque it has paid. Where a bank loses the protection of s.60 it bears both the loss of the amount paid itself and cannot debit its customer's account, and is liable to the true owner of the cheque. Neither the right to possession of the cheque, nor the property in it, is divested out of the true owner by the forgery of the indorsement.

The protection under s.60 is limited to the banker on whom the cheque is drawn.

Protection under the Bills of Exchange Act 1882, s.80
Section 80 provides that, where a bank on which a crossed cheque is drawn pays it in good faith and without negligence, the bank paying the cheque is placed in the same position and has the same protection as if the payment of the cheque had been made to the true owner.

Where payment of a cheque bearing a forged indorsement is made strictly in accordance with ss. 60 and 80, the payment is technically a payment in due course, and not only discharges the drawee bank from liability to the true owner of the cheque but, if the cheque has been either constructively or actually delivered to the payee, the payment also discharges the drawer from liability on the cheque itself and for the debt represented by the cheque under the transaction for which it was drawn. In *Charles* v. *Blackwell* (1877) it was held that the payee cannot sue the drawer on the cheque or in respect of the underlying transaction after the cheque has technically been paid by a paying bank which is protected by s.60

Protection under the Cheques Act 1957, s.1
The protection afforded by the Cheques Act 1957, s. 1 is additional to that given by the Bills of Exchange Act 1882, ss. 60 and 80, so the paying bank is entitled to rely on all or any of these provisions if sued by the true owner of a cheque.

Section 1 gives protection to the paying bank if it pays a cheque in good faith and in the ordinary course of business when the cheque is not indorsed or is irregularly indorsed, but it is questionable whether this protection extends to payments made across the counter to a person other than the payee himself, so that the paying bank is apparently only protected if it makes payment to the payee (if the cheque is uncrossed) or to another bank. By a circular issued by the Committee of London Clearing Banks in 1957, an indorsement is still required where cheques are cashed or exchanged across the counter. A paying bank which departs from this practice may find it difficult to establish that it paid the cheque in the ordinary course of business; it would then be unable to obtain the protection of s. 1 if it paid someone not entitled to payment, i.e. a thief. This section is necessary because normally cheques are presented for payment by a collecting bank and the paying bank has no means of discovering whether the payee of the cheque is the collecting bank's customer or is a third person in whose favour the payee should have indorsed it. But the protection extends beyond situations where the cheque is collected for a third party to whom the payee has transferred it to cases where the third person's title to the cheque is void or voidable and the cheque has not been indorsed at all or the indorsement, although genuine, is irregular in form. Section 1 would also seem to extend to forged indorsements if they are irregular in form, but only so as to protect the paying bank against the irregularity. For protection against the consequences of an indorsement's being a forgery, the bank must rely on the Bills of Exchange Act 1882, ss. 60 and 80.

The protection of the collecting bank

The collecting bank is now protected by the Cheques Act 1957, s.4, and unless a bank can bring itself within the conditions of the section, it is liable for conversion or for money had and received if the person from whom it receives cheques for collection has no title or a defective title to them. The collecting bank is therefore afforded a means of avoiding claims for liability in conversion to which it would otherwise have no defence.

Components of the defence

The Cheques Act 1957, s.4, confers protection on a banker if the collecting bank acts in good faith and without negligence. These requirements are distinct. A thing is done in good faith where it is in fact done honestly, whether it is done negligently or not. The onus of proving the absence of negligence is on the bank which seeks to rely on the section. The collecting bank does not owe a contractual duty to the true owner of the cheque but will still be liable in conversion if it can prove that it acted without negligence: this means that it will be liable to the true owner of the cheque if it took proper care to protect the interests of the true owner, apart from the interests of the customer for whom collection is made. The test of negligence has been formulated in a number of cases and in *Lloyds Bank Ltd* v. *E. G. Savory & Co* (1933) it was held that the absence of negligence is to be determined by reference to the practice of reasonable men carrying on the business of bankers in such a manner that they and others are protected against fraud. In *Marfani & Co* v. *Midland Bank* (1968) this test was modified; the court held that it was necessary to look at all the circumstances at the time of the acts complained of and whether under the circumstances a reasonable banker, having the information about his customer which he as a reasonable banker should possess, would have suspected that the customer was not the true owner of the cheque.

Where therefore there is something on the face of the cheque or in the quality and the behaviour of the customer for whom the cheque is collected which should put the bank on inquiry, the bank is in breach of its duty to the true owner of the cheque if it fails to make proper inquiries. It is not a defence for the bank to suggest that if proper precautions had been taken the inquiries would not have revealed anything suspicious.

The courts have held various acts or omissions on the part of the bank to amount to negligence. The following cases merely serve as an indication as to whether the transactions or the circumstances of a particular case will amount to negligence.

The bank is under an obligation to see that everything is apparently in order when it receives the cheque for payment and presents it for collection, and if the circumstances in which the customer came into possession of the cheque should cause the bank to entertain suspicions as to his title to it, the bank must clear up those suspicions by making all proper inquiries before it presents the cheque for payment. In *Lloyds Bank Ltd* v. *E. B. Savory & Co* (1933) bearer cheques drawn by a firm of stockbrokers and intended to be delivered to another firm of stockbrokers were paid into the personal account of a housewife at Redhill as a result of her husband, a clerk employed by the drawers, paying the cheques in at the city branch of Lloyds Bank with instructions to credit her account at Lloyds' Redhill branch. On discovery of the frauds, the drawers brought an action against Lloyds Bank for money had and received. The defence pleaded by the bank, that it had acted with due care, failed when it was shown that it had not undertaken a full inquiry into the circumstances as laid down in the bank rule book; it had failed, on the opening of the wife's account at Redhill, to inquire who the husband's employers were or the nature of his occupation. This failure, together with its City branch's failure to inquire how the husband came to have possession of the cheques before instructing its Redhill branch to credit them to his wife's account, resulted in the bank's being held negligent since, as a single legal entity, it was responsible for the collective acts and omissions of its employees.

A more flexible view was adopted in *Marfani & Co Ltd* v. *Midland Bank Ltd* (1968) where an employee of the plaintiff company obtained from it a cheque for £3,000 drawn in favour of one Eliaszade. The employee, by pretending to be the payee, opened a current account at a branch of the Midland Bank, which obtained a favourable reference for Eliaszade after the account was opened from another longstanding customer of the bank. The bank collected a cheque for Eliaszade who withdrew all the money from his account and absconded. The court accepted that the bank had acted in accordance with current banking practice and was not negligent in failing to ask for further evidence of the employee's identity or to enquire as to his employment. Moreover, it did not constitute any lack of reasonable care if, before opening an account for a customer, the bank refrained from making inquiries which would probably not have revealed the customer's dishonest intention.

In *Lumsden* v. *London Trustee Savings Bank* (1971) the bank was held negligent for not fully establishing the customer's credentials when the account was opened, the bank's having trusted the customer because he said he had professional qualifications and appeared respectable. The bank would merely have had to inspect a telephone directory in order to verify the information given by the customer, namely that he was a retail chemist who carried on a business at a stated address.

The bank's duty to enquire is a continuous one, and arises every time a transaction occurs which is apparently out of harmony with the description of the customer's business or occupation given by him or otherwise inconsistent with the normal manner of conducting his account. In *Nu-Stilo Footwear Ltd* v. *Lloyds Bank Ltd* (1956) the plaintiff company employed M as its secretary. M opened an account at the defendant bank in the name of B, saying that he was a freelance agent and giving his real name as a referee. The bank followed up the reference by telephone and acting as his own referee M said that B had recently begun a business and was expected to do well within a few years. The court gave judgment for the plaintiff company on the ground that the amounts paid to B were inconsistent with the occupation of a freelance agent newly started in business, and the bank was therefore under a duty to inquire as to the authenticity and origin of the cheques every time a cheque for a substantial amount was paid into B's account for collection.

The strict attitude of the courts is illustrated by its decision in *Baker* v. *Barclays Bank Ltd* (1955) in which Baker and Bainbridge were trading in partnership under the name Modern Confections. Bainbridge misap-propriated nine cheques amounting to about £1,160 payable to the partnership. He indorsed the cheques and handed them to one Jeffcott, an insurance agent, who paid them into his account at Barclays Bank for collection. Jeffcott further paid in cheques payable to Bainbridge personally who had indorsed them. The bank manager on inquiry was assured that Jeffcott was paying in cheques for his friend Bainbridge who was the sole proprietor of Modern Confections and had just commenced business and was using Jeffcott's bank account temporarily before opening an account in his own name. In an action for conversion by the other partner, Baker, the bank was held to have been negligent in not making further and fuller enquiries. The bank manager should not have been satisfied by the reasons given for cheques in the name of a third party being paid into its customer's account and in the circumstances the manager should have made enquiries from Bainbridge personally.

In *Marquess of Bute* v. *Barclays Bank Ltd* (1954) the plaintiff employed one McGaw as manager of certain sheep farms on the Island of Bute. McGaw resigned in April 1949, but in September the Department of Agriculture for Scotland sent him warrants totalling £546 in respect of hill sheep subsidies which McGaw had claimed on the Marquess of Bute's behalf four months before his resignation. The warrants were forwarded by the Post Office to McGaw, who opened an account with the defendant bank, and after references in respect of him had been checked, the bank allowed him to draw against the warrants. The warrants were payable to "Mr D. McGaw Kerrylamont, Rothesay, Bute" but immediately after were added in parentheses the words "for the Marquess of Bute". The Marquess claimed the amounts of the warrants in an action for damages for conversion. The court held that, in order to succeed in a claim for conversion, the claimant need only establish that, at the material time, he was entitled to immediate possession of the subject matter; this the plaintiff in this particular case was able to do. In any event the test as to true ownership is the intention of the drawer. The Department of Agriculture knew that the subsidies were due to the plaintiff and had indicated their intention in the words in parentheses.

The bank's duty is obviously less stringent where a series of cheques are paid into the customer's account for collection over a considerable period of time and in *Crumplin* v. *London Joint Stock Bank Ltd* (1913) nine third party cheques were collected by the bank over a period of two years but the court held the bank had not been negligent.

Where a bank collects cheques drawn payable "to A for B" or "to A on behalf of B" or "to the account of B" the question which the courts have had to deal with is whether the bank can collect the instrument to the account of A.

Contributory negligence

In *Lumsden* v. *London Trustee Savings Bank* (1971) the plaintiffs brought an action for the conversion of certain cheques. The court held that the Law Reform (Contributory Negligence) Act 1945 applied not only to actions for negligence but also to other torts, including the tort of conversion, so that if the plaintiffs are contributorily negligent in facilitating a fraud, the damages recoverable by them must be proportionally reduced. The decision has now been given statutory force by the Banking Act 1979, s. 49, and so in future loss may be apportioned by the court in proportion to the blameworthiness of the respective parties.

The collecting bank as a holder for value

If a bank allows a customer to draw against an uncleared cheque it may claim to be entitled to credit the amount of the cheque when it is honoured in favour of itself. In *Capital & Counties Bank* v. *Gordon* (1903) the bank, following normal practice, placed the amount of the cheques to the credit of its customer and allowed him to draw against that amount, the bank afterwards receiving payment from the drawee bank. The court held that the bank, having credited the cheques to its customer's account before receiving the proceeds, did not collect the cheques on behalf of its customer but received it on its own behalf as holder for value. The question which arises is whether a bank can become a holder in value of a cheque where the customer of the collecting bank has obtained the cheque by fraud against which the customer has already drawn. In *Westminster Bank* v. *Zang* (1966) the court held a bank can only become a holder for value if it can show cheques drawn by the customer were paid which would have been dishonoured had the cheques in question not been paid in.

The collecting banker's lien on cheques

The case of *Westminster Bank Ltd* v. *Zang* (1966) gave the Court of Appeal an opportunity to interpret the effect of the Cheques Act 1957, s. 2. In that case the defendant, having lost heavily at gaming, borrowed £1,000 from a friend, Tilley, and gave him his cheque in exchange. The loan was made out of money belonging to a company which Tilley controlled, and he subsequently paid the unindorsed cheque to the credit of the company's account, contrary to the rules of the clearing banks, which require that if an instrument is rendered for the credit of an account other than that of the ostensible payee, it should be indorsed. The cheque was dishonoured and the collecting bank surrendered it to Tilley for the purpose of enabling him to bring an action against the drawer. The action failed, and the bank then took redelivery of the cheque from Tilley and commenced an action against the drawer, claiming to be a holder for value of the cheque by virtue of the Cheques Act 1957, s.2. The House of Lords held that, in order that a bank might plead s.2, it was necessary that the cheque should be delivered to the bank for credit of the account of the payee of the cheque unless he had indorsed it. The bank therefore lost its lien, and the only title it could have by the redelivery of the cheque to it by Tilley was that of a holder for value (assuming that it gave value) but it could not in any case be a holder in due course because when it took the cheque back from Tilley it had notice that the cheque had already been dishonoured. The court further said that a bank may have rights in the cheque as a holder for value or as a holder in due course only if it retained possession or, if for whatever reason it relinquished possession, if it reserved its rights.

RECOVERY OF AMOUNTS INCORRECTLY PAID

Money paid by a bank under a mistake of fact can be recovered in certain limited circumstances. The bank can recover when the recipient knew that he had no right to the money paid by the bank but it is not essential for the bank to prove that he has such knowledge. An example of bad faith on the part of the recipient is provided in *Kendal* v. *Wood* (1870), where a cotton spinner, W, had dealings with X, a cotton dealer. K entered into partnership with W at a time when the latter owed money to X. During the partnership, unknown to K, W appropriated £1,000 owing to the partnership and used it to pay his private debt to X. On the partnership being later dissolved, K paid £4,000 to X in settlement of the partnership debt. K then discovered the misappropriation by W and sought to recover the £1,000 from X. The court held that because X had known that he was receiving partnership money and that W was exceeding his authority in making the payment, he had accepted the money at his peril and K was entitled to recover the money.

For the plaintiff to recover money paid under a mistake of fact, the mistake must be one arising between the party paying and the party receiving the money. In *Chambers* v. *Miller* (1862) a bank paid a cheque in cash over the counter to the payee, but before he left the bank it was discovered that there were not sufficient funds in the drawer's account to meet the cheque. The court held that the mistake arose between the bank and its customer, and therefore the bank could not insist on the payee's repaying the money.

The question of recovery of money paid under a mistake of fact may arise where a paying bank seeks to recover money paid out on a cheque on which an indorsement has been forged. In the leading case of *London and River Plate Bank* v. *Bank of Liverpool* (1896) a bill drawn in Montevideo on the plaintiffs in London, on which indorsements were forged, was presented and paid by them to the defendants. The forgeries on the bill were discovered some months later and an action brought to recover the money as paid under a mistake of fact. Mathew J held that the amount was not recoverable and gave judgment for the defendants. It was agreed that there was no evidence of negligence on the part of the plaintiffs and that the defendants had acted in good faith. Neither the loss of the recipients' opportunity to give notice of dishonour nor any actual prejudice or damage to the innocent holder need be proved to enable him to keep the money and resist a claim for repayment. If he has held the money for such time that his position may have been affected he may keep the money.

The question that arises finally is whether the existence of a forged signature, whether of the drawer, acceptor or indorser on a bill which is paid by the banker precludes it from recovering the money from an innocent recipient or his banker. This question came before the English courts for the first time in *National Westminster Bank Ltd* v. *Barclays Bank International Ltd* (1974). In that case the second defendant, one Ismail, was a Nigerian businessman anxious to move substantial funds out of Nigeria, contrary to strict exchange control regulations. He bought at a premium a cheque for £8,000 drawn on the National Westminster Bank, at a branch in London, but, before paying for it, he sent it to his own bank in London, Barclays Bank International, for special collection. The cheque was duly presented and paid and Ismail paid for it in Nigeria. A fortnight later it was established that the cheque form had been stolen and it had been completed as a forgery, apparently bearing the signature of a customer of National Westminster to whom the cheque form had been issued. National Westminster brought an action for recovery of the money. The plaintiffs were held to be entitled to recover in view of the suspicious circumstances in which the cheque had been obtained; the defendants could not regard the payment of the cheque as a representation that it was genuine and a bank does not by paying a cheque make any representation to the recipient as to the genuineness of its customer's signature thereon.

The *National Westminster Bank Ltd* v. *Barclays Bank International Ltd* case was followed in *Barclays Bank Ltd* v. *W. J. Simms* (1979), a case concerning a mistake of fact, not forgery. In the *Simms* case the judge had to decide whether a bank which overlooks its customers instructions to stop payment of a cheque and consequently pays the cheque on presentation can recover the amount from the payee as having been paid under a mistake of fact. The judge followed the earlier cases and held that, where a person paid money to another under a mistake of fact which caused him to make the payment, he was prima facie entitled to recover it as money paid under a mistake of fact. However, the claim will fail if the payer intends that the payee should have the money at all events, or the payment has been made for good consideration and, in particular, if the money discharges a debt owed to the payee or if the payee changes his position in good faith.

Where a party seeks to recover money paid out under a mistake of fact he can recover the amount paid either from the person to whom the money was paid or from anyone who holds that money by derivation from the recipient, provided the money can still be identified. For this reason, too, the customer of the collecting bank can always be compelled to restore the amount collected if he has since drawn it out of his account with the collecting bank. In *Banque Belge* v. *Hambrouck* (1921) H fraudulently obtained a number of cheques from his employer, which he paid into his own bank account and his bank collected the amounts from the employer's bank. H then withdrew these sums by cheques in favour of his mistress, D, who paid the cheques into her own bank account. The employer's bank sought to recover the money from D, asking for a declaration that the £300 placed to her credit was the bank's property. It was argued that, as D took the money without notice of H's wrongs, she acquired a title valid against the world. However, this argument was rejected since it overlooked the fact that only a person who gave consideration and had no notice of the source of the money was protected, not a volunteer.

PROBLEMS

1. To what extent do the rules in the Banking Act 1979 relating to the requirements with which an institution must comply in order to carry on a banking business differ from the rules formulated by the courts at common law?

2. Explain the legal nature of amounts held by a bank to the credit of a customer's account.

3. What rights does a bank have to recover amounts overdrawn by a customer without pursuing an action in the courts?

4. Explain the duties owed by the bank to its customer. Does the bank owe any duty to a third party who is not its customer and, if so, what is the scope of this duty?

5. What are the duties owed by a customer to his bank?

6. Explain the nature of a negotiable instrument and the conditions it must fulfil to be recognised as negotiable in law.

7. What requirements must a holder satisfy if he is to enjoy the protection granted to a holder in due course?

8. To what extent will the rights of a holder in due course of a bill of exchange be defeated by a defect in the title of the transferor? What are the types of defects from which the holder in due course enjoys protection?

9. Explain the liability of the parties to a bill of exchange and the extent to which they will be estopped from denying their liability.

10. What are the types of crossings found on cheques and what effect do they have?

11. To what extent do paying and collecting banks enjoy statutory protection for wrongful payment of a cheque?

CHAPTER EIGHT

The Law of Insurance

OBJECTIVES

It is proposed in this chapter to examine the law relating to insurance contracts. In particular the chapter deals with:

(a) the formation of an insurance contract, including:
   (i) conditions and warranties in contracts of insurance;
   (ii) cover notes;
   (iii) the insurance policy;

(b) the necessity for an insurable interest and the nature of such an interest, including the time when the insurer must actually have an interest in insurable property;

(c) the nature of the risk including:
   (i) the period of insurance;
   (ii) conditions and limits of insurance;
   (iii) the proximity of the loss;

(d) the duty of the insured to disclose any material information, including:
   (i) the effect of non-disclosure or misrepresentation;
   (ii) the duty of disclosure in marine insurance contracts;

(e) the amounts of the premium and the measure of indemnity;

(f) special rules relating to marine insurance, including:
   (i) different kinds of marine insurance;
   (ii) the duty to disclose in marine insurance cases.

THE CONTRACT OF INSURANCE

A contract of insurance is one under which the insurer agrees to indemnify the insured against the loss he may suffer on the occurrence of certain events on which the insurer's liability is to arise. The Marine Insurance Act 1906, for example, provides that a contract of marine insurance is one whereby the insurer undertakes to indemnify the insured in a manner and to the extent agreed against losses of ships and goods as the result of marine risks. The Act does not, however, provide whether the insured is to be indemnified by a monetary payment or by a substitute. However, in the case of an insurance on life or against accident the insured may be entitled to receive a definite sum of money irrespective of the loss sustained or, alternatively, an equivalent benefit in services. There is nothing to prevent the parties from reaching an agreement in the policy on the value of item insured and, in the absence of fraud, the insured will be entitled to recover the agreed value in the event of a total loss, or a proportionate amount in the event of a partial loss. Although agreed valued policies are not common in the case of the insurance of goods and buildings, the Marine Insurance Act 1906 expressly provides for agreed value policies covering marine risks. An agreed value policy is one which specifies the value of the subject–matter insured as agreed between the parties and the value so fixed is, as between the insurer and the insured, conclusive evidence of the insurable value of the subject–matter.

The liability of the insurers to indemnify the insured is usually limited to a specified amount known as the "sum assured". If the value of the item lost exceeds this amount, the insurers are only liable to pay the total amount for which the subject–matter has been insured, but if the value is less, they are bound to pay, except in the case of a value policy, its actual value. The principle of indemnity operates to limit their liability to the loss actually suffered by the insured, for their undertaking is to pay that loss only.

Formation of an insurance contract

It is not proposed to deal here with the general principles of contract law which apply to insurance policies in the same way as other contracts, but to make those points which are especially relevant to insurance contracts.

The principles of contract law require that there must be a valid offer and acceptance. In insurance contracts, where the insurers accept the insured's proposal subject to the payment of a certain premium, the contract becomes binding only on the tender to the insurer of that premium. An undertaking to insure subject to the payment of a premium is therefore a counter–offer, accepted by the insured on the payment of a premium.

Where the insurers provisionally accept the risk subject to the premiums being paid within a fixed time, a binding contract is concluded on the acceptance of the risk, although the performance of the insurers' obligations is contingent on a receipt of the premium.

Whilst an acceptance of an offer must be given within a reasonable time in order to constitute a binding contract, an offer by the insurers is also subject to an implied condition that the nature of risk does not change materially prior to the acceptance. An offer to insure, therefore, will be treated as having lapsed if, before the acceptance, circumstances are altered to such an extent that the nature of the risk has increased substantially.

A contract of insurance does not in English law have to be in writing, although the Marine Insurance Act 1906, s.22, renders a contract of marine insurance inadmissible in evidence unless it is embodied in a marine insurance policy. The policy must specify the name of the insured or his agent who affects the policy on his behalf and the subject–matter to be insured has to be identified with reasonable certainty, although the extent of the insured's interest in the subject–matter need not be specified (Marine Insurance Act 1906, s. 26). Finally the policy must be signed by or on behald of the insurer. In Scottish law, however, an insurance contract must be in writing in order to be valid.

Conditions and warranties

Effect of breach of condition

A breach of condition by either party gives the innocent party a right either to avoid the contract or to treat the contract as continuing but to sue for damages thereby treating the breach of condition as one of warranty.

Warranties

The tendency in insurance law has been to treat a warranty in the same way as a condition. The Marine Insurance Act 1906, ss. 33–35, provide that a warranty is an express or implied promise by the insured to do something whereby the existence of a particular state of facts is affirmed. A warranty is defined in s. 33 of the Act as a condition which must be complied with precisely, whether or not its requirements be material to the risk. If it is not complied with, the insurer is discharged from his liability from the date of that breach. In *Dawson* v. *Bonnin* (1922) a misrepresentation by the insured as to the place where a vehicle was garaged was held to be immaterial, but the insured could not recover under the policy since he had warranted it to be true.

The burden of proving that a warranty has been broken is on the insurers.

The policy of insurance

The insured who wishes to take out an insurance policy will either negotiate directly the terms on which the insurers are willing to grant him cover for the types of risks against which he wants protection, or will instruct an insurance broker to arrange insurance on his behalf within certain limits, (i.e. as to the rates of premium and the risks to be insured). An insurance broker who proposes insurance to marine underwriters or to members of Lloyd's will write the details of the insurance required on "the slip", and an underwriter who accepts the risk will write on the slip the amount of the risk he is willing to undertake and will sign or initial it. The broker will take the slip to successive underwriters until the whole of the risk has been covered, and he will then send the insured a memorandum of the insurance effected.

A slip, unlike a cover note, is an acceptance of the proposal and a contract of marine insurance is completed when the slip is initialled by the last underwriter, and the risk is fully covered. Until the last underwriter has signed the slip the previous underwriters can vary the terms on which they are willing to grant cover. The contract of insurance can thus be made subject to identical terms for all underwriters. When the contract is complete between the parties neither party can vary the terms of the agreement without the assent of the other.

Cover notes

The applicant may want immediate protection pending the acceptance of his proposal and prior to the issue of a formal policy. The insurers may be willing to provide such cover on condition that they are free to withdraw from the temporary bargain after inquiries have been made. The cover note usually states that it is to be in force for a limited period of time or until a policy is delivered unless the insurers give notice to the insured that they had decided not to accept his proposal.

The issue of the policy

A contract of insurance is embodied in a policy issued by the insurers. If the insurance is undertaken by Lloyd's, the policy will be issued by the Lloyd's signing office. The rule of contract law is that where the terms of a contract are reduced to writing, oral evidence is inadmissible to vary or contradict it. In insurance contracts, however, the mere fact that a policy has been issued to the insured is not necessarily evidence of the whole contract and where the policy contains terms inconsistent or contradictory with a prior contract the insured or the insurers may seek an order of rectification.

Self-renewing policies

Insurance policies are not renewable by the insured as of right after the expiration their original term unless they are expressed to be so renewable; life and deferred annuity policies, on the other hand, are presumed to be so renewable. Where there is a provision for renewal, the policy is renewed by the insured paying the renewal premium within the period specified in the policy.

Construction of technical terms

A policy of insurance is to be construed in accordance with the same rules as any other contract. Terms are therefore to be construed in their natural and ordinary sense, unless they are technical words and phrases, which must be understood in their proper sense. The policy as a whole will be taken into account in determining the meaning of words and phrases.

THE INSURABLE INTEREST

In insurance law the word interest is used to describe the insured's interest in the subject–matter of the insurance and, because the contract of insurance is generally an indemnity undertaking by the insurer, he is not obliged to pay any amount under the policy if the insured has no interest in the subject–matter at the time when the insurance is taken out and at the time of the loss. The courts tend to construe the terms of a policy so as to necessitate that the insured has an interest in the subject–matter as a condition precedent to his claim. However, the terms of the policy may indicate an intention by the insurer to pay although the insured has no interest at the time of the loss and in such circumstances the policy will be valid. In *Thomas* v. *National Farmers Union Mutual Insurance Society* (1961) the tenant of a farm insured hay and straw against fire. The policy expressly provided that it should cease to cover any property which passed from the tenant to a third party. The tenant moved from the farm and the property in the hay and straw passed to the landlord by virtue of the Agricultural Holdings Act 1948. The hay and straw were subsequently destroyed but it was held that the insured could recover under the policy although he had ceased to have an interest in the subject–matter of the policy.

In some cases the insured may be required to have an insurable interest in the property either by the terms of the contract or by a statutory provision. Where a statute requires the insured to have an insurable interest in the property or the event insured against, and this is lacking, the contract will be illegal and void. An express provision in the contract dispensing with the need for the insured to have an interest in the subject–matter will not remove the defects and the contract is unenforceable by both parties. In *Macaura* v. *Northern Assurance Co* (1925) it was held that a shareholder cannot insure assets owned by the company of which he is a shareholder and since the contract of insurance was one of indemnity the insured had to prove an interest in the subject–matter of the insurance at the time of the loss.

There are also a number of statutory provisions which require the insured to obtain insurance in the property or against the occurrence of an event. The Marine Insurance Act 1906, ss. 4–7, provide that a contract of marine insurance will be deemed to be a gaming or wagering contract and will therefore be void where the insured has no insurable interest in the marine adventure. The insured must therefore have a legal or equitable interest in the property, adventure or other subject–matter in question and, consequently, must be in a position to benefit by the avoidance of the risks insured against or to suffer loss or damage by the occurrence of those risks. Moreover, the insured must be interested in the subject–matter insured both at the time the insurance was taken out by him and in general and at the time the risk occurs or loss is suffered by the insured. If the insured had no interest in the subject–matter at the time of the loss he cannot subsequently acquire any interest after he becomes aware of the loss. The Marine Insurance Act 1906 provides that, where an insured obtains a contract of marine insurance without having a bona fide interest in the safety, or the ship, or the subject–matter the contract will be deemed to be a contract by way of "gambling in loss by maritime perils" and the insured will be guilty of an offence.

The nature of an insurable interest

The insured must have an enforceable interest in the subject–matter and it has been held that a party has an interest if he will gain an advantage on the happening of a particular event or suffer a loss if it fails to materialise. In *Wilson* v. *Jones* (1967) the plaintiff, a shareholder in the Atlantic Telegraph Company, was held entitled to have an insurable interest in the anticipated profits of a business adventure and the resulting loss was caused by the perils insured against. In *National Filtering Oil Co* v. *Citizens Insurance Co of Missouri* (1887) it was said that if the insured has a right in or against the property which a court will enforce and that right or the value of that right is dependent on the existence of the subject–matter then the insured has an insurable interest. Therefore, a contractual or proprietary right, whether legal or equitable, is essential to found an insurable interest, e.g. an owner of goods has an insurable interest in the profits he can expect to make from a sale of those goods.

An insurable interest must also be a pecuniary interest or capable of valuation in money. The mere fact that the interest cannot easily be valued in monetary terms is no bar to obtaining an insurance cover. Thus although the profits of a trade may be difficult to value the interest is insurable; profits or the value of shares held by a shareholder are insurable interests.

A person has an insurable interest if he has possession of the subject–matter insured, even though the possession is unlawful. A bailee has an insurable interest in the goods in his possession insofar as he is liable to the owner if the goods are lost or destroyed. However, the mere possession of goods without a corresponding legal duty or responsibility for the safety of the goods does not give the person in possession an insurable interest. Thus, where the insured allowed timber belonging to a company to lie on his land without owing any duty to the owner for the safe custody of the timber, it was held that the land owner had insurable interest in the timber (*see Macaura* v. *Northern Assurance Co* (1925)).

Time when interest must attach

The nature of the interest which the insured must possess in the subject–matter is similar in the case of both statutory and contractual interests but a distinction has to be drawn. In cases where the contract between the insurer and the insured requires the insured to have an interest in the property or the adventure, it is the time of the loss which is important: the insured must be in a position to prove his interest in the property at the time of the loss if he is to recover. In the case of statutory provisions the time when the insured must possess the statutory interest depends on the wording of the statute. In *Dalby* v. *India and London Life* (1854) the Life Assurance Act 1774, which provides that no insurance will be affected where the insured "shall have no interest", was held to mean no interest at the time the insurance contract was made. The Marine Insurance Act 1906, s. 6 requires the insured also to have an interest in the subject–matter at the time of the loss, but he may nevertheless claim if someone else had an interest when the insurance was affected and he has later acquired that interest.

An insured may be entitled to insure interests other than his own, e.g. as trustee or executor although he cannot use this right to make a private gain. If a trustee or executor pays the premium personally he will be entitled to be reimbursed the amount of the premium when any insurance money is received, but must account for the balance received by him under the policy.

THE RISK

An insurer can only calculate his premium so he has a margin for a profit if he knows accurately the nature of the risk he is required to insure. Similarly, it is essential that the insured knows precisely the extent of his cover so that, if necessary, he can take out additional insurance.

An insurance policy will normally cover loss caused by any negligence of the insured or anyone else unless there is an express provision to the contrary in the policy. It is irrelevant whether the negligence is that of the insured, his servants or a stranger. An insurance of goods in transit will normally cover negligence by the carrier, his servants or agents. Whilst the insured is usually able to recover for loss caused by negligence, he cannot recover for any loss caused by his own wilful misconduct, i.e. where he intentionally sets fire to his house or scuttles a ship. There are certain implied limitations on the liability of the insurer in addition to the exclusion of losses caused by the wilful misconduct of the insured, namely normal wear and tear in normal circumstances in respect of the goods insured, inherent vice of the subject–matter insured and risks that cannot lawfully be insured against. In *British Marine Insurance Co* v. *Gaunt* (1921) a policy which insured "all risks" or "all losses" was held not to include loss or damage caused by wear and tear, inherent vice, own act of the insured or risks that it was not lawful to cover. However, since in that case the goods insured were damaged from an unknown cause the loss was held to fall within the policy.

"Loss" of subject–matter insured

All insurance policies place a limitation on the cover given, namely that the insurers are only liable for loss of or damage to the subject–matter of the insurance. However, under a marine policy where the adventure is insured, the insurance extends not only to insurance of the goods but also to their safe arrival. This rule has no application to non–marine policies on goods. The mere fact that recovery is unlikely does not constitute a loss under a non–marine policy, but does constitute a constructive total loss under the Marine Insurance Act 1906. In *Webster* v. *General Accident Insurance Co* (1953) the insured parted with possession of a motor–car to a rogue on the fraudulent representation that he had a buyer for it. The rogue sold the car by auction and misapplied the proceeds. The insured knew where the car was, but was told by the police that recovery would be impossible. The court held that there was a loss of the car within the meaning of a policy, the case turning on the question whether recovery is uncertain after the insured has taken all reasonable steps.

Period covered by insurance

The general rule is that a period measured "from" or "after" a named day does not include the day named. This rule has been applied to time policies of insurance and in *Isaacs* v. *Royal* (1870) a policy giving cover for six months from "14th February until 14th August" was held to exclude 14th February but to include the 14th August. A policy for a fixed period covers all losses within that period up to the amount insured, e.g. if a number of fires occur, the insurer must pay in respect of each, subject to a maximum liability equal to the sum insured.

In marine insurance it is common to insure, not for a fixed period, but for a named voyage. The question to be asked is where are goods to be transported and not when does transit commence. In *Crow's Transport* v. *Phoenix Assurance Co* (1965) goods were insured against all risks in transit by a firm of hauliers. The goods were delivered when the drivers were resting and were stolen. The court held that the goods were "in transit" within the meaning of the policy. It was said that if you take a parcel to the post office or to a railway station and hand it over, the goods are in transit from the moment the post office or the railway accept them. The commencement of the transit is the moment of acceptance by the carrier unless the policy otherwise provides.

Where the contract is governed by the Carriage of Goods by Road Act 1965, s. 17(1), the carrier is liable for loss or damage to goods from the time when he receives them until the goods are delivered to their destination. Similarly, the Lloyd's standard form of policy for international carriers covers the carrier of goods against loss from the moment he takes over the goods.

The question as to when transit ends may be difficult. The Marine Insurance Act 1906 provides that the risk on goods will continue until they are safely unloaded in the customary manner and within a reasonable time at the port of discharge. Similarly, in a number of cases involving the carriage of goods on land, the courts have held that a policy of transit on goods covers "loading and unloading".

Deviation

A deviation which is wholly unrelated to the usual and ordinary method of pursuing an adventure would prevent the goods from being "in transit" within the meaning of the insurance policy. The Marine Insurance Act 1906 (Sched. I, r. 5—rules for construction of policy) provides that where a ship deviates without lawful excuse from the voyage contemplated under the policy, the insurer is discharged from liability from the time of deviation.

PROXIMITY RULE

In insurance law, only the proximate cause, namely the direct or dominant cause of the loss is of concern to the insurer. If the proximate cause of the loss is within the risks covered, the insurers are liable in respect of the loss, but the insurers will not be liable if the proximate cause of the loss is within the excepted perils. A loss may be caused by the combined effect of a number of causes but for purposes of insurance law a single dominant cause responsible for the loss must be established. In *Fidelity and Casualty Company of New York* v. *Mitchell* (1917) the appellents insured the respondent against bodily injury sustained accidentally which would prevent his continuing his profession. The respondent sprained his wrist and was disabled so that he could not work. The appellants paid him under the insurance for the disability but then refused to make further payments. The respondent, who was still disabled, sued under the policy. It was held that the respondent was entitled to recover under the policy and the disability to his wrist was due purely to the accident and not any other cause or illness to which the respondent might have been susceptible.

Where there is more than one proximate cause of the loss but one of these is an excepted peril then only one of the causes, namely the one under which the insurer is liable to indemnify the loss, will be treated as a proximate cause. In *Leyland Shipping Company Ltd* v. *Norwich Union Fire Insurance Society Ltd* (1918) a ship was insured against perils of the sea by a time policy which excluded liability for all consequences resulting from hostilities. The ship was torpedoed by a German submarine but taken into Havre harbour by tugs. The ship eventually sank in bad weather and the shipowners brought an action under the policy for loss caused by perils of the sea. The court held that the loss of the ship due to severe weather conditions was not an intervening event and the damage done by the torpedo was the proximate cause of the loss. The underwriters were therefore protected by excluding damage due to hostilities.

Rules for determining proximate cause

The proximity rule has been developed largely in marine cases, but does have general application. The courts will apply the following principles in order to determine the proximate cause of the loss, namely;

(*a*) the risk insured against must in fact operate to cause the loss. Thus the abandonment of a voyage through fear of capture is not loss by capture, or the danger of goods being lost by seizure is not loss by seizure;

(*b*) once the risk operates any further damage to the subject–matter due to efforts to check the progress of the danger is covered. The proximate cause of such damage is the risk insured against. Thus in *Symington* v. *Union Insurance of Canton* (1928) cork was insured against fire. A fire broke out and in order to prevent it spreading some of the cork was thrown into the sea. It was held that the loss of the cork was covered on the ground that damage by water was in consequence of the threat posed by the fire to the property and to the cork. Where the peril is so imminent that in order to avert the danger the goods themselves must be destroyed, then it is the original peril which is the cause of the loss;

(*c*) an accident facilitating the loss must be distinguished from an accident causing the loss. Thus where an air–raid facilitates the theft of goods from a building, it is the theft which is the proximate cause of the loss and not the air–raid;

(*d*) novus actus interveniens. Where human intervention after the peril insured against causes the loss, it is the intervention and not the insured peril which is the proximate cause of the loss. Thus where a man falls onto a railway track in a fit and is run over by a train it is the train and not the fit which is the proximate cause of the injury (*Lawrence* v. *Accidental Insurance Co* (1881));

(*e*) where injury or loss is caused by a human act which is followed by natural causes which contribute to the loss, the chain of causation is not broken (*Leyland Shipping Co* v. *Norwich Fire Insurance Society Ltd* (1918)).

Burden of proof

The burden of proof is on the insured to show that the proximate cause of loss was a peril insured against within the terms of the policy. The insured need not prove how the loss or damage occurred, but merely that it fell within one or other of the perils insured against. Thus, under a marine insurance policy which covered the usual perils of the sea but was warranted "free of capture" the insured was said to have discharged the burden of proof by proving that the vessel was at the bottom of the sea without proving that it had not been captured or sunk (*Macbeth* v. *King* (1916)).

Once the insured can produce a prima facie case, the burden is on the insurer to show that the loss was caused by an excepted peril and it was that which was the proximate cause of the loss.

NON-DISCLOSURE AND MISREPRESENTATION

Duty of disclosure

It is the duty of the insured to make a full disclosure to the insurer of all material facts. The contract of insurance is one of the utmost good faith.

If the insured knowingly conceals a material fact, this is a fraud on his part and the insurer, when he acquires knowledge of the matter, may elect to avoid the contract. The duty to disclose is not based on an implied term of the contract but on the nature of the contract, i.e. it is a contract uberrimae fidei and this applies to all contracts where there is a relationship of trust or confidence between the parties.

A contract affected by non–disclosure does not give rise to a claim for damages; the only remedy is for the insurer to avoid the contract, i.e. the insurer must elect either to continue with the contract and accept any further obligation, or risk imposed on him as a result of acquiring full knowledge of the facts or avoid the contract.

The duty of disclosure applies only to negotiations preceding the formation of the contract, but full disclosure may be made at any time until the contract is concluded. If the insurers' consent is necessary to renew the contract, any material facts which have arisen since the contract was first entered into need be disclosed.

Duty of disclosure under marine insurance

The Marine Insurance Act 1906, s. 18, provides that the insured must disclose to the insurer before a contract is concluded between them every material fact known to the insured or which he ought reasonably to know in the ordinary course of business. All facts which are likely to influence a "prudent insurer" in deciding whether or not to insure the risk, or fixing the premium are material. The insured is not, in the absence of express inquiry by the insurer, bound to seek out and reveal facts which he does not know, or to disclose facts which diminish the risk, or facts already within the knowledge of the insurer or presumed to be within his knowledge. The insurer is presumed to know matters of common notoriety and matters which an insurer in the ordinary course of business is presumed to know. The insured is not bound to disclose information into which the insurer ought to have made fuller inquiry under the circumstances and in the light of the knowledge the insurer possesses. In such circumstances, the insurer is deemed to have waived his right to fuller information. Finally, the insured need not disclose immaterial facts.

In order to determine what facts are material, the standard to be applied is the judgment of a prudent insurer (Marine Insurance Act 1906, s. 18(2)). The test is identical for both marine and non–marine insurance and the test of the prudent insurer is adopted by other statutory provisions (Road Traffic Act 1977). The mere fact that the insured thinks the facts are immaterial does not excuse disclosure on his part, although he may have acted in good faith. In *Joel* v. *Law Union & Crown Insurance Co* (1908) the insured failed to disclose certain information about the state of her health. The court held that the insured had not fraudulently concealed the state of her health but, considering all factors which may influence the decision of the insurers in deciding the terms of the insurance, or whether or not to undertake the risk, she should have disclosed all material facts about her health although the insured may have considered them to be irrelevant.

However, not every fact which increases the risk is material unless there is some probability that the insurer would attach some importance to it in assessing the premiums. It has been held that previous refusals by other insurance companies to insure the same or similar risks for the insured is material (*Locker & Woolf* v. *Western Australian Insurance* (1936)). The existence of other insurance against the same risk is also material (in the case of life or accident policies), as are any facts which render the subject–matter insured exceptionally liable to destruction by the peril insured against or the fact that the goods insured are of dangerous kind.

Misrepresentation

If a material fact which the insured represents to the insurer is untrue, the policy is voidable, whether or not the insured knew his statement to be untrue. The insured cannot argue that he acted in good faith and with honesty if the statement turns out to be false.

Where, however, a statement expressed by the insured depends on his state of mind, the mere fact that his belief is mistaken will not vitiate the policy. Thus, a statement made by the insured as to the state of his health is merely an opinion given to the best of his knowledge. The courts have said that in the case of life assurance policies, the misrepresentation of a matter of opinion must be fraudulent in order for it to avoid the contract. The Marine Insurance Act 1906, s. 20, however, provides that unless every representation made by the insured during negotiations for a marine policy are true, the insurer can avoid the contract, regardless of whether the representation is a fact or an opinion or expectation. A representation on a point of fact is true if it is substantially correct.

THE PREMIUM

The premium is the consideration for which the insurer will undertake to insure the risk. The consideration can be paid either by the payment of money or by a payment in kind, e.g. by two or more persons mutually undertaking to insure each other against losses. It is, however, more common for the payment of a premium to be in monetary form. The actual payment of the premium is not a necessary pre–condition for the creation of a binding insurance contract and the courts will not imply a term in the contract exempting the insurer from the risks until the premium is actually paid. The contract of insurance may, however, expressly require that the policy's taking effect and the payment of the premium be concurrent. The Marine Insurance Act 1906, s. 52, provides that the issue of the policy and the payment of the premium must be concurrent conditions and the insurer is not bound to issue the policy until the premium is paid.

Where the premium is payable periodically or the policy is renewable by payment of a further premium, insurance companies will usually send a notice of reminder to the insured and most policies allow a certain number of "days of grace" beyond the date of expiry of the insurance policy for payment of the renewal premium. If the premium is paid within the days of grace the policy will not be treated as lapsed and the insured will be covered against loss during those days.

THE MEASURE OF INDEMNITY

A claim for indemnity under the insurance policy is for an unliquidated sum. Where the policy is an agreed value policy, however, the measure of indemnity is the agreed value of the subject–matter of the insurance. In no case can the indemnity exceed the sum insured. Where the policy is expressed to be "subject to average" only that proportion of the amount insured which bears the same proportion to the loss as the sum insured bears to the real value of the subject–matter has to be paid. The measure of indemnity is calculated by assessing the value of the subject–matter at the place where the loss occurs on the date of the loss.

The Marine Insurance Act 1906, s. 16, has specific rules relating to the assessment of the measure of loss. It provides that, in the case of the insurance of a ship, the insurable value is the value of the ship at the commencement of the risk. In the case of the insurance of freight, the insurable value is the gross amount of the freight at the risk of the insured, plus the charges of insurance. In the case of the insurance of goods or merchandise, the insurable value is the prime cost of the property insured, plus the expenses of and incidental to shipping. The Act provides that the insured can recover in respect of a policy which is not an agreed value policy the full extent of the insurable value or, in the case of a value policy, to the full extent of the value fixed by the policy.

If there is a total loss of the subject–matter insured, the value recoverable in the case of a valued policy is the sum fixed by the policy, and in the case of any other policy the insurable value of the subject–matter. If, however, there is only a partial loss and the insured can purchase the goods on the open market, the amount recoverable is the market value of the goods. The Marine Insurance Act 1906, ss. 69–71, specifically provide the amounts recoverable by the insured where there is a partial loss but the amount recoverable depends on the nature of the subject–matter. Thus, where a ship is damaged but not lost the insured can recover a reasonable amount of the costs incurred in carrying out repairs, or if the ship is sold in its damaged state, the insured is entitled to be indemnified for the fall in the value of the ship caused by its condition of disrepair. The act provides separate rules for partial loss of goods or merchandise (Marine Insurance Act 1906, s. 71).

The salvage rule

If the subject–matter insured is not totally destroyed but remains wholly or in part in a deteriorated or damaged condition, the insured can only claim the value of the actual loss, unless all that remains of the subject–matter is surrendered by the insured by agreement between the parties. Under the Marine Insurance Act 1906 there is deemed to be a constructive total loss of the subject–matter of the ship or goods insured against if the insured is deprived of the possession of the subject–matter and cannot recover it because the cost of recovery would exceed the actual value of the subject–matter. In this case the insured cannot claim any benefit from what may be capable of salvage. Although the doctrime of constructive total loss does not apply to non–marine insurance, the doctrine of abandonment applies generally.

MARINE INSURANCE

The law relating to marine insurance is codified in the Marine Insurance Act 1906. In an export transaction the terms of the contract of sale provide whether the costs of marine insurance will be borne by the buyer or seller. If goods are sold on fob terms, the cost of insurance has to be borne by the buyer, although the seller may in fact agree to arrange the insurance for him. If the contract of sale is on cif terms, it is the duty of the seller to arrange the insurance and to pay for it but his only obligation is to take out a marine insurance policy which provides cover against the risks customarily covered in the particular trade in respect of the kind of cargo. The seller is not required to take out an all risks policy unless the parties expressly agree or it is a custom of the trade.

Kinds of marine insurance

1. Valued and unvalued policies

A valued policy under the Marine Insurance Act 1906, s. 27(2), is one which specifies the agreed value of the subject–matter to be insured whereas an unvalued policy states merely the maximum limit of the sum insured and leaves the insurable value of the goods to be ascertained subsequently (Marine Insurance Act 1906, s. 28). The difference between these two types of policy is that, in the case of a valued policy, the value fixed by the policy is conclusive of the insurable value of the subject insured, whereas in the case of an unvalued policy, the value of the goods insured has to be proved by the production of invoices, vouchers, estimates and other evidence. In the latter case the insurable value of the goods is prima facie the cost of the goods plus the expenses of shipping and any incidental costs. In a valued policy, the buyer's anticipated profits are normally included in the value declared by adding 10 or 15 per cent to the invoice value of the goods. The valued policies are more commonly used in export transactions these days.

2. Voyage, time and mixed policies

Under a voyage policy the subject–matter is insured in transport from one point to another, whereas under a time policy the subject–matter is insured for a fixed time. Under a mixed policy the goods are insured both for a particular journey and for a certain period of time.

In voyage policies it is necessary to define exactly when the goods are covered for loss or damage and when they cease to be so covered, for example the Marine Insurance Act expressly provides that where goods are insured "from the loading thereof" the risk does not attach until the goods are actually on board the ship and the insurer is not liable for them while they are in transit from the shore to the ship. The rule can, of course, be varied by incorporating a clause in the policy stating that the goods are covered for risks from shore to the ship.

A time policy is rarely used in export transactions, but the period for which the goods may now be covered under the voyage policy will not exceed 12 months unless otherwise stated, and if the ship is still on its voyage after the initial period for which the cover was provided has expired, the insurance cover may be extended to cover the full voyage by an additional premium being paid.

A mixed policy will cover land risks incidental to the sea voyage.

3. Floating policies

A floating policy will be used to insure goods where a number of similar export transactions are intended. The floating policy lays down the general conditions of insurance but does not give the details of an individual consignment intended to be covered. At the time the insurance policy is effected these particulars are usually unknown to the insured. The floating policy covers all shipments and the insured is required to declare any shipment with due expedition so that it can be effectively covered by the policy. The floating policy may contain a clause limiting the maximum risk covered by the policy per vessel. An insured who wishes to ship in excess of the limit per vessel will need to make separate arrangements for additional cover.

The floating policy is normally a valued policy. However, where a declaration of value is not made until after notice of loss or arrival of the goods, the policy must be treated as unvalued unless there are provisions for such a contingency in the policy.

4. Open covers

The open cover is again a method of effecting a general insurance for recurring shipments, the details of which are unknown when the insurance is effected, and again the insured is bound to declare all individual shipments unless the contract of insurance otherwise provides. The open cover is a document by which the insurer undertakes subsequently to issue duly executed floating or specific policies.

The open cover may be limited in time and may contain a maximum limit of the insurer's liability per vessel or location.

The difference between the floating policy and the open cover is that in the case of a floating policy the insured "buys" a fixed insurance cover which is written off as declarations of further shipments are made. In the case of open cover, the insurance does not run out but will cover every shipment falling within the terms of the cover made during the time limit.

5. Blanket policies

Where the insured does not want the inconvenience of declaring the particulars of shipment under a floating policy and open cover, i.e. where the value of the shipment is small and the duration of the voyage is short, the insured may take out a "blanket policy", in which case a lump sum premium will cover all the shipments instead of a premium at several rates.

Certificates of insurance, brokers' cover notes and letters of insurance

There are a number of documents which lack the legal characteristics of an insurance policy but acknowledge that insurance cover has been obtained.

The certificate of insurance states the main terms of the open cover under which the goods are insured and also contains a declaration of the goods stating the value for which they are insured, the voyage and the distinguishing marks and numbers of the goods. The certificate is signed either by the insurance broker or by the insured himself if he obtains insurance cover directly.

A buyer under a cif contract is not obliged to accept a certificate of insurance instead of an insurance policy unless he has expressly agreed or unless it is a custom of the trade. The English courts have held that the buyer need not accept an American insurance certificate unless it is issued by the insurer and incorporates all the terms of the insurance policy and conforms to the requirements of a policy (*see Diamond Alkali Export Corporation* v. *Bourgeouis* (1921)).

A brokers' cover note is merely an advice note sent to a client informing him that insurance cover has been obtained and is not a policy which a buyer under a cif policy need accept.

The duty to disclose

A contract of marine insurance, like every insurance contract, is one of the utmost good faith and if full disclosure is not made of any material facts which may affect the contract of insurance, the other party may avoid it.

The "held covered" clause

A material misdescription of the goods in the policy enables the insurer to avoid the policy on grounds of misrepresentation although the misrepresentation was due to an innocent mistake or to an accident. The parties may therefore insert a "held covered" clause in the contract of insurance which provides cover against an innocent misdescription of the goods but the insured will be required to pay an additional premium when the time and completed description of the goods is supplied. In *Hewitt Brothers* v. *Wilson* (1915) the insured described second–hand machinery simply as "machinery" under the belief this was a sufficient description. It was held that although this was a material misdescription which would normally have entitled the insurer to rescind the contract, the defect was protected by a "held covered" clause and the insurer had to suffer the loss suffered due to damage to the machinery. The insurer was, however, entitled to claim the additional premium.

The insured can only obtain the protection of the "held covered" clause if he acted with the utmost good faith towards the insurer.

Type of policy

The form of policy generally used today in marine insurance is the Lloyd's SG Policy and is appended as a model form to the Marine Insurance Act 1906. The standard SG Policy covers perils of the seas, men of war, fire, pirates, enemies, restraints etc. When a loss is caused by a peril insured against the policy will cover it, but if the policy does not expressly cover the peril or exclude it, the risk is not covered and a claim cannot be made. The question which has to be asked is: what was the proximate cause of the loss? In *Hamilton, Fraser & Co* v. *Pandrof & Co* (1887) it was held that the proximate cause of the loss was sea–water (a peril of the sea) when rats gnawed through a pipe and sea water entered the hole damaging the cargo. In *Leyland Shipping Co* v. *Norwich Union Fire Insurance Society* (1918) an insurance policy did not cover war risks. A torpedo struck the ship and, although the ship made port, it sank due to bad weather. It was held the proximate cause of the loss was the torpedo damage and this was a risk of war. Consequently the insurers were not liable.

The loss must not be caused by the wilful misconduct of the insured but the insurer is liable if the loss would not have occurred but for the negligence or misconduct of the crew. The onus of proof is on the insured to show that an accident has occurred and that on a balance of probabilities it occurred because of a peril which is insured against.

However, the ordinary consequences of a sea voyage will not result in damage being treated as caused by a peril of the seas. Such a peril does not include the ordinary action of the wind and waves but only fortuitous accidents of the sea. If therefore the ship is old and leaky and goods in the hold are damaged this is not a peril of the sea. Only exceptionally will heavy weather be classified as a peril of the sea.

The parties may expressly add further clauses to the standard clause found in the SG Policy itself. The clauses most often added are the Institute clauses and these prevail if they are variance with a term in the SG Policy.

PROBLEMS

1. To what extent must an insured who seeks insurance cover have an insurable interest in the property he seeks to insure?

2. What are the types of risk that may be covered under a policy of insurance?

3. Explain the proximity rule.

4. What is meant by the rule that a contract of insurance is one of the "utmost good faith"? What is the result if, during negotiations for an insurance contract, the insured fails to disclose facts material to the contract or misrepresents relevant facts?

5. What are the types of policies available in marine insurance?

PART FOUR

Commercial Associations

CHAPTER NINE

Company Law

OBJECTIVES

It is proposed in this chapter to deal with the law governing companies and their activities. In particular the chapter deals with:

(*a*) the formation of a company, including:
- (*i*) its memorandum and articles of association;
- (*ii*) the nature of corporate personality;
- (*iii*) the alteration of the memorandum or articles of association;
- (*iv*) pre-incorporation contracts;
- (*v*) the ultra vires rule;
- (*vi*) rule in *Royal British Bank* v. *Turquand*;

(*b*) share and loan capital including:
- (*i*) payment for shares;
- (*ii*) alteration of share capital;
- (*iii*) classes of shares;
- (*iv*) raising of capital by a large issue of securities;
- (*v*) dealings with shares;

(*c*) profits and dividends and bonus shares;

(*d*) debentures, including:
- (*i*) fixed and floating charges;
- (*ii*) the invalidation of mortgages and charges in a winding-up;
- (*iii*) registration of mortgages and charges;
- (*iv*) the realisation of a floating charge;

(*e*) promoters and directors, including;
- (*i*) disqualification of directors;
- (*ii*) remuneration and loans to directors;
- (*iii*) powers of directors;
- (*iv*) duties of directors;

(*f*) protection of minority shareholders;

(*g*) meetings and resolutions;

(*h*) winding-up.

CLASSIFICATION OF COMPANIES

The Companies Act 1980 classifies companies as public and private companies. The Act provides certain requirements which must be satisfied if a company is to be registered as a public company under the Companies Acts 1948–1981. All other companies are private companies. It is proposed to examine the classification of public and private companies prior to 1980 and then to examine the new classification under the 1980 Act.

The Companies Act 1948

Under the Companies Act 1948, companies were classified as follows.

1. A company limited by shares

The members or shareholders are liable to contribute only the difference between the nominal value of their shares and the amount which they have already paid the company in respect of them; for example if X owns 1,000 shares with a nominal value of £1 each and he initially paid £400 for them and then transferred them to Y who paid another £400, Y's liability if the company were wound up would be £200.

2. A company limited by guarantee

The constitution of the company states that it is a company limited by guarantee and the extent of the liability of its members up to and under the guarantee; a company limited by guarantee can also have a share capital, in which case the shareholder would also be liable for the unpaid balance on his shares.

3. An unlimited company

Under the 1948 Act this could either have a share capital or not; the liability of the members or shareholders of the company is unlimited and they have a twofold obligation, namely to pay the unpaid balance on their shares and to pay any further amounts necessary to satisfy the company's debts in full if it is wound–up.

Under the Companies Act 1948, any of these companies could either be public or private and the status of the company depended on whether or not its articles of association imposed the three restrictions required by s.28 of the Act, namely:

(a) the membership of the company was limited to 50 persons excluding its employees or ex-employees who were members;

(b) a prohibition on the issue of a prospectus offering the company's shares for subscription by the public;

(c) some restrictions on the free transfer of shares in the company.

If the company's articles contained any of the above prohibitions then the company was automatically classified as a private company. All other companies were public companies.

The Companies Act 1980

The Companies Act 1980 defines a public company as a company which is either limited by shares or limited by guarantee and has a share capital. No new companies of the latter kind can now be formed as public companies.

Additionally, a public company must satisfy the following requirements:

(a) the company's memorandum of association must state that it is a public company;

(b) the company must have a nominal and issued capital of at least £50,000. A consequence of this is that the company cannot commence business until it has issued at least £50,000 of its nominal share capital and at least 25 per cent of the nominal value of each of its issued shares has been paid-up; the company can, of course, be registered with the Registrar of Companies before it has satisfied the minimum capital requirements but it cannot commence trade until the capital requirements are satisfied; and

(c) the name of the company must conclude with the words "public limited company" or "Plc", or, in the case of a company with a registered office in Wales, optionally with the Welsh equivalent. All other companies under the 1980 Act are private companies.

FORMATION OF A COMPANY

A company formed under the Companies Acts 1948–1981 must be registered by the Registrar of Companies who, when the company has filed the proper documents with him, will issue the company with a certificate of incorporation. In order to obtain this certificate the promoters of the company must deliver to the Registrar the following documents.

The memorandum of association

The memorandum of association deals with the fundamental provisions of the company's constitution and must provide for certain matters, namely the objects or activities which the company is formed to pursue, its share capital and the place of its registered office. The Companies Act 1948, Sched. 1, contains a specimen form of memorandum and articles of association and whilst a company's memorandum or articles need not conform exactly with the specimen forms, they must contain the provisions which are expressly required by the Act. The memorandum of association must be signed by at least two persons as subscribers, and must state the number of shares each subscriber takes in the company.

The memorandum of association of a public company must contain the following six essential clauses; whilst the memorandum of a private company will only contain five clauses:

Clause 1–the name of the company
The first clause of the memorandum will state the name of the company and, if it is a public company, the name must conclude with the words "public limited company" or "plc". In the case of a private company the word "limited" will appear at the end of the name unless the company is unlimited. The company's name is chosen by the promoters, but the freedom to choose a name is restricted in a number of ways, e.g.:

(a) a number of statutes prohibit the use of certain names in order to prevent individuals from taking the benefit and goodwill attached to those names, e.g. Red Cross;

(b) the Registrar of Companies may refuse to register a company under a name either if it is contained in an index kept by him, including a name connected with Her Majesty's Government or a local Authority, or if the use of the name chosen would constitute a criminal act;

The Secretary of State for Trade and Industry may require a company to change its name within twelve months from the date of its registration if he considers the name to be the same as that of an existing company (except for incidental features) or if he considers the name infringes regulations issued by the Secretary of State for Trade and Industry under the Companies Act 1981. The company will then have six weeks to change its name. Where the company changes its name for any reason the Registrar of companies must enter the new name on the register and issue a new certificate of incorporation;

(c) an action in tort may lie at common law for passing–off where the plaintiff carries on the same kind of business and under a similar name as that of another company, so that people are likely to be misled or deceived and the plaintiff's clients are likely to be mistaken as to its identity. In *North Cheshire & Manchester Brewery Co* v. *Manchester Brewery Co* (1899) the Manchester Brewery Company had carried on its business under that name for a number of years. The appellants bought an old brewery business called "The North Cheshire Brewery" and were registered as "The North Cheshire and Manchester Brewery Company". An injunction was granted to restrain the appellants from using that name, since it would deceive the public. However, where a company in the business of carrying out car insurance adopted as its name "Motor Manufacturers and Traders Insurance Co Ltd" and had an action brought against it by another existing trade protection society whose name was the Society of Motor Manufacturers and Traders, it was held that no injunction to restrain the insurance company from having or using its name could be issued since it carried on a different kind of business activity from the trade protection society and there was no risk of injury to the society's reputation.

The name of the company must be clearly displayed on the company's business premises, engraved on the seal and mentioned on all company documents.

Clause 2–public limited company

The second clause in the memorandum of association of a public company must state that it is incorporated as a public limited company. In the case of a private company this clause is omitted from the memorandum.

Clause 3–registered office

This clause will state the country where the company's registered office will be situate (i.e. England, Wales or Scotland) and the papers of incorporation must be filed with the Registrar of Companies where the company's registered office is situate. The Registrar of Companies for England and Wales operates from Cardiff and the Registrar for Scotland from Edinburgh. This fixes the nationality of the company and it is governed by the law of that country. All documents, including legal papers, can be served on the company at its registered office. A company may change the address of its registered office but it cannot change the country of its registration.

Clause 4–objects clause

The objects clause sets out the kind of activities or business which the company is formed to carry on. It, therefore, usually sets out the company's objects in the widest manner because any transactions in excess of these objects are beyond the company's legal powers and ultra vires. Companies tend to draft the objects clause in wide terms to give themselves flexibility. The objects of a company are its main purpose or activity but the objects clause may also contain many ancillary powers given to it in order to achieve its main objects; for example, the main object of the company may be to manufacture motor vehicles but it may be given express power to own land, factories and plant, pay its employees and hold a bank account. In *Stevens* v. *Mysore Reefs Mining Co Ltd* (1902) the objects clause of the company included the acquisition of a named gold mine in Mysore as one of its activities. A sub-clause in the objects clause authorised the company to buy other gold mines. The directors of the company abandoned all operations in Mysore when it was discovered that the named gold mine was unprofitable and they planned instead to buy gold mines in West Africa. A shareholder brought an action to restrain the company from completing the contract on the ground it was outside the scope of the company's activities. The wider powers given in the sub-clause to acquire gold mines in general were held to be subject to the main object of the company which was to acquire and work a specific gold mine in Mysore, and the company could only purchase further mines in so far as those mines assisted the exploitation of the named mine. On the other hand, where a company's objects clause stipulated that it was in the business of taking over and carrying on a specific engineering business, it was held that it could continue business as general engineers under a sub-clause which empowered it to do so. The main objects clause was supplemented by the general powers given in its subsequent sub-clauses (*see Re Kitson & Co Ltd* (1946)). In *Cotman* v. *Brougham* (1914) the company's objects clause stated it was in the business of developing rubber plantations. One of the sub-clauses in the objects clause empowered the company to acquire and deal in stocks and shares in any company or corporation. The final sub-clause stated that each of the sub-clauses of the objects clause was to be interpreted separately without restricting the effect of any of the other clauses. The company underwrote and allotted shares in another company which subsequently went into liquidation. The court held that the sub-clauses were wide enough to cover underwriting and dealings in shares and such undertakings were intra vires. The allottees were consequently entitled to be placed on the list of contributories.

The effect of the ultra vires rule has been that the companies are registered with very wide objects clauses to which the courts may give a restricted interpretation. In *Re Introductions Ltd* (1970) the company's memorandum provided that its objects were to provide facilities for foreign visitors during the Festival of Britain in 1951. It was given power by one of its sub-clauses to borrow and raise money. A sub–clause in the objects clause provided that each of the clauses should be construed independently and each should be given effect as a main object. The company went into the business of pig breeding and raised a loan from a bank. It subsequently went into liquidation and the liquidator took out a summons for a declaration that the debenture was void. The court held that it would not interpret each sub–clause as an independent and main clause because the company would become entitled to borrow money as an independent object in itself. The money borrowed the court said had to be for a purpose and since pig breeding was an ultra vires purpose the debenture was void.

The courts may imply certain powers to facilitate the company's achieving its express powers because they are necessary for a particular trade or business. In *Deuchar* v. *Gas, Light & Coke Co* (1925) the company was in the business of manufacturing coal gas but it also had power by the memorandum to manufacture, convert and sell by–products. It was held the company had power to convert a by–product, napthalene into a marketable product by running a plant and purchasing quantities of caustic soda necessary to manufacture napthalene. Similarly, in *Evans* v. *Brunnner Mond & Co* (1921) a company formed to manufacture chemicals was held to have implied power to make grants to universities and scientific institutions to facilitate research and the training of scientists, although the company would not obtain any immediate benefit. The courts will require two conditions to be satisfied before they will imply a power, namely, that there must be some reasonable connection between the company's objects and the power it seeks to exercise, and that the company will in fact benefit in some way from the exercise of that power. The courts will not imply powers if they are not sufficiently closely connected with the company's main objects.

Clause 5–limited liability

The clause will state that the liability of the company's members is limited. If the company is one limited by shares the liability is automatically limited to the amount unpaid on the shares each member holds. If liability is limited by guarantee the liability of each of its members is limited to the specific sum stated in a separate clause.

Clause 6–capital

If the company is limited by shares, the clause will state the share capital with which the company proposes to be registered and the nominal value of each share. If the company issues shares in excess of its stated share capital the issue is void to the extent it exceeds the maximum stated.

In addition to these clauses, a company's memorandum may contain certain additional clauses which may equally be inserted in the articles of the company, i.e. class rights attached to certain classes of shares, the terms of employment of directors etc.

The articles of association

A company limited by guarantee and an unlimited company must have their own articles of association. A company limited by shares need not have its own articles, in which case Table A to Sched. 1 of the 1948 Act will constitute the company's articles.

The articles of association regulate the internal management of the company. For example, the articles usually define the different classes of shares the company is empowered to issue, provide for meetings, determine voting rights and provide for the appointment of the board of directors.

Rules relating to the interpretation of articles of association

The articles of association are subordinate to the memorandum and in case of conflict the memorandum prevails. In *Guinness* v. *Land Corporation of Ireland* (1882) the company's memorandum of association provided that its main object was the development of land in Ireland. The company was empowered to carry out activities incidental to that object. It was held that a provision in the articles of association under which part of the company's capital could be used to invest in a guarantee fund for the payment of dividents was void. Subject to the rule that in cases of conflict the memorandum prevails, the memorandum and articles of association should be read together where there is ambiguity, so as to remove it if possible. In *Re Duncan Gilmour & Co* (1952) the company's memorandum was silent on whether its shares were to be all of one class or of different classes. A power in the articles of association which enabled the company to issue shares of different classes was held to resolve the uncertainty and the company was entitled to issue a number of different classes of shares (*see Re Pyle Works* (No. 2) (1891)).

If, however, the memorandum is certain the articles cannot be used to cast a doubt on the memorandum and, to the extent to which the articles are inconsistent with the memorandum, they are void and must be disregarded.

Other documents

In addition to the memorandum and articles, the company must file certain other documents with the Registrar of Companies, namely:

(*a*) a statement of the address of the company's intended registered office; this must be signed by the subscribers of the memorandum;

(*b*) a statement signed by the subscribers of the memorandum setting out the names of the company's first directors and secretary, signed by these persons and stating that they agree to act in that capacity;

(*c*) in the case of a limited company with a share capital, a statement of the amount of cash or value of assets contributed by the subscribers for their shares for which they subscribed the memorandum; and

(*d*) a statutory declaration by a solicitor engaged in the formation of the company or by a director appointed by the articles that the requirements under the 1948–1981 Acts are satisfied.

Incorporation procedure

The Registrar of Companies will examine the documents filed with him and, after satisfying himself that they are in order, he will issue a certificate of incorporation and give notice of the company's incorporation in the London Gazette. The certificate of incorporation is conclusive evidence that the requirements of the Companies Acts 1948–1981 in respect of registration have been complied with and that the proper procedure has been followed (*Oakes* v. *Turquand* (1867)). In *Jubilee Cotton Mills Ltd* v. *Lewis* (1924) the court held that the company is validly incorporated on the date which its certificate of registration bears, not the date on which the documents are filed with the Registrar.

A private company may enter into contracts and commence business once a certificate of incorporation has been issued, but a public company must obtain a certificate of entitlement to do business from the Registrar of Companies before it can commence trading. This certificate is conclusive evidence that the company is entitled to commence business and to borrow money and that the company has satisfied the minimum capital requirements under the 1980 Act. The directors or secretary of the company must make a statutory declaration that the nominal value of its issued share capital is not less than the authorised minimum, and as to the amount paid up by the shareholders being not less than one quarter of the nominal value of the shares taken by them plus the whole of any share premium and any payment or benefit conferred on the promoters. A failure to obtain the certificate to commence business does not render any transactions entered into by the company void, but the directors are personally liable for any loss caused to a third party unless the certificate is obtained within 21 days after he requires them to obtain such a certificate.

A company which registers as a private company and then re-registers as a public company on satisfying the requirements of the Companies Acts is not required to obtain a certificate of entitlement to do business.

CORPORATE PERSONALITY

A company once incorporated is a legal person distinct from its members and capable of entering into contracts on its own behalf, of owning property and being subject to liabilities. The rule that a company is a separate legal entity from its members was firmly established in the case of *Salomon* v. *Salomon & Co Ltd* (1897) in which case a sole trader, Salomon, formed a limited liability company and transferred his business to it. There were six other shareholders in the company, each of whom owned one share each. The sale price of the business was paid partly in cash and partly by the creation of a debenture over the company's assets. The company subsequently went into liquidation and the liquidator brought an action for a declaration that, firstly, the debenture in favour of Salomon was void and, secondly, that the company was a sham because it was formed in order to enable Salomon to avoid his legal obligations whilst allowing him to enjoy the profits of the company. Salomon was held not personally liable for the full debts of the company and moreover the debenture issued to him was held to be valid. Thus the court will not look at the motive behind the formation of the company once it has been properly registered unless fraud or an illegal purpose can be shown. The company is at law a distinct entity from its subscribers, who are only liable to the extent of any amounts outstanding on the nominal value of their shares.

The consequences of the separate legal personality rule enable the company as the absolute owner of the property to hold it in its own right and not as a trustee for its members. For that reason a shareholder does not have an insurable interest in the company's property (*see Macaura* v. *Northern Assurance Co* (1925)). Similarly, he cannot enforce a contract made by the company for he is not a party to the contract. A member of a company cannot sue in respect of torts committed by third parties against the company, nor can he sue for torts committed by the company. In *British Thompson–Houston* v. *Sterling Accessories Ltd* (1924) it was held that the directors of the company were not personally liable for an alleged breach of a patent.

The rule of separate corporate personality also applies where the shareholder itself is a company, for example, a parent company which has shares in a subsidiary. The subsidiary company is a separate legal entity from its parent or holding company and legal rights and obligations which belong to it cannot be enforced by the parent company.

Exceptions to the separate legal personality principle

The courts have recognised a number of exceptions to the principle that the company is a distinct entity from its shareholders and will impose personal liability on the shareholders or directors for the acts or omissions of the company. The exceptions are as follows:

1. Companies Act 1948, s. 31

Section 31 of the 1948 Act, as amended by the 1980 Act, provides that if the number of members of a company falls below two in the case of either a public or private company and remains below that for six months, every person who becomes or remains a member of the company while the situation prevails is personally liable for the debts of the company. In the case of a public company this is very unlikely to arise, although in the case of a private company this may occur if there are only two members and one of them dies.

2. Fraudulent trading under the Companies Act 1948, s. 332

This section provides that if the company is wound up and the court is satisfied that its business has been carried on with intent to defraud its creditors, it may hold any persons who were knowingly parties to carrying on the company's business with intent to defraud personally liable for any of its debts and liabilities. The court will only impose personal liability on those involved in the management of the company's business if they have been guilty of dishonesty. In *Re Gerald Cooper Chemicals Ltd* (1978) the directors of a company which was having difficulty in repaying a substantial loan entered into a contract for the delivery of certain goods to a third party. They were aware that the company could not supply the goods and accepted payment in advance which they then re-used to pay part of the outstanding loan. It was held that the directors were personally liable because the contract to supply goods and the subsequent advance payment amounted to a fraud on the third party.

The dishonest intention may be apparent from the circumstances in which the company's business was carried on (Re William C. Letich Bros Ltd (No. 1) (1932)). Thus, once the directors realise that the company will not be able to pay its debts they are deemed to have a dishonest intention if the company continues to incur further debts. However, only those directors (or other parties) who actively participate in the management of the company once they realise that the company is in financial difficulties and is unlikely to be able to repay its creditors will be held personally liable.

Once the court has made an order against the company's management, those held personally liable must pay the amounts ordered against them to the company's liquidator. In Re William C. Letich Bros Ltd (No. 2) (1933) the court said that money recovered under s. 332 was not to be applied exclusively for the benefit of the creditors whose debts were contracted with intent to defraud the creditors, but that the fund formed part of the company's assets generally and so was available to pay all its debts rateably.

If the defrauded creditor, however, obtains repayment of the debt from the directors personally by his own resources, i.e. by threatening to bring legal proceedings against them, the payment will not be impressed with a trust in favour of the company's creditors and he is entitled to retain the full amount (Re Gerald Cooper Chemicals Ltd (1978)).

3. Paramount public interest

The court will disregard the separate legal entity of a company and will investigate the attributes of the shareholders if a question of the public interest is involved. In Daimler Co Ltd v. Continental Tyre & Rubber Co (GB) Ltd (1916) the court disregarded the legal entity of a company registered in the UK and looked at the attributes of the shareholders who were German nationals, resident in Germany. The company was held to be an enemy alien and therefore could not bring an action in the English courts without a special licence from the Crown (see FG Films Ltd (1953)).

4. Evasion of legal obligations

The court will disregard the legal personality of the company if the purpose for which the company is formed is to facilitate the shareholder from evading his legal obligations. In Gilford Motor Co Ltd v. Horne (1933) the defendant entered into a valid restrictive covenant not to compete with his employer for a specified period and not to solicit his customers. He formed a company in his wife's name and started a competing business. It was held that since the defendant in fact controlled the company, its formation was a mere sham to enable him to break his agreement with the plaintiff and the court granted an injunction. Similarly, in *Jones* v. *Lipman* (1962) the vendor of property entered into an agreement to sell certain land, but subsequently conveyed it to a company which he controlled. The court disregarded the legal entity of the company, and an order of specific performance was granted against the vendor and the company.

5. Implied agency or trusteeship relationship

The courts have, in certain cases, implied that the company was acting as an agent or trustee for its shareholders, thereby holding the shareholders personally liable for the acts or omissions of the company. This principle has been applied in cases where the strict principle of separate legal personality would result in injustice. Thus in *Smith, Stone & Knight Ltd* v. *Birmingham Corporation* (1939) a company acquired the shares of another company and continued to run it as a subsidiary. The subsidiary was controlled by the parent company, and its profits were treated as those of the parent company. The defendant corporation compulsorily acquired the premises of the subsidiary company and the parent company claimed to be entitled to compensation. The defendant corporation argued that the subsidiary company was the proper claimant because it was a separate legal entity from its parent company, but the court rejected this view and held that the subsidiary company was such a closely integrated part of the parent company that two companies would be treated as a single commercial unit. The court laid down six guidelines which could be used to determine where control over the subsidiary company was vested. However, in *D H N Food Distributors* v. *Tower Hamlets London Borough Council* (1976) the facts of which were similar to the Birmingham Corporation case, the court did not apply the trusteeship concept but relied entirely on the commercial unity of the group of companies in order to identify the holding company which carried on business with its wholly owned subsidiary, the owner of the premises where the business was carried on. The court, therefore, held that, because the parent and subsidiary companies were a single commercial unit, compensation could in fact be claimed by the parent company.

In *Woolfson* v. *Strathclyde Regional Council* (1978) the court refused to look behind the corporate veil. It stated that the rule in *Salomon* v. *Salomon* should be given its full effect except in special circumstances and held that the appellant was not entitled to compensation for disturbance under a compulsory purchase order because any loss suffered by him was solely as a shareholder in the company which carried on business on those premises and not as the owner of the land.

The courts have been inclined to hold that a subsidiary company is an agent of its parent company in cases involving the Revenue. In *Apthorpe* v. *Peter Schoenhofen Brewing Co Ltd* (1899) an English company was held liable for income tax on the profits earned by its wholly owned American subsidiary in the USA. Similarly, in *Firestone Tyre & Rubber Co Ltd* v. *Llewellin* (1956) an

American parent company was held liable to UK income tax for profits earned in this country by its subsidiary, whose conduct of the European business of the group was closely controlled by the American parent company.

THE LEGAL RELATIONSHIP BETWEEN THE COMPANY AND ITS MEMBERS

The statutory contract

The Companies Act 1948, s. 20, implies a statutory contract between the company and its members and between the members themselves. The section only implies a contract between the company and its members in respect of the rights and duties of members so that, if the memorandum or articles of a company provide for other matters, these do not form part of the implied contract. Therefore, any rights given to a person in his capacity otherwise than as a member cannot be enforced against the company. In *Eley* v. *Positive Government Life Assurance* (1875) the articles of a company provided that a particular member should be employed as the company's solicitor. It was held that under s. 20 such a contract could not be implied and if the clause in the memorandum was to have effect the parties would have to make this a term of a separate contract. Similarly, in *Re Tavarone Mining Co* (1873) a clause in the articles that the company should purchase certain mines belonging to a particular member could not be enforced under s. 20. In order to be effective the parties would have to enter into a separate contract incorporating the terms of sale.

However, s. 20 will give effect to rights which arise by a virtue of the member's holding shares in the company, namely, the right to be notified and to attend annual general meetings, to vote at meetings and to receive a dividend. Similarly, the company has a right by virtue of this contract to be paid any unpaid balance on the nominal value of the shares.

Contracts incorporating part of the memorandum or articles

A contract is not created automatically where there is a provision in the memorandum or articles which does not relate to the rights of its members, but a separate contract embodying that provision may subsequently be entered into or implied in some cases. In *Re New British Iron Co, ex p. Beckwith* (1898) the articles of a company provided that the directors should be paid a certain sum as remuneration every year. The plaintiff served the company as a director without any express agreement on the matter of his remuneration. It was held that the provision in the articles was implicitly incorporated in the contract of employment. In *Read* v. *Astoria Garage (Streatham) Ltd* (1952) the company agreed to employ the plaintiff as its managing director. It was held that the duration of his employment was governed by the articles of the company since his service contract was silent on the point.

A separate contract entered into between the company and its members will be deemed to incorporate only so much of the articles of association as are relevant to the subject–matter of the contract. In *Beattie* v. *E & F Beattie Ltd* (1939) a member of a company served as its director without entering into an express service contract. It was held that a clause in the articles that disputes should be referred to arbitration was not incorporated in the terms of his employment, since it was envisaged that the provision would apply to disputes which arose with members in that capacity and not in any other capacity.

Contracts between members themselves

The Companies Act 1948, s. 20, implies a contract on the company's members who are contractually bound to one another to obey the provisions of the memorandum and articles, in so far as the articles relate to their rights and duties as members. In *Rayfield* v. *Hands* (1960) the articles of a private company contained a provision that a member who wished to sell his shares must notify the directors who would purchase them at a fair value. The plaintiff offered his shares for sale to the directors who refused to purchase them on the grounds that the cluase merely gave them an option to purchase the shares. It was held that the articles bound the directors in their capacity as members and since this obligation was personal the plaintiff could enforce it against the directors.

The legal nature of shares

A share is a bundle of legal rights given to the shareholder and measured by the value of the shares purchased. A member of a company is only liable to contribute towards the payment of the company's debts in a winding-up to the extent of any unpaid balance on their shares.

VARIATION OF THE MEMORANDUM AND ARTICLES OF ASSOCIATION

A company may find it necessary to alter the contents of its memorandum or articles for a number of different reasons, e.g. where it wants to redistribute the powers and functions allocated to its board of management, to alter voting rights or to raise further capital.

Memorandum of association

The following clauses in the memorandum of association may be altered by the company's satisfying the procedural requirements laid down in the Companies Acts:

1. The name of the company

A company may change its name by a special resolution passed by a three–quarters majority vote at a general meting. The same restrictions apply to a company when it proposes to change its name as those which apply to the company's promoters when choosing the name. A change of name does not affect the rights, obligations and liabilities incurred by a company under its old name. These obligations may be enforced against the company under its new name and in any case proceedings may be brought against the company under its former name until the Registrar of Companies issues a new certificate of incorporation in the company's new name and advertises the change in the London Gazette.

2. Registered office

Although a company can change the address of its registered office it cannot change the country of its registration. It must give notice to the Registrar of Companies of a change of the address of its registered office and, until this is done, documents may be served on the company at its former address. The notified change of registered office must be advertised by the Registrar of Companies in the London Gazette.

3. The objects clause

The circumstances under which alteration of the objects clause of a company will be allowed are governed by the Companies Act 1948, s. 5. A company can alter its objects clause by passing a special resolution, but the alteration must relate to one of seven specific purposes set out in the Companies Act 1948, s.5(1), which are:

(a) To enable the company to carry on its business more economically and more efficiently. Section 5(1) (a) gives the company the power to amend its objects clause in order to enable it to carry on its business more economically, but the business it carries on must be precisely the same as the one before the alteration, although carried out by different methods. The company cannot therefore use s. 5(1) (a) to rewrite its objects clause. In *Re Cyclists Touring Club* (1907) the memorandum stated that the objects of the club were to promote, assist and protect the use of bicycles. The company passed a resolution to the effect that the memorandum should be altered to allow membership to be extended to other road users, including motorists. It was held the proposed alteration was not within 5(1)(a), since it would alter the nature of the club's business which was to protect cyclists and would cause a conflict of interest with the other road–users. In *Re Government Stock Investment Co* (1891) it was held that a company formed to invest in the securities of British and foreign governments and local authorities could not alter its objects clause to enable it to invest in the debentures and shares of commercial companies. An alteration of the objects clause in this form would lead to an alteration of the company's business;

(b) To enable the company to attain its main purpose by a new and improved means. An alteration under s.5(1)(b) will only be allowed if it is to enable the company to attain its existing main objects in a new way. The purpose of the subsection is to permit the company to make additions to its ancillary powers in order to enable the company to achieve its main objects. The company cannot therefore alter its main objects clause and empower itself to undertake new projects;

(*c*) To enable the company to carry on some business which under existing cirsumstances may conveniently or advantageously be combined with the business of the company. Section 5(1)(*d*) gives the company wide powers to alter its objects clause so that it can combine a new business with its main purpose. However, the courts will prevent the company from undertaking a new venture if it is inconsistent with the company's existing objects, as in *Re Cyclists Touring Club.*

In *Re Parent Tyre Co* (1923) the company's objects included the manufacture and sale of tyres or any other business which may conveniently and advantageously be carried on in connection with another business. The company went into the business of managing investments in another company A special resolution was passed purporting to give the company power to carry on the business of bankers, financiers, underwriters and dealers in shares and investments. The court held that the alteration of the objects clause would be permitted since in the opinion of the company's directors it was possible to carry on the new business with its existing business;

(*d*) To enlarge or change the local area of its operations;

(*e*) To restrict or abandon any of the objects specified in the memorandum;

(*f*) To sell or dispose of the whole or any part of its undertakings; and

(*g*) To amalgamate with any other company or body of persons.

These last four permitted alterations are largely self-explanatory.

An alteration of the objects clause must be affected by a special resolution and comes into effect immediately, but an application to cancel the resolution can be made to the court by holders of at least 15 per cent in nominal value of the company's issued share capital, or by 15 per cent in nominal value of the issued shares of any class within twenty-one days of the resolution's being passed. On such an application being made, the alteration is suspended. On the hearing of the application, the court may confirm the resolution in whole or in part, or subject or not to conditions or, if it thinks fit, the court may cancel the alteration.

The court may approve arrangements for the purchase of the shares of any dissenting members (but not the debentures of any debenture holders who oppose the alteration). However, the company's capital cannot be used on the acquisition of such shares: they must be purchased by the other members out of their own resources or by the company out of its profits. The court can only sanction such a purchase if all the parties agree.

4. The limited liability clause

A limited company which has not previously been an unlimited company may re–register as an unlimited company if all its members consent and its memorandum and articles are altered so as to conform to those of an unlimited company. The written consent of all the members, a statutory declaration by the directors that the consenting members comprise the whole membership of the company and copies of the altered memorandum and articles must be filed with the Registrar of Companies, who will issue the company with a new certificate of incorporation. The Registrar must publish the issue of the new certificate of incorporation in the London Gazette. The effect of the conversion will be that members of the company will become liable to contribute without limit towards the payment of the companies debts.

Conversely, an unlimited company may re–register as a limited one, provided the conversion is authorised by a special resolution of a general meeting setting out the company's share capital and making the necessary alterations to the company's memorandum and articles of association. The effect of the conversion is that persons who become members of the company after the date of the company's re–registration are liable to contribute towards the payment of its debts only to the extent of the unpaid balance on their shares. However, persons who held shares in the company before the conversion do not enjoy limited liability.

5. Capital and guarantee clauses
A public or private company with limited liability or a company limited by guarantee may increase, reduce or reorganise its capital clause.

6. Additional clauses
A company which inserts in its memorandum of association a clause which could equally be inserted in the articles may alter it under the Companies Act 1948, s. 23, unless there is an express provision in the memorandum that the clause may not be altered or providing for its alteration. Once a special resolution effecting the alteration has been passed, the minority shareholders have the same right to apply to the court to cancel it as in the case of an alteration affecting the objects clause.

Alteration of the articles of association
An alteration of the articles of association is governed by the Companies Act 1948, s. 10, and must be effected by a special resolution. Any provision in the memorandum or articles which enables an alteration of articles to be made in any way other than by a special resolution is ineffective (see Ayre v. Skelseys Adamant Cement Co Ltd (1904)). A provision in the articles allowing alteration will be ineffective if it conflicts with the memorandum of association.

Limitations on the power of alteration
An alteration of the memorandum or articles of association is subject to the overriding requirement that it must be for the benefit of the company as a whole. In Allen v. Gold Reefs of West Africa Ltd (1900) a company under its articles of association had a lien for the debts and liabilities of any member of the company on all shares held by that member which had not been fully paid. The company sought to alter its articles by omitting the words "not fully paid up" and thus creating a lien on a particular member's fully paid shares. It was held the company had a power to alter its articles by extending its lien to fully paid–up shares. The court said that the statutory power given to shareholders

to amend the company's articles must be exercised not only in the manner required by the law but also for the bona fide benefit of the company as a whole.

In *Shuttleworth* v. Cox Brothers & Co (Maidenhead) Ltd (1926) it was said that the test in the *Allen case* laid down two requirements, namely.

(*a*) that the words bona fide must relate to the state of the mind of the person whose act is complained of; and

(*b*) the alteration must be for the benefit of the company.

The facts of the *Shuttleworth* case were that the company altered its articles to provide that any director shold cease to hold office if requested to resign by all the other directors. This was in order to enable the company to dismiss the plaintiff from his position as a director. The court upheld the alteration. The test that the alteration should be for the benefit of the company as a whole was expressed more subjectively and it was said the question is whether the alteration is *in the opinion of the shareholders* for the benefit of the company. The alteration will not be upheld if it is something that no reasonable man would consider for the benefit of the company. However, in *Greenhalgh* v. *Arderne Cinemas Ltd* (1951) the court affirmed the more objective test laid down in the *Allen* case. The facts of the *Greenhalgh* case were that the original articles of a private company required any shareholder who wished to sell his shares to offer them to other members at a fair price before selling them to a stranger. The majority shareholders who wanted to well their shares to an outsider passed a special resolution enabling any shareholder to well his shares without first offering them to the minority shareholder, who claimed his right of pre-emption provided the company approved of this by an ordinary resolution passed at a general meeting. The court held the alteration was valid and that the test was whether an individual hypothetical member would honestly have voted in the same way, taking into account the long-term future development of the company. The hypothetical member is someone who may be a member of that company at any time, present or future, and whose particular interests are not going to be affected by any particular distribution of the shares or voting power amongst the shareholders.

The *Greenhalgh* case was followed in *Rights & Issues Investment Trust Ltd* v. *Stylo Shoes Ltd* (1956), in which the plaintiff brought an action to challenge the validity of a resolution, the effect of which would have been to double the voting rights attached to management shares. It was held that the resolution was passed in good faith and it did not discriminate against the plaintiff because the ordinary shareholders would all suffer the same dilution of their voting rights.

The courts have used the objective test of a benefit to the company in a number of cases involving the expropriation of shares and voting rights. In *Brown* v. *British Abrasive Wheel Co* (1919) the majority of the shareholders were only willing to provide further capital for the company if they could purchase the shares of the minority on certain terms. The majority purported to pass a resolution altering the articles so that the minority could be compelled to sell their shares if required to do so by the holders of 90 per cent of the company's capital. It was held that the resolution allowing the alteration was not passed for the benefit of the company as a whole, but simply for the benefit of the majority, and that the alteration was therefore void. In *Dafen Tinplate Co Ltd* v. *Llanelly Stell Co Ltd* (1920) a company in the steel business, fearing that some of its members might start dealing with other steel manufacturers, passed a resolution which purported to give some of the existing shareholders power to purchase the shares of those whom it suspected might purchase steel from other sources. It was held that the proposed alteration was improper because it conferred on the majority an unrestricted power to expropriate shares of the minority and placed some members in a privileged position. However, in *Sidebottom* v. *Kershaw Leese & Co* (1920) an alteration of the articles empowered the directors to require any member who carried on a competing business with that of the company to sell his shares to the other members at a fair value. It was held that the alteration was valid and that it was in the interests of the company as a whole that trade secrets should not be available to the company's competitors.

Although the cases so far dealt with have involved an alteration of the articles of association of the company, the same rules apply where an alteration of a clause in the company's memorandum is proposed. Thus, in *Clemens* v. *Clemens* (1976) an alteration in the company's memorandum, the effect of which would have been to reduce further the powers of the minority shareholder to prevent special resolutions being passed, was held to be invalid because the expropriation was oppressive on the minority.

COMPANIES' CONTRACTS

Pre-incorporation contracts

A company cannot enter into contracts made before it is properly incorporated, nor is it bound by contracts made by agents who purport to act for the company before its incorporation, because it has no legal existence before its registration. In *Kelner* v. *Baxter* (1866) before a company's incorporation, A, B and C entered into a contract with the plaintiff to purchase goods and signed it A, B and C ".... on behalf of the company's name". The goods were supplied and consumed in the course of the company's business. The company subsequently went into liquidation and the plaintiff brought an action against A, B and C. It was held that they were personally liable on the contract. If the company had been in existence when the contract was made, they would have acted as its agents but since the company had not then been in existence the contract would be wholly inoperative unless the defendants could be held personally liable. Moreover, since the contract was obviously intended to have some effect, the only way of giving it that effect was to hold the parties personally liable. Thus this sort of situation is to be distinguished from that in *Newborne* v. *Sensolid (GB) Ltd* (1954), where a contract was entered into and signed "Leopold Newborne Ltd, per Leopold Newborne Director" with a third party at a time before the company with that name was incorporated. The question was whether Leopold Newborne could enforce the contract against the third party personally. It was held that the contract purported to be entered in by the company and not by Leopold Newborne acting as an agent on its behalf, and was therefore simply a nullity, so Newborne could not enforce it nor have it enforced against himself.

The European Communities Act 1972, s.9(2), provides that where a contract is entered into by someone purporting to act in the name of or on behalf of a company which has not yet been incorporated, that person is personally liable, regardless of the capacity in which he purports to sign the contract. The Act abolished the distinction between contracts entered into "on behalf of" or in the name of the company before its incorporation. In *Phonogram Ltd* v. *Lane* (1981) the defendant entered a contract with the plaintiff to borrow £6,000 "on behalf of" a company which was not yet in the process of being formed and in fact was never formed. The plaintiff brought an action to recover the amount which had been paid to the defendant. It was held that the defendant was personally liable and that the European Communities Act 1972, s. 9, had abolished the distinction between contracts entered into "on behalf of" or in the name of the company.

A company cannot after its formation ratify a contract entered into on its behalf before it was properly incorporated. If a company is to acquire rights and liabilities in consequence of a contract entered into before it's incorporation the company must enter into a new contract after incorporation. It is insufficient that the company's memorandum provides that it will carry out any contracts negotiated before its incorporation. Only an express agreement with the other party by which the company undertakes to fulfil the obligations imposed on it by a contract entered into before its incorporation will bind the company to such a contract. Thus, a company which simply remains silent on receiving invoices for goods supplied to it after its incorporation under contracts entered into before its incorporation is not treated as having affirmed the contract or acquiesced to being bound by it (*see Scott* v. *Ebury* (1867)). Similarly, the company will not be treated as having entered into a new contract if it performs its obligations under the contract in pursuance of a separate agreement made with a third party (*see Bagot Pneumatic Tyre Co* v. *Clipper Pneumatic Tyre Co* (1902).

Where, however a third party has conferred a benefit on the company under the belief that the contract was binding on both parties, equity may grant a remedy because it would be unjust for the company to benefit under such a contract without giving consideration in return. Equity may grant one of the following remedies where, before incorporation, the promoters have performed services which have increased the value of the company's property. They can:

(*a*) bring an action against that property for the value of their services; or

(*b*) sue for a quantum meruit, i.e. the fair value of their services; or

(*c*) a third party can bring an action for subrogation, or substitution for the promoters' rights to be indemnified for expenses they have incurred.

Initial contracts

A newly incorporated public company cannot commence business or borrow money until it has obtained a certificate of entitlement to do business from the Registrar of Companies. If the company enters into a contract between its incorporation and the issue of its trading certificate the contract is not void and will bind the company, but the other party may terminate the contract if the company's paid-up capital is not raised to the statutory minimum within a certain period after he requires this to be done.

THE ULTRA VIRES RULE

The rule at common law

All contracts made by a company which are not expressly authorised by its memorandum or which are not incidental to or consequential on the carrying on of the company's business are void, unless they are made enforceable against the company under the European Communities Act 1972, s. 9(1). It is possible for both the company and the third party to rely on the ultra vires rule to escape liability. It is necessary to distinguish between contracts which are patently ultra vires, when they are compared with the company's memorandum and contracts which are not necessarily shown to be outside the company's powers (*see Rolled Steel Ltd v. British Steel Corporation* (1982)). A contract is patently ultra vires if a comparison of the contents of the memorandum and the actual contract entered into by the company shows that it is obviously outside the scope of the company's powers; it is then void and neither party can enforce it unless the European Communities Act protects the third party. Thus, in *Ashbury Railway Carriage and Iron Co v. Riche* (1875) a company which was in the business of manufacturing railway carriages entered into a contract to construct a railway line in Belgium. It was held that the contract was patently ultra vires since a comparison of the company's memorandum and the contract entered into would show the contract was outside the authority given under the memorandum.

The memorandum and articles of association of a company are public documents and are open to inspection by the public. Thus a third party who entered into a contract was deemed at common law to have constructive notice of the company's objects clause and that was sufficient notice that the contract was patently ultra vires. However, the rule that constructive notice is sufficient does not apply where the contract was not patently ultra vires. The third party can enforce the contract against the company unless he has actual notice of the ultra vires purpose intended. Where therefore, the third party, has actual notice of the purpose intended by the company's directors being ultra vires, he is also deemed to have constructive notice of the company's objects and this, coupled with his knowledge of the purpose of the directors, will show the third party that the contract was ultra vires. In *Re Introductions Ltd* (1969), a company formed to provide facilities for overseas visitors borrowed money on the security of a debenture and went into the business of pig breeding. In an action for repayment against the liquidator, the bank argued that the debenture was valid because it was within the company's power to borrow money. It was held that since the bank had actual knowledge that the loan would be used for an ultra vires purpose (i.e. pig breeding) the contract was void. However, in *Re David Payne* (1904) a company made a loan to another company which had a general power to borrow, but the purpose for which the loan was to be applied was unknown to the lending company (except one of its directors who had learnt in his personal capacity that the loan was to be used for an ultra vires purpose). It was held that the lending company was not bound to inquire into the purpose for which the money was to be used, and the knowledge of one of its directors could not be imputed to the lending company. A third party can therefore, recover under the contract unless he was actually aware of the ultra vires purpose, even though he was not also aware that it was ultra vires.

In *Jon Beauforte (London) Ltd* (1953) a company which had been formed to manufacture ladies gowns went into the business of making wooden veneered panelling, and purchased a quantity of coke for this purpose. The court held that the coke merchant knew the coke was to be used for an ultra vires purpose because he had constructive notice of the nature of the business which the company was actually authorised to undertake, namely the manufacture of ladies clothing, and he should have realised from the fact that the company described itself in the correspondence leading to the contract as a manufacturer of veneered panels that the coke was intended for an improper purpose.

If, however, the other party to a contract which is not patently ultra vires enters into a contract without actual knowledge of the purpose for which the goods are to be used, the other party (but not the company) can now enforce it by virtue of the European Communities Act 1972, s. 9(1). Where a company's memorandum states that it has only a limited power to make certain types of contract and an inquiry would have shown that the limitations were being exceeded, the third party could not at common law enforce the contract if he failed to make an inquiry. Thus, in *Fountaine* v. *Carmarthen Railway Co* (1968) a railway company with a limited power to borrow, having borrowed up to the full amount, raised a further loan on the security of a debenture. It was held that amounts borrowed in excess of its limited power were void and the lender should have made enquiry as to whether the company had borrowed the whole amount authorised. The present law enables the lender to recover in these cases, however, provided he acts in good faith and does not actually know that the company's borrowing powers are being exceeded.

If a company has power to borrow a limited amount, a loan of a sum less than the total amount it is permitted to borrow is not patently ultra vires but will in fact be ultra vires if the company has already borrowed so much that the new loan takes its total borrowing over the permitted total, so that the lender cannot recover the amount he has advanced.

Statutory validation of ultra vires contracts

The European Communities Act 1972, s. 9(1), provides that any person who enters into a contract with the directors of the company or with someone who has been authorised by the directors to enter into the contract in good faith, without actual knowledge that it is beyond the scope of the company's objects, can enforce the contract against the company because the contract is deemed to be within its powers. The fact that the memorandum is open to inspection will not negative good faith unless the third party actually knew or suspected that the transaction was outside the scope of the company's powers. In *International Sales and Agencies* v. *Marcus* (1982) the court said that it was for the company to prove bad faith and this can only be done by showing either that the third party had actual knowledge that the transaction was ultra vires the company, or that he could not under the circumstances have been unaware that he was party to an ultra vires contract. Secondly, the court held that a person who seeks to rely on s. 9 must show that he was dealing with the company and not merely with an officer of the company acting beyond his powers.

Finally, dicta in the *Marcus* case would suggest that a transaction decided upon by a managing director or sole effective director who has been properly authorised to act for the company will fall under s. 9(1), although it literally requires the transaction to be decided on by the directors collectively (i.e. by the board of directors).

Remedies available to a third party under an ultra vires loan
The normal contractual remedies available to a third party who enters into an ultra vires contract are not available if he was aware of the ultra vires character of the contract. For example a third party who knowingly makes a loan in excess of the company's borrowing powers cannot recover it by bringing an action in debt. The third party may only enforce the contract under s. 9 of the 1972 Act if he was unaware of the ultra vires act. If s. 9 does not apply, however, he may have a number of other remedies available, namely:

1. Subrogation
If the company uses any part of an ultra vires loan made to it to pay a lawful debt owed by the company to another person, the lender may be subrogated to the rights of the lawful creditor to the extent of the ultra vires loan. The lender under the ultra vires contract is also entitled to the benefit of any security the creditor had, but he does not enjoy any statutory priority which the creditor has over other creditors.

2. Tracing at common law
The lender under an ultra vires contract has a right to trace, at common law, amounts paid by him if they are held by the company, because property remains in the creditor. If the loan is used to purchase a particular asset the lender is entitled to treat the company as an agent (*see Sinclar* v. *Brougham* (1914)).

3. Tracing in equity

The tracing remedy at common law is only available while the money is still identifiable, or while the goods purchased by the company can be identified as having been purchased with that money. If, however, money paid by the lender is paid by the company into its bank account and mixed with the company's other funds, the money lent is no longer identifiable as that of the lender and so title to the money passes to the company. The only remedy then available to the lender is tracing the funds in equity. If amounts are withdrawn from the bank account by the company for any purchase which does not result in the acquisition of an asset it is deemed to have withdrawn the money belonging to it and the lender's money in the order they were respectively credited to the account. If, however the credit balance in the bank account is used to acquire an asset, the company is deemed to draw rateably on its own and the lender's money, and the lender can trace his money into any assets and have them sold so that an appropriate fraction of the proceeds may be paid to him to discharge the ultra vires loan, wholly or in part. The lender can exercise his right to trace at any time, but if the company is wound up the rights of the lender are subordinated to any intra vires creditors of the company.

4. Voluntary repayment

If the company voluntarily repays an ultra vires loan made to it, the lender is entitled to retain the amount.

5. Guarantees

The lender can sue a guarantor of an intra vires loan on the guarantee undertaking but in *Heald* v. *O'Connor* (1917) it was held that a guarantee given for an ultra vires transaction was itself void. The plaintiffs sold to the was indorsed by the personal guarantee of the purchaser. The company issued by instalments, secured by a floating charge on the company's assets, which was indorsed by the personal guarantee of the purchaser. The company issued a debenture under the authority of its memorandum and articles and when the company defaulted, the defendant contended that the debenture was illegal and void and therefore the guarnatee was void. It was held that a debenture holder could not enforce the guarantee because the loan was void and in consequence the guarantee also was void.

6. Loans made by a company

There have been no cases where a company has sought repayment of a loan made by it when it had no power to lend. However, the courts have held that trustees of a friendly society who made unauthorised loans of funds were entitled to a repayment (*Re Coltman* v. *Coltman* (1881)). Similarly, a building society has been held entitled to recover amounts lent under an ultra vires transaction. On these cases it would appear that the courts would allow a company to recover sums lent under ultra vires transactions.

7. Dispositions of property

If property is sold to a company under an ultra vires contract, it is uncertain whether the title to the property passes to it.

THE RULE IN ROYAL BRITISH BANK v. TURQUAND

Apart from the invalidity of the transaction under the ultra vires rule a transaction entered into with a company may be defective because some necessary condition or procedural reqirement has not been satisfied. An inspection of the memorandum or articles of a company will reveal the existence of the condition or procedural requirement but will not give an indication whether or not it has been complied with; the question is whether a third party who deals with the company is required to find out whether the condition has been satisfied or whether he can merely assume compliance.

The courts have established the rule that a person dealing with the company has no right to insist on proof that conditions relating to matters of internal procedure of a company have been satisfied. In *Royal British Bank* v. *Turquand* (1855) the directors of the company could be empowered by the board of directors to raise loans for the company on an appropriate resolution's being passed by the shareholders in general meeting. It was held that the company was bound by such a loan, although no resolution had been passed authorising the directors to raise it. A third party is bound at common law to inspect the documents filed with the Registrar of Companies to ensure that the transaction is not inconsistent with them, but he is not required to do any more. Once it is determined that a company may authorise its directors to borrow by a resolution the third party can assume that such a resolution has been passed. There are three types of defects in which the *Turquand* rule has been evoked.

1. Where there has been a defective appointment of a director, or where a director continues to act for a company after the terms of his appointment have expired

Thus in *Mohony* v. *East Holyford Mining Co* (1875) a company was formed to purchase a mine belonging to the promoter. The subscribers to the company's memorandum were to appoint the company's first directors; instead the company's promoters and the two subscribers managed the company's business without being formally appointed as directors and they gave instructions to a bank, with which the company had an account, that cheques signed by two directors should be honoured by the bank. The bank acted in accordance with these instructions but on the company's subsequently being wound-up the liquidator brought an action against the bank for the return of amounts paid out by it on the grounds that the bank had acted without a mandate, since the persons who had acted as directors had never been properly appointed by the company. The action against the bank did not succeed because if the bank had inspected the articles it would have discovered that the subscribers to the memorandum were authorised to appoint the first directors.

Further, if the bank had sent an employee to the company's registered office he would have seen the promoter and the subscribers managing the company's business. The bank therefore had no right to insist on proof that the directors had been properly appointed, since to all outward appearances they had been properly appointed.

Similarly, in *Duck* v. *Tower Galvanising Co* (1901) a debenture holder was entitled to assume that the persons acting as directors had been properly appointed from the mere fact that they were in control of the company's business and the debenture issued by them on the company's behalf was, therefore, held binding on the company. In *Morris* v. *Kanssen* (1946) however it was held that a person ineffectively appointed to be director of a company could not claim the protection of the *Turquand rule* in respect of an irregular allotment of shares to him because at the time shares were alloted to him he was acting as a director of the company and was, therefore, in a special position to find out whether any procedural conditions relating to the transaction had been complied with.

In *Hely Hutchinson* v. *Brayhead Ltd* (1968) R was the chairman of B Ltd and acted as *de facto* managing director although no formal appointment had been made. He made decisions on financial matters and entered into contracts for the company and he subsequently reported to the board of directors. R was also a director of P Ltd. In order to acquire a controlling interest in P Ltd, B Ltd brought a large number of H's shares in the company in return for his being appointed a director of B Ltd and agreed at a private discussion with R to lend money to P Ltd if R would guarantee a private loan made to H. R guaranteed the loan to H on company headed note paper and as chairman of B Ltd. The transaction was not reported to the board of directors. H, relying on the guarantee, advanced £45,000 to P Ltd. H subsequently resigned from the board of B Ltd, and P Ltd went into liquidation. It was held that, on the facts, R had actual authority, implied from the conduct of the parties, to enter into contracts and non–disclosure did not render it void.

2. Where there has been a failure to hold properly convened board meetings

The directors can only exercise their powers collectively by resolving at a properly convened board meeting that certain transactions should be entered into in the name of the company. The second type of defect where the *Turquand rule* may be invoked, therefore, is where the resolution is passed at an irregularly convened board meeting, or no board meeting is held at all and thus, no valid resolution is passed to the effect that the company should enter into the transaction. If proper notice of a board meeting is not given to each director, that will not affect a third party and the company will be bound by the transaction. Similarly, if the memorandum or articles require a minimum number of directors to be present to form a quorum, the rights of the third party are not affected if the meeting which authorises the transaction is inquorate. In *County of Gloucester Bank* v. *Rudry Merthyr Steam & House Coal*

Colliery Co (1895) the directors of a company passed a resolution fixing the number of directors required to form a quorum at three. At a board meeting where only two directors were present a resolution was passed which authorised the company to execute a mortgage of its assets in order to secure a loan. It was held that the transaction was valid and binding on the company since the mortgagee was unaware of the absence of a quorum at the board meeting.

If a transaction is entered into by someone who is not a director, the company cannot be held liable, unless it can be estopped from denying his authority as a director or officer of the company invested with power to bind the company.

The forgery exception

The protection given by the *Turquand* case to documents does not extend to forged documents. A company is not bound by a forged document although the person who took it did so under the belief that it was issued with the authority of the board of directors.

3. If limitations on the authority of the directors are disregarded

If a transaction entered into by the directors infringes a limitation on the powers of the directors, the other party to the transaction may, nevertheless, treat the company as bound by the contract if he entered into it in good faith. The other party is not bound to inquire about any limitations on the powers of the directors to bind the company and he is presumed to act in good faith. The *Turquand rule* does not protect a third party against absolute prohibitions in the company's memorandum or articles, or against infringements of restrictions on the powers of its directors which the transaction he enters into involves.

However, an outsider is protected if the directors of a company are empowered by the memorandum of articles to enter into the transaction in question but subject to certain procedural requirements being satisfied, e.g. where the directors are empowered to borrow money provided the shareholders consent in a general meeting.

Persons who can rely on the Turquand rule

The principle of the *Turquand* case is designed to protect third parties dealing with the company (i.e. persons who are not in any special relationship with the company) against defects in the internal management of the company's affairs. However, persons who are connected with the company and who have access to special information from which they should realise that procedural requirements have not been complied with cannot rely on the *Turquand rule*. In *Morris* v. *Kanssen* the person acting as a director could not rely on the *Turquand* case although some of the irregularities took place before he was appointed. The mere fact that a person is a member of the company will not disentitle him from relying on the *Turquand rule*. In *Bargate* v. *Shortridge* (1855) the articles of a company required its members to obtain the consent of the board of directors before transferring their shares. It was held that a member could rely on what appeared to be a written consent given by the board of directors although it was in fact the consent of the managing director alone. The company could not, therefore, claim the right to restore the member's name on the register.

COMPANIES AND THE LAW OF AGENCY

An agent is usually deemed to have that authority to do all acts on the principal's behalf which an agent of that class ordinarily has. If, therefore, the principal restricts the agent's authority, the principal will still be bound if the agent acts within the normal scope of his authority unless the third party dealing with the agent has actual notice of the agent's lack of authority. An agent who is not properly appointed to represent a company will only bind it if the company is estopped from denying that it conferred the requisite authority on the agent.

If the articles of a company do not enable the board of directors to delegate its powers, a company is not bound by a transaction entered into by an individual director although the company may have led an outsider to believe that it has power to delegate by exercising such a power.

SHARE AND LOAN CAPITAL

Nomenclature

1. Share capital
The share capital of a company is the amount of money contributed by its shareholders in return for an allotment of the company's shares. The money paid by the shareholders becomes the property of the company on payment. The company is not the debtor of the shareholders to the extent of their shares. A shareholder acquires a number of contractual and statutory rights against the company on the allotment of shares (e.g. the right to receive a dividend when it has been declared and the right to be repaid the capital he has contributed when all of the creditors have been paid in a winding-up).

2. Nominal value
Where a company is limited by shares, the liability of the shareholder to contribute towards the payment of its debts is the nominal value of the shares he holds. Once the nominal value of the shares has been paid the shareholder's obligation to contribute in a winding-up is discharged, unless the company is unlimited.

3. Nominal capital
The nominal capital of the company is the total of the nominal values of the shares it may issue.

4. Issued capital

A company's issued capital is the total of the nominal value of all the shares which have so far been allotted to shareholders. The difference, therefore, between the company's nominal and issued capital is its unissued capital.

5. Paid-up capital

The paid-up capital is the total amount paid up by shareholders on the shares they have taken up.

Where the company has not received payment of amounts from its shareholders equal to the nominal value of the shares issued to them, the difference is its unpaid capital.

6. Uncalled capital

The uncalled capital of a company is the difference between the amounts of paid-up or called-up capital on the issued shares and the amounts outstanding in the hands of the shareholder.

7. Called-up share capital

The Companies Act 1980, s. 87, provides that a company's called-up capital is the aggregate amount of the calls made by a company on its shares, whether or not those calls have been paid, together with any share capital paid up without a call being made and any share capital to be paid up at a future date specified under the articles.

PAYMENT FOR SHARES

The payment of shares is governed in part by the common law and in part by statute, namely the Companies Act 1980 which affects shares allotted by both public and private companies. However, the law on the payment of shares by a private company is still mainly governed by the common law and it is proposed firstly to deal with the common law and then to examine how the position has been altered in the case of public companies by the 1980 Act.

Allotment of shares for cash

Shares are paid for in cash when the shareholder pays the nominal value of the shares in cash to the company, together with any premium payable on the shares or, alternatively, when a company indebted to the shareholder allots shares to him as fully paid-up by the agreed discharge of the debt payable by it. In *Re Paraguassu Steam Tramroad Co* (1874) contractors agreed to supply steam engines to the P company. It was agreed that the contractors could set-off the purchase price payable for the steam-engines against any calls made on the shares allotted to them. The P company was wound up and the liquidator made a call on shares held by it. The court held that the contractors could not set off the amounts payable by the company for the engines against amounts remaining unpaid by them on the shares. The agreed set-off was effective only if both the debt payable by the company and the unpaid capital on the shares held by the creditor were due for payment before winding-up commenced. The unpaid capital in the present case only became due when called up by the liquidator.

Conditions for payment by appropriation of debts issued by the company
Shares will not be treated as paid up in cash by the appropriation or cancellation of a debt unless the company owes a liquidated sum which is payable immediately and agrees that it will be discharged in the payment of shares. The shareholder cannot set off a debt owed to him by a company if it brings an action against the shareholder for unpaid calls unless the company agrees that the debt will be appropriated for the purpose of discharging the shareholder's liability for payment of calls.

Shares will not be paid up in cash if a person merely has an unliquidated claim for damages against the company and he agrees to abandon the claim against the company in return for the allotment of full-paid shares of an equal or smaller nominal value. In *Re Barangah Oil Refining Co* (1887) it was agreed by the company and a claimant for unliquidated damages for breach of a contract he had made with the company, that he should be allotted fully paid-up shares in satisfaction of his claim. The liquidator brought an action for a declaration that the claimant was holder of the shares on which nothing should be treated as paid-up since the claim he sought to set-off was not a liquidated one. It was held that the shareholder had not paid cash for the shares allotted to him and the unliquidated claim he had against the company could not be treated as the equivalent of cash so that by surrendering it, the shares he held had not become fully paid.

A debt must be payable immediately if it is to be appropriated in payment of capital. The company cannot agree to allot fully paid-up shares for sums it may become liable to pay in the future but it can agree to allot shares in return for the shareholder's supplying goods to the company in future. The shares are treated as fully paid-up to the extent that the goods have been supplied and the company has become liable to pay their price.

If, however, an amount is immediately payable by the company, it may agree to appropriate the debt in payment of calls made in the future and, if such calls are made while the company is a going concern, the shares will be treated as paid to the extent payable by the company as and when the calls are made. If the company is wound up before the full amount payable has been appropriated to calls made on shares held by the debtor, the shareholder cannot treat future calls made by the liquidator as satisfied by the debt which the company owes him and he must pay these further calls in cash (*Re Paraguassu Steam Tramroad Co* (1874)).

Allotment of shares for a consideration other than cash
A private company may agree with a third party to allot shares to him in consideration for a promise to serve the company, e.g. as a director or in some

other capacity, or to perform certain services, e.g. to underwrite an issue of its shares, or to transfer property or assets held by the shareholder in return for the company's issuing its own shares to him. The contract of allotment may provide either that shares are to be allotted in consideration of the shareholder's providing certain property as services, or a specific price for which the shares are allotted and this will be satisfied by the shareholder's performing some obligation, e.g. by transferring property to the company.

However, an allotment of shares credited as fully paid in consideration of services already performed by the shareholder is not an allotment for a consideration other than cash, because services rendered in the past are no consideration for the subsequent allotment of fully paid–up shares. In *Re Eddystone Marine Insurance Co* (1893) the shareholders of a private company before its conversion into a public company issued further fully paid–up shares to themselves for services already rendered by them. The court held the company was not estopped from denying that the shares were not paid–up because the services were past consideration which was no consideration for the present allotment of shares. Moreover, the release by a shareholder of a debt payable by the company to him out of future profits is not valid consideration for the allotment of shares treated as either fully or partly paid–up. In *Bury* v. *Famatina Development Corporation* (1909) a company proposed to issue a number of fully paid–up shares to bond–holders in return for it's being discharged from its obligation to pay interest on the bonds in the future if the company should make a profit. It was held that the proposed issue of shares would not be allowed because it turned what was a contingent liability into a present liability and moreover, no consideration had been given for the issue of the shares.

Value of consideration given for allotment of shares
The courts usually treat the value of the consideration as a matter to be negotiated by the company and the allottee of shares. If, however, shares are allotted and the consideration in kind is worth less than the amount by which the shares are credited as paid–up, the court may hold that the shares will be deemed to be paid–up to an amount equal to the actual value of the consideration. The case of *Ooregum Gold Mining Company of India Ltd* v. *Roper* (1892) held that a company limited by shares has no power to issue shares as fully paid–up when the consideration given by the allottee is less than their nominal value. The facts of the case were that the directors of a company passed a resolution which would empower them to issue preference shares with a nominal value of £1 each, of which 15 shillings were to be treated as paid–up, leaving a liability of only 5 shillings per share. It was held that the issue was beyond the powers of the company and the preference shares were held subject to the liability of the holder to pay the company the full amount unpaid on the shares.

Failure of the company to assess the money value of the consideration
Whilst the courts will interfere to assess the cash value of the consideration given for shares, it requires the board of directors to make its own assessment of the value of such consideration. If the directors fail to make a cash assessment of the consideration supplied by the allottee the shares will not be treated as paid–up at all. In *Tintin Exploration Syndicate Ltd* v. *Sandys* (1947) a company allotted shares in consideration of the transfer to it of certain mining leases and of expenditure by the vendor on the improvement of the mines, but the directors failed to make an assessment of the cash value of the leases and improvements. It was held that the shares were not paid–up at all, because no attempt had been made to correlate the nominal value of the shares allotted to the value of the property and services granted. Since no contract had been entered into between the company and the allottee before the allotment of shares, it was held there was no evidence of the directors' having made an assessment of the cash value of the property transferred to the company.

If the directors have assessed the cash value of the consideration the court will not interfere with the assessment and set it aside, unless it was made in bad faith, or dishonestly or unless it can be shown that as reasonable men they could not have concluded that the consideration was equal in value to the amount credited as paid–up on the shares. In *Hong Kong and China Gas Co Ltd* v. *Glen* (1914–15) a company acquired a trading concession in exchange for an allotment of shares and agreed that if it subsequently increased its capital the vendor would be entitled to receive further commission equal to a quarter of the fully paid shares from its new issue. The court held that the vendor was entitled to a call for the additional shares on an increase in the company's capital, but he would have to pay cash for them because the number of further shares to be allotted to him was uncertain when the contract was made, and so the directors were not in a position to equate the nominal value of the further shares with the value of the concessions bought by the company. Similarly, in *Re White Star Line Ltd* (1938) where a company which had earned no profits accepted deferred creditor's certificates previously issued by it in payment of amounts unpaid on shares held by a shareholder; the certificates entitled the surrendering shareholder to payment of a debt out of the future profits of the company. It was held that the shares were not paid–up by the surrender of the certificates because the directors could not have considered them equal in value to the amounts unpaid on the shares.

The conduct of the parties may show that the directors did not genuinely believe that the consideration given for the shares was equal to the amount credited as paid–up on them. In *Re Innes & Co Ltd* (1903), however, the vendor agreed with the promoters to sell a business to the company yet to be formed for fully paid shares of a nominal value of £6,000. When the company was incorporated the vendor agreed to sell the business to it for fully paid £1 shares of a total nominal value of £25,000, and the shares were to be divided between the vendor of the business and his nominees. The court upheld the transaction because it was uncertain whether the directors had merely paid an extravagant price or had actually acted dishonestly.

If the directors do not make a genuine assessment of the consideration given for the shares, the shares are treated as wholly unpaid and the shareholder must pay their nominal price (*Re White Star Line Ltd* (1938)). If the shareholder is unaware that the directors have not made a genuine assessment of the value of the shares and at the time this comes to his notice he has not been registered as a member he may repudiate the allotment. If the allottee has been registered as a member in the company's register of members he may apply to the court for an order that his name shall be removed from the register and the contract rescinded. In *Tintin Exploration Syndicate Ltd* v. *Sandys* (1947) it was held that where an allotment of shares is made by the company without the directors' having made an assessment as to the value of the consideration given by the allottee the directors may be held personally liable.

The company may be entitled to rescind a contract where it has been induced to accept the consideration for shares it has allotted by a fraudulent misrepresentation or if the transaction is voidable because there has been a breach of fiduciary duty by the director or promoter. However, the other party does not cease to be a member of the company automatically. He will be liable to pay the nominal value of the shares in cash if he retains them. If the shareholder repudiates the allotment of the shares when the company rescinds the contract, he will cease to be under any liability to pay in cash for them provided he repudiates the contract immediately after the company rescinds the contract.

The effect of the 1980 Act

The common law still applies to the payment of shares and valuation of a non–cash consideration in the case of a private company. The Companies Act 1980 makes a number of changes where a public company allots shares, and, by s. 20(2), provides that whilst the payment of shares allotted by a public company may be in "money or money's worth", prohibits a public company from accepting payment for its shares, whether as the nominal value of the shares or any premium, by means of an undertaking to "do work or perform services" for the company. The result of this prohibition is that shares in a public company must necessarily be paid up either in cash or in non–cash assets. Section 87(3) provides that shares will be taken to have been paid–up in cash if the consideration is:

(*a*) cash received by the company; or

(*b*) a cheque received by the company in good faith which the directors have no reason for suspecting will not be paid; or

(*c*) the release of a liability of the company for a liquidation sum; or

(*d*) an undertaking to pay cash to the company at a future date.

Section 87(1) states that "non–cash assets" means "any property or interest in property other than cash."

Where a public company issues shares contrary to s. 20(2) and accepts work or services in payment for its shares, the holder of the shares will become liable to pay the amount of their nominal value together with any premium and interest to the company. Section 20(4) provides that where a subsequent holder acquires shares issued contrary to s. 20(2) he also becomes liable, jointly and severally, with the original allottee to pay the company unless either he is a purchaser for value who at the time of purchasing the shares had no knowledge that s. 20(2) had been contravened or he derived title to the shares from a person who acquired them after the contravention and was not himself so liable.

The Companies Act 1980, s. 29, requires shares issued by a public company to a subscriber to the memorandum in pursuance of his undertaking in it, together with any premium, to be paid in cash.

Valuation of non-cash assets under the 1980 Act

The Companies Act 1980, s. 24, provides that where a company allots shares as fully or partly paid-up for a consideration other than in cash, the assets or other benefits conferred on it must have been appraised by an independent third party during the six months immediately preceding the allotment and a copy of a report by that person on the value of the consideration must be sent to the proposed allottee. The valuation and report must be made by a person qualified to be the auditor of the company, but to assist him he may appoint an independent person to carry out the whole or part of the valuation. The person appointed must appear to the main valuer to be suitably qualified in terms of requisite knowledge and experience as to the value of the consideration and he must not be an officer or other employee of the company, or any other body corporate which is that company's holding or subsidiary company. The report made by the valuer must state:

(*a*) the nominal value of the shares to be either wholly or partly paid for by the consideration given by the proposed allottee;

(*b*) the amount of any premium on those shares;

(*c*) the description of that consideration, the method and date of valuation; and

(*d*) the extent to which the nominal value and the premium on those shares is to be treated as paid-up by the consideration, and secondly in cash.

Where the whole or part of the valuation is carried out by someone other than a qualified auditor, the report must state the person's name, the knowledge and experience of the valuer and the method of valuation employed by him.

Section 24 will not apply to an allotment of shares by a company where it issues shares on a merger or takeover. A merger results where one company acquires the undertaking of another company, whilst in a takeover the offeror company purchases the shares of the offeree company, possibly with a view to acquiring control. If the consideration offered for the acquisition is other than cash, a valuation is not required.

Shares issued at discount

The 1980 Act provides that a company cannot allot shares at a discount. If shares are issued in contravention of the section they will be treated as paid–up to the extent of the nominal value minus the amount of the discount.

Shares issued at a premium

If shares are issued at a price which exceeds their nominal value, the excess is a share premium which must be credited to a special capital reserve called the share premium account and cannot be distributed as a dividend though it may be repaid if the same procedure as for a reduction of capital is carried out. The share premium account can be used to pay–up the nominal value of bonus shares distributed gratuitously by the company to its members, or to write–off the preliminary expenses of forming the company. A share premium arising on the issue of shares in connection with a take–over bid by the company for another company which results in the former company's holding 90 per cent or more of the latter's ordinary shares need not be credited to the share premium account.

ALTERATION OF SHARE CAPITAL

The Companies Act 1948, s. 61(1), states that a company may, if its articles empower it to do so, alter the capital in various ways. Under this provision a company may:

(*a*) increase its nominal capital by a fixed amount divided into shares with a fixed nominal value;

(*b*) consolidate its existing shares into shares with a larger nominal value, (e.g. by consolidating each five 5p shares into one 25p share);

(*c*) subdivide its shares into shares with a small nominal value;

(*d*) convert fully paid up shares into stock; stock has the same total nominal value as the shares converted into stock but is transferable in any money denominations (e.g. 1p) even though this is smaller than the original nominal value of the shares;

(*e*) cancel shares which have not been allotted and reduce the amount of the nominal capital by the number of unissued shares.

A proposed alteration of the company's capital clause under s. 61 may be made by an ordinary resolution unless the company's articles expressly provide that it must be by special resolution.

Reduction of share capital

A reduction of the company's share capital may affect the interests of its creditors and members. A company may, therefore, only reduce its capital if the statutory conditions designed to ensure that the rights of creditors and shareholders are not adversely affected, are satisfied. However, certain transactions which result in either a temporary or permanent diminution of capital may be permitted without the company's complying with the strict conditions imposed by the law, for example:

1. Cancellation of unissued capital

A limited company may, if its articles permit, cancel shares which have not been issued or agreed to be allotted and reduce its nominal capital by the nominal value of such shares. An ordinary resolution will be sufficient unless the memorandum or articles require a special resolution. The Registrar of Companies must be given notice of the cancellation of the unissued shares within one month. The resolution does not affect the company's already issued or paid–up capital; it merely reduces its nominal capital so the number of shares a company may issue are now reduced.

2. Forfeiture and surrender in lieu of forfeiture

A company may be empowered by its articles to forfeit any shares held by a shareholder who fails to pay for them in accordance with the terms of the allotment and it may also have the power to reissue such forfeited shares. Alternatively, a company may accept the voluntary surrender of the shares if it could forfeit them and it may then reissue them. Shares which are forfeited or surrendered are not cancelled for they are merely held in abeyance until they are reissued. This merely results in a temporary reduction of the company's issued capital.

3. Other surrenders

A company may accept a surrender of fully paid shares if it gives no consideration out of its assets to the shareholder. The company does not release the shareholders liability for unpaid capital, nor does it return paid–up share capital to him.

Reduction of share capital with the sanction of the court

A limited company whose articles authorise it may, by a special resolution, confirmed by the court, reduce its share capital in any way. In particular the company may use one of the following methods prescribed in s. 66 of the 1948 Act:

1. By extinguishing or reducing the liability of its shareholders for unpaid capital in respect of shares issued to them

In such a case the company will reduce the nominal value of the shares issued, for example a company which has issued shares of a nominal value of £1 on which 50p has been paid–up may reduce the liability of its shareholders for the unpaid capital to 25p on each share by reducing the nominal value of the shares to 75p, or it may cancel the unpaid capital completely by reducing the nominal value of the shares to 50p. The same result may be achieved by leaving the nominal value of the shares as £1 per share, but by cancelling one share out of every two held by a shareholder.

2. By the return of capital to shareholders

A company which wishes to reduce its share capital may return paid–up capital which is in excess of its requirements. The company can, for example, distribute the cash it receives from the sale of surplus assets or part of its understanding amongst its shareholders in this way and reduce the nominal and paid–up value of their shares to an equivalent amount. A company need not necessarily convert its assets into cash in order to return paid–up capital. It may instead distribute its assets.

3. The company may cancel any paid–up capital which is lost or unrepresented by assets it holds

If the value of the company's net assets after deducting its liabilities is less than its paid–up capital (i.e. where the company either never had assets equal to the value of its paid–up capital because its shares were watered down or because it has suffered a trading loss) the company may reduce its paid–up capital by the amount of the deficiency and may also reduce the nominal value of its shares correspondingly.

The protection granted to creditors

In order to protect the interests of the company's creditors and shareholders s.66 provides that a proposed scheme introduced by the company, the effect of which would be to reduce its share capital, must be approved by the courts.

The Companies Act 1948, s. 67(2), provides that, where a reduction of the company's capital involves reducing the liability of its shareholders for unpaid capital, or the return of paid–up capital, any creditor who could claim in the company's winding–up may object to the reduction but, if the debt is paid–off, the creditor cannot object.

A court will not sanction a resolution which purposes a reduction of capital unless a full list of the company's creditors, verified by an affidavit is filed in court and a notice of the proposed reduction, is sent to each creditor advertised by the company.

A reduction of capital will be approved if the court is satisfied that the creditors named in the affidavit have either been paid–off or have consented to the reduction (R.S.C. Ord. 102, r. 12). The court may dispense with these requirements if the company has deposited a sum of money with the court to satisfy any claims that may be brought by its creditors.

If a creditor who is entitled to object to the reduction does not receive notification of the proposed reduction because his name is omitted from the list of creditors filed with the court and in consequence does not receive payment, he may require each shareholder who holds shares on the date the reduction is sanctioned by the court to contribute towards the payment of his claim against the company. The amount he can require each shareholder to pay cannot exceed the difference between the nominal and paid–up value of his shares before the reduction (Companies Act 1948, s. 70(1)).

If the court dispenses with the provisions allowing creditors to object to the proposed reduction, then the creditor has no rights against the company's shareholders.

The court may direct that the provisions designed to protect creditors where the company proposes to reduce its share capital by reducing the liability of its shareholders for unpaid capital or by the return of capital will apply in any other case where the scheme for reduction of capital does not involve the diminution of liability of shareholders for unpaid capital or the return of paid–up capital to them.

The right of shareholders on a reduction of capital

A reduction of capital is, in fact, a partial winding–up and if capital is reduced by being repaid or by cancellation of any paid–up capital which is lost or unrepresented the order of reduction amongst the different classes of shareholders should follow the order of distribution of capital in a winding–up. In *Re Floating Dock of St Thomas Ltd* (1895) it was held that, where a company issues preference shares which carry the right to be repaid capital in a winding–up before the ordinary shareholders are repaid, a reduction of capital because of loss of assets must first be borne by the ordinary shareholders and only after the paid–up value of such shares have been reduced will the value of preference shares be reduced.

If preference shares have no priority for repayment of capital, they will be repaid capital rateably with the ordinary shareholders. In so far as a reduction of capital affects the same class of shareholders, the company need not adhere to the order of distribution in a winding–up and so more capital may be repaid on some shares than on other shares of the same class. However, if the shareholders of a same class are not treated equally, the scheme will not be approved under the 1948 Act, s. 66, but will have to comply with s. 206. The normal order of reduction of capital between different classes of shares may be varied with the consent of the class of shareholders whose rights will be adversely affected, and a provision in the articles that such rights may be varied with the consent of the holders of a certain fraction of the shares of that class may be invoked for this purpose.

The function of the court

In addition to ensuring that the right of different classes of shareholders are represented, the court has the function of ensuring that the proposed scheme of reduction is fair and equitable. This is something the courts will be ready to assume if the scheme is proposed in good faith. In *Carruth* v. *Imperial Chemical Industries Ltd* (1937) the company's deferred shareholders opposed a scheme for a reduction of its share capital on the grounds that it affected them adversely, and that a separate meeting of the deferred shareholders should have been called. The company's capital consisted of preference, ordinary and deferred shares. It proposed to reduce its capital by cancelling its paid–up capital to the extent of 5s on each 10s deferred share, and reducing the nominal amount of each to 5s share and converting them into ordinary shares. Under the memorandum the special rights attaching to any special loss of shares could not be altered without the sanction of the class affected at a separate class meeting. General and class meetings were called and held on the same day and the necessary resolutions were passed. The holders of shares other than deferred shares were present at the deferred shareholders' class meeting and no member of that class objected, although they did not vote. A petition for confirmation was opposed by deferred shareholders who argued that the reduction was ultra vires as there had been no valid class meetings. The court held that the scheme was fair to both the ordinary and deferred shareholders and the reduction was confirmed.

If the scheme of reduction involves an alteration of the rights attached to a class of shares and the consent of that class is required, the court will not approve the reduction of capital if the majority shareholders of that class act with an ulterior motive and not in the interests of the members of that class generally.

Procedure for reduction of capital

After a special resolution for a reduction of capital has been passed, the company must present a petition to the Companies Court to have the reduction confirmed. A summons for directions is taken out and the Registrar may order the company to take certain steps to protect the creditors. The Registrar will order the petition to be published. After the Registrar's Certificate has been filed, the petition is heard by the court, which may confirm the reduction on such terms as it thinks fit. If the court approves the scheme, a copy of the court's order and a minute approved by the court showing the state of the company's capital after the reduction must be delivered to the Registrar of Companies. On the registration of these documents the reduction becomes effective. The Registrar of Companies will then issue a certificate, which is conclusive evidence that the requirements of the Companies Acts have been complied with.

CLASSES OF SHARES

The rights attached to different classes of shares may be contained in the company's memorandum or articles, or alternatively the articles may empower the directors to issue the company's unissued shares with such rights attached as they think appropriate in a general meeting. The Companies Act 1980, s.33(1), provides that where a company allots shares which carry rights not expressly stated in the memorandum or articles or in any resolution or agreement (not negotiated under the 1948 Act, s. 143) the company must deliver to the Registrar of Companies within one month of allotting the shares a statement containing particulars of those rights.

Preference shares

The holder of preference shares is entitled to receive a fixed dividend before the ordinary shareholders. Where there are two or more classes of preference shares, the holders of the class which has priority will be entitled to receive a dividend before the other class. Preference shares are a part of the company's capital and therefore a dividend can only be paid if the company has earned sufficient profits.

A dividend is only payable to the shareholder once it has been declared in accordance with the procedure laid down in the articles. A shareholder cannot bring an action for payment of a dividend unless it has been properly declared. A provision in the articles that the preference dividend will become payable without the company's declaring a dividend is void (*Re Bond* v. *Barrow Haematite Steel Co* (1901)). But the company's profits must be adequate to pay the dividend. The company cannot be compelled to declare a dividend and, therefore, if the directors of the company decide to set aside the profits earned in a particular year as reserves, the shareholders cannot compel the company to declare a dividend (*Re Buenos Ayres Great Southern Steel Co Ltd* (1947)).

A preference dividend may be cumulative under the terms of issue, so if profits are insufficient in any one year, the unpaid balance is carried forward to future years and payable out of profits earned in subsequent years. A dividend cannot then be paid to the company's ordinary shareholders until the preference shareholders have been paid their accumulated dividends in full.

The whole of the cumulative dividend is paid to the person who holds the shares when a dividend is declared. An unpaid balance which is carried forward from earlier years is not therefore payable to the person who held the shares during those years (*Re Wakley, Wakley* v. *Vachell* (1920)).

If the dividend on the shares is expressed to be non–cumulative, any unpaid balance of the dividend which the company cannot pay in that year will not be carried forward.

Right of the preference shareholder to participate in residual profits
A preference shareholder is only entitled to his fixed preference dividend out of the company's distributable profits. He is not also entitled to a share in the residual profits of the company after the other shareholders have been paid an equivalent dividend. In *Will* v. *United Lankat Plantations Co* (1914) the terms under which the preference shares were issued provided that they should carry a cumulative preference dividend of 10 per cent. It was held that the preference shareholders were not entitled to a share of the residual profits because the terms of issue made specific provision about the payment of dividend and the terms of issue were presumed to provide exhaustively the rights of the shareholders. Since the terms of issue did not expressly provide that the preference shareholders were entitled to a share in the residuary profit of the company, the presumption was that the shareholders had no such right.

Preference shares under which the shareholder is entitled to a share of residual profits after the ordinary shareholders have been paid are known as participating preference shares.

Repayment of capital to preference shareholders

Preference shareholders are not presumed to be entitled to repayment of their capital in the company's winding–up in priority to the ordinary shareholders. Unless the terms of issue expressly provide, preference and ordinary shareholders must be repaid their capital rateably in a winding–up. If the assets of the company are insufficient to repay the whole of its capital, all its shareholders must be repaid the capital on their shares proportionally to the nominal value of the shares.

Finally, if the assets of a company which is in liquidation are more than sufficient to repay the shareholders their capital, any surplus after repayment is distributable between all the shareholders, except where the preference shares carry priority for repayment of capital.

A dividend which is declared before the company commences winding–up is a debt owed by the company, and in the winding–up must be paid immediately after all the other debts have been discharged.

Ordinary shares

The ordinary shareholders are entitled to be paid a dividend only after all the preference dividends have been paid or, if they have priority for repayment of capital in a winding–up, after the preference shareholders have been paid. In a winding–up the ordinary shareholders are entitled to the whole of the surplus assets after the debenture–holders, preference shareholders and unsecured creditors have been paid. Ordinary shares usually carry more voting rights proportionately to their nominal value than other classes of shares.

Deferred shares

These shareholders only qualify for a dividend to be paid to them after the ordinary shareholders have been paid a dividend. The risk they carry of not being paid a dividend is even greater than the ordinary shareholders.

Variation of class rights

The articles of association usually provide that the terms or rights which are attached to any class of shares may be varied normally with consent of shareholders, i.e. by special resolution. If rights conferred on a particular class of shareholders are contained in the memorandum of association they cannot be varied under the Companies Act 1948, s. 23, but if the memorandum itself provides a method of alteration, then that method must be followed.

However, the Companies Act 1980, s. 32, provides for a variation of a clause relating to class rights in certain circumstances:

(*a*) Where there is no provision for a variation in either the memorandum or articles:

(*i*) and where class rights are specified in the memorandum, any variation requires the consent of all the members of the company;

(*ii*) where the class rights are specified elsewhere (i.e. in the articles or term of issue), a variation requires either the written consent of the holders of three–quarters of the issued shares of that class, or the sanction of an extraordinary resolution passed at a class meeting.

Moreover, any other requirements expressly stated in document containing class rights must be observed.

(*b*) where there is a provision for variation in either the memorandum or the articles:

(*i*) and the method of variation of class rights is expressly stated in the memorandum of articles, if the variation relates to the revocation, renewal, variation or grant of the directors authority to allot shares or a reduction of share capital, the consent of three–quarters of the holders of that class is required or an extraordinary resolution of shareholders of that class as well as conformity with any other requirement of the memorandum or articles; or

(*ii*) where the class rights are specified in the memorandum, and the articles contain a provision for a variation, the variation must be in accordance with that provision; or

(*iii*) where the class rights are specified elsewhere, and the articles contain a provision for a variation the variation must be in accordance with that provision.

Appeal against consent to variation of rights
Where the memorandum or articles provide for variation of class rights with the consent of shareholders or where class rights are varied under a statutory provision the holders of not less than 15 per cent of the issued shares of that class who did not consent to, or vote for the variation may apply to the court to cancel the variation and if the court is satisfied that the variation would unfairly prejudice the shareholders, it may cancel the variation (Companies Act 1948, s. 72). A petition to the court for cancellation must be filed within 21 days of the consent to the variation by the class whose rights are affected. When a petition is presented to the court the variation is suspended immediately and becomes effective only if it is confirmed by the court. A petition may be presented by any one or more of the shareholders appointed by the others to act for them all, if written authority by other shareholders is given before the applicant presents the petition.

The court's power is confined to either approving or disallowing the variation, it cannot amend the variation or approve it subject to conditions. It can cancel the variation if it would unfairly prejudice some of the shareholders of the class affected, i.e. if those consenting acted in bad faith, or fraud or oppression is alleged. In *Carruth* v. *Imperial Chemicals Industries Ltd* (1937) it was held that where shareholders who vote in favour of the variation are motivated by fraud then a petition for variation can be presented outside the 21 day period.

What amounts to a substantial variation?
Class rights are varied only if they are different in substance after the alleged act of variation from what they were before the variation, so if they are same in

substance but merely commercially less valuable, this is not a substantial variation and class consent is unnecessary. An increase in the shares so that the existing shares of a particular class would be worth less is not a substantial variation and therefore class consent is unnecessary. In *White* v. *Bristol Aeroplane Co Ltd* (1953) and *Re John Smith Tadcaster Brewery Co Ltd* (1953), the companies in question proposed to increase their capital by a bonus issue of shares and the question was whether they needed to obtain class consent for the variation. It was held that since the issue of new shares would not affect the rights and privileges of existing shareholders of the classes of which further shares were to be issued the increase did not have to be sanctioned by them. The relative voting strength of the shareholders would be affected, but in substance the rights attached to the shares would be unaltered (e.g. the right to vote at meetings and the right to receive a dividend) and therefore class consent was unnecessary in either case.

Where the alteration would affect the rights of an existing class of shareholders in substance, the consent of the class is necessary in accordance with either the memorandum, or articles or the Companies Act 1980. In *Re Old Silkstone Collieries Ltd* (1954) a coal mining company after nationalisation reduced its capital by repaying 10s out of every £1 in the nominal value of its stock. The resolution for reduction of stock provided that preference stockholders should remain entitled to the same adjustment of their interest as if the reduction had not taken place. The company was held not to be entitled to reduce its capital further by repaying the remaining 10s on each share because that would extinguish the rights of the preference shareholders to share in the government compensation scheme.

The redistribution of voting or other rights may amount to a substantial variation of class rights, although under the original test it would not amount to a literal variation. In *Greenhalgh* v. *Arderne Cinemas Ltd* (1946) the company proposed to divide its 10s shares, each carrying five votes into five shares each carrying one vote. It was held that this did not amount to a variation of the rights of the shareholders who held shares of a nominal value of 2s each carrying one vote although their proportionate voting strength was thereby reduced. The court said that if the only rights that were affected by the variation were the rights of enjoyment to the shares, then any variation would not be a substantial variation and class consent would not be required. Moreover, the shareholders who seek to object to the variation must show their rights are directly affected by the variation.

RAISING OF CAPITAL BY A LARGE ISSUE OF SECURITIES

A public company may raise the capital it requires by a large scale issue of shares or debentures. This can be done in one of the following ways:

(*a*) by a rights issue and open offers; or

(*b*) by placings; or

(*c*) by a public offer, either by a prospectus published by the company or by an offer for sale published by an issuing house or broker.

Rights issues and open offers

The company will invite its existing share or debenture-holders to subscribe for the further capital it requires. If the company issues further ordinary shares for cash it must first offer them to existing shareholders before inviting the general public to subscribe and any shares not subscribed by the existing shareholders can be offered to the general public. The company cannot offer those shares to the general public during the time in which the offer was to remain open to the existing shareholders or until the company has had a refusal to accept further shares from the shareholders. Under the Companies Act 1980, a company must make a new rights offer of any new ordinary shares it proposes to issue to the holders of its existing ordinary shares where the issue price is to be paid in cash. This may be avoided only by the ordinary shareholders passing a special resolution waiving their preferential subscription rights.

When a rights issue is made the company will send to each share or debenture holder a circular letter, called a letter of rights, inviting him to subscribe for further shares or debentures in proportion to his existing holding. The letter of rights may simply enable the person to whom it is addressed to subscribe for further shares and in this event the right to subscribe cannot be transferred. However, renounceable letters of rights are more common than non-renounceable ones and the letter may contain a form of renunciation which the addressee may sign in order to exercise his right to subscribe. A company may make a rights offer in the form of a provisional letter of allotment. The new securities are actually allotted to the share or debenture holder unless he rejects them. A provisional letter of allotment may be renounceable or non-renounceable.

A variant to the rights issue is the open offer. The invitation is confined to existing share or debenture holders but no limit is placed on the number of securities for which the shareholder may apply. The number of shares so allotted, therefore, does not depend on the existing holding. A rights offer may be combined with an open offer so that existing shareholders who wish to take more shares than they are entitled to on a proportionate basis are given the opportunity. The price at which securities are offered by a letter of rights is usually below the current market value of existing securities in order to induce shareholders to subscribe.

Placings

When a company has its shares or debentures placed, it agrees to allot the whole issue to an issuing house (usually a merchant bank or stockbroker) at an agreed price. They will then sell the securities to purchasers at a profit and retain the difference between the issue price which they paid the company and the price at which they resell the securities. The issuing house or brokers have to pay the company the issue price whether or not they resell the securities.

Only securities for which a stock exchange listing has been sought are placed by issuing houses or brokers and therefore before the issuing house or broker binds itself to place shares or debentures the company must apply for a stock exchange listing.

The issuing house or stockbrokers who place securities resell them to jobbers or dealers who are members of the Stock Exchange. The Stock Exchange requires that at least 25 per cent of the shares should be offered to the public for sale. The shares are then available for purchase on the Stock Exchange by members of the investing public.

Public offers

Where the company invites the public generally to subscribe for securities anyone may apply for any number of shares or debentures. A public offer may be made by using one of the two following methods:

(*a*) the company may issue a prospectus or advertisement inviting the public to subscribe for the securities; or

(*b*) it may agree to allot the whole issue to an issuing house which then issues a prospectus inviting the public to purchase the securities from it. The issuing–house makes a profit by selling shares to the public at a price higher than that which it paid the company.

A company will only invite subscriptions from the public directly if it is large enough and can inspire public confidence by its own name. A public offer of securities has little chance of success unless listed on the Stock Exchange.

Underwriting

A company, issuing house or stockbroker undertake a risk when floating a public issue. They can insure against these risks by an underwriting agreement whereby a person agrees to purchase shares if those originally invited fail to take them. An underwriter is paid a commission. A company need not underwrite its shares when it offers them to existing share or debenture holders by letter of rights, or when the company issues a prospectus and invites the public to subscribe for shares direct. If the securities are being placed for sale by an issuing house or by stockbrokers, it is they who should arrange to have the issue underwritten because they bear the risk of the venture's proving a failure. If underwriters wish to purchase the shares for investment purposes they will underwrite "firm" and they subscribe for a number of shares like an ordinary applicant but they are still entitled to their underwriting commission.

Prospectuses

The Companies Act 1948 defines a prospectus as "any prospectus, notice, circular, advertisement or other invitation, offering to the public for subscription or purchase any shares or debentures of a company".

The prospectus must be in writing and it must induce the persons to whom it is addressed to subscribe for or purchase securities for cash. An invitation to acquire securities for a consideration in kind is not a prospectus under the Companies Acts (*see Government Stock & Other Securities Investment Co Ltd* v. *Christopher* (1956)).

A prospectus must contain an invitation addressed to the public at large so that anyone may apply for the securities; but it can also include any section of the public, whether selected because they are members of the company or because they are clients of the person issuing the prospectus. If the invitation does not extend to the general public then it is not a prospectus. Therefore, a non–renounceable letter of rights is not a prospectus but if an invitation to subscribe can be used by someone other than the person to whom it is addressed then it will be a prospectus.

Requirements of a prospectus

A prospectus must be dated and a copy must be presented to the Registrar of Companies (before it is issued), signed by every person named in it as a director, or by his authorised agent. If a prospectus is issued by an issuing house or stockbroker, the copy delivered to the Registrar must also be signed on behalf of the issuing house or brokers by at least two of its directors and must contain a statement that a copy has been delivered to the Registrar. The Registrar of Companies cannot refuse to register a copy of a prospectus on the ground that it is either false or misleading.

Prospectus issued generally

The prospectus must contain certain information, except where it is issued to existing members of a company with an invitation to subscribe for further shares or debentures, or where it relates to shares or debentures which will be uniform with shares or debentures previously issued by the company and which are listed on a recognised stock exchange or when it is issued to a person requested to underwrite securities to be offered by the prospectus.

A prospectus or application form must contain certain additional information if it does not fall within the three types of document dealt with above and is issued to outsiders in addition to the company's existing members or debenture holders and relates to new class of securities.

Contents of a prospectus issued generally

The prospectus must contain information specified in the Companies Act 1948, Sched. 4, Part I, and it must contain the accountant's reports specified in Part II of the Schedule. The information which must be contained is:

(a) *A statement of the company's share and loan capital.*
The prospectus must give details of the rights of different classes of shareholders in respect of dividend, capital and voting rights. It must state the number of founders, of management or deferred shares and the content of the interest of each holder in the company's property. The prospectus must also state the profits of the company. If any persons have an option to subscribe for the shares or debentures of the company it must state who the option holders are and the price they must pay for the securities if they exercise their option, must give details of the shares offered and allotted for cash within the previous two years, details of any shares allotted for a consideration other than in cash

and details of the consideration given for the allotments.

(*b*) *Details of the securities offered by the prospectus*:

If the prospectus offers shares for subscription or purchase it must state the amount payable by a subscriber on application and allotment, including any amounts payable as share premiums. An estimate of the amount required from the proceeds of the issue of shares to meet the purchase price of any property which is to be paid out of the proceeds and the expenses of issuing the shares must also be given. The amount required out of the proceeds of the issue to meet these expenses is known as the "minimum subscription".

(*c*) *Particulars of the company's business.*

If the company has carried on business for less than three years, or if the issue is being made to enable it to purchase a business which has been carried on for less than three years, the length of time for which the company has carried on business must be stated. The prospectus must contain a report by the company's auditors on its assets and liabilities on the last date to which its accounts were made up, and on its profits and losses and the rates of dividend paid on each class of its shares for each of the five financial years (if the company has been carrying on business for that length of time) preceding the issue of the prospectus, or for each of its financial years since its incorporation if that was less than five years previously. If the proceeds of the issue are to be used to purchase another business, similar reports by a named accountant in respect of that business must be disclosed in the prospectus. Any material contracts and the dates on which these were entered must be stated. Material contracts are those which are likely to influence prospective investors in deciding whether or not to purchase shares but do not include contracts made in the ordinary course of the company's business.

(*d*) *The proposed application of the proceeds of the issue.*

If the company proposes to apply the whole or part of the proceeds of the issue in paying for property which it has acquired or proposes to acquire, or if it has not completed the purchase of property which it proposes to acquire at the date when the prospectus is issued, it must state the names and address of the vendors, the total purchase price and the proportion to be paid in cash or otherwise, and the amount payable to each vendor and the manner of payment. Information must be given of all transactions relating to the property completed within two years before the issue of the prospectus in which the vendor, promoter or director of the company had an interest. This ensures that where a vendor (e.g. a promoter selling property to the company after its incorporation) has recently bought the property at a much lower price than he is charging the company, the price which the vendor paid is disclosed so that intending investors can decide the real value of the property.

(*e*) *Promoters and directors.*

The names, addresses and descriptions of company directors must be stated in the prospectus, together with the number of shares which the articles require each director to hold as his qualification shares. Any amounts paid and benefits given to the promoters within two years before the issue of the prospectus, or intended to be paid or given to them, and the consideration for payments or benefits must be disclosed. Moreover, any amounts paid (or promised) to the directors in cash or shares to induce them to become directors or in payment of services provided must be disclosed and, if a director has an interest in any property to be acquired by the company, that too must be declared.

If the securities offered to the general public are not uniform with the existing shares listed on the Stock Exchange, it is an offence to issue an application form for them unless it is accompanied by a prospectus containing the above information, but this does not apply where an application form is sent to a person invited to underwrite the issue.

Certificate of exemption
A company wishing to issue a prospectus which has applied for Stock Exchange listing for the securities to be offered by it may apply for a certificate of exemption to be issued by the Stock Exchange. The company will then issue a prospectus in accordance with the Stock Exchange rules and the Companies Act 1948.

Stock Exchange requirements as to the contents of prospectus
In the case of all public offerings of shares or debentures which have a Stock Exchange listing or seek it, the rules of the Stock Exchange impose additional duties of disclosure on top of those imposed by the Companies Acts. The Stock Exchange requirements apply to prospectuses issued by a company or an issuing house in connection with an offer for sale of securities and to information published in connection with placings. The Companies Act 1948 only applies to new securities, whilst the Stock Exchange rules apply to the secondary marketing of securities, where the existing holders of shares or debentures offer the whole or part of their holdings for sale. The Stock Exchange rules require the disclosure of additional information to that called for by the Companies Act 1948 (e.g. a summary of the geographical and sectoral distribution of the company's activities and a forecast of its short–term business prospects).

Failure to comply with rules relating to prospectuses issued generally
The Companies Act 1948 does not expressly provide for the consequences if a prospectus does not comply either with Sched. 4 of the Act, or with the requirements of the Stock Exchange rules. The Act makes it an offence to issue a defective prospectus accompanied by an application form for the securities offered.

If, however, the securities are placed, the information notice published in the press will not be accompanied by an application form so that even if the notice omits the required information no offence is committed.

A subscriber cannot rescind an allotment of securities which he is induced to take by a prospectus which omits certain information required to be enclosed by the 1948 Act, Sched. 4, under the Stock Exchange rules.

False statements in invitations to subscribe

If an invitation to subscribe for shares or debentures contains false statements made by a company, an issuing house or any other person responsible for the statement is subject to both civil and criminal action.

Civil remedies

Rescission

If an invitation to subscribe for shares or debentures contains a false statement of fact which is believed to be true by a person to whom it is addressed and he applies for, and is allotted, shares or debentures to which the invitation relates, he may rescind the allotment and recover the money he has paid, when he discovers the falsity of the statement.

The false statement must fall within the rules of misrepresentation, namely it must have been a material statement of fact which induced the purchaser to subscribe for the share. A misrepresentation as to the effect of law, or opinion, or a forecast of the company's profits which turns out to be unfounded cannot be made the subject of rescission. However, a statement by the directors that they intend to use the money raised by the issue of shares for a particular purpose, can be relied upon and the contract rescinded if it turns out to be false. Similarly, a representation as to the contents of the company's memorandum if false will entitle the allottee to rescind. The prospectus must not only be free from statements which are literally untrue, but also from statements which may be misleading. It is only when the prospectus is required to disclose certain information under the Companies Acts that the statement it contains must be true, and if it omits to mention a certain feature, the subscriber for shares cannot complain.

The plaintiff can rescind an allotment only if he was induced to take it by a false statement of fact addressed to him by the company, or by the issuing house or stockbroker responsible for the prospectus. An investor who is induced to buy securities from an existing holder by reading the prospectus under which they were issued cannot rescind his transaction and require the company to take the securities from him if he relies on a statement in the prospectus which is false.

If a prospectus is addressed to a limited class of persons only those persons may rely on it and rescind an allotment if it contains false any statements, i.e. a non–renounceable letter of rights can be relied upon only by the share or debenture–holders to whom it is addressed.

A renounceable letter may be construed as an offer to issue securities to an existing share or debenture holder or to persons whom they nominate by renunciation. A person to whom the letter is renounced can accept the offer and subscribe for shares and, if there is a misrepresentation, the allottee can rescind.

The false statement must be addressed to the plaintiff who seeks to rescind the allotment by someone who has authority from the company or issuing house. An individual director has no implied authority to solicit subscriptions for the company's securities on its behalf without authorisation by the board of directors.

The plaintiff must show that the false statement in the prospectus or other invitation induced him to subscribe for the securities and if his conduct shows that he did not rely on the statement, the company is not liable. In *Jennings* v. *Broughton* (1853) the plaintiff subscribed for shares in a mining company, offered by a prospectus which inaccurately described the capacity of a mine. The court held he was not entitled to rescind because he had inspected the mine himself and must therefore have relied on his own observations and not the contents of the prospectus.

Winding-up

A subscriber for shares which are partly paid loses his right to rescind if the company is ordered to be wound-up by the court, if it resolves to be wound up voluntarily or if it fails to pay its debt in the ordinary course of the business because it is insolvent. On a winding-up, the company's creditors may compel the shareholders to pay the unpaid capital in respect of their shares in order to satisfy the company's debts so if a shareholder were allowed to rescind he would prejudice the rights of the company's creditors. If the company agrees to rescind the contract, the company should remove the subscriber's name from the register of members. If it refuses to do so the subscriber is entitled to bring an action for rescission against it and the allotment will be treated as rescinded only when such an action has commenced.

If an action for rescission is commenced before the winding-up the court can declare that the rescission is effective although judgment is not given until after the winding-up order is made.

Action for damages for deceit

In addition to the requirements of rescission the plaintiff must also prove that the defendant knew that the statement complained of was false, that he did not honestly believe it to be true, or that he made it recklessly, not caring whether it was true or false (*see Derry* v. *Peek* (1889)). The court is ready to infer that the defendant knew of the falsity of the statement on its being shown that he had knowledge of facts from which he must have realised that the statement was false.

Persons who may be sued

The persons who issue the invitation to subscribe for securities (whether directors or promoters) may be sued for deceit. If the invitation is in a prospectus issued by the company, the directors will be responsible because it is by their board's resolution that the prospectus is issued. If a director can show that he did not take part in the relevant board meeting, or did not agree to the issue of the prospectus, he may be excused personal liability. However, the company may be held vicariously liable for the fraud of its directors.

Measure of damages

The loss suffered by the plaintiff as a result of the deceit is the difference between the price he paid for the securities and their real value on the date he took them. He cannot recover damages for the company's failure to honour the high expectations which it held in the prospectus.

If the plaintiff can show that the market value of securities when he took them was greater than the amount he has been paid for them he will be able to recover the difference as additional damage.

Action for damages in negligence

The common law action for negligent mis–statements under the rule in *Hedley Bryne & Co* v. *Heller & Partners* (1964) is only available where the Companies Act 1948, s. 43, does not grant relief.

Statutory claim for compensation

Any person who is induced to subscribe for shares or debentures by an untrue statement in a prospectus may claim compensation for the loss he has suffered in consequence from the persons responsible for the issue of the prospectus which contains false statements. The claim only lies where the invitation to subscribe was contained in a prospectus and not when the plaintiff was induced to subscribe by a non–renounceable letter of rights, by a statement in lieu of a prospectus or by a provisional letter of allotment. The action does not apply where the plaintiff was induced to subscribe for the securities from an existing holder; but if the securities are offered for sale to the public by an issuing house after the company has allotted them to it for that purpose, the purchase of securities by an investor under the offer for sale is treated as though it were a subscription for the shares from the company. An action may be brought against any person who was a director of the company on the date when the prospectus was issued, or against any person who authorised the use of his name in the prospectus as a director or against a promoter of the company who was a party to the preparation of the prospectus or a party to the part of the prospectus that contained the untrue statement.

If a prospectus is issued by the issuing house its directors will be liable for any untrue statements. An expert who gives a report is liable if the false statement is in his part of the report. However, an action cannot be brought against the company itself under the Companies Act 1948, s. 43.

The plaintiff merely has to prove that he subscribed for shares or debentures in reliance on the false statement in the prospectus and that he has suffered a loss in consequence. A statement is deemed to be false if it is misleading in the context in which it is made, and the measure of damages which will be awarded will be the same as in an action for deceit.

However, the defendant is liable basically for negligence and he can escape liability if he can show that he was not negligent in failing to discover the false statement in the prospectus. The statutory defences fall into two groups namely, those which are available to a person other than an expert whose statement is contained in the prospectus, and statements made by an expert.

A defendant other than an expert may escape liability by showing that the false statement was contained in a report made by an expert who had agreed in writing to its being included in the prospectus and his consent had not been withdrawn before a copy of the prospectus was filed at the Companies' Registry and, furthermore, that the defendant believed that the expert was competent to make the statement, or that the untrue statement was expressed to be a statement made by an official person or that it was a copy or extract from an official document and was a fair representation of that statement or document, or in any other case the defendant believed the statement on reasonable grounds to be true up to the time when the plaintiff's shares or debentures were allotted to him.

A defendant other than an expert may additionally, escape liability by proving certain personal defences namely, that being liable as a person who had consented to become a director he withdrew his consent before the prospectus was issued and he did not authorise its issue; that being a director or promoter he did not consent to the issue of the prospectus and on its issue he gave reasonable public notice that it was issued without his consent; or that he only became aware of the untrue statement after the prospectus was issued and before any shares or debentures were allotted he withdrew his consent to the prospectus and gave reasonable public notice of his withdrawal.

An expert has three defences available to him namely; that he was competent to make the statement or report complained of and believed it to be true on reasonable grounds up to the time when the debentures or shares were allotted, or that he withdrew his consent to the inclusion of his report before a copy of the prospectus was filed at the Companies Registry, or that after a copy of the prospectus had been filed he discovered the false statement complained of and withdrew his consent to the inclusion of the statement or report in the prospectus.

Misrepresentation Act 1967

The Misrepresentation Act 1967, s. 2(1), gives a statutory right to sue for damages to a person who has been induced to enter into a contract by a misrepresentation made by the other party. Such an action can only be brought if the plaintiff has first rescinded the allotment made to him and consequently, if he has lost his right to rescind he cannot sue at all. The Act only permits the recovery of damages equal to the loss suffered by the plaintiff.

Criminal proceedings

In addition to civil proceedings, criminal proceedings may be brought under various statutes against persons responsible for issuing invitations to subscribe for or purchase securities which contain false statements of fact, e.g. a director who publishes a written statement which he knows to be false with intent to induce any person to become a shareholder will be guilty of obtaining by deception under the Theft Act 1968. It is also an offence for a person to induce or attempt to induce another person to dispose of shares, or to underwrite any shares by making a false statement. Finally, the Companies Act 1948 makes it an offence for any person to authorise the issue of a prospectus or the filing of a statement in lieu of a prospectus which contains an untrue statement. The prosecution need only show that the statement was in fact false and the accused must either prove that the statement was immaterial, or that he, on reasonable grounds up to the time when the prospectus was issued or a statement in lieu of a prospectus was filed, believed it to be true.

ALLOTMENTS, CALLS AND MEMBERSHIP

Contracts to subscribe for shares and debentures

The Companies Act 1980, s. 14, provides that directors can only exercise their power to allot shares or securities if they have been so authorised by the members in a general meeting, or if the articles expressly confer authority on them. The authority conferred on the directors may be of a limited duration but it cannot exceed five years. It may be for a single allotment.

The contract for the allotment of shares or debentures, is subject to the ordinary rules of the law of contract as modified by the Companies Act 1948. The issue of a prospectus by a company is merely an invitation to prospective purchasers to make an offer for the purchase of shares. The contract is concluded when the company accepts the offer and allots shares to the investor and notifies him of the allotment (*Household Fire Insurance Co* v. *Grant* (1879)).

Lapse and revocation

An application for the allotment of shares or debentures will lapse unless accepted within a reasonable time and may be revoked at any time before it is accepted. A company may accept an offer at any time after it has been made and before it is revoked by allotting shares and giving notification of the allotment. If, however, the prospectus is one issued generally, namely to persons who do not already hold shares or securities in the company, the company cannot allot shares until the third day after the day on which the prospectus is first issued, or until after the date specified in the prospectus if one has been specified, being not earlier than the third day after the issue of a prospectus. An application for the allotment of shares or debentures cannot be revoked by the applicant until the fourth day after the opening of the subscription lists.

Letters of right

When shares or debentures are offered to existing members or debenture holders by a letter of rights, the letter itself is the offer. If the letter of rights is in the form of a provisional letter of allotment, the company does not have to notify acceptance. A letter of rights will limit the number of shares for which each recipient can subscribe.

Unconditional acceptance of applications

The company must accept an application to subscribe for shares unconditionally, so that if it makes a counter–offer the subscriber can reject it, for example, if the issue is over–subscribed and the company allots fewer shares than the number subscribed to by an applicant, he can refuse to accept the shares actually allotted to him unless the company reserves to itself the right to allot fewer shares.

Minimum subscription

If a company offers its shares for subscription to the public, it may not allot any of the shares offered unless all the shares are subscribed for, but the company may reserve the right by the prospectus to allot less shares than it offers (Companies Act 1980, s. 13).

If the company issues a prospectus generally it must state the maximum amount of money which the directors wish to raise. Unless the company has previously issued shares under a prospectus it cannot allot shares until an amount equal to the minimum subscription can be raised. If the minimum subscription is not subscribed within 40 days of the issue of the prospectus, any amount received from the prospective subscribers must be returned to them. If this is not done within 48 days of the issue of the prospectus the directors will be personally liable on the amounts which should have been repaid, plus interest, unless they can show that the failure was not due to any misconduct or negligence on their part. If the company has allotted shares, but the minimum subscription is not subscribed for, the shareholder can rescind the contract of allotment.

If a prospectus, whether issued generally or not, states that an application has been made or will be made for the shares or debentures to be listed on the Stock Exchange, any allotment of shares will be void if an application has not been made to the Stock Exchange before the third day after the issue of a prospectus, or if the application is refused within three weeks following the closing of the subscription lists. If the issue does become void any money received from subscribers must be returned within 8 days after the allotment becomes void. The company remains a trustee of amounts received while there is a possibility that it may have to be returned.

If an issuing house undertakes to obtain a Stock Exchange listing, it must take the shares from the company if the listing is refused but an applicant to the issuing house for the allotment of shares can rescind it.

Underwriting

An underwriter agrees, for a commission, to subscribe for shares or debentures offered by a company, an issuing house or broker if the persons initially invited to subscribe for them fail to do so. If the persons initially invited take all the securities offered the underwriters' liability is discharged and if they only subscribe for some of the securities the underwriters must take up the remainder.

An underwriter will normally sign a standard form letter addressed to the company, issuing house, or broker in which he undertakes to subscribe for certain securities. The letter constitutes an offer and an underwriting agreement does not come into existence until the company, issuing house, or broker notifies the underwriter of acceptance.

The company may be authorised to vary the terms of the draft prospectus on which the underwriters' agreement with the company is based but this does not authorise the company or the issuing–house to vary the terms on which the securities are to be allotted, or to increase the risk borne by the underwriters. In *Warner International and Overseas Engineering Co Ltd* v. *Kilburn Brown & Co* (1914) an underwriting contract authorised the draft prospectus to be varied. The published prospectus had considerable alterations. In particular, a provision for £15,000 minimum subscription had been reduced to £100. It was held that the defendants were not under an obligation to perform their underwriting obligations since the published prospectus had considerably increased the risks undertaken by the underwriters without their agreement having been obtained.

The underwriting agreement enables the company or issuing–house to allot to the underwriter or his agent any securities he is obliged to take without receiving a further application from him. The company can allot the shares or debentures although the underwriter refuses to take up the securities. In *Re Hannon's Empress Gold Mining & Development Co* (1896) it was held that an underwriter could not compel the company to remove his name from the register of members when he had empowered the company to appoint an agent who was authorised to apply for the allotment of the shares on his behalf. He was therefore liable to take up the securities under an underwriting agreement, and since the agent appointed by the company had signed such an application the shares were allotted to the underwriter in consequence.

Sub–underwriting

An underwriting agreement requires the underwriter either to take up the securities for which he is responsible, or to find someone else. The underwriter can relieve himself of either part or the whole of his liability by entering into sub–underwriting agreements with other persons, by which in return for a commission they agree to underwrite some of the securities which the underwriter is obliged to accept. The company can allot shares to a sub–underwriter even though he refuses to take them. If the underwriter is empowered by him to apply to the company for the allotment of the shares, he is liable to take them up.

Subscribers of the memorandum

The subscribers of the company's memorandum of association are under a statutory obligation to take and pay for the shares set opposite their signature in the memorandum. They must take their shares directly from the company and pay for them in cash.

The subscriber of the memorandum remains liable to take his shares throughout the company's life and the obligation can be enforced against him although the company is being wound-up. The company can release a subscriber from his obligation only if the whole of its nominal capital has been taken up and there are no shares left to allot. However, if the company subsequently increases its share capital so that it has new shares available for issue the subscriber's obligation revives.

Return of allotments

The company must make a return to the Registrar of Companies within one month after allotting shares, stating the number and nominal value of the shares allotted, the name and addresses of the allottees, the amount pending on the shares and the amount of any calls or instalments of the issue price due. If shares are allotted for a consideration other than cash, the return must show the number and nominal value of the shares so allotted. A contract under which shares have been allotted for a consideration other than cash must also be filed.

If the company issues renounceable or provisional letters of allotment the Register of Companies will accept a return of allotments within one month after the date on which the allotment ceases to be renounceable.

Letters of allotment and renunciation, calls and forfeiture

A private company will issue a share certificate to the subscribers immediately an allotment is made and before the whole of the issue price has been paid. Any further instalments of the issue price have to be noted on the certificate. However, a public company will issue letters of allotment first, and a share certificate or debenture bond will only be issued when the shares are fully paid-up. When payments are made by a shareholder they are noted on the letter of allotment.

Position of the holder of a letter of allotment

A person who is allotted shares or debenturess has all the rights of a share or debenture holder but he is not a member of the company and so he cannot attend or vote in general meetings and his name cannot be entered in the register of members. A subscriber for shares has the right to insist that the company enters his name in the register of members when he receives the share certificate and he can compel the company to do so by applying for a court order. However, the contract for allotment can defer the date when this must be done.

Renunciation

A letter of allotment usually has printed on it a form or letter of renunciation.

The letter of renunciation is signed by the original allottee when he sells or disposes of his shares or debentures and he informs the company that he has renounced his rights in respect of these shares to the person who signs the registration application form attached to the letter of allotment. The letter of allotment may be transferred several times before the registration application form is completed and the letter of allotment surrendered to the company. If the original allottee retains the letter of allotment he can complete the registration form and register himself.

If the original allottee wants to sell only some of the shares or debentures to which the letter of allotment relates, he may complete the letter of renunciation in respect of these and may surrender it immediately to the company, which will issue two or more split letters of allotment for numbers of shares equal to the total originally allocated. The split letters of allotment may be renounced further and the holder of it who completes the registration application form will be registered by the company in respect of those shares.

A letter of allotment will prescribe the final date on which it may be split or renounced. Once this date has expired the original allottee will be registered and a share certificate issued to him. The legal relationship between the original allottee and his renouncee is that of an assignor and assignee of a chose in action. The company is not under any contractual relationship with the renouncee of the letter of allotment but, if the company accepts the renunciation, a new contract arises between it and the renouncee by which the original allottee is relieved from his liabilities for those shares. The company can then sue the new allottee for the price of the shares which he actually subscribed. A renunciation of all the shares will only be accepted when the whole of the issue price has been paid and therefore the company retains its right to recover the issue price from the original allottee.

The company is bound to accept renunciation of the letters of allotment and is in breach of contract if it refuses.

Calls
The terms of issue of the shares or debentures will specify the instalments by which the issue price is payable and the dates on which the instalments are payable. The allottee is contractually bound to pay those instalments and the company or issuing house can sue him in debt if he fails. The amount payable when applications for shares are invited by a prospectus must be at least 5 per cent of their nominal value.

Making of calls
A call is a demand by the company for payment of a part of the issue price of shares or debentures which remain unpaid and the date of payment of which was not specified in the terms of issue. If the articles are silent about the making of calls, a call may be made by an ordinary resolution passed at a general meeting of members.

A call cannot be made in breach of a contract made with the shareholder and the company cannot therefore make a call before the instalments are due.

A resolution of the board of directors or members making the call must specify the amount and the date on which it is payable, but the articles can enable calls to be made by instalments.

An irregularity in the proceedings for making calls will invalidate the call and, therefore, if notice of the calls has to be given a failure to do so will result in the company's being unable to enforce payment until proper notice is given.

Equality of calls

Unless the company's articles otherwise provide, there must be equality of calls, i.e. a call made on some shareholders but not others in the same class or a call of greater amount on some of the shareholders than on others is void (unless it relates to shares of different classes).

If, however, the articles allow calls for different amounts or at different times to be made, then such calls are valid.

Calls must be made in good faith

The directors may validly exercise their power to make calls and to specify the instalments by which the issue price of shares and debentures is to be paid, but they must act in good faith and for the benefit of the company. In *Alexander* v. *Automatic Telephone Co* (1909) the directors subscribed the company's memorandum for a substantial number of shares which were allotted to them but on which they did not pay anything. They then issued shares to other subscribers who were required to pay certain amounts on the allotment of shares. It was held that the directors were guilty of a breach of duty in not paying an equivalent amount on their own shares and the call on the other shareholders could not be enforced.

A company may sue for a call made on its shareholders within 12 years after the date on which it becomes payable. The articles will usually provide that interest should be charged on unpaid calls from the date on which they should be paid.

A person who is a member of the company on the date on which a call is made is liable on it although he transfers his shares before the date on which it becomes payable.

The registered transferee of partly paid shares is also liable to pay the call, whether the transfer to him is made before or after the date on which the call is payable.

If the purchaser is not registered on the register of members and the company cannot recover the calls from the vendor the company is subrogated to the vendor's right to an indemnity and may recover the calls from the purchaser direct.

A member who is sued for unpaid calls cannot allege against the company that he was induced to subscribe for the shares or debentures by misrepresentations made by the company.

If a company's articles so provide the company may accept payment of any part of the issue price of shares from a member before that part falls due for payment or has been called up. These advance payments are loans to the company and, if the articles so provide, the company may pay interest on it. If a company is wound-up, payments in advance of calls are repaid immediately after the other creditors of the company have been paid and before the share capital is returned to members.

Forfeiture and surrender

The articles of a company may give a power to it to forfeit shares if a shareholder fails to pay calls or instalments of the issue price of shares within a certain time after they fall due.

The directors of the company are normally required to serve notice on a shareholder who has failed to pay a call, warning him that unless he pays within a certain time his shares may be forfeited. If a call is still unpaid at the end of that time the articles may empower the directors to forfeit the shares by a resolution passed at a board meeting. The procedure laid down for forfeiture must be strictly followed, otherwise it will be void. The directors can exercise their power to forfeit shares only for the benefit of the company. The power cannot be exercised merely to release an unwilling shareholder from his liability to pay the issue price of the shares.

If a company has power to forfeit shares for failure to pay calls it may accept a voluntary surrender where it is in the interests of the company, but the surrender is void if its purpose is to relieve an unwilling shareholder from paying.

Where shares have been properly forfeited or surrendered the former shareholder cannot be sued for unpaid calls, unless the company's articles expressly provide (*Re Blakely Ordnance Co* (*Lumsden's Case*) (1868)).

The company's articles may allow directors to receive forfeited shares on such terms as the directors think fit. A public company must reissue or cancel forfeited or surrendered shares within three years; if the shares are cancelled the company's issued share capital is reduced accordingly.

The reissue is really a sale of the shares by the company, and so the purchase price belongs to the company. The shares are treated as paid up in the hands of the purchaser to the extent to which they were paid up at the date of forfeiture. If the company subsequently recovers unpaid calls from the former shareholder, the shares are credited as paid-up by the amount of those calls for the benefit of the purchaser, and the company cannot recover calls from him to the extent that they are recovered from the former shareholder.

Commissions

A company may pay commissions to persons who underwrite the company's issue of shares. However, an issuing house which undertakes to offer shares for sale is not entitled to receive a commission, because it will make its profit in turn by selling shares to the public at a higher price than they paid the company. A company is not allowed to pay commissions merely because a person subscribed for shares but only if he agrees to take them if the persons primarily invited to subscribe fail to.

Share certificates and share warrants

When letters of allotment or acceptance in respect of shares cease to be renounceable the company will issue a share certificate or, if the articles permit, a share warrant to the person who surrenders the letter of allotment. If a share certificate is issued, the company will enter the shareholder's name in its register of members. If a renounceable share certificate is issued and the allottee has not renounced his certificate, he will retain the certificate as evidence of his title to the shares.

Share certificates

A share certificate is a document issued by the company stating that a named person is a registered holder of a specific number of shares and the extent to which they are paid–up. The share certificate may bear a distinguishing number corresponding to the same number in the company's own records. It must in any case state the distinguishing numbers of shares to which it relates. If the company has issued shares of different classes the register must also indicate the shares of each class held by members.

A share certificate is prima facie evidence of the shareholder's title to the shares specified in it but it is not conclusive evidence, and the shares belong to the person who can show a valid title. The certificate will state the amount paid up on those shares and, unless the rights of an innocent third party are affected and the company is estopped by its conduct from alleging that the shares are not paid up to the extent stated, it is entitled to rectify the share certificate if, due to an error, the shares are represented to be paid–up to a larger amount than in fact has been paid on them.

Share warrants

A company limited by shares may, if so authorised by its articles, issue a share warrant in respect of fully paid–up shares or stock. The share warrant certifies that the bearer of the warrant is entitled to the shares represented by it. The holder of a share warrant can transfer legal title to the shares by a mere delivery of the share warrant provided it is delivered with the intention of transferring the ownership of the shares. The bearer may surrender the share warrant at any time, and have his name registered in the members' register; he will then receive a share certificate in respect of the shares. A share warrant is a negotiable instrument, and so a purchaser or a person who receives the share warrant as security will acquire a good title to it if he gives value and acts in good faith, and he will not be affected by defects of title affecting the person who transfers it to him.

Membership of a company

The following are members of a company:

(*a*) the subscribers of its memorandum of association, who become members of the company on its incorporation; and

(*b*) every person who agrees to become a member and whose name is put on the register of members.

The legal capacity of a person to become a member of the company depends on the ordinary rules of contract but he must consent to becoming a member and his name must appear on the register of members. Thus, a minor may become a member but he is entitled to rescind the allotment or transfer of shares to him before or within a reasonable time after attaining his majority. If a minor repudiates an allotment the shares are treated as if they had never been issued. If an existing shareholder transfers his shares to a minor and the minor rescinds the transfer the company may be able to recover calls from the former holder in whom the shares are now re–vested.

The register of members

The company must keep a register of members showing the names and addresses of its shareholders, the number of shares held by each person, the distinguishing numbers of the shares and the amounts paid–up. The register of members must be kept at the company's registered office, or at another address in Great Britain where it is made up, and be available for inspection by any person during business hours.

The company's register of members is prima facie evidence of the matters recorded in it, but it is not conclusive evidence and, therefore, if there has been an omission or error it can be rectified by order of the court.

DEALINGS WITH SHARES

Power of shareholder to transfer shares

Registered shares

A share certificate is a document issued by a company stating that a named person is the registered holder of a specified number of shares of a certain class and that the shares are fully paid–up to a stated amount. A share certificate is prima facie evidence of the shareholder's title to the specified shares.

Power of shareholder to transfer

The legal title to the shares is vested in the person entitled to the shares either by allotment by the company or by a transfer from a holder, but if legal rights are to be enjoyed by that person he must be registered as a holder in respect of those shares.

Procedure for transferring shares registered in the company's register of members

Unless shares are represented by a share warrant, the transferor of shares will execute a share transfer form by which he transfers a number of shares in the company to the transferee. The transfer does not have to be by deed unless so required by the company's articles and, regardless of any provision in the articles, fully paid shares may be transferred by an appropriate instrument signed by the transferor. If fully paid–up shares are transferred in this way under the Stock Transfer Act 1963 the transfer does not have to be in a special form provided the stock transfer form has been signed by the transferor. The transfer should state the names, addresses, and descriptions of the transferor and transferee but the transfer will be valid if these particulars are omitted or defectively stated, provided that the company can ascertain the identities of the parties.

The transfer, when executed by the transferor, is delivered by him, together with the share certificate, to the transferee who himself executes the tranfer and sends both documents to the company for registration. Execution by the transferee is unnecessary if the appropriate form of transfer under the Stock Transfer Act 1963 is used.

On presentation of the transfer for registration, the company should ascertain that the documents are in order and that the transferor is registered as a member in respect of the shares transferred. It will then enter the transferee in its register of members in respect of the shares transferred, and it will enter a note against the transferor's name that he is no longer a member in respect of those shares.

The transferor's share certificate and the instrument of transfer are retained by the company and a new share certificate, showing the transferee as the holder of the shares, is issued to him.

Restrictions on transfer

Shares are freely transferable unless the company's articles impose restrictions on their transfer; the motive of the transferor in disposing of his shares is immaterial. Thus, if a holder of shares transfers them to a person of small means, or even to an insolvent person, in order to avoid future calls, the transfer is valid.

A company's articles, in particular those of a private company, may impose restrictions on the transfer of shares, but it appears that the articles cannot prohibit transfers completely (Companies Act 1948, s. 73).

If a company exercises its rights to refuse to register a transfer under a provision of its memorandum or articles, it must notify the transferee within two months after the transfer is presented for registration. If the company fails to notify the transferee within two months it cannot afterwards assert its right to refuse registration and the transferee may compel the company to register him as a member. A company's obligation to notify a refusal to register a transfer only applies if the refusal is due to the exercise of a discretion vested in the directors. If the transferee has no right to be registered at all (i.e. if his title is defective) then the failure to notify him within two months does not entitle him to be registered.

The transfer of shares free from defects of title

Procedural defects on the issue of shares (e.g. the passing of an irregular board resolution approving the transfer for registration) will not prejudice the allottee of shares who is unaware of them, or his successors, because they can rely on the rule in *Royal British Bank* v. *Turquand*. If, however, the issue of the shares is defective in substance, i.e. the issue is tainted by forgery, the allottee will not acquire any title to the shares, the forgery rendering the whole transaction inoperative. If, therefore, the company registers a forged transfer the true owner can have the register of members rectified. Where, in such circumstances, the company has issued a new share certificate to a subsequent purchaser, and he has relied on the certificate (e.g. by contracting to sell the shares) it cannot deny his defective title to the shares. In *Re Bahia and San Francisco Railway* (1868) the registered holder of certain shares left the share certificate with a broker. A transfer was forged and the share certificate and forged transfer were sent to the company for registration. The company issued the purchaser with a new certificate and he transferred the shares to a sub–purchaser. The true owner was held to be entitled to have the register of members rectified but the sub–purchaser was entitled to recover damages from the company because, in issuing a new certificate in favour of the purchaser, the company was held to have represented to him that he was entitled to the shares. The company was, therefore, estopped from denying the purchaser's title and the sub–purchaser was entitled to recover damages when the true owner of the shares was restored to the register.

In order to avoid this situation a company will usually notify the transferor that a transfer of his shares has been presented in order to enable the registered holder to object to his name's being removed from the register of members.

The share certificate is not a negotiable instrument and it is the actual registration of the transferee as a member which passes title. The share certificate is, however, prima facie evidence of title and the company may be estopped from denying the title of the person in whose name the share certificate is issued if an innocent third party relies on it. The company cannot therefore deny the title of a holder of shares once it has issued a share certificate to him except against the person who forges the certificate of transfer or the share certificate.

If a shareholder is induced to transfer his shares by mistake or misrepresentation, the transfer is void and a transferee obtains no title to the shares despite his good faith or registration of the transfer.

However, if the transfer is merely voidable (e.g. because of misrepresentation or undue influence by the transferee) the transferor cannot rescind the transfer against a purchaser for value from the transferee who had no notice of the circumstances and such a purchaser will obtain a good title against the transferor.

Although, the transferor of shares has no title or a defective title to the shares, the true owner may estop himself by his conduct from challenging the transferee's title.

The transfer of title to the shares

Until the transferee's name is entered in the register of members the transferor is deemed to remain the holder of the shares.

Equitable interests in shares

An equitable interest may be created in the shares by the registered holder or bearer of a share warrant's declaring himself a trustee of the shares, or by his transferring them to another person to be held on trust as directed by him. When a shareholder agrees to sell particular shares the equitable ownership in them passes to the buyer immediately. Shares may also be equitably mortgaged by the shareholder's agreeing to treat them as a security for a loan, and undertaking to the transfer the legal title to the lender if called on to do so.

Protection of equitable interests

The owner of an equitable interest derived out of registered shares can protect himself by serving a stop notice (i.e. an order issued by the High Court) on the company. The notice informs the company that the equitable owner is entitled to an interest in the shares and the stop notice is issued in order to prevent the registration of transfers of the shares, or to stop payment of dividends to the registered shareholder. A copy of the sealed notice, together with an affidavit, must be served on the company by the equitable owner. The company must, so long as the notice remains in force, notify the person who served it before the company registers a transfer of shares or pays a dividend in respect of those shares. If a transfer of the shares is registered without notice being given to the person who served the notice, the directors will be liable to compensate the owner of the equitable interest because they have assisted in the breach of trust.

Rules which govern competing claims to priority

When a transfer creating a later interest in the shares is presented for registration, the company must notify the person who has served a stop notice on it within eight days after the transfer is lodged. He may apply to the court to restrain the company from registering the transfer. If he does not apply for an injunction the company may register the transfer, and the legal title to the shares will then pass to the transferee and the stop notice will cease to be effective. If the transferee at that time is unaware of the equitable interest which the stop notice was served to protect, he will take the shares free from it.

When a company notifies the owner of an equitable interest he may preserve priority for his interest over any rights arising under the transfer by giving an informal notice of his interest to the transferee, or he may commence an action to restrain registration of the transfer.

A later interest arising out of shares is bound to be equitable itself and will, therefore, be postponed to an earlier equitable interest, whether or not the owner of the later interest has notice of the earlier one.

Financial assistance given by a company for the acquisition of its own shares

The Companies Act 1981, s. 42, deals with the provisions governing the assistance given by a company to itself or its subsidiary to purchase its own shares. The section contains a general prohibition on the company's giving financial assistance, either directly or indirectly, for the purpose of enabling a person to acquire shares in the company. Such assistance may take a number of forms, i.e. assistance by way of gift, or guarantee or security or indemnity, or by way of a release or waiver of an obligation due to the company or by way of a loan. Thus, the transfer of money or money's worth or the company's undertaking to forgo a debt owed to it by a prospective shareholder may be within the scope of s. 42. Similarly, the making of a payment by the company under a contract for property which the vendor agrees to repurchase at a later date will involve the company's giving financial assistance to the vendor to purchase shares in the company if that is the purpose of the arrangement.

However, s. 42 does not apply if the assistance is given in good faith in the interests of the company and the principle purpose of giving the assistance is not to enable the person assisted to purchase the shares, or if the giving of financial assistance is merely a part of a larger transaction entered into by the company. Moreover, the section expressly provides that financial assistance does not include the company distributing dividends or assets in a winding–up, allotting bonus shares, doing any act done under a scheme of arrangement, making payments on a reduction of capital confirmed by the court, or, in connection with the redemption or purchase of shares by the company in accordance with the 1981 Act, or carrying out a number of other transactions.

A private company may additionally give financial assistance in connection with the acquisition of its own shares if it has profits available to do so, or if its net assets are not reduced (Companies Act 1981, s. 43). A private company cannot give financial assistance in connection with the acquisition of shares in its holding company if the private company is a subsidiary of a public company. If a private company gives financial assistance in connection with the acquisition of shares in itself or its holding company, the company and, if shares of a holding company are to be acquired, that company, must approve the grant of assistance by a special resolution at a general meeting (Companies Act 1981, s. 43(3)). The directors of the private company proposing to give financial assistance and the directors of any holding company whose shares are to be acquired must make a statutory declaration giving details of the assistance proposed together with a statement that in their opinions the private company or the holding company will subsequently be able to pay its debts in full during the year following the declaration or, if the company is wound–up during that time that it will be able to pay its debts in full within 12 months after the winding–up commences.

However, the intended financial assistance cannot be given until four weeks from the passing of the special resolution or before any application to the court to cancel the resolution made during that time has been dealt with. An application for cancellation must be made by a creditor of the company or by the holders of 10 per cent of the company's issued share capital of any class. The court may cancel or confirm the resolution subject to any conditions if it thinks fit.

Redeemable shares

A company limited by shares may, under the Companies Act 1981, s. 48, if authorised by its articles, issue shares which are or may at the option of the company be redeemed. Redeemable shares may be redeemed only if fully paid. The shares may only be redeemed out of profits available for distribution, or out of the proceeds of a fresh issue of shares, and any redemption premium must be paid out of distributable profits.

If redeemable shares were issued at a premium, a redemption premium may be paid out of proceeds of a fresh issue of shares. The terms of redemption are fixed by the company's articles. Redeemed shares are cancelled and the company's issued share capital is reduced by the nominal value of the redeemed shares.

A private company limited by shares may, however, if authorised by its articles, redeem shares out of capital. A payment out of capital for redemption of shares may be made only if it is approved by a special resolution at a general meeting.

SALES OF SHARES

A contract for the sale of shares need not be in any particular form; an oral contract is sufficient. The contract need not be for the sale of specific shares which are identified at the time the contract is made. If a contract for sale of shares is not for specific shares, the equitable title passes to the purchaser only when the seller appropriates particular shares to the contract. Where the contract is for specific shares equitable title in the shares passes immediately to the purchaser.

The purchaser will become entitled to receive the dividends when equitable title passes to him, although the dividend declared is for a financial year which terminated before the contract of sale was made and before the purchaser acquired any interest in them. In *Black* v. *Homersham* (1878) the purchaser acquired shares at a public auction although the date for completion of the contract was postponed. It was held the completion related back to the time when the contract was made, and the purchaser was entitled to receive a dividend declared after the contract of sale was actually made.

The purchaser must indemnify the seller against all calls made on the shares after he acquires the equitable title in them, and if he resells the shares before he is registered as the holder the indemnity extends to all calls made before the sub–purchaser registers his title.

The seller remains entitled to vote on the shares as he wishes, although equitable title in the shares has passed, until the purchase price is paid in full, because he has a lien for the unpaid price. Once the purchase price has been paid in full he must vote as the purchaser directs but so far as the company is concerned the only person entitled to the shares is the registered shareholder and all dividends are paid to him and all calls are made on him.

On completion of a sale, the seller is under an obligation to deliver his share certificate, together with a duly executed transfer, to the purchaser and to assist him to be registered as a member of the company. Where the directors have a power to refuse the registration of a transfer the seller does not impliedly undertake that they will register the transfer and so if the directors refuse to register the seller is not liable to the purchaser in damages but holds the shares as a trustee for him.

It is not necessary that a purchaser of shares be registered as a member of the company himself before he can resell them. He may transfer the shares to a sub–purchaser by delivering the seller's share certificate, together with a transfer from the seller to the sub–purchaser duly executed by the seller, or by delivering the share certificate and two instruments of transfer; the first from the seller to the purchaser and the second from the purchaser to the sub–purchaser. If, however, the purchaser has received a blank transfer from the seller, not naming a transferee it is an offence for him to deliver the document to the sub–purchaser still in blank and he should, therefore, fill in the sub–purchaser's name before making delivery.

If the sale of shares is of shares represented by a share warrant the seller's duty is merely to deliver the warrant to the buyer and legal title passes to him.

Other transactions in shares

Gifts of shares

The legal title to shares may be transferred by way of gift. If shares are registered in the company's register of members the donor will execute a transfer to the donee and deliver the transfer and share certificate to him. The donee will send these documents to the company so that his name may be entered in the register of members and a new share certificate may be issued to him. If the donor holds merely a letter of allotment, he is required to deliver that and a letter of renunciation signed by the original allottee. The donee will be able to obtain registration in the register of members by completing the registration application form and presenting it to the company. If shares are represented by a share warrant, the donor transfers the legal title by delivering the warrant to the donee. No instrument of transfer is necessary.

If the donor of shares has not done everything necessary on his part to vest the legal title in the donee the law will not assist a donee to perfect an imperfect gift. Thus if a donor dies the law will not compel the donor's personal representatives to complete the transfer. In *Milroy* v. *Lord* (1862) it was held that a purported transfer of inscribed stock by a deed of gift was ineffective to pass title and after the donor's death his personal representatives could not be compelled to complete the transfer. Similarly, in *Re Fry* (1946) it was held that a transfer of shares was ineffective where Treasury consent required by law had not been obtained by the transferor. The courts would not assist the donee to perfect the imperfect gift when at the time of the donor's death this consent had not been obtained.

If, however, the only thing necessary to perfect the gift is an act to be done by the donee, the gift is complete although legal title has not yet passed. If the donor purports to invoke the gift or dies, the donee may still do what is necessary to acquire the legal title (*Re Rose* (1952)).

Mortgages of shares

A legal mortgage of shares transfers the legal title to the mortgagee and the transfer is registered in the company's register of members. The mortgagee is made personally liable for calls or instalments of the issue price if the shares are only partly paid.

If an equitable mortgage is created over the shares the mortgagor remains the registered holder of the shares and he retains the legal title in them. He will, however, deposit his share certificate with the mortgagee. An equitable mortgage operates as an agreement to create a legal mortgage. The mortgagee can convert an equitable mortgage into a legal mortgage by completing the blank transfer with his own name as transferee, and sending it to the company for registration. Until the mortgagee has done this he can protect his interest by serving a stop notice on the company.

A mortgagee may sell the shares without a court order. Alternatively, an equitable mortgagee may retain the blank transfer until the borrower defaults and then sell the shares, either by completing the blank transfer in favour of himself and executing a transfer to the purchaser personally or, alternatively, by filling in the purchaser's name in the original blank transfer. The transfer to the purchaser will then be presented to the company for registration.

Company's lien

A company does not have a lien or equitable charge on the shares of its members for sums owed by them to it, unless such a right is expressly conferred by the company's articles. The lien or charge may extend to the capital only, or to an unpaid balance on the shares, or to any indebtedness of the shareholder to the company. A lien attaches not only to the shares but also to any dividends payable on the shares. The articles will usually empower the company to enforce its lien by selling the shares. A lien attaches to the shares from the moment they are issued, even though the shareholder does not become indebted to the company until a later date. A lien, therefore, precedes any other equitable interest which is created out of the shares and it consequently has priority over an equitable mortgage created by the shareholder, unless the company actually knows of the existence of a mortgage at the time the holder of the shares becomes indebted to it.

The articles of a company cannot effectively impose a lien on shares represented by a share warrant unless the company has possession of the share warrant.

Judgment creditors

A judgment creditor may levy execution on the shares registered in the company's register by obtaining an order of the court charging the shares with the payment of the debt. An application for a charging order is made by summons in the proceedings in which a judgment was given. An ex parte application is made in the first instance, and the court will make an order calling on the shareholder to show cause why the order should not be made absolute.

If the company does register a transfer it may be liable to the judgment creditor for either, the whole amount of the judgment debt or the value of the shares, whichever is less.

A charging order can only be made in respect of the beneficial interest in shares vested in the judgment debtor and, therefore, the debtor must be the beneficial and registered owner of them.

A judgment creditor who obtains a charging order nisi has priority for the amount payable to him under the judgment over all persons who later acquire an interest in the shares. Charging orders can be made in respect of shares represented by share warrants or renounceable or non–renounceable letters of allotment.

Personal representatives and trustees in bankruptcy

On the death of a shareholder his shares vest in his personal representatives, and the company must recognise their title to the shares on the production of the grant of probate of the deceased's will, or letters of administration to the deceased's estate. The personal representatives are entitled to any dividends and the return of capital, and it is unnecessary that they should be registered as members of the company before they can claim them. The personal representatives have a right to subscribe for further shares if a rights issue is made by the company, and they need not be registered in the company's register of members for this purpose either.

If the deceased's shares are only partly paid the personal representatives are only personally liable to pay any unpaid capital. The personal representatives can insist on the company's registering them as members in respect of the deceased's shares unless the articles provide otherwise.

The beneficiaries of the deceased's estate only have an equitable interest in the shares until the personal representatives transfer legal title to them, but until then the beneficiaries can serve a stop notice on the company to protect their interest.

Disclosure of interests in shares

If a person knowingly acquires an interest in shares of a public company, which carry the right to vote in all circumstances at general meetings, or ceases to have such an interest, or becomes aware that he has acquired or ceased to acquire such shares, he must notify the company of his interest if:

  (*a*) prior to the acquisition he was interested in less than 5 per cent of such issued shares of the company of any class, and subsequent to the acquisition he was interested in 5 per cent or more; or

(b) prior to the cessation he was interested in 5 per cent or more of such issued shares of any class and subsequently he was interested in less than 5 per cent; or

(c) both before and after the acquisition or cessation he was interested in 5 per cent or more of the issued shares and his holding has changed by at least 1 per cent.

The notification to the company must be made in writing within 5 days of the obligation's arising. For the purposes of notification the shareholder is treated as having an interest in any shares held by his spouse or minor child.

PROFITS AND DIVIDENDS

Profits available for a distribution

The Companies Act 1980, ss. 39–45, makes no distinction between capital and reserve profits and losses to be distributed as dividends. A distribution can only be made from the company's accumulated realised profits after its losses have been written-off. The company cannot distribute any realised profits, although it may issue bonus shares paid-up out of them. A company cannot avoid the terms of the section by an express provision to that effect in the memorandum or articles. Additionally, a public company is not entitled to make a distribution if the result would be to reduce the value of its assets to such an extent that the liabilities and paid-up capital would not be covered by the total value of its assets. However, a company is under no obligation to distribute the whole of its profits. The current earnings of a company are the receipts of the company's business less the expenses incurred in earning such amounts. Any profit the company hopes to make in the future, i.e. from work in progress, cannot be taken into account until the work is completed. A company can debit its current expenses, namely, employees' remuneration, taxes accrued and payable and the rent of premises occupied by the company etc. from its trading account. A company is further entitled to set aside amounts in a reserve fund for depreciation of its fixed assets and thus reduce the dividend payable to the shareholders. If the company sells its fixed assets at a profit, the difference between the cost price and the resale price is distributable. Finally, the company's articles may empower it to carry forward a part of its profits for future developments or requirements.

Machinery for payment of dividend

Unless the articles of association make dividends payable automatically on the ascertainment of profits, dividends are not payable until they are properly declared at a general meeting of the company's members. Alternatively, the company's directors may be empowered to declare dividends without a general meeting's being called. The articles of a company normally provide that a dividend can only be declared out of the profits after the directors have set aside such reserves as are necessary for the company's future development and prospects. In anticipation of any dividend which may finally be declared, the board of directors may have power to pay interim dividends. The amount of an interim dividend declared by the directors may be raised or varied at any time before the dividend is paid and, unlike a final dividend which has been declared, it is not a debt.

The dividend is payable to the person who is registered in respect of those shares in the company's register of members at the time the dividend is declared. Dividends are paid to members by means of dividend warrants which are cheques drawn by a company on its bank. The dividend warrant must be accompanied by a statement showing the amount of the dividend and the amount of the advance corporation tax paid by the company in respect of it; this will give rise to a corresponding income tax credit in favour of the recipient.

If shares are represented by a share warrant, the holder of the share warrant will surrender to the company the relevant coupon which was issued with the share warrant and he will then be paid the amount of the dividend by a dividend warrant in his favour.

A dividend must be declared at a uniform rate on all shares of the same class and the shareholders must be paid proportionately to the nominal value of the shares, and not their paid–up value, unless the articles otherwise provide (i.e. if some of the shares of a class are fully paid and others only partly paid all the shareholders normally qualify for the same amount of dividend).

If a company is empowered by its articles simply to pay dividends, it may distribute dividends only in cash. It cannot declare a dividend and satisfy it by the allotment of further shares or debentures credited as correspondingly paid up. It is common, however, for the articles of a company to contain a power entitling the company to capitalise any part of its profits and to issue fully paid shares or debentures with a total nominal value equal to the amount capitalised. These new shares or debentures are known as bonus shares or debentures and, since no cash dividend is declared by the company, an issue of bonus shares is treated as an issue for a consideration other than cash. The articles of a company which is authorised to issue bonus shares or debentures do not usually determine the rights attached to these shares or debentures. If the company has, therefore, issued preference and ordinary shares, a bonus issue to the ordinary shareholders may be in the form of preference shares (*White* v. *Bristol Aeroplane Co* (1953)). The advantage of a bonus issue of shares is that it enables the company to retain money required for its business which it would otherwise have to raise by issuing new shares or debentures.

Finally, it may be possible for a company to distribute dividends in the form of specific assets of the company, such as shares or debentures which it holds in other companies.

DEBENTURES

Floating charges and specific charges

A company may create various forms of security for loans made to it, but it is common for both public and private companies to raise loans by issuing debentures or debenture stock, conferring a charge over the whole or part of the company's property. A debenture is a document which either evidences or acknowledges a debt and debentures for the purpose of the Companies Acts 1948–1981 include, "debenture stock, bonds and other securities of a company whether constituting a charge on the assets of the company or not." Debenture stock represents a fractional share in a global debt owed by the company to trustees on the terms of a covering trust deed by which a charge on the company's property is created in favour of the trustees. Loans to companies under debentures or debenture stock trust deeds may be secured by specific or floating charges over the company's property. A specific charge attaches to a particular piece of property which is identified when the charge is created, even if it does not exist at that time, and the identity of the property charged does not change during the subsistence of the charge, i.e. a mortgage of a building or a ship or aircraft which has not yet been constructed is a specific mortgage. A floating charge, on the other hand, is an equitable charge on a class of asset the constituents of which are constantly changing, for example the stock-in-trade from time to time of a business, or the whole assets and undertakings for the time being of the company. When an item is sold out of the stock-in-trade or the company's undertaking, the charge ceases to extend to it, and the buyer takes it free from the floating charge. If a new item is added to the stock-in-trade or undertaking, the charge automatically extends to it without the execution of a further mortgage, but the charge will continue to apply to the asset only so long as the company retains it.

In *Illingworth* v. *Houldsworth* (1904) a charge created by an association over its freehold and leasehold property was held to be a floating charge because the court said that, on the construction of the deed creating it, it was intended that the company should be able to carry on business. The judge stated that a charge is a floating charge if it is a charge on a class of the company's present and future assets, if that class of assets is one which would normally change from time to time and if it is contemplated that, until a further step is taken by the person in whose favour the charge is created, the company may carry on business as normal.

When a floating charge crystallises it attaches specifically to all the items comprising the class of assets in question at that time, and thereafter the company can only sell or mortgage those assets subject to the charge in favour of the lender. A floating charge may crystallise in one of three ways: by the occurrence of an event which, under the terms of the debenture, is to cause the lender's security to attach specifically to the company's assets, by the appointment of a receiver of the assets in question by order of the court or by the lender under a power contained in the debenture or covering trust deed, or by the company's being wound–up.

In *Siebe Gorman & Co Ltd* v. *Barclays Bank Ltd* (1979) Slade J held that a charge will not be a floating charge if the instrument creating it shows that an immediate and irremovable security is intended over the property in question. Consequently, a charge over present and future book–debts of a company was held to be a specific charge over them when it was stated to be a "fixed charge" and the company was prohibited from assigning or dealing with book–debts and was required to pay them to the lender immediately on receipt.

Priority of floating charges

A bank or other institution which lends on the security of a specific mortgage of a company's property is entitled to repayment of its loan out of the proceeds of sale of the mortgaged property before the company's other creditors in the event of the company's insolvency. A debenture holder secured by a floating charge cannot prevent the company using the assets over which the charge is created to pay its unsecured creditors while the charge continues to float, but once it crystallises he is entitled to repayment of his loan out of the assets charged before they are used to pay the company's unsecured creditors. A statutory exception to this rule exists in favour of certain unsecured creditors of an insolvent company.

A company which creates a floating charge over its undertaking or a class of its assets retains the power both to sell and to mortgage the assets subject to their charge as long as it continues to float. Such a mortgage, whether legal or equitable, ranks for payment out of the property comprised in it in priority to the amount secured by the floating charge, but a company cannot create mortgages ranking in priority to the floating charge after it has crystallised. On crystallisation, the floating charge becomes a specific mortgage of property which the company then owns or which it acquires thereafter and the normal rules of priority apply: where a mortgage is created before the floating charge crystallises, the mortgage will have priority, but if a mortgage is created after the charge has crystallised, the charge has priority.

A debenture secured by a floating charge may prohibit the company even while the charge floats, from creating mortgages or charges which rank for payment in priority to the debenture debt or equally with it. This restriction operates as an equitable restriction on the company's normal power to create later specific mortgages ranking before the floating charge. The mere registration of a charge under the Companies Act 1948, s. 95, although it is constructive notice of the charge, is not of itself notice of the prohibition. The prohibition itself may be registered with the Registrar of Companies but only actual notice of the prohibition will be sufficient to prevent the later specific charge from having priority. A later mortgagee who takes a legal mortgage without notice of such a restriction is not affected by it because a purchaser of a legal interest for value is not bound by prior equities of which he does not have notice. If, however, a later mortgagee takes his mortgage with notice of the equitable restriction in the debenture, the later mortgagee will be postponed to the debenture holders. A later equitable mortgagee also takes free from a prohibition clause if he is unaware of it.

If a charge, lien or other security attaches to any of the company property by operation of law it ranks before a floating charge created over the company's assets and undertaking which has not yet crystallised, whether or not the debenture creating the floating charge prohibits the creation of charges ranking in priority. Moreover, it has been held that if a lien arises after crystallisation of the floating charge it still has priority because the debenture holders take the company's property subject to the same claims against it as the company was subject to.

By the Companies Act 1948, s. 94(1), when a floating charge crystallises on the appointment of a receiver or the debenture holders' taking possession of assets subject to the floating charge, the claims against the company which would be preferential payments in a winding–up must be paid out of the property to which the charge attaches before the other unsecured creditors. Similarly, by s. 319(5), when a company is wound–up, preferential debts must be paid out of any property of the company subject to a floating charge in priority to the debt secured by that charge, for example the Crown has a preferential claim for corporation tax due for any accounting period ending on or before the preceding 5th April not exceeding any one year's assessment, and employees of the company have preferential claims for wages and salaries in respect of services rendered by them during the immediately preceding four months.

When a company is wound–up without a receiver's having previously been appointed to realise the floating charge, the liquidator must pay the preferential claims out of property subject to a floating charge before repaying the loan secured thereby. This applies only if the floating charge has not crystallised and become specific before the winding–up commences. If the debenture holders appoint a receiver or take possession of the company's property before the company is wound–up preferential claims will have priority only if they have accrued due by the date of crystallisation, and claims which arise during the period between the appointment of the receiver or taking possession of the company's property and the subsequent winding–up of the company will not have priority over the debenture debt.

A receiver is personally liable to pay preferential debts if, at the time when he is appointed to enforce a floating charge, he has notice of the preferential claims of creditors but fails to pay them before discharging the debenture debt out of the property subject to the floating charge. A debenture holder who knowingly allows the receiver to pay the debenture debt before the preferential claims are paid is also personally liable.

If a debenture contains a specific charge over some of the company's assets and a floating charge over the remainder, creditors with preferential claims are entitled to prior payment of their claims only out of the property subject to the floating charge, and the debenture holders may be paid the amount owing to them so far as possible out of the property subject to the specific charge without deferment. The result of this is that any residue of the preferential claims which is not satisfied from the company's assets which are subject to a floating charge must be met out of the company's general assets which are subject neither to the floating nor the specific charge.

Invalidation of floating charges in a winding-up

A floating charge created by a company within one year before the commencement of its winding–up is void as security for any debt other than cash paid to the company in consideration of the charge at the time it was created, or subsequently (Companies Act 1948, s. 322). This provision avoids the floating charge as security for any debt other than such an advance, but it does not invalidate the debt itself, and so the debenture holder whose charge over the company is void can still prove in the winding–up as an unsecured creditor and be paid a rateable dividend with the other unsecured creditors. Therefore, a bank which lends to a company on the understanding that the company will create a floating charge to secure it, is in the same position as if the charge had been created at the date of the loan and so where a debenture containing the charge is issued subsequently within a year before the company's winding–up the bank may enforce the charge on its winding–up.

A floating charge is valid as security for loans made after the date it was created even though the lender did not promise to make such loans but merely reserved the power to do so and to treat the floating charge as security for them if he did so. In *Re Yeovil Glove Co Ltd* (1965) a company which had overdrawn on its current account with the claimant bank created a mortgage over its assets in the form of a floating charge to secure its existing and future indebtedness to the bank. The company was insolvent at the time the charge was created and subsequently went into liquidation within the following twelve months. By the Companies Act 1948, s. 322, the floating charge to the bank was void as security for advances already made. The advances made since the floating charge was created were secured by it, and ranked for payment before the claims of the company's other creditors in any case, including those of creditors for preferential debts. A loan is treated as being made to the company at the date a floating charge is created only if fresh money is genuinely made available to enable the company to continue carrying on its business. Thus, where a floating charge was given to secure a loan expressed to be made to the company but in fact the lenders paid nothing to the company but appropriated the loan to pay directors' fees which the company owed them, the charge was held void in the company's subsequent liquidation (*Re Destone Fabrics Ltd* (1941)). The loan was a sham since no new money was really put at the company's disposal.

Floating charges are invalidated by the Companies Act 1948, s. 322, only when the company is wound up. If before this happens the company redeems a floating charge which would have been invalidated by its liquidation, the liquidator cannot require the creditor secured by the charge to repay what he has received.

A fraudulent preference is where the company knowing that it cannot pay its debts in full voluntarily makes a payment, or gives a benefit to one particular creditor which will result in him being treated preferentially to the company's other creditors. There is no fraudulent preference if the payment or benefit conferred on one creditor is not given voluntarily; if a company pays an outstanding debt to a bank under the threat of legal proceedings or a threat to realise the bank's security, there is no fraudulent preference. If directors pay off a debt in order to discharge their personal liability that is a fraudulent preference. Consequently, in *Re M Kushler Ltd* (1943) there was held to be a fraudulent preference when directors who had guaranteed repayment of the company's bank overdraft paid it off at a time when they knew the company was insolvent.

A payment or benefit given to a company at the time when it is insolvent or just before it becomes insolvent is not a fraudulent preference unless the company intends to give an improper advantage to that creditor or to relieve a surety for the debt owed to him. Thus where shortly before its liquidation a company paid a substantial sum to a contractor in order to be relieved from a contract for the transportation of the company's goods by him, it was held that the payment was not a fraudulent preference since the company's motive was to be able to employ another contractor who was willing to carry the goods at a cheaper rate (*Re Paraguassa Steam Tramway Co* (1874)). The courts will not readily impute an improper motive to a company when its acts are susceptible of several different motives or if it acts under a mistake.

A transaction is a fraudulent preference only when a creditor obtains some benefit which he would not otherwise have received if the company had been wound–up immediately, or if a surety is relieved from paying a sum which he would have been liable to pay if the creditor had merely received a dividend in the winding–up. When a creditor is compelled to return money or property to the liquidator it can be distributed generally and the holder of a floating charge has no prior rights to repayment.

Registration of charges under the Companies Act 1948, s. 95

Charges created by a company over its property have to be registered at the Companies Registry (Companies Act 1948, s. 95). The classes of charges created by a company which must be registered include charges to secure an issue of debentures, floating charges on the undertaking or property of a company as well as specific mortgages on various particular types of property. Floating charges are registrable whether they are general charges over the company's assets or floating charges over a class of assets. If, after the creation of a registrable mortgage or charge on the company's property, the company creates a charge over other property by way of additional security, or in substitution for the original charge, the second charge must be registered separately unless the first charge expressly extends to additional or substitute property.

The company is under a duty to register particulars of charges created by it within 21 days of their creation, and if the company fails to do this any other interested person may register the charge. A failure to register makes any security on the company's property or undertaking conferred by the charge void against the liquidator and creditors of the company. The charge, however, is valid against the company when not registered so that if the person entitled to the charge sells his security before the company is wound–up, the purchaser gets a good title against the other creditors and the mortgagee can retain the proceeds of sale.

While the company is a going concern only secured creditors who have a security on the property subject to an unregistered charge can contend that it is void against them so as to give priority to them for their own security. The company's unsecured creditors cannot restrain the company from dealing with the property as it wishes and so the company can, if it wishes, pay off any debt secured by an unregistered charge. When the company is wound–up its unsecured creditors, through the liquidator, can treat the unregistered charge as invalid and can have the property subject to it applied in payment of all the company's debts, subject to the discharge of mortgages and charges which have been properly registered. Since non–registration simply invalidates the charge and not the debt it secures the charge ranks as an unsecured credit equally with other creditors.

The period of 21 days during which a charge must be registered runs from the time when the instrument creating the charge is executed, and not from the date on which the loan is made. Similarly, where debentures are issued in a series the charge to secure the series should be registered within 21 days after the trust deed securing the debentures is executed because it is the charge on the company's property which has to be registered and not the loan secured by it.

If a charge is not registered within 21 days of its creation the company may agree to cancel it and replace it with another charge and if that is subsequently registered within 21 days of its creation, its registration is fully effective to preserve the debenture holder's priority. Nevertheless, since the second charge secures a loan which has already been made, it may be invalidated under the Companies Act 1948, s. 322.

The court may, on the application of the company or any interested person, permit a registrable charge to be registered after the expiration of 21 days from its creation if the failure to register was accidental or due to inadvertence or if on other grounds registration is considered to be just and equitable. The only case in which the court will refuse an application to register out of time under this provision is if it suspects that the failure to register was deliberate and designed to cancel the existence of the mortgage or charge from the other creditors of the company.

The court will grant an application to register out of time if the application does not prejudice the rights of other persons who acquire such rights before registration takes place, for example mortgagees who have registered their charges.

Realisation of floating charges

A floating charge may be realised by the appointment of a receiver in one of two ways, namely by the debenture holders or their trustees exercising their power to appoint a receiver given by the debenture or the covering trust deed or by the court appointing a receiver. A receiver appointed by debenture holders or their trustees is their agent and, consequently, they are liable as principals on contracts which he makes during the receivership. This is not so, however, if the debentures or trust deed expressly provide that the receiver shall be the company's agent.

Alternatively, a mortgagee or debenture holder may apply to the court to appoint a receiver. The purpose of the appointment is to enable the receiver to realise the company's assets comprised in the debenture holder's security and to distribute the proceeds to the debenture holders in satisfaction of their claims. Any proceeds or unrealised assets are returned to the company by the receiver after the debentures have been discharged in full and the company may then either continue to carry out its undertaking or may go into liquidation if it is insolvent or has insufficient assets left to carry on business. A receivership does not necessarily result in the company terminating its undertaking, but this will inevitably result if the company has insufficient assets even to pay its debenture holders the full amount owing to them.

If a receiver of the whole, or a substantial part of the company's property is appointed for the benefit of debenture holders secured by a floating charge, the receiver must notify the company of his appointment and within fourteen days the company must prepare and submit to him a statement of its affairs showing its assets and liabilities, together with particulars of its creditors and the securities held by them for the payment of debts. The purpose of this is to show the receiver which assets are subject to the floating charge and whether specific mortgages have priority over the debenture holders' claim. The receiver is required to verify this statement personally.

Collection of assets comprised in the debentures

A debenture or trust deed which provides for the appointment of a receiver out of court will normally also empower the receiver to take possession of all the company's assets or those assets over which the security has been given. The receiver may use this power not only to obtain possession of the company's tangible assets under the control of its officers but also to obtain payment of debts owed to the company. If the court appoints a receiver, the receiver will have similar powers and in both cases the receiver takes the property or any rights the company may have in the same condition and subject to the same incumbrances as the company itself.

The rules by which the receiver should apply the proceeds of realisation have been developed by the courts but they are enumerated in R.S.C., Ord. 44. The order of application of proceeds is as follows:

(a) the cost of selling the property, collecting the debts and enforcing the claims of the company against third parties in order to realise the security created by the debenture;

(*b*) all other proper expenses of the receiver and manager and their remuneration;

(*c*) the costs and expenses of trustees of the debenture trust deed and their remuneration, if the trust deed directs that it shall be paid before the debenture debt;

(*d*) the costs of the debenture holders action, if any;

(*e*) if the debentures are secured by a floating charge, the debts of the company which would be preferential payments in a winding–up; and

(*f*) the debenture debt, with interest thereon, up to the date of payment.

PROMOTERS

The promoters of a company are the people who conceive the idea of forming the company and they take the necessary steps to incorporate it, to provide it with share and loan capital, and to acquire the business.

They then hand over control of the company to its directors who may also have been its promoters. The courts have defined a promoter as one who undertakes to form a company with reference to a given project, and to establish it as a going concern. A promoter need not undertake the whole of the work involved in incorporating it, which may be divided between a number of people. A person will be a promoter if he is concerned in some way with the management or preparations for the management of the company's affairs. If he is employed merely in a professional or technical capacity (e.g. as a (solicitor) he is not a promoter.

The promoters of a company are personally liable on contracts made by them for the purpose of forming the company, or whilst carrying on a business already acquired until the company is ready to carry it over.

Duties of a promoter
The fiduciary duties imposed on a promoter are as follows:

(*a*) not to make any secret profit out of the promotion of the company without the company's consent; and

(*b*) to disclose to the company any interest which he has in a transaction entered into by it.

A promoter is not a trustee for the company he promotes and, therefore, there is no absolute prohibition on his making a profit out of the promotion.

Secret profits
A promoter must not make a secret profit if he purchases property, or business at a time when he is promoting the company with view to resale to the company. He then owes a duty to the company not to profit on the resale to it. If the promoter purchases the property, or business at a time when he merely has an intention of promoting a company he owes no such duty to the

company. A promoter is permitted to make a profit out of a promotion with the consent of the company. In *Lagunas Nitrate Co* v. *Lagunas Syndicate Ltd* (1901) it was said that consent to retention of a promotion profit can only be given by the directors or shareholders if the promoter makes full disclosure of the nature and amount of profit he has made. It is insufficient for him to give them information from which they can deduce that he has obtained a profit.

Disclosure of interest

A promoter must disclose to the company any interest he has in a transaction entered into by it.

Remedies for breach of fiduciary duties

If a promoter makes a secret profit the company may recover it from him by suing him in its corporate name, although the events giving rise to the duty to account occurred before it was incorporated. A promoter is entitled to deduct any expenses he has incurred in connection with the promotion, but he is not entitled to any allowance in respect of the transaction. In *Emma Silver Mining Co* v. *Grant* (1879) it was held that if a promoter has made a secret profit by selling his own property to the company in return for shares, and he has since sold the shares the company may recover from him the difference between the price at which he sold the shares and the price at which he bought the property.

Rescission

The company may rescind any contract made with the promoter or his nominee and recover any consideration which it has conferred on him under a contract entered into by a promoter in breach of his fiduciary duties.

However, a company can only rescind the contract if it can restore to the promoter the consideration he gave under the contract in substantially its original form. The right to rescind will also be lost if the company delays for an unreasonable time.

Damages

The company can recover damages against a promoter for breach of either of his fiduciary duties.

Common law duties of a promoter

The common law duties of a promoter have not been worked out by the courts but they do not depend on a contract between the company and the promoter because at the time the promotion begins the company is not incorporated and cannot enter into contracts with its promoters. A promoter's duties must, therefore, be the same as those of a person who acts on behalf of another without a contract of employment, i.e. to abstain from deception and to exercise reasonable skill and care.

Termination of a promoter's duty

The promoter's duties do not end on incorporation of the company or even when a board of directors is appointed; they continue until the company has acquired the property, or business which it was formed to manage, and has raised its initial share capital, and the board of management has taken control over the affairs of the company from the promoters. The promoter's fiduciary and common law duties then cease and he is subject to no more extensive duties in dealing with the company than a person unconnected with the company.

DIRECTORS AND SECRETARIES

Appointment of directors

The Companies Acts 1948–1981 do not define the term director but merely provide that it includes any person occupying that position regardless of the official name or title designated to him. A person is, therefore, a director of a company if he exercises such functions. The Companies Acts 1948–1976 treated any person in accordance with whose instructions the directors of the company acted or was empowered to act as a director for certain purposes under the Companies Acts. The Companies Act 1980, however, calls such persons "shadow directors" and they are treated as directors, unless the directors merely follow advice given by such persons in their professional capacity, e.g. a solicitor.

The board of directors of a company manage its business subject to any control vested in the hands of the shareholders. The minimum number of directors who must hold office at any time in both public and private companies is two.

Power to appoint directors

The power of appointment is usually vested in the shareholders in a general meeting, or in other directors but the articles of association will provide how directors are to be appointed. The first directors of a company are usually named in the articles of association, but if the appointments made actually differ from the statement of the first directors in the articles, which has to be signed by the subscribers of the memorandum of association and filed with the papers leading to incorporation, the persons named in the statement are the first directors of the company and the appointment of other persons named in the articles is void.

Subsequent directors

The power to appoint subsequent directors is usually exercisable by the members of the company in general meeting by an ordinary resolution. If the articles prescribe a maximum number of directors, any appointments in excess of the maximum is void, unless the members have power to increase the number of directors.

When directors of a public company are appointed or re-appointed each resolution relating to the appointment must be passed individually unless it is agreed at the beginning of the meeting that a composite resolution will be valid.

Right of inspection of directors' service contracts

The Companies Act 1948, s. 26(1), as amended by the Companies Act 1980, s. 61, provides that every company must keep at an appropriate place, usually its registered office or its main place of business, a copy of the directors' written service contracts or, in case of a director whose service contract is not in writing a memorandum setting out the terms under which he is employed. In the case of a director employed by a service contract with a subsidiary, a copy of that contract or, failing that, a memorandum setting out its terms must also be kept. A company must give notice to the Register of Companies notifying him where copies relating to directors' service contracts are kept and have them available for inspection every day for at least two hours.

These requirements do not apply where the unexpired term of the contract is less than one year, or where the company terminates the contract within the next year without paying compensation, or if the director is to work mainly outside the UK.

The Companies Act 1980, s. 47, provides that long term contracts of employment (i.e. contracts for more than 5 years during which time the contract cannot be terminated by the company) cannot be entered into, unless a written memorandum setting out the proposed agreement has been made available for inspection for not less than 15 days prior to a general meeting at which the duration of the contract is approved by ordinary resolution.

The board of directors is usually empowered to fill casual vacancies and to appoint additional directors up to the maximum permissible, but such directors hold office only until the next annual general meeting.

Disqualification from being a director

A person is disqualified from becoming a director of a company in the following circumstances:

(*a*) it is an offence for an undischarged bankrupt to act as a director of a company or to take part in its management without the leave of the court which adjudged him bankrupt;

(*b*) the court may disqualify a person from being a director and from taking part in the management of a company for not more than 15 years:

(*i*) if he has been convicted on indictment of an offence in connection with the promotion, formation or management of a company; or

(*ii*) if in a winding–up of a company he is found to have been guilty of fraudulent trading or guilty of breach of duty towards the company, while taking part in the management of a company; or

(*iii*) because he has been the director of two companies which have been wound–up in an insolvent condition within 5 years of each other and, in consequence of his conduct in connection with those companies, the court considers him unfit to be a director; or (*iv*) if as a director he persistently defaulted in making returns or delivering accounts or returns required by the Companies Acts, and three convictions for failing to do so within 5 years are conclusive evidence of such persistent default;

(*c*) a person cannot be appointed as a director of a public or a subsidiary of a public company if he is 70 or more years old, unless his appointment is made at a general meeting and special notice of the resolution is given when the meeting is called specifying his age.

The articles of association of a company may expressly add further disqualifications.

Share qualification

The articles of association of a company may require each director to hold a certain minimum number of shares to ensure they have an incentive for the success of the company. Unless the articles of the company so require, a director need not obtain his qualification shares before he is appointed but he must obtain them within 2 months of his appointment. He will otherwise cease to be a director and cannot be re-appointed until he has obtained his qualification shares. If no time is fixed by the articles during which a director must take up his qualification shares, the company may allot them to him after a reasonable time. A director may hold the shares in any capacity but if the articles require a director to hold the shares "in his own right" he must be registered as the holder of the shares in such a way that the company can treat him as the owner.

Vacation of the office of director

Termination of period of office

The articles of association of a company may authorise appointment of a director for any period and provide that he may be removed from office. In any event, he ceases to be a director automatically when his period of office expires.

In most public companies a fraction of the directors retire each year by rotation and members are empowered to fill the vacancies at each annual general meeting. All directors retire at the first annual general meeting and at each subsequent annual general meeting one–third of the directors retire each year. If no annual general meeting is held, an appropriate number of directors retire at the end of each year. Those who have held office longest retire at the annual general meeting, but if two or more directors were appointed on the same day and only one is required to retire, lots will be drawn. The retiring directors can be re-elected. Table A provides that the retiring director is automatically re-elected if members do not elect someone else, or resolve that the vacancy be not filled.

Resignation

The articles of association usually provide that a director vacates his office if he resigns by giving written notice to the company. He can resign even though there is no such provision in the articles unless the articles expressly prohibit him from doing so or where he has undertaken to serve the company for a fixed time period. A resignation is effective as soon as it is notified to the company and cannot then be withdrawn without the consent of those persons entitled to appoint a new director.

Publicity in respect of directors
Register of directors and secretaries
Every company must keep at its registered office a register of its directors and secretaries showing each director's christian or forenames and surnames and any former christian and forenames or surnames, residential address, nationality, and, in the case of a public company, his date of birth, in order to ensure compliance with retirement provisions.

The company must notify the Registrar of Companies within 14 days of any change in its directors or the particulars lodged in respect of them, including other directorships and past directorships held by them within the last 5 years. The Registrar must advertise the change in the London Gazette. The register of directors and secretaries must be open for inspection.

A company must state the names of all of its directors on its business correspondence or on a document which is displayed in the company's registered office and available for public inspection.

Register of directors interests in shares and debentures
A company must keep at its registered office a register showing the interests of each of its directors in its shares and debentures and any interest the directors have in shares or debentures of other companies in the same group. A director is treated as having an interest in the shares if his children under 18 years or spouse hold shares in the company. The entries in the register in respect of each director must be made chronologically and the register must be kept at the same place as the company's register of members. Any member of the company or any other company may inspect the register or require the company to supply him with copies of the register.

If the Department of Trade and Industry suspects that a director has not disclosed a matter which he is required to notify to his company it may appoint an inspector to investigate the matter and he has the same powers to obtain information an an inspector appointed to investigate the mismanagement of a company's affairs.

Remuneration and loans to directors
The remuneration paid to directors may take any form and the amount will depend on the terms of the articles and the director's service contract. Table A leaves the form of directors' remuneration open by providing that it shall be determined from time to time by the members in general meeting. The directors are not entitled to remuneration unless the articles so provide and they may be compelled to restore any amounts wrongly paid although they acted in good faith and honestly believed that they were entitled to the

payments. The remuneration payable to a director is a debt owed by the company. It is not contingent on the company's earning sufficient profits to pay it unless it is expressly made contingent by the terms of the director's service agreement. A company may not pay a director remuneration free of income tax. The prohibition on the payment of tax–free remuneration applies to all income paid to directors in any capacity.

Compensation for loss of office

A company cannot make a payment to a director who vacates his office as compensation for loss of office or consideration for his retirement unless the proposed payment is disclosed to members of the company and approved by an ordinary resolution at a general meeting. A payment is only treated as compensation for loss of office if the company is under no legal obligation to make it. If a director is dismissed in breach of his service contract, payment of damages does not require the members' approval.

LOANS AND PROPERTY TRANSACTIONS MADE WITH DIRECTORS AND CONNECTED PERSONS

Property transactions

The Companies Act 1980, s. 48, provides that a company cannot enter into an arrangement with a director or a person connected with such a director whereby the director acquires non–cash assets from the company or vice versa, unless the arrangement has first been approved in a general meeting.

A non–cash asset is of the requisite value if, at the time the arrangement is entered into, its value exceeds £50,000 or 10 per cent of the amount of the company's relevant assets (whichever is less) but its value is in any case not below £1,000.

The arrangement entered into by the company in contravention of s. 48 is voidable at the instance of the company unless restitution of any money or asset is impossible, or a bona fide third party who was not a party to the transaction has acquired rights or the arrangement is affirmed within a reasonable period by the company in general meeting.

Where an arrangement is entered into with a director or connected person which is contrary to s. 48, the director and any person connected with him and any director of the company who authorised the transaction will be liable:

(a) to account to the company for any gain which he has made directly or indirectly; and

(b) to indemnify the company for any loss or damage resulting from the transaction.

A director will not be liable, however, if he can show that he took all reasonable steps to ensure that the company complied with s. 48 or he was not aware of facts contravening the section.

Prohibition of loans to directors and connected persons

The 1980 Act, s. 49(1), provides that, in general, no company can make a loan to any of its directors, or to any director of its holding company, or enter into any guarantee or provide security in connection with a loan made by any other person to a director. The section further provides that in general no relevant company (i.e. a public company or a private company which is in a group containing a public company) may make a quasi-loan to any of its directors or to any director of its holding company, or enter into any guarantee or provide security in connection with a loan made by any other person to such a director. A quasi-loan is a transaction under which one party (the creditor) pays or agrees to pay a sum for another (the borrower), to a third party or reimburses or agrees to reimburse expenditure incurred by a third party for the borrower and the borrower has agreed or is obliged to indemnify the creditor.

Section 49(3) deals with the position where company enters into an indirect arrangement and provides that no company may arrange for the assignment to it of liabilities or obligations owed to a third party by its directors.

Section 50 provides an exception to s. 49, namely, a company is not prevented from entering into any transaction for any person if the aggregate loan does not exceed £5,000 and the company enters into the transaction in the ordinary course of business. The section also creates an exception in favour of recognised banks which may lend to directors in the ordinary course of business without limit, except where the loan is a mortgage for a house.

THE POWERS OF DIRECTORS

The board of directors and members of a company can together exercise all the company's powers. The division of power between the board of directors and members of a company is dependent entirely on the articles of association. The articles usually confer on the board of directors all the powers of the company except those required to be exercised by the members in general meeting. It is possible for the articles to vest the same power in the directors and the members concurrently and, in case of conflict, the decision of the members would prevail over the directors.

Thus, directors' power to sell or retain any of the company's assets, including its undertaking, power to appoint a managing director and the power to declare a dividend and to sue in the company's name are normally wholly conferred on the directors unless the articles of the company confer the exercise of such powers concurrently on the directors and the members.

However, a power of the directors to appoint additional directors and to fill casual vacancies on the board, or to fix remuneration of directors will be a concurrent power unless the articles show that it is exclusively conferred on the directors.

Board meetings

The directors can only exercise their powers collectively by passing resolutions at board meetings, unless the articles provide otherwise. If all the directors agree informally, their unanimity is equal to a resolution passed at a board meeting and is binding on the company. Notice of board meetings should be given to all the directors. The notice need only set out where the meeting is to take place. It is unnecessary to set out the business which is to be transacted. Unless proper notice is given to each director the meeting and all the resolutions passed at that meeting are void.

Any director can call a board meeting unless the articles provide otherwise. A board meeting cannot proceed to business unless a quorum of directors, the number of which is usually fixed by the articles, is present. If the articles do not specify the number of directors required to form a quorum the number of directors who usually attend board meetings constitutes a quorum.

A director who is disabled from voting under the articles (e.g. because he has a personal interest in the matter) does not count towards the quorum. Unless the articles otherwise provide, each director has one vote at a board meeting and a resolution is carried by more votes being cast in favour of the proposal than against. If an equal number of votes is cast the resolution is lost. However, the chairman of the board may be given a casting vote in the event of a tie.

A company must keep minutes of the meeting and if the minutes are signed by the chairman it means that, until the contrary is proved, the meeting was properly convened and the resolutions recorded were duly passed. The minutes are open to inspection by directors but members have no right of inspection.

Delegation of directors' powers

The board of directors must act collectively and only has power to delegate if the articles of the company empower delegation or by a resolution being passed.

If for some reason the board of directors is unable or unwilling to make a decision the members may make the decision themselves, e.g.

1. Where the act in question is beyond the board's powers

The members in general meeting may intervene where directors are unable to act because the transaction which they wish to carry out is outside their own powers. The authority must then be sought from members in a general meeting and given by passing an ordinary resolution. The members may, therefore, authorise directors to do those acts which are outside the directors' own powers but within the company's power. In each situation directors act as agents of the members and not as directors of the company, and thus members may revoke or vary the authority by ordinary resolution at any time.

2. Lack of quorum at board meetings

The directors may not be able to exercise powers given to them by the articles because they have become so few in number that a quorum cannot be constituted at a board meeting or because so many of them are interested in the transaction that they are disabled from voting, and hence a quorum cannot be formed. In such a situation the members can exercise the directors' powers until a board of directors can be properly constituted.

3. Conflict with duties to the company

If the directors are unable to exercise the powers conferred on them by the articles because to do so would be in breach of the members' interests, the members may, by ordinary resolution, ratify what the directors have done or authorise them in advance to do the act in question.

4. Board cannot act because of dissension

Where the directors cannot act because of dissension between themselves, the members may exercise the board's powers until a board is elected which is able to act. It is necessary to show a persistent failure to reach a decision (e.g. a quorum cannot be formed, or dissenting factions have equal votes and therefore no resolution can be passed). In such a case the court has power to appoint a receiver to manage the company's business until a competent board can be constituted or, if the power is one which the court itself can exercise, the court may exercise such power.

Director's duties to the company

The duties of directors can be considered under three heads and are owed to the company (not to members of the company):

(a) fiduciary duties similar to those owed by an agent, i.e. to keep within the powers given to him, to act in good faith and to disclose any personal interest;

(b) common law duty to take care; and

(c) statutory duties.

Fiduciary duties

Duty not to exceed powers

The directors must not do any act which is illegal or ultra vires the company or do any act which is beyond the powers conferred on the directors by the company's articles unless the members in general meeting give authority. If the directors act beyond their powers and the company suffers a loss it can recover the full amount of the loss from them. It is not necessary to show negligence on the part of the directors. However, the directors can only be sued for paying a dividend out of capital if they have been guilty of negligence in not ascertaining that the company had sufficient profits available to pay the dividend.

Duty not to obtain a personal profit by exercise of powers

A director, like any other agent, must account to the company for any profit he has made by the use of powers conferred on him as director without the company's consent. A director must similarly pay to the company any commission he has been paid by third parties. In *Barton Deep Sea Fishing Co* v. *Ansell* (1888) a director who accepted a bribe in return for placing an order with the person giving the bribe was held liable to account to the company.

A director may subscribe for shares in his own company, but he must pay the full market value for them. In *Parker* v. *McKenna* (1874–80) the directors of a company had power to allot shares as they thought fit. They allotted themselves shares standing at a premium on the stock exchange at £3 for £1.50 per share. The directors were held accountable for the difference between the price which they would have obtained for the shares on the open market and the price they paid the company. In *Cook* v. *Deeks* (1916) a company was formed by three shareholders, who were all directors, to supply railway sleepers. Two of the three shareholders formed a second company because of a disagreement with the third director, and persuaded a customer of the first company to place orders for sleepers with the second company and, therefore, the third director was excluded from a share of the profits. The third director was held entitled to succeed and the two directors who had formed a separate company were held in breach of duty to the first company. If directors give away business to another company which, in the normal course of business, would come to the company of which all were directors, they are in breach of duty to the other director. In *Industrial Development Consultants Ltd* v. *Cooley* (1972) IDC employed C to obtain orders for the company, for which he was paid a fixed remuneration. He was invited by a regional gas board to set up his own consultancy with a view to the gas board's placing orders with him. He persuaded IDC to release him from his service contract under the pretext that he was ill. He was given substantial contracts by the gas corporation which would otherwise have gone to IDC. It was held that C had placed himself in a position where his private interests conflicted with those of the company and he was liable to account to IDC for profit made out of contracts which otherwise would have been given to them.

If a director uses information available to him in his capacity as director when such information is not available to the general public and makes a profit he is liable to account to the company for the profit. The directors are in the position of trustees and, therefore, if they make a profit as a result of using secret information available to them whilst acting as directors they are liable to account for the profits.

Abuse of powers

This duty extends beyond the duty not to make a secret profit. If the directors are responsible for a loss to the company by the abuse of their powers without a corresponding gain for themselves they are still liable to the company for a loss. In *Howard Smith Ltd* v. *Ampol Petroleum Ltd* (1974) the directors of the company favoured one of two prospective takeover bidders for control of the company and issued further shares to that bidder, in order to prevent the rival bidder from gaining control. There was nothing to indicate that the directors had gained personally. It was held that the directors were in breach of their duty and the allotment of shares was rescinded. If the directors abuse their power the company may treat the resulting transaction as void even though this may prejudice an innocent third party. The shareholders may, however, ratify the directors' acts despite an abuse of powers and the resulting transaction may be validated.

Contracts with directors

A director is not in breach of his fiduciary duties merely because he has an interest in a contract entered into by the company. The mere existence of an interest does not itself amount to a breach of duty but the director should declare his interest to the other directors and he must abstain from voting if a resolution is necessary. The company has the right to rescind the contract if he fails to disclose any interest.

The right of the company to rescind a contract in which one or more of its directors is interested may be waived either by the articles of association of the company or by the members in a general meeting, but it cannot be waived by the board of directors.

The question which arises is whether a director who is also a shareholder in the company can vote as a member of that company in order to decide whether or not the contract should be rescinded. In *Beattie* v. *Beattie Ltd* (1938) the question was whether a vote validating a contract in which one of the directors had a personal interest was valid because the director had taken part in the voting. The court held that the director in his capacity as a shareholder was entitled to vote at a meeting where shareholders decided whether or not to approve the contract. However, in the American case of *Globe Woollen Co* v. *Utica Gas & Electric Co* (1918) a director had a controlling shareholding in B Co and also owned shares in A Co. A Co made a bid to purchase B Co. The director failed to disclose to the board of A Co that the bid was too high. It was held that A Co could rescind the contract although other shareholders had approved the transaction. The director had voted in favour of approving the transaction and because he held a majority of the shares his vote in effect had approved the sale.

Common law duty: negligence

A director owes a duty to his company to exercise reasonable care in the management of its affairs and he is liable in damages if he fails to exercise such care. However, the duty owed is not so onerous as to deter capable men from serving as directors. In *Overend & Gurney Co* v. *Cribb* (1872) it was held that a director is not expected to exercise the skill and care of a professional man. The directors were held to have complied with their duty of care when they purchased a company carrying on a business but which proved to be insolvent. The directors were not under any obligation to make their own inquiries into the financial standing of the company.

The directors are not required to examine the company's accounting records and may trust the managing director and the company's accountants to maintain proper records; thus they can declare a dividend on the basis of a profit and loss account laid before them by the managing director. However, in *Re Denham & Co* (1883) the company's directors were held to be negligent in not checking the companies accounts but an individual director who had not taken part in nor attended any board meetings for the previous three years was held not liable. A director is under no duty to attend board meetings.

If the day-to-day running of the company is in the hands of a managing director, the other directors are not under a duty to supervise his actions but if there is no managing director they will all be liable if the company's funds are used for purposes other than the company business. In *Re City Equitable Fire Insurance Co Ltd* (1930) the managing director of a company, who was a stockbroker, used to sell the shares in City Equitable to finance his own private business and then purchase them before the auditors prepared the company's annual accounts. The liquidator brought an action against the other directors of the company when the stockbroker became bankrupt, and was unable to repurchase City Equitable's shares. It was held that the other directors were not liable in negligence since they had no reason to suspect that the managing director was dishonest.

Actions against directors
An action against a defaulting director may be brought by the company itself or, if the breach is of a fiduciary duty, a member of the company may sue in a derivative action on behalf of himself and all the other members of the company. The action must be brought within six years after the alleged breach of duty.

An express provision in the company's articles or in a director's service contract will not exempt him from the fiduciary duties and the duty of care imposed on him by law. The court may, however, relieve a director from liability if he can show that he acted honestly and reasonably and ought fairly to be excused. The relief will not be given to a director who, although not guilty of personal dishonesty, has acted in accordance with the directions of a controlling shareholder or other person and not for the benefit of the company. The amount recoverable from a director guilty of a breach of duty will be either the loss he has caused the company or the profit obtained by the breach, whichever is greater.

If the company calls on the directors to account for secret profits they have made as a result of a breach of duty, they are liable to account for what they have received and are jointly and severally liable for the costs of the action brought against them.

Actions against third persons for directors' breaches of duty
If a breach of duty by a director results in a tort being committed against the company by a person, the company may sue that person for damages or for the return of property. If a director disposes of company property in breach of his equitable duties the company can recover the property or its value from a person.

Directors' duties to members and to persons dealing with the company

The directors owe no contractual or fiduciary duty to the members of their company. In *Ferguson* v. *Wilson* (1866) the plaintiff had an option to subscribe for shares in the company. The directors ignored this right and issued all the company's shares to themselves and other persons. It was held that the plaintiff had no cause of action either at equity or in common law. In *Percival* v. *Wright* (1902) the directors entered into a contract with a shareholder in that company to purchase shares from him but did not notify him of their intention to resell them at a higher price to another person who had made a bid for the shares. They were held not to owe any duties to the shareholder and so were not accountable to the shareholder for the higher price obtainable from the third party.

If the directors induce members to sell their shares at an undervalue by misleading them as to the value of the shares, the members can sue the directors for deceit and rescind the contract but may also require the directors to account in equity for the difference between the price paid by them for the shares and their real value at the time of the sale.

However, the directors may constitute themselves the agents of individual members of a company to carry out a particular transaction and will then owe the same fiduciary duties to such members as any other agent to his principal. In *Allen* v. *Hyatt* (1914) the directors purchased shares from a shareholder for £2 and resold them to a third party for a profit. The directors had constituted themselves agents of the shareholder to find a purchaser, and therefore were liable to account for the price they received from the third party.

Duties to persons dealing with the company

The directors of a company owe no fiduciary or contractual duties to persons who deal with their company and therefore are not liable to pay debts incurred by the company at a time when they know the company is insolvent. The only situation where a director may be made liable to a third party dealing with the company is where the director commits a tort against that third party and has also committed a breach of duty against the company. In *Fairline Shipping Corporation* v. *Adamson* (1975) the director of a company entered into a contract with a third party to place goods in deep freezers owned by the company. The director entered into the contract in such a manner as to make himself personally liable, i.e. a contract was signed by him in his own name and the rent for storage was received at his private address, in his own name. The deep freeze broke down and the goods deteriorated. The director was held personally liable to the third pary because he had assumed a personal duty to take care in storing the goods.

Breach of warranty of authority: subrogation

A director is personally liable on a contract which he negotiates on the company's behalf which is not binding on the company at all. When a director negotiates a contract on behalf of the company he represents that he has authority from the company, and if he lacks that authority he is guilty of breach of warranty of authority and is liable for any loss which the other party suffers. The damages recoverable from directors guilty of a breach of warranty of authority represent the difference between the value of the other party's actual rights against the company and the value those rights would have had if the company had been bound by that transaction.

Secretaries

The secretary of a company is its administrative officer, and his function is to carry out the decisions of the directors. A secretary has no power to participate in the mangement of the company's affairs but may have a limited power to engage in transactions for the company.

PROTECTION OF MINORITY SHAREHOLDERS

The rule in Foss v. Harbottle

The rule in *Foss* v. *Harbottle* (1843) resulted from the refusal of the court to interfere in the management of a company at the insistence of minority shareholders dissatisfied with the conduct of the company's affairs by the majority. It is not the court's function to take management decisions and to substitute its opinions for those of the directors and the majority of the members. If, therefore, the majority of the members are empowered to do something, the court will not interfere because its decision could be set aside by a resolution of the members. However, the rule applies only where the majority can cure the irregularity complained of by passing an ordinary resolution. The court will interfere at the insistence of the minority when this cannot be done.

The refusal of the courts to intervene has two strands, namely:

(*a*) that members cannot bring an action to remedy a wrong done to the company, because the company alone can enforce rights of action vested in it and only the directors of the company or the members at a general meeting can decide whether or not to pursue an action in the company's name;

(*b*) that the majority of the shareholders may wish to waive the company's right to sue.

The rule in *Foss* v. *Harbottle* does not deprive an individual member of a personal right to bring an action against the company for wrongs done to him personally and he can sue for wrongs done to him in his capacity as a member.

Representative and derivative actions

In certain circumstances an individual member may bring an action to remedy a wrong committed against the company or to compel the company to conduct its affairs in accordance with its constitution, although no wrong has been done to him personally and although the majority of the shareholders do not wish to bring an action. The plaintiff does not sue in his own right but on behalf of himself and other members of the company, except those against whom relief is sought.

The individual members' action against the company and those shareholders it is sought to compel is known as a representative action because, it is brought to compel them to conduct the company's affairs in accordance with its constitution. If relief is sought against third parties, unconnected with the company, for the company's benefit the action is known as a derivative action because the individual member sues to enforce a claim which belongs to the company and his right of action is derived from it.

The exceptions to Foss v. Harbottle

There are a number of cases where a member may compel a company to conform to its constitution and the rules governing the conduct of its affairs, or to enforce a claim belonging to the company by a derivative action, namely:

(a) where the members cannot remedy the defect or forgo the company's right to sue by passing an ordinary resolution in a general meeting, and

(b) cases where the courts have excluded the rule in Foss v. Harbottle because it would be unfair.

If the plaintiff's action does not fall within one of these exceptions the court will stay the action.

The situations where the majority shareholders cannot prevent a member from suing by passing a resolution that the company itself will not sue are six in number:

(a) where the plaintiff seeks to restrain the commision of an ultra vires act, or to compel the directors to compensate the company for loss suffered by it in consequence of an ultra vires act, or to recover property of the company which has been disposed of to a third party by an ultra vires transaction. If the plaintiff seeks to recover compensation for an ultra vires act which has already been committed, or to recover property disposed of by an ultra vires transaction the action must be a derivative one, but if the plaintiff seeks to prevent an ultra vires transaction he can bring either a personal or a representative action;

(b) where the plaintiff seeks to restrain a threatened breach of a provision in the memorandum or articles. Since the articles of association can only be altered by a special resolution, an ordinary resolution by the company to that effect would be ineffective;

(c) where the plaintiff seeks a declaration that a resolution altering the memorandum or articles, although passed in the proper form, is invalid because the alteration was not made in good faith and for the benefit of the members as a whole;

(d) where the plaintiff seeks to have a resolution of a general meeting declared void and to restrain the company from acting on it because it should have been passed as a special or extraordinary resolution, but has not been passed in that form. In such a case the action must be a representative one, unless the personal rights of the plaintiffs have already been interfered with, in which case he may bring a personal action;

(e) where the plaintiff seeks by a representative action to restrain the company from doing an act contrary to the Companies Acts 1948–1981, or the general law; or

(f) where a general meeting has resolved validly that something shall be done or abstained from and the plaintiff brings a representitive action to restrain action by the company which is contrary to the resolution.

Fraud or oppression

Where the persons who control a majority of the votes which can be cast at a general meeting use their power of control to defraud or oppress the minority shareholders the court will intervene at the insistence of the minority. The fraud or oppression must involve unconscionable use of the majority's power or the likelihood of its resulting in financial loss, or in unfair or discriminatory treatment of the minority; and it must be more serious than a failure by the majority to act in the interest of the company as a whole.

In *Menior* v. *Hooper's Telegraph Works Ltd* (1874) a company was formed to lay down a transatlantic telegraph cable which was to be made by Hooper's Telegraph Works Ltd, the majority shareholder. Hooper Ltd discovered it could make a larger profit by selling the cable to another company, but that company refused to buy the cable unless it had government concessions to lay down the cable. Hooper, therefore, induced the trustees for the original company to transfer the government concessions to the second company and Hooper then sold the cable to the second company. Hooper then procured the passing of a resolution that the first company should be wound–up and a liquidator appointed. Menier, a minority shareholder, brought a derivative action against Hooper to compel him to account to the company for the profits it had derived from the improper arrangement. It was held that a derivative action would lie, since this was a clear case of fraud against the minority. In *Clemens* v. *Clemens Bros. Ltd* (1976) it was held that the court would set aside resolutions for the issue of further shares as being oppressive to the minority shareholders. In another case, it was held that the court would restrain the company and its directors from carrying out a resolution that the company should invest its funds in another company on the promise of a director of that company that the majority shareholders might exchange their existing shares for shares in the other company on favourable terms, when no such offer had been made to the minority shareholders. The court held that the minority shareholders, to whom no such offer had been made, could restrain the company and its directors from carrying out the resolution because the inequality of treatment between the majority and minority was a fraud on the minority and grossly unfair (*Re Kerry Maori Dream Gold Mines Ltd* (1898)).

Breach of directors' and promoters' fiduciary duties

A derivative action may be brought against directors and promoters who have been guilty of a breach of their fiduciary duties to the company, if they are able to prevent the company from suing them in its own name because they control a majority of the votes at a general meeting, or because they are otherwise able to prevent a general meeting from resolving that the company shall sue them. Thus, a derivative action has been permitted against directors in control of the company who misapply its property in breach of the Companies Acts (*Wallersteiner* v. *Moir* (1974)) to compel directors to account to the company for personal profits made by business opportunities which the company should have enjoyed (*Cook* v. *Deeks* (1916)), to disclose a secret profit obtained from transactions entered into whilst acting for the company (*Atwool* v. *Merryweather* (1867)), or to deprive the members who controlled the company of their power to control it in the future (*Howard Smith* v. *Ampol Petroleum* (1974)). It may be possible, where there has been a breach of fiduciary duty, to bring a derivative action for fraud or oppression of minority shareholders.

Negligence
In *Daniels* v. *Daniels* (1978) it was held that a minority shareholder could bring a derivative action against the directors for breach of a duty provided they have gained personally by that breach. The plaintiff alleged that one of the directors had deliberately sold property at an undervalue and the court held that the action could proceed.

It has been held that a derivative action against directors or promoters for breaches of fiduciary duty can only be brought if they have the power to prevent an action being brought in the company's name, i.e. where directors own the majority shares.

Statutory protection of the minority
The Companies Acts 1948–1981 give protection to minority shareholders in four ways:

1. Relief against oppression
Any member of a company who claims that its affairs are being conducted in a manner unfairly prejudicial to some of the members may petition to the court and, if the court is satisfied that the company's affairs are being conducted oppressively, it may, if it thinks it fit and equitable, make a winding–up order, or make any other order it thinks fit in order to remedy the complaint and to regulate future control of the company. The kind of unfair prejudicial conduct which justifies the court in making a winding–up order includes fraudulent or oppressive conduct by majority shareholders, and breaches of fiduciary duty by controlling directors or promoters which would justify a minority shareholder in bringing an action under one of the exceptions in *Foss* v. *Harbottle*. It is unnecessary for a petitioner for relief to show that the majority acted with a motive to obtain an improper advantage. The court will not interfere with a question of business policy in hearing a petition for relief (e.g. if the alleged oppression consists of a failure of majority shareholders to declare a dividend).

A member of a company who petitions for relief must show that he, or a group of members of whom he is one, has been treated in an unfairly, prejudicial manner. He cannot claim if he has been treated harshly in some other capacity, e.g. if he has been dismissed from his employment with the company. The fact that the oppressive acts have been done in some other capacity than that of members of the company does not prevent the court from giving relief. In *Scottish Co-operative Wholesale Society Ltd* v. *Meyer* (1954) minority shareholders were held entitled to relief from oppression caused by the majority shareholder, a co-operative society, managing its own affairs so as deliberately to ruin the company.

A petition for relief must be presented in good faith. Thus, if the reason for which the petitioner obtains relief is to obtain payment of a debt, it will be refused. Similarly, delay in applying for relief will result in the court refusing relief.

The court can only make an order under this statutory provision if it would have jurisdiction to wind-up the company on the ground that it is just and equitable to do so because of the oppression (Companies Act 1948, s. 210). The remedies available are at the discretion of the court and may include payment of compensation to the oppressed shareholders, removal of directors, appointing a receiver to temporarily manage the company's affairs, and altering the voting or other rights of classes of members.

2. Section 75 of the 1980 Act

Under the 1980 Act it is no longer necessary for a petitioner to show that the facts would justify a winding-up order, and it is no longer necessary for the petitioner to be a member of the company. The conduct complained of need not be a course of conduct: an isolated act will be sufficient to bring an action on the grounds that the affairs of the company are being conducted in a manner which is unfairly prejudicial to the interests of some part of the members (including the petitioner) or that any proposed act or omission would be so prejudicial. The section allows personal representatives or trustees in bankruptcy who have not been registered to petition. The orders which a court can make in hearing a petition have been extended and the court may authorise civil proceedings to be brought in the name and on behalf of the company by such person or persons as the court may direct.

3. Misfeasance proceedings

In a winding-up of a company an application may be made to the court by the official receiver, the liquidator, or any other creditor or contributory for an order that any promoter, past or present director, liquidator or officer of the company who has misapplied, or retained or become accountable for the company's money or property, or has become guilty of misfeasance or breach of trust should repay or restore the money or property. Misfeasance proceedings can be brought although the member could not have brought a derivative action, i.e. where there has been no fraud or oppression by the majority. The only orders which the court may make in misfeasance proceedings are for the return of property to the company, or for the payment of compensation or damages. The court cannot therefore rescind the contract or order payment of a debt to a company.

Only the officers of the company can be made respondents in misfeasance proceedings. The Companies Act 1948 defines officers as including directors, managers and secretaries, but it has been held that auditors are officers for the purpose of misfeasance proceedings. A member may bring misfeasance proceedings only if he has an interest in the property or compensation claimed being returned, or paid to the company.

4. Investigation by the Department of Trade and Industry
The Department of Trade and Industry may appoint one or more inspectors to investigate the affairs of a company on the application of the company, or of two hundred members of it, or of members holding at least one–tenth of the company's issued share capital; the Department may require the applicant to produce evidence to show that they have good reason to request an investigation. The Department of Trade and Industry may also appoint an inspector if it appears that the company's business is being or has been conducted with intent to defraud its creditors or for any fraudulent purpose, or in a manner oppressive to any of its members, that the company has been formed for an unlawful purpose, if it appears that the directors or persons engaged in the management of the company's affairs have been guilty of fraud, misfeasance or other misconduct towards its members, or if it appears that the members of the company have not been given all the information with respect to its affairs which they might reasonably expect. Finally, the court can order the Department of Trade and Industry to appoint an inspector. If an inspector is appointed by the Department the directors are not entitled to be informed of the reasons for appointment. The inspector can investigate any matters relating to the company's management, assets, profits or losses, or any of its subsidiary or related companies. Past and present promoters, directors, paid officers of the company, and persons whom the inspector considers have information which would assist the investigation must produce to the inspector all documents relative to the company which are in their possession or power, and must give all assistance to the inspector which they can reasonably give. The inspector may examine such persons under oath.

As a result of the investigations the Department may petition for the company to be wound–up by the court or for an order giving relief to members against the unfairly prejudicial conduct of the company's officers, or the department may bring civil proceedings in the name of the company whose affairs have been investigated to recover damages for its benefit.

MEETINGS AND RESOLUTIONS

General meetings
There are three types of general meetings, namely annual general meetings, extraordinary general meetings and class meetings.

The law requires every company to hold an annual general meeting in each year. There must be not more than fifteen months between the meetings. If a company fails to hold an annual general meeting, any member may apply to the Department of Trade and Industry which may then itself call a general meeting and give such directions as it thinks fit. The business which may be transacted at an annual general meeting is not governed by law, and normally the company's ordinary business as defined by its articles is dealt with, but the company may deal with any other business.

Article 52 of Table A provides that any business transacted at an extraordinary general meeting is special business and at an annual general meeting all business is special except:

(*a*) declaring a dividend;

(*b*) the consideration of accounts, balance sheets, and the directors' and auditors' reports;

(*c*) the election of directors; and

(*d*) the appointment and remuneration of auditors.

Annual accounts

The Companies Act 1976 provides that a copy of the balance sheet, together with the other documents, i.e. the profit and loss account, must be annexed and a copy laid before the company in general meeting. The company's accounts are now prepared in accordance with the Companies Act 1981, unless the company is a type of company which is expressly exempted under the Act, in which case it will continue to prepare its accounts under the Companies Act 1948. The company must send out certain documents to every member at least 21 days before the meeting, but if these documents are sent less than 21 days before the date set for the meeting, they will be deemed to have been duly sent if it is agreed by all the members entitled to attend. The documents required to be sent are the company's balance sheet, the profit and loss account, group accounts where appropriate, the directors' report and the auditors' report. Certain other documents may also be annexed to the balance sheet.

Conduct of meetings

Table A provides that notice may be given to any member either personally, or by post, or to his registered address. The notice must specify the place, day and hour of the meeting and, in the case of a special meeting, the nature of the business. A resolution which is not covered by the terms of the notice cannot validly be passed.

The articles will normally state that the chairman of the board of directors will preside as chairman at every general meeting, but any member elected by those present at a meeting may act as chairman.

Table A provides that a resolution will be decided on by a show of hands unless a poll is demanded and on a show of hands every member will have one vote. A proxy cannot vote on a show of hands, unless he votes as a member in his own right and then he will only have one vote. However, a representative invited by a company to attend and vote at meetings who is a member can vote on a show of hands. Where a resolution is passed by a show of hands, a declaration by the chairman as to the outcome and a record in the minutes is conclusive evidence of the outcome. A vote by a show of hands ceases to have effect once a poll is properly demanded. A poll demanded on the election of a chairman and on a question of adjournment must be taken immediately, but a poll demanded on any other question may be adjourned until such time as the chairman directs. On a poll members have the number of votes attached to their shares. Moreover, they are not bound to cast all the votes or to cast them all in the same manner.

A poll may be demanded by the chairman. All general meetings other than the annual general meeting are extraordinary general meetings and the directors may convene one whenever they think fit. The Companies Act 1967, s. 132(1), states that notwithstanding any express provision in the articles the directors must convene an extraordinary general meeting on the request of members holding not less than one-tenth of the paid-up capital carrying the right to vote. The members are required to state the objects of the meeting and deposit them at the company's registered office. If the directors fail to convene a meeting within 21 days of the deposit of the formal request, the members calling the meeting may hold it themselves.

The company can transact any business it could in a general meeting in addition to all special business. Moreover, the courts have power on the application of either its directors or its members to order a meeting to be called and held in any manner the court directs.

Class meetings
If a class meeting of the holders of a particular class of shares is held, the holders of any other class of shares have no right to attend. The usual business of a class meeting is to consider a variation of class rights. In order for there to be a valid meeting it must be properly convened. In effect, this means that persons entitled to attend must have been summoned by the proper authority and that proper notice must have been sent to all those entitled to attend.

A notice of the meeting must be served on every member, or the personal representatives of a deceased member, or the trustees in bankruptcy of a bankrupt member of the company unless the articles otherwise provide. The meeting must be attended by at least two members present in person or proxy. Members present representing at least one-tenth of the total voting rights of all members entitled to vote or members holding voting shares on which one-tenth of the total amount paid-up on all voting shares has been paid-up may require the directors to call a meeting.

Proxies
The term proxy covers both the person who is appointed to act on behalf of a member at a meeting and the instrument by which his appointment is made. Any member who is entitled to attend and vote is entitled to appoint another

person as his proxy with power to attend and vote for him. A proxy need not himself be a member.

Resolutions

An act which must be done by the members themselves, e.g. the appointment and removal of directors, requires a vote by the members. A question on which a vote is necessary is called a motion. There are three types of resolutions, namely:

(*a*) Ordinary resolution—this is passed by a simple majority.

(*b*) Special resolution—this is passed by a majority of 75 per cent.

(*c*) Extraordinary resolution—this is passed by a 75 per cent majority of the members entitled to vote.

The Companies Act 1948, s. 143(4), as amended by the 1980 Act, requires a copy of certain types of resolutions or agreements to be filed with the Registrar of Companies.

WINDING-UP BY THE COURT

The winding–up or liquidation of a company is a process by which the management of the company is taken out of the hands of the company's directors, and its assets are realised by the liquidator in order to pay off its debts from the proceeds. The High Court has jurisdiction to order the winding–up of any company registered in England or Wales, but if the paid–up share capital of the company does not exceed £120,000 the county court within whose district the company's registered office is situated may wind–up the company. The county court has all the powers of the High Court, and in the course of winding–up it may decide any question even though the subject–matter in dispute would ordinarily take the issue outside the county court's jurisdiction.

A petition for a winding–up may be presented by the company itself, any of its creditors or contributories, or the Department of Trade and Industry.

A company may be wound–up by the court if:

(*a*) the company has, by special resolution, resolved that the company be wound–up;

(*b*) being a public company on its incorporation, the company has failed to obtain a certificate entitling it to do business;

(*c*) the company does not commence its business within a year from its incorporation or suspends its business for a whole year;

(*d*) the number of members is reduced to below the minimum of two;

(*e*) the company is unable to pay its debts; or

(*f*) in the opinion of the court it is just and equitable that the company be wound up.

A creditor may petition for a winding–up order to be made if a liquidated sum is owing to him and it is immaterial whether he is a secured or unsecured creditor. A creditor is a person who could enforce his claim against the company by an action for debt, but a person is not a creditor when he merely has a right of action against the company for unliquidated damages. If, however, such a person obtains judgment against the company, the judgment itself creates a debt for an ascertained sum and he is then able to petition for winding–up. The court will not make a winding–up order if the petitioning creditor is owed less than £200, or unless the total indebitness of the company to those of its creditors who present or support the petition does not exceed £200. However, if a company does not have assets sufficient to satisfy the petitioner's debt and refuses to call up its unpaid capital (if any) to enable it to do so, the court will make a winding–up order although the petitioner's debt is less than £200. A company is statutorily deemed unable to pay its debt if:

(a) a creditor to whom the company owes more than £200 immediately has secured on it, at its registered office, a written demand for payment signed by him and the company has for three weeks thereafter, neglected or otherwise failed to pay the debt. The creditor must after service of the demand wait for twenty–one days before presenting his winding–up petition, and if the company contends that it is not liable to the creditor or has a substantial defence to plead to his claim the court will not hold it in default for its failure to pay within 21 days and will refuse to make a winding–up order;

(b) if a judgment creditor of the company has issued a process of execution which has been returned unsatisfied in whole or in part;

(c) if the court is otherwise satisfied that the company is unable to pay its debts, taking into account its prospective future liability as well as debts immediately payable. There are two tests of insolvency in these circumstances, and the company is insolvent if it satisfies either of them. The first is that the company cannot pay off its debts as they fall due out of cash or readily realisable assets in its hand; the second is that the company cannot pay all its debts, present and future, out of its total assets. A creditor who can give proof that his debt has not been paid gives prima facie evidence that the company is insolvent, but the company may rebut this presumption of insolvency by proving that it can in fact pay its debts.

Procedure for winding-up

The procedure for obtaining a winding–up order is governed by the Companies (Winding–Up) Rules 1949 (as amended) and the same rules govern procedure on winding–up in all courts. The petition must follow one of the forms set out in the Appendix to the rules and, in addition to the facts on which the petitioner relies and the relief he seeks, it must state the date of the company's incorporation, the address of its registered office and details of its capital and its objects. Within four days of its presentation at the office of the Registrar of the court at which it will be heard, it must be verified by an affidavit. A sealed copy of the petition must be served on the company by leaving it at its registered office, or with an officer or servant of the company. The petition must be advertised once in the London Gazette and once in a national newspaper, seven days before the hearing. The advertisement must contain, amongst other things, a note stating that any person who wishes to be heard in support or against the petition must notify the petitioner's solicitor. The petitioner must, prior to the commencement of the hearing, give a list to the court of persons wishing to be heard. Any affidavits in opposition to the petition must be filed in court within seven days of the affidavit verifying the petition.

The winding–up petition is heard in open court, and evidence at the hearing consists of affidavits filed in support of or against the petition, unless the court admits oral testimony. The affidavit verifying the petition is prima facie proof of the alleged facts.

On the hearing of a winding–up petition, the court may make or refuse a winding–up order or make any other order it thinks suitable. The petitioning creditor should withdraw his petition if the company offers to pay his debt before the hearing.

Consequences of winding-up order

When a winding–up order is made, no action or proceeding against the company may be commenced or continued in any court without the leave of the court. The provision does not prevent a defendant sued by the company in liquidation from setting–off any claim he has against the company or counter–claiming for such a claim. The court may give a plaintiff leave to proceed against the company if he has a prima facie case and his claim cannot be dealt with adequately in the winding–up proceedings, for example leave will be given to a secured creditor to bring an action for the realisation of his security.

When a winding–up order has been made, the court will appoint a liquidator after considering nominations by the company's creditors and shareholders. The court has a free discretion in making the appointment but it will usually appoint one or more accountants who have been in practice for at least five years. A liquidator cannot act until he has notifed the Registrar of Companies of his appointment and has given security. The liquidator must then advertise his appointment in such newspapers as the court directs.

VOLUNTARY WINDING-UP

A company may be wound–up voluntarily when by a special resolution it resolves to that effect, or by an extraordinary resolution it resolves that it cannot continue its business because of its liabilities. The passing of the resolution must be advertised in the London Gazette within fourteen days after it is passed.

If the directors file a statutory declaration that they reasonably believe that the company will be able to pay its debts in full within twelve months from the commencement of winding–up, the winding–up is a "members'' voluntary winding–up. If no declaration of solvency is made the winding–up is a "creditors'" voluntary winding–up.

In the case of a creditors' voluntary winding–up, the company must cause a meetings of its creditors to be summoned for the day or the day after it passes the resolution, and it must advertise the meeting.

Distribution of the debtor's assets in liquidation

In every winding–up proofs may be lodged for all debts owed by or claims against the company so that these debts and claims will qualify for payment of dividends out of the assets of the company. All claims must be valued as at the date when the winding–up order was made, and contingent claims and debts payable at a future date must be valued with regard to the facts as they exist at the date of the winding–up. However, any later events which modify the value originally put on the claims will be taken into account when distributions are later made.

A company is insolvent if its assets are insufficient to meet its outstanding liabilities after the costs of the winding–up have been paid.

A secured creditor, namely one who has a mortgage, charge or lien on the property of the company, may either:

(*a*) sell the property subject to his security and prove in the winding–up or bankruptcy for the balance of his debt: or

(*b*) surrender his security to the liquidator or trustee in bankruptcy and prove for the share of the debt as an unsecured creditor; or

(*c*) estimate the value of the property subject to his security and prove for the balance of the debt; or

(*d*) rely on his security and not prove in the winding–up or bankruptcy.

The creditor can either sell the security and apply the proceeds of sale to discharge the debt owed to him by the company, or surrender the property to the liquidator or trustee in return for payment of the debt, either in full or in part, proving for any balance in the winding–up.

In a winding–up, a debtor can set–off a claim only if it is for a liquidated sum already owing, or if it is for an unliquidated sum which is immediately payable under the transaction which gave rise to it.

In every winding–up, certain debts and claims against the company, or bankrupt must be paid before other claims. Such preferential claims must be paid in full but if the insolvency is so extreme that the preferential debts cannot be paid in full, they must be paid rateably (Companies Act 1948, s. 319(1)–(5)). They include a company's liability to corporation tax, the payment of wages and salary of any employee of the company rendered during the four months preceding the relevant date, holiday remuneration payable to an employee and certain claims by former employees under the Employment Protection (Consolidation) Act 1978.

A creditor who has a mortgage or charge on the company's property for both preferential and ordinary claims may appropriate the proceeds of sale of the property in satisfaction primarily of the ordinary claims so that any sums owed are on preferential claims for which he may claim priority as an unsecured creditor.

It is the function of the liquidator to admit, or reject debts or claims against the company and to apply the available assets in discharging its liabilities (Companies Act 1948, ss. 257(1), 273(b) and 303(2); Bankruptcy Act 1914, ss. 32, 48, 55, 62 and Sched. II, r. 23). Every debt or claim must be proved by the creditor's delivering to the liquidator an unsworn claim in writing, or where the liquidator requires it, by affidavit verifying the debt or claim. A secured creditor must disclose in his proof that he has a security for his debt, but it is unnecessary for him to offer to surrender it.

The liquidator must admit or reject a proof and if the creditor claims preferential payment, the liquidator must admit or reject his claim to priority within 28 days after it is lodged. The liquidator may at any time appoint a date by which all debts must be proved so that they may be included in any distribution made to the creditors, and notice must be given to all the creditors to this effect.

A liquidator will declare and pay dividends to the creditors as and when he realises sufficient of the company's assets. A secured creditor who has not proved his claim in time to share in a distribution is not excluded from a later distribution, but he cannot insist that a dividend already declared should be re-calculated to take his claim into account. However, he can insist that any money in the liquidator's hands which is not required to pay dividends already declared should be applied first in paying an equivalent dividend on his own claim.

PROBLEMS

1. What is a company? What are the requirements which a company must satisfy before it can be registered and commence business as a public company under the Companies Act 1981?

2. Explain the nature of the documents and their contents which a public company must file with the Registrar of Companies in order to obtain a certificate to commence business.

3. What is meant by the principle that a company is a separate entity from its shareholders? What are the exceptions to this principle?

4. Explain the ultra vires principle. How has the law been modified by the European Communities Act 1971, s. 9(1)?

5. How far are contracts made in a company's name before its incorporation enforceable by and against it?

6. What are the rules relating to payment of shares where the consideration given for the allotment is otherwise than in cash?

7. What are the usual rights of preference and ordinary shareholders?

8. What information should a prospectus offering shares to the public contain?

9. What remedies are available for false statements contained in a prospectus?

10. What is meant by underwriting?

11. What are the rules relating to calls made on shareholders?

12. What is a debenture? Distinguish between a floating and fixed charge over a company's assets.

13. What are the fiduciary duties owed by a director to his company?

14. What is the rule in *Foss* v. *Harbottle?* What are the exceptions to it?

15. Outline the procedure necessary to obtain an order of the court for the winding–up of a company.

16. What is meant by a voluntary winding–up? How may it be brought about?

CHAPTER TEN

Law of Partnership

OBJECTIVES

It is proposed in this chapter to examine the law relating to the constitution and operation of partnerships. In particular the chapter deals with:

(*a*) the situation where a partnership exists and the types and number of partners;

(*b*) the capacity of persons to enter into a partnership;

(*c*) the relations of partners to persons dealing with the partnership;

(*d*) the contractual liability of the partnership and the partners, including:

(*i*) liability for debt;

(*ii*) liability of the firm for wrongs committed outside the ordinary scope of the partnership business;

(*iii*) liability of incoming and outgoing partners;

(*iv*) liability of retiring partners;

(*e*) the relations of the partners between themselves, including:

(*i*) the power to expel a partner;

(*ii*) the fiduciary duties owed by one partner to the others;

(*f*) dissolution of a partnership.

CONSTITUTION OF A PARTNERSHIP

The Partnership Act 1890 codified the rules of common law and equity governing partnerships. It defines a partnership as an association of persons who carry on a business in common, with view to a profit. This means that the partners must carry on a business together for the purpose of realising gains in which they are entitled to share. It is not necessary, however, that all of them are entitled to take part in the management of the business, or that they have an equal share in the partnership profits or gains.

A business is deemed for this purpose to include every trade, profession or occupation, and even if the partnership venture is confined to a single transaction (e.g. the purchase and resale of a consignment of goods) there is still a partnership. A partnership does not exist when the persons involved merely undertake acts preparatory to the commencement of a business. However, in *Keith Spicer Ltd* v. *Mansell* (1970) it was held that, where promoters of a company merely ordered goods so that they could be used in the company's business when it was incorporated, the promoters did not constitute a partnership since their acts were merely preparatory to the commencement of the company's business. Moreover, it is essential that the business is being carried on with a view to making a profit, so that a venture formed merely in order to cover its costs is not a partnership.

Presumption of a partnership

The Partnership Act 1890, s. 2(1), provides that, where it is not clear from the conduct of the partners or the manner in which the business is carried on, certain rules will apply in order to determine whether a partnership in fact exists. These rules are as follows:

(*a*) if property is held by persons as joint tenants or tenants in common this does not in itself create a partnership in respect of property thus held by the partners (Partnership Act 1890, s. 2(1)). Thus, in *Davis* v. *Davis* (1894) where property was left by a father's will to his two sons as tenants in common and it was employed in the course of a partnership business carried on by them, the property did not become partnership property or constitute the assets of a new partnership between them;

(*b*) the sharing of gross profits does not itself create a partnership, whether or not the persons sharing such returns have a joint interest in the property from which the profits are derived (Partnership Act 1890, s. 2(2));

(*c*) however, the receipt by a person of a share of the net profits of a business is prima facie evidence that he is a partner in the business under s. 2(3), but the receipt of a payment which is contingent on or varying with the profits of a business does not of itself necessarily make him a partner in the business. The common law principle, laid down in *Cox* v. *Hickman* (1860), was that the receipt of a share of partnership profits implied that the recipient was a partner in the absence of a contrary intention. Consequently, in deciding whether a partnership existed the receipt of a share of profits was not conclusive, but merely one of the factors to be taken account (*see Davis* v. *Davis* (1894). The Partnership Act 1890, s. 2(3), goes further than *Cox* v. *Hickman* and provides that the recipient is not a partner where he receives payment of a debt due to him by instalments out of the profits of the debtor's business, nor is a partnership constituted if a servant receives remuneration in the form of a share of profits, nor where a widow or child of a deceased partner receives an annuity out of partnership profits, nor where a loan is made and the lender is to receive a share of profits in place of interest or a variable rate of interest dependent on the profits from the partnership business. In these cases the recipient is a creditor of the owner of the business and not a partner with him. Finally, the receipt of an annuity or a portion of the profits of the business in consideration for the sale of goodwill does not necessarily make the recipient a partner.

In such circumstances the court will ascertain the real intention of the partners and the person who is entitled to a share of the profits. In *Badeley* v. *Consolidated Bank* (1888) the lender was held not to be a partner although he was entitled to a share of the annual profits of a business. The court held the lender had made a loan bona fide on a security being created on partnership profits, and the mere fact that he was also entitled to a share in the profits did not constitute him a partner. However, in *Pooley* v. *Driver* (1876) the court held that a lender who was entitled to a share of the profits of a business was a partner because the "lender" had, in addition to the right to share in the profits, other rights comparable with those held by a partner, i.e. a right to a share in the capital and a right to a share in the surplus profits on the final settlement of accounts when the business was sold or wound up.

A person who, under s. 2(3), is entitled to participate in the profits of a business. A distinction must, however, be drawn between "dormant" or however, subject to the disability that if the owner of the business is adjudged bankrupt, he cannot compete with the other creditors for recovery of his debt and his claim must be postponed until all the other partnership creditors have been paid in full.

Types of partners

The Partnership Act 1890 does not distinguish between different kinds of partners, and assumes that normally a partner will be a general or active partner who has a right to take part in the management of the partnership business. A distinction must, however, be drawn between "dormant" or "sleeping" and other partners, although the Act does not expressly provide for them. A dormant partner is not entitled to take an active part in the management of the partnership business, but he is nevertheless fully liable for acts done within the scope of the partnership business by any of the other partners.

Maximum number of partners

A partnership cannot consist of more than 20 partners, but an exception is made in case of certain professional partnerships, i.e. solicitors, accountants, surveyors and engineers, in which the number of partners may exceed 20.

The partnership firm

In English law (unlike Scottish law) the partnership firm is not a distinct legal person from its members, and so the firm or the firm's name is simply a collective expression for the partners.

Choice of names

A partnership which carried on a business in a name other than that of the partners had formerly to register the firm or business name under the Registration of Business Names Act 1916, now repealed by the Companies Act 1981. That Act now provides that in the case of limited (but not ordinary) partnerships the Registrar of Companies will keep an index of the names of those bodies.

In the case of persons who carry on business in Great Britain or who have a place of business in Great Britain under a name which, in the case of a partnership does not consist of the names of all the partners (whether corporate or individual), the proprietor of the business cannot, without the approval of the Secretary of State for Trade and Industry use a business name which is likely to give the impression that the business is connected with the government, or a local authority (Companies Act 1981, s. 28(2)). Any persons who carry on business in a name other than that of all the partners must, on all business letters and correspondence, including invoices and written orders for goods and receipts issued in the course of the business, state the name of each partner (whether an individual or company) and display the name and addresses of all the partners in a prominent position on its business premises (Companies Act 1981, s. 29). Where the partnership consists of 20 or more partners, the names of the partners need not be imprinted on business letters or correspondence, and it is sufficient for the names and addresses of the partners to be displayed on its business premises, provided that the names of none of the partners appear on the letterheads. Where the partnership maintains a list of partners it must be open to inspection by any person during business hours.

CAPACITY TO ENTER INTO A PARTNERSHIP

There are certain classes of persons who cannot enter into a partnership and it is proposed to deal briefly with these. Subject to these exceptions everyone is capable of entering into a partnership.

Aliens
A partnership which includes an enemy alien is terminated on the outbreak of war, although the rights of an enemy alien are not extinguished. The firm is instead dissolved and all the partners (including enemy aliens) are entitled to have the firm's business wound-up.

Minors
A minor who is a partner cannot incur contractual liability for partnership debts, so that a judgment against the "firm" cannot be enforced against the "firm" as a whole, but only against the partners other than the minor. A minor can repudiate the partnership contract either during his minority or within a reasonable time of attaining majority. However, the minor cannot recover amounts paid as a premium to procure admission to the partnership unless there has been a total failure of consideration (i.e. the net assets of the firm have never had a positive value).

Mental patients
A person who is mentally ill can enter into a partnership agreement, but the agreement is voidable at his insistence if he can show that he did not appreciate the implications of the agreement, and that the other party was aware of his mental condition. However, a partner's mental disorder is sufficient grounds to have the partnership dissolved under the Mental Health Act 1959, s. 103(1).

THE RELATIONSHIP OF PARTNERS TO PERSONS DEALING WITH THEM

Authority of partners
A partner, as an agent of the other partners, has general authority to bind the

partnership firm by any acts done by him in the usual course of the partnership business. The power and the authority of a partner to bind the firm and the other partners is derived from the fact that partnership business is conducted on behalf of the partners by some or all of their number. In addition to the actual or usual authority which a partner has conferred on him by the partnership agreement or by his fellow partners, he also has apparent (or ostensible) authority to do such acts as are normally within the scope of the business which the partnership carries on, and third persons who deal with him may treat the firm as bound by such acts unless they know that the act in question is outside the actual authority of the partner or do not know him to be a partner. The scope of a partner's authority to act on behalf of the partnership and to bind the other partners was discussed in *Re Agriculturist Cattle Insurance Co (Bairds Case)* (1880) in which it was said that "as between the partners and the outside world each partner is the unlimited agent of every other in every matter connected with the partnership business . . ." and which is not outside the scope of the partnership business.

The scope of a partner's apparent authority is confined to such acts as are connected with the usual conduct of a business of the kind carried on by the partnership. It is a question of fact whether or not a partner's act falls within the scope of the partnership business. In *Mercantile Credit Co Ltd* v. *Garrod* (1962) the partners were in the business of letting garages and carrying out motor–car repairs. One of the partners, without the knowledge of the other, purported to sell a car to which the firm had no title to a hire–purchase company. It was held that the other partner was accountable for the money received because the act of selling the car was sufficiently closely connected with the partnership business of running a garage as to be within the scope of the partnership business.

To be binding on the other partners, the act in question must not only fall within the scope of the business carried on by the firm but it must be done in the usual manner in which an act is done in a business of that kind. The firm will, therefore, be liable if the circumstances, time, place or manner in which the act is performed is normal to the kind of business which the partnership carries on. In *Higgins* v. *Beauchamp* (1914) acceptance of an incomplete bill of exchange which lacked the drawer's signature was sufficiently unusual to place it outside the normal manner of carrying on the partnership business, and the holders of the bill could not sue the acceptor partnership on it. Nevertheless, an act which is outside the usual scope of the partnership business will bind the firm if it is authorised expressly by the other partners.

A partner will be deemed to have apparent authority to bind the firm and his fellow partners in a number of such circumstances, namely;

(a) every partner is deemed to hold such powers as are normally held by all the partners (e.g. authority to sell any goods or chattels of the firm and to purchase goods normally used in the business, although they are subsequently misapplied by the partner who purports to purchase them on behalf of the firm). Thus, in *Mann* v. *D'Arcy* (1968) where one partner in a greengrocery wholesale firm purported to commit the partnership firm to a joint venture with the plaintiff for the sale of a consignment of potatoes the court held that the arrangement was merely one of buying and selling goods of the kind which the partners dealt in, and the joint venture agreement was fully binding on the firm; and

(b) a partner in a trading firm (i.e. one which buys and sells goods) is deemed to have wider powers than a partner of a non–trading firm. Thus, a partner in a trading firm may borrow money on credit, may draw, issue or accept bills of exchange, and he may mortgage or pledge partnership property.

Liability of the firm and the partners

The Partnership Act 1890, s. 6, provides that any act or instrument which relates to the firm's business may be done or executed in the firm's name or by any method which indicates an intention to bind the firm by any authorised person (whether he is a partner or not) and the act or instrument will be effective in binding the firm. If the partner enters into a transaction for his own personal benefit and not on behalf of the firm, the transaction will not be binding on the other partners or the partnership firm if the other party to the transaction is aware of this. In *Beckham* v. *Drake* (1843) the court said the question to be considered was whether the person who enters into the transaction is acting solely for his personal benefit or on behalf of the firm. The facts of the case were that A and B entered into a contract whereby they agreed that the partnership would continue to employ X, as foreman. It was held that although C, the third partner, was not a party to the contract he was bound by it and so he could be sued along with the other partners.

The firm will, however, be bound if the partner acts within his actual authority or has his actions ratified by his fellow partners. Where a partner pledges the credit of the firm for a purpose unconnected with the firm's ordinary course of business, the firm will not be bound unless the partner is in fact authorised to enter into the transaction by the other partners. The section does not affect the personal liability of the individual partner. In *Bignold* v. *Waterhouse* (1913) one of the partners granted a special favour to a consignor of goods whilst acting for the partnership, in return for a valid consideration as between himself and the consignor but which was of no value to the partnership firm. The court held that the partnership firm was not bound by the concession granted although it was granted in the partnership name. Similarly, in *Kendall* v. *Wood* (1871) the defendant received £10,000 of partnership money from W, a partner, in discharge of a personal debt. It was held on the dissolution of the partnership that the £10,000 could not be retained by the creditor as against the other partner who had neither authorised the use of it to pay off a private debt, nor led the creditor to believe that the indebted partner had the authority to dispose of partnership property in this way.

The Partnership Act 1890, s. 8, provides that any restriction on the power of the partners to bind the firm is effective and acts done in contravention of the limitation are not binding on the partnership firm if the third party involved in the transaction has notice of the limitation. In *Cox* v. *Hickman* (1860) the court said that partners may, as between themselves, agree that some of them will have only a limited power to enter into contracts binding on the firm but such an arrangement between the partners will not affect the right of a third party who enters into a contract with a partner without notice of this limitation. Any restrictions on the power of partners is normally twofold.

1. Liability of partners for debts and obligations

A partner who enters into a contract which is binding on his firm will subject all the partners to a joint liability, which affects all the partners including the partner who enters into the contract on behalf of the other partners. In *Kendall* v. *Hamilton* (1879) it was held that partnership debts and contractual obligations are joint in nature but if a partner subsequently dies, not only the surviving partners but also the deceased's estate are liable to satisfy the contractual obligations. Since the Civil Liability (Contribution) Act 1978, judgment recovered against one of the partners when the other partners are living does not bar the creditor from bringing an action against the other partners who are jointly liable. The Partnership Act 1890, s. 9, applies not only to contractual obligations but also to partnership debts. The joint liability of the partners only relates to debts and contractual obligations incurred by the firm whilst the partner whom it is sought to make liable was a member of the firm. The law in Scotland imposes both joint and several liability on partners' partnership debts and contractual obligations and, therefore, s. 9 does not apply.

2. Liability of firm for wrongs

Partners may be liable for wrongs done to a third party by a partner either because the wrong was authorised by the other partners or because the wrong has been committed in the course of the partnership business (e.g. where one of the partners acts negligently whilst acting in the course of an ordinary partnership transaction). The Partnership Act 1890, s. 10, provides that where a wrong is done in the course of the partnership business the other partners are liable to the same extent as the partner who personally committed the wrongful or negligent acts. In *Hamlyn* v. *Houston & Co* (1903) one of the partners in a partnership firm, consisting of himself and another partner, bribed a clerk in a rival firm to disclose confidential information concerning the contracts and tenders of his employers. It was held that obtaining information which might be useful to the partnership was within the scope of the firm's business and the method used to obtain that information, although unauthorised by the other partners, was sufficiently related to the conduct of the firm's business to make the other partners liable.

Section 11 deals with the misapplication of money or property received by the partnership firm and deals with two situations where the partners will be liable to the owner of the property: firstly, where one partner receives money or property belonging to a third party whilst acting in the scope of his authority and misapplies it and, secondly, where the firm receives money or property belonging to a third party in the ordinary course of its business and one of the partners misapplies it. In both of these situations the firm will be liable to make good the loss. It is proposed to examine these two situations in detail.

Acts within the ordinary course of business
An act which is within the apparent scope of the authority conferred on a partner is binding on the firm, except where a third party has actual notice of the partner's lack of authority. In *Rhodes* v. *Moules* (1895) it was said that, in determining what constitutes the ordinary course of a business in any case, account may be taken of any ancillary services performed in relation to transactions which are clearly within the scope of the business. In that case a partner in a firm of solicitors was held accountable for the misapplication of share warrants which had been delivered by a client of the firm to a co-partner on the faith of the latter's false representation that a creditor of the client had called for additional security. In *Stain* v. *Bromley* (1847) it was held that money received by a solicitor from a client for investment was within the ordinary course of the business and the partnership firm was liable when one of the partners misappropriated it.

Acts outside the ordinary course of business
The members of a partnership are not liable for acts outside the apparent authority of a partner or unconnected with the ordinary business of the partnership. A transaction may lie within the ordinary course of business of a firm but the firm will not be liable if a third party elects to deal with the partner as a principal. In *British Homes Assurance Corporation Ltd* v. *Paterson* (1902) it was held that a client who had elected to continue his dealings with a solicitor who had originally practised alone could not sue a person whom the solicitor had subsequently taken into partnership. The court said that a third party who insists on dealing with one of the partners as principal after he has given notice of the partnership cannot subsequently treat the co-partners as liable for the wrongful acts of the partner he deals with.

Where, however, only one of the partners is qualified to perform a particular type of transaction, then the partnership firm will be liable if that purported act is within the ordinary course of the partnership business. Thus, in *Kirkintilloch Equitable Co-operative Society Ltd* v. *Livingston* (1972) the partners in a firm of accountants were held liable for the negligence of one of their number who had been appointed as auditor of the co-operative society.

The Partnership Act 1890, s. 12, provides that every partner is liable jointly with his co-partner, and also severally liable for wrongs in respect of which the firm incurs liability whilst he is a partner.

Improper employment of trust property for partnership purposes
If a partner, being a trustee, employs trust property in the business or on the

account of the partnership, the co–partners are not liable to the persons beneficially interested, but this provision will not apply where the other partners had notice of the breach: the beneficiary will then be entitled to follow the trust money. A partner is not, therefore, liable to the beneficiaries merely because a partner who is a trustee has committed a breach of trust, even when this takes the form of using trust property for partnership business. In *Blyth* v. *Fladgate* (1891) the knowledge of a solicitor who had acted on behalf of trustees was imputed to the other partners. In *Ex parte Heaton* (1819) a father and his sons carried on business as partners. The sons were trustees of a will and applied trust money for partnership purposes. It was held that the amount so appropriated could not be recovered from the joint estate of the partnership since the father could not be shown to have knowledge of the wrongful appropriations.

Persons liable by "holding out"

The Partnership Act 1890, s. 14, provides that a person who acts as a partner or allows others to represent that he is a partner is estopped from denying to persons who rely on his credit that he is not a partner, even if this is in fact so. A person will be treated as a partner where, for example, he allows his name to remain in the firm and be used in business correspondence or displayed over a shop window. However, the defendant's name must be used with his knowledge or acquiescence. In *Tower Cabinet Co* v. *Ingram* (1949) the use of a firm's notepaper by the continuing partners after one of the partners had retired was insufficient to impute liability on the retired partner even though the notepaper showed him as still being a partner, because the person dealing with the firm had not known that he was a partner before his retirement. As from the date of the retirement he ceased to be liable for any further debts contracted by the firm to such a person. The fact that the third person later discovered that the former partner had in fact been a partner was irrelevant.

Moreover, the person who seeks to make the retired partner liable under the rules of estoppel must have known his name through a representation which indicated that he was a partner in the firm.

A retiring partner will be liable for debts subsequently incurred by the partnership firm after his retirement if he omits to give due notice of his retirement to those persons who previously dealt with the firm (i.e. existing customers). In *Scarf* v. *Jardine* (1882) a partnership firm consisted of two partners, A and B. A retired from the partnership and his place was taken by a new partner, C. A customer of the firm dealt with the firm after the change in partnership, but without notice of it, and was held entitled to elect to treat as liable either the partnership as it was before A's retirement, or the new partnership as newly constituted.

Liabilities of incoming and outgoing partners

A partner is generally only liable in respect of obligations incurred by the partnership firm whilst he was a member of it. The Partnership Act 1890, s. 17, enumerates three rules:

(a) a person who becomes a partner in an existing firm does not incur liability for anything done by the firm prior to his becoming a partner;

(b) a retiring partner continues to be liable for debts and obligations incurred by the firm while he was a partner; and

(c) a retiring partner may be discharged from liability for any partnership debts or obligations by agreement between himself and the other members of the firm (including any new partners) and the partners.

An incoming partner will only be liable for existing debts or debts incurred before he becomes a partner if there has been a novation of the debt.

A creditor to whom the partnership firm is indebted can look to a partner who retires for payment of his debt. Any agreement between the partners that the retiring partner will not be liable for partnership debts incurred before his retirement is ineffective unless there has been a novation agreed to by the creditor. In *Oakford* v. *European–American Steam Shipping Co* (1863) a partnership firm consisting of A, B and C as partners entered into a three–year contract with D. The contract had only been performed for a year when A retired from the partnership firm. A covenant was entered into by B and C under which they agreed to indemnify A for any liability under the contract. It was held that A remained liable to D, although D had notice of A's retirement for acts done under the contract by B and C, subsequently to A's retirement. However, A was in the position of a surety, and would be discharged from liability if the terms of the original contract were varied.

THE RELATIONSHIP OF THE PARTNERS INTER SE

Persons who enter into a partnership agreement are free to determine their powers and relations by an express agreement. In so far as the partnerships relationship is not governed by an express or implied agreement between the partners certain statutory rules will govern the relationship. Moreover, the relationship is that of the greatest good faith and certain fiduciary duties are owed by the partners.

Partnership property

Partnership property must be dealt with exclusively for the purposes of the partnership and in accordance with the partnership agreement. Moreover, on a dissolution of the firm, every partner is entitled as against the other partners to have partnership property applied in payment of the debts and liabilities incurred by the firm and to have any surplus assets applied in payment of amounts due to the partners.

What is partnership property?
The Partnership Act 1890, ss. 20 and 21, provide that all property and rights bought into partnership stock or acquired on account of the firm or in the

ordinary course of the partnership business are partnership property and must be applied by the partners exclusively for purposes of partnership business. Where partners own property as co–owners of an estate and the property is not itself partnership property, the property is held by them, in the absence of an express agreement, not as partners, but as co–owners for the same respective estates as are held by them in the land at the date of ownership. However, property bought with money which belongs to the firm is bought on account of the firm unless there is evidence to the contrary.

There is no limitation on what is capable of being partnership property and therefore, land, leaseholds, good will, chattels and any other form of assets are all capable of being partnership property. However, the mere fact that property is used as partnership property does not necessarily mean it is partnership property. In *Davis* v. *Davis* (1894) a testator left his residuary estate, including a business, to his two sons in equal shares as tenants in common. The sons did not enter into a partnership agreement, but they were held to be partners in the business which had been left to them by reason of their carrying on business as partners. However, the facts did not show that the land left to them as tenants in common was held as partnership property; instead the partnership merely had the use of that property.

Partnership property under the 1890 Act consists of the following items:

(*a*) all property and rights and interests in property brought into partnership stock. The mere fact that property has not been expressly brought into the partnership as partnership property does not necessarily mean that the partnership does not have an interest in it. In *Pocock* v. *Carter* (1912) three partners carried on a tailoring business in Salisbury. The terms of the indenture provided that the lease of the business premises was to remain the property of one of the partners, but the rates, rents, and taxes in respect of it were to be paid out of annual profits. It was held that, despite the fact that one of the partners continued to own the lease, the partnership had a tenancy in the premises and the partner who owned the lease could not evict the others from the premises before the partnership ended.

However, where there is no evidence at all that property used by the firm is regarded as partnership property, the courts have been reluctant to hold that a proprietary interest in favour of the firm exists. In *Miles* v. *Clark* (1953) and *Singh* v. *Nahar* (1965) the court held that the partnership firm did not possess any interest over property brought into the business by one of the partners;

(*b*) property purchased either on account of the partnership firm or for the purposes and in the course of the partnership business is partnership property, and property bought with money belonging to the firm is deemed to have been bought on account of the firm. In *Ex parte Hinds* (1849) the partners were trading merchants. One of the partners, without the authority or knowledge of the other partner, used partnership money to acquire shares in a company. The shares were held to be partnership property, and were treated as having been purchased on account of the firm, although the property purchased was not property bought in the ordinary course of the partnership business. Similarly, it has been held the property purchased out of the proceeds of other property held as tenants in common but used in the partnership is partnership property (*see Waterer* v. *Waterer* (1873)).

The nature of partnership property

A partner has a share in the partnership property equivalent to a proportion of the partnership assets after they have been converted into money and the partnership debts have been discharged. The partners may, however, by agreement convert partnership property into the separate property of one of the partners.

Where a judgment order is obtained against the partnership firm the Partnership Act 1890, s. 23, lays down rules which govern the interests of the partners in the property and the obligation of the firm to indemnify a partner in respect of payments made and liability incurred by him in the ordinary course of the partnership business.

Power to expel a partner

The Partnership Act provides that a majority of the partners cannot expel any partner unless there is an express agreement to that effect. An express power of expulsion must be exercised in a bona fide manner and for the benefit of the partnership as a whole. In *Bliset* v. *Daniel* (1853) it was held that the power of expulsion, if exercised by the partners, must be excercised for the benefit of the partnership as a whole and not for the benefit of the partners exercising their right to expel.

However, if the partner has been guilty of conduct scandalous or detrimental to the firm the expulsion may be justified. In *Carmichael* v. *Evans* (1904) the expulsion of a partner who had been convicted of travelling by train without a ticket was held to be valid.

A partner who is to be expelled must be given notice of the reasons for his proposed expulsion and an opportunity to be heard. In *Wood* v. *Woad* (1874) it was held that a partner had been wrongly expelled when the other partners decided to exercise their power of expulsion without giving the accused partner a right to defend his conduct. The exercise of the power of expulsion was, therefore, void.

Fiduciary duties owned by a partner

The relationship between the partners is one of the "utmost good faith" and the Partnership Act 1890, s. 28, provides that partners are under a duty to render true accounts and disclose full information on all matters affecting the partnership. A partner to whom such information is not available is entitled to avoid the transaction, unless he waives such a right, once he acquires full knowledge of the facts.

The partners in a firm owe fiduciary duties in respect of their dealings, to co–partners not only during the existence of the partnership but also after its dissolution, until it is completely wound–up. In *Thompson's Trustee in*

Bankruptcy v. *Heaton* (1974) it was held that the obligation of good faith may survive the dissolution of a firm, and the partners may be in breach of their obligation of good faith although the business relationship has terminated. The case of *Dean* v. *MacDowell* (1878) laid down three aspects of the fiduciary duties owed by the partners to co–partners and the firm. These are now placed on a statutory basis in ss. 29 and 30 of the Partnership Act 1890, and it is proposed to deal with each of the obligations individually.

Accountability for private profits

A partner must not derive a personal profit from a transaction entered into on behalf of the partnership without the consent of his co–partners. The partner holds a position of trust or confidence and he must not discharge his obligations in such a manner as to make a private gain. In *Re Nichol* (1900) a partner who received a premium in consideration of his work in negotiating an assignment of a lease was held accountable to his partners for the money received by him to his benefit.

The use of partnership name, property or business connections

If a partner uses the partnership name, property or business connections for a personal purpose, his partners have the option of treating the resulting gain as partnership property. In *Featherstonhaugh* v. *Fenwick* (1810) it was held that where a partner renewed for his own benefit a lease which had been previously granted to the partnership his partners could treat the renewed lease as partnership property.

Competing business

A partner cannot unless his partners consent, commence a business competing with the partnership business. In *Brown, Janson & Co* v. *Hutchinson (No. 1)* (1891) it was held that one of the partners could restrain his co–partners from publishing in an evening newspaper in which he had no interest, information obtained at the expense and for the use of a morning newspaper which was published by a firm of which they were all partners. On the other hand, in *Aas* v. *Benham* (1891) a member of a firm of shipbrokers assisted in the formation of a company to build ships, using information derived by him from his membership of the shipbroking firm. It was held that the information was used for purposes which were outside the scope of the shipbroking business and consequently, the partner using such information was not liable for a breach of duty not to compete in business with the partnership, and not to obtain any personal advantage by the use of information available through the partnership.

Rights of an assignee of a share in partnership

The Partnership Act 1890, s. 31, deals with the assignment by any partner of his share in the partnership. It allows the assignee to receive a share of the profits to which the assignor would have been entitled. He can inspect the books of the partnership but he is not entitled to interfere in the management or the administration of the partnership business. The section provides for an assignment by a partner of his share in the partnership and not his position as a partner. In *Dodson* v. *Downey* (1901) the court held that an assignee under s. 31 (i.e. an assignee of a partner's interest) is entitled to the share of profits the assignor would have been entitled to and, if the firm makes a loss, the assignee must indemnify the assignor for his share of the loss because he continues to be a nominal partner.

In the case of a dissolution, the assignee becomes entitled to the assignor's share of assets and to an account to enable that share to be ascertained.

DISSOLUTION OF A PARTNERSHIP

Dissolution without the aid of the court
A partnership may be dissolved without an order of the court for the following reasons.

On the expiration of a partnership entered into for a fixed term
If the partnership is entered into only for a fixed term, it will dissolve automatically on the expiration of that term without the partners taking any positive acts. However, it may end sooner if one of the partners dies before the date fixed for dissolution. Where the partners continue in business after the expiration of a fixed term they are merely partners at will, and may terminate the partnership by giving notice.

Termination of adventure
A partnership entered into for the completion of a specific project will terminate when the project is completed.

Notice to dissolve
If there is no limit on the period for which the partnership is to exist, any partner may give notice of his intention to dissolve the partnership at any time. The partnership will exist only to the extent it is necessary to wind-up the affairs of the partnership. The termination does not, however, absolve the partnership from liability for breach of contract in respect of third parties.

Death
A partnership is dissolved on the death of one of the partners and any continuance of the partnership business by the surviving partners constitutes a new partnership.

Bankruptcy
The bankruptcy of one of the partners ends the partnership and vests his share in the trustee in bankruptcy.

Charging order

The effect of a charging order on a partner's interest by way of execution on a judgment obtained against him personally does not dissolve the partnership automatically but the co-partners are given the option to dissolve it by some unequivocal act.

Illegality

A partnership cannot continue if it becomes illegal for the firm to carry on its business (i.e. on the outbreak of war if one of the partners is an enemy alien). Alternatively, it may be illegal for the members of the firm to carry on that business (e.g. if the business itself is lawful but those who perform it are required to comply with certain requirements or possess certain qualifications and do not do so).

Dissolution by the court

The Partnership Act 1890, s. 35, and the Mental Health Act 1959, s. 149(2), give the courts power to order a dissolution of the partnership on the application of a partner. It is proposed to deal briefly with the grounds on which the courts may grant a decree dissolving the partnership.

Mental illness

Under the Mental Health Act 1959 a court may make an order dissolving a partnership of which a partner committed under the Act is a member.

Permanent incapacity

Whether a partner has become permanently incapable of continuing as a partner is a question of fact: confirmed and incurable insanity would provide a cause for dissolution but mere senility would not.

Prejudicial conduct

Where a partner is guilty of conduct which is prejudicial and likely to affect the business carried on by the firm, e.g. where a solicitor-partner is guilty of embezzling trust money, or where a partner commits a criminal offence which is likely to affect the standing of the partnership, the co-partners have a right to apply to the court for a dissolution.

Persistent or wilful breach of partnership agreement

Only a wilful and persistent breach of the partnership agreement will justify a dissolution of the partnership, i.e. where one of the partners has continuously kept erroneous accounts and has failed to enter receipts into the bookkeeping.

Loss

The courts will imply that the partners intend to carry on business with a view to making a profit and if the state of the partnership is such that only losses can be anticipated then the partnership will be dissolved.

Just and equitable

Whenever circumstances arise which in the opinion of the court render it just and equitable that the partnership should be dissolved, the court can, on an application, dissolve the partnership. For example, the court would grant an application for an order to dissolve a partnership despite the partnerships' flourishing business if there is deadlock between the partners and no effective decisions can be taken about the conduct of the firm's business.

Rights of persons dealing with the firm against apparent members of firm

The Partnership Act 1890, ss. 14 and 36, provide that where a person deals with a firm after a change in its constitution he is entitled to treat all apparent members of the old firm as still being members of the firm unless he has notice of the change. In *Tower Cabinet Co* v. *Ingram* (1949) the partnership firm continued to use old notepaper after one of the partners had retired. It was held that the partner who had retired could not be held personally liable because he was not known by the plaintiffs to be a partner prior to his retirement and was, accordingly, under no obligation to give notice of his retirement to those who might after his retirement learn that he was a member of the firm.

Administration of partnership estates

In the case of a partnership one of two situations may arise in a bankruptcy. Firstly, the partner may be made bankrupt in respect of his separate debts whilst his co-partners remain fully solvent. In such a case the partnership creditors are entitled to prove in his bankruptcy, but the other solvent partners are likely to pay them off. Alternatively, bankruptcy proceedings may be taken in respect of a firm debt and normally all the partners will then be made bankrupt.

Where partners are adjudicated bankrupt, the partnership is dissolved and the assets of the partnership (including money representing the partnership's credit balances on bank accounts) are distributed to the partnership's creditors (principally its suppliers and customers). The origin of the rule is found in *Ex parte Cook* (1728) where two joint traders became bankrupt, and a joint commission of bankruptcy was taken out against them. Subsequently, bankpruptcy proceedings were commenced against the two traders by their personal creditors. The court held that the joint estate of the partnership was applicable in payment of the debts of the partnership and the separate estate of each partner was applicable in the payment of his separate debts. If there were a surplus of the joint estate after paying the partnership debts in full, it would be divided between the partners' separate estates in accordance with their rights and used in payment of their separate debts.

PROBLEMS

1. What are the rules of law which will be used to decide whether persons trading together constitute a partnership, when there is no express agreement to that effect?

2. What is the liability of the partners for acts and transactions done in the ordinary course of the partnership business?

3. Explain the liability to a third person of an outgoing partner who retires from the partnership, and the liability of a person who joins an existing partnership, as an incoming partner.

4. What is partnership property under the Partnership Act 1890?

5. Explain the nature of the fiduciary duties owed by a partner to the other partners.

6. On what grounds may a partnership be dissolved?

CHAPTER ELEVEN

Law of Employment

OBJECTIVES

It is proposed in this chapter to examine the law governing the relationship between an employer and the person who performs services for him under a contract of employment, that is an employee. In particular the chapter deals with:

(a) the nature of the contract of employment;
(b) the capacity of the parties;
(c) sexual and racial discrimination in employment;
(d) the obligations of the employer and employee;
(e) disciplinary measures by the employer;
(f) the termination of the contract of employment;
(g) dismissal and redundancy.

THE CONTRACT OF EMPLOYMENT

The nature of the contract

The master/servant or employer/employee relationship exists where one person works for another under a contract of service, as distinct from a contract for the provision of certain services. If an employer can instruct the employee not only what work he shall do, but also how he shall do it, then the contract is one of service. Thus, a chauffeur is employed under a contract of service, but a taxi driver is not so employed since he merely contracts to provide a specific service (i.e. to drive his fare to a particular destination). The more skilled and qualified an employee, the less the employer can instruct an employee, how the work he undertakes is to be done, but the employee is still subject to contract of service since the employer still has substantial control over the conditions in which the work is done (e.g. hours of work, equipment and materials with which it is done). The control test has been modified somewhat in recent years so that in *Stevenson, Jordon & Harrison Ltd* v. *Macdonald & Evans* (1952) it was said that a person is employed under a contract of service if he is employed as part of the employer's business and his work is done as an integral part of the business. The organisational test is a gloss on the original control test in that it contemplates a situation where skilled persons are employees and are an integral part of an enterprise (e.g. nurses and doctors). In *Whittaker* v. *Minister of Pensions* (1967) a trapeze artiste broke her wrist as a result of a fall during her act, and it was held that she was an integral part of the circus business and thus an employee for the purpose of claiming industrial injuries benefit.

However, no single test can be sufficient to determine the matter, and the court will now look at all the surrounding features. Thus, the power of selection, the payment of wages, national insurance contributions, whether income tax is deducted at source, and the power to suspend and dismiss are all relevant features which may be taken into consideration. In *Ready Mixed Concrete* v. *Minister of Pensions* (1968) a haulage firm dismissed its drivers, sold its lorries to them and re-employed them under contracts by which they could be both employed and self-employed persons. The drivers had to wear the company's uniforms, place their lorries at the company's disposal for a specified number of hours each week, obey the orders of the company's foreman and, if the company required, re-sell the lorries to the company at an agreed valuation. However, the drivers had to maintain the lorries at their own expense and to pay all running costs. They could employ a substitute driver and could own more than one lorry. They paid their own income tax and national insurance contributions, and made their own decisions as to when they would drive the lorries and which routes they would take. The court held that the drivers were self-employed haulage contractors, and were not employed under contracts of service. It was said that three conditions were necessary to establish that a contract of service existed, namely: that the employee agreed to provide his own work and skill in the performance of a service for his employer, that there was a sufficient degree of control exercisable by the employer, and that the other terms of the contract were not inconsistent with the existence of a contract of employment.

More recently the courts have looked at the position from the self-employed person's point of view and the court will look at whether he provides his own equipment, hires his own assistants, undertakes any financial risks and undertakes the work on a regular basis. In *Market Investigations Ltd* v. *Minister of Social Security* (1969) it was held that women employed on a part-time basis by a company to do market research were employees as, although they could choose their hours of work, they had to work according to a prescribed pattern. Similarly, in *Airfix Footwear Ltd* v. *Cope* (1978) although a woman worked at home it was held she was an employee because she was provided with the necessary equipment and materials, and worked in accordance with instructions given to her by the employer and because she had worked for the employer for five days a week for the previous seven years.

It is important to distinguish whether a person is an employee or a self-employed person for a number of reasons. The national insurance contributions for an employee and self-employed persons are different, and an employer is liable for the tortious acts of his employees committed in the course of their employment, but an employer is not vicariously liable for any tortious acts committed by an independent contractor. In *Hillyer* v. *St. Bartholemew's Hospital* (1909) the plaintiff was held entitled to bring an action against a hospital for the negligent performance of a consultant who was engaged by it for certain periods but who otherwise carried on his own medical practice. In *Cassidy* v. *Minister of Health* (1951) it was held that a hospital was the employer of a resident surgeon who had been negligent in performing an operation and the hospital was held liable. An employer owes a duty to his employees to take reasonable care for their safety, whereas these duties do not arise in the case of independent contractors (subject to the requirements of the Health and Safety at Work, etc. Act 1974).

Formation of an employment contract

A contract of employment can be in writing or be oral, although apprenticeship contracts and the articles of merchant seamen must be in writing. A contract of employment must comply with the general rules governing all contracts.

Express terms

The task of the courts and tribunals is to interpret the meaning of any express terms in a manner which is consistent with industrial realism. The parties may expressly have agreed on certain terms as to salary, commission, hours of work, the nature of duties, holidays, overtime, sick pay etc. In *Redbridge Borough Council* v. *Fisherman* (1978) an employee, who was appointed as a teacher in charge of a resource centre, was held to have been unfairly dismissed when she was asked to teach more subjects and for longer periods, and was eventually dismissed when she refused to increase her workload. The request to undertake the teaching was ancillary to her main job and consequently, the directions to undertake more teaching went beyond the strict contractual obligations. The ordinary contractual rules which govern the incorporation of express terms apply to a contract of employment.

Implied terms

The courts and tribunals may imply terms into the contract of employment where the parties do not insert an express term. It is not, however, possible to imply terms into the contract merely because the express terms are too vague or unpredictable, or to imply terms which the parties would not have agreed upon had the matter been drawn to their attention. Thus, it would appear that the courts will imply a term that an employer will treat the employee with respect and trust. To accuse an employee of theft, or to refuse unreasonably an increase in remuneration which has been granted to other employees would appear to constitute conduct on the part of the employer which amounts to a breach of an implied term that the employer should treat the employee fairly and reasonably. Similarly, there is an implied term that the employer will not prevent the employee's performing his contract of employment, or delay his pay, or hinder his earning his full remuneration, but the employer is entitled to take steps to ensure that the employee's work is done efficiently.

Incorporation of the terms of a collective agreement

A collective agreement is an agreement entered into by an employer's association (or a single employer) and a trade union. In addition to laying down the procedure which will govern the relationship between the parties, it also provides the terms and conditions for the employment of employees whom the union represents. There can be a national or federated collective agreement between an employers' association and a group or association of trade unions. The terms of the collective agreement will be legally binding between the individual employer and his employees if the collective agreement is, either expressly or implicitly, incorporated into the individual contracts of employment. The terms of a collective agreement will be incorporated expressly into an employees' contract if they are included or referred to in the statement of the terms of employment given to the employee under the Employment Protection (Consolidation) Act 1978, s. 1.

Collective agreements and non-unionists

The terms of a collective agreement apply to an employee who is not a member of a union if his contract of employment expressly so provides, but in the absence of such an express incorporation the collective agreement will not apply to a non-union employee. In *Singh* v. *British Steel Corporation* (1974) an employee resigned from his trade union and instructed the employers to cease deducting his membership subscription from his wages. The union negotiated a new agreement with the employers which provided for a new shift system, but the employee refused to agree to this and was dismissed. It was held that the employee's contract did not provide that his conditions of work could be altered unilaterally, or by means of a collective agreement. The tribunal thought that, while the employee was a member of the union, he was bound by any collective agreement negotiated by the union because it was negotiating on his behalf, but once he had resigned from the union he ceased to be bound by collective agreements entered into thereafter. The union and the employer had no power to vary the terms of his contract of employment agreement without his consent.

Written particulars of the contract of employment

The Employment Protection (Consolidation) Act 1978 (EPCA), s. 1, requires an employer, not later than the end of the thirteenth week from the commencement of employment, to give to each employee a written statement containing the following information:

(*a*) the rate of remuneration payable to him or the method of calculating it;

(*b*) the intervals at which remuneration is to be paid;

(*c*) the terms and conditions relating to hours of work and to holiday entitlement;

(*d*) entitlement to sick pay and to any pension;

(*e*) the length of notice required on termination of employment; and

(*f*) the title of the job which employee is required to do.

The employer may, instead of giving these details, refer the employee to a document which contains such information (e.g. a collective agreement), provided the document is reasonably accessible.

In addition, every statement must contain a note of the disciplinary rules applicable to an employee, specify the body or person to whom he can appeal if he is dissatisfied with any disciplinary decision relating to him and specify the procedure available to an employee for seeking redress of any grievance relating to his employment.

The employer is not required to give particulars under the EPCA to any employee who works less than 16 hours per week, or to employees engaged in a certain type of employment (e.g. registered dock workers and Crown employees). A change in the terms of employment must be notified to the employee within one month, or he must be notified of a reasonably accessible document which incorporates these changes.

Itemised pay statement

An employee has the right to be given an itemised pay statement which gives particulars of the gross amount of his wages or salary, the amount of any deductions and the purposes for which they are made, and the net wages or salary payable. If an employer fails to give an itemised pay statement, the employee can require a reference to be made to an industrial tribunal to determine the particulars which ought to be included in a pay statement.

Variation of contractual terms

The terms of a contract of employment may only be varied with the consent of both the employer and employee. A unilateral alteration by one of the parties is ineffective and will amount to a repudiation of the contract by him. Thus, if an employee is demoted without cause, this will amount to a repudiation by the employer and the employee's consequent resignation will in fact be a dismissal by the employer. If the employee continues to work for the same employer subsequent to the variation he will be treated as having accepted the contract of employment in its modified form.

The express terms of the contract may permit a substantial variation and in these circumstances the other party is bound by the variation, whether he consents to it or not, i.e. the terms may permit a change in the location of employment or the duties of the employee. In *Bex* v. *Securior Transport Ltd* (1972) it was a condition of the employee's contract that the nature of his work could be changed by the company. The company was held entitled to direct him to do different work, and it was not in breach of contract although the employee considered it to be tantamout to demotion.

An implied variation, accepted by both parties, may be inferred from the conduct of the parties. In *Armstrong Whitworth Rolls* v. *Mustard* (1971) an employee who was engaged on an eight–hour shift for five days per week, then began working a twelve–hour shift and continued to do this for seven years, was held entitled to a redundancy payment based on a normal working week of 60 hours although there had been no express mutual agreement to increase his hours.

Finally, a contract may be varied by virtue of the terms of a collective agreement entered into by a union to which the employee belongs.

LEGAL CONSTRAINTS ON TERMS AND CONDITIONS OF EMPLOYMENT

Minors

A contract of employment entered into by a minor is valid, provided that it is substantially for his benefit. The effect of the contract as a whole must be considered, and it will be effective although it contains terms which are onerous or detrimental to the minor's interests. In *De Francesco* v. *Barnum* (1890) a 14-year old girl entered into an apprenticeship agreement to perform as a dancer in the defendant's troupe and agreed only to accept other engagements with the plaintiff's permission. The terms of remuneration were stringent and the court held that the deed was void as unreasonable and not in the interests of the girl. In *Denmark Productions* v. *Boscobel Productions* (1969) a contract entered into by four minors with their manager was held binding.

Apprentices

A contract of apprenticeship is an agreement whereby, the apprentice binds himself to his employer in order to learn a trade and the employer agrees to instruct him. The contract of apprenticeship must be in writing, and signed by the parties, but the employer can only terminate it in case of grave misconduct.

Sex discrimination

The Sex Discrimination Act 1975, although enacted to prevent unlawful discrimination against women, makes it unlawful to discriminate against either sex for that reason, or on grounds of a person's marital status. Thus, if a firm wishes to offer cheap mortgage facilities to its staff, these facilities must be available to married women if the facility is open to married men (*Sun Alliance Insurance Co* v. *Dudman* (1978)).

There are three types of unlawful acts under this legislation.

Direct discrimination

This form of discrimination will arise if a person of one sex is treated less favourably than a person of the other sex, and the reason for the unfavourable treatment is the first person's sex. Thus, to refuse to employ a woman because the job in question is a man's job is direct discrimination (*Batisha* v *Say* (1977)).

Indirect discrimination

This arises where an employer applies a condition or requirement to a person which is such that the proportion of persons of the one sex who can comply with the condition are considerably smaller than the number of persons of the other sex. Thus, to advertise for a "male or female clerk, must have a large beard" amounts to indirect discrimination. The burden is on the employer to prove that the condition is necessary for the proper performance of the work to be done.

The court or tribunal must consider whether, in reality, women can satisfy the condition. In *Price* v. *Civil Service Commission* (1976) the employers advertised for executive officers between the ages of $17\frac{1}{2}$ and 28 years. The applicant, a 36-year-old woman, alleged there was indirect discrimination because fewer women than men could actually comply with the requirement in practice because of the demands of raising children. The Employment Appeal Tribunal (EAT) held that in reality far fewer women would be available for employment between those ages than men, and it was to her detriment that she could not comply. The case was remitted to the industrial tribunal which subsequently held that the respondents had failed to show that the age requirements were justified.

Victimisation

It is unlawful to victimise a person because he or she has brought proceedings under the Sex Discrimination Act 1975, or the Equal Pay Act 1970, or given evidence or information in connection with proceedings under either of the Acts, or done anything in relation to either Act to the person accused of discrimination or any other person, or has made allegations of contraventions of either Act against the person so accused or any other person.

DISCRIMINATION IN EMPLOYMENT

There are five types of unlawful acts of discrimination which may be committed against a person in relation to his or her employment:

1. In the arrangements made for the purpose of determining who will be employed.

The arrangements made to fill a vacancy must ensure that job opportunities are available to all, irrespective of their sex. Thus, an advertisement is part of the arrangements for determining who will be appointed. If the advertisement is non-discriminatory, an unlawful act may be committed subsequently. In *McDonald* v. *Applied Art Glass Co* (1976) a man contacted the firm by telephone in response to an advertisement and was told by the telephone operator that it was "women's work". He was subsequently invited to complete an application form but refused on the grounds that the firm would not view favourably applications by men. The allegation of sex discrimination was rejected, but the industrial tribunal said that employees who deal with employment enquiries should be instructed to deal with them in a manner which creates the impression that applications from persons of both sexes will be viewed favourably.

Similarly, questions asked at an interview are part of the employment arrangements. It has been held that to ask female applicants certain questions which the male candidates are not asked may be an indication of discrimination on the employer's part.

2. In the terms on which employment is offered

If an employer makes an offer of employment to a woman on terms which are less favourable than those offered to a man, this is clearly discrimination. If the employer can show that the variation is due to a genuine material difference between the applicants, then the difference is justifiable. Moreover, it may be permissible not to offer certain opportunities to women (i.e. night shift or overtime work) if to do so would be a contravention of a restriction imposed by the law.

3. By refusing or omitting to offer employment because of a person's sex

A man who is refused a job as a cook because other women employees will refuse to work with him (*Munro* v. *Allied Suppliers* (1977)), or a woman who is refused a job as a cave guide because it is "a man's job" (*Batisha* v. *Say* (1977)), are both discriminated against, but an employer still has the right to choose the best candidate for the job. The fact that the person rejected has better qualifications or experience than the person appointed for the job is not sufficient ground to found a claim of discrimination. The employer may show that women have been appointed on previous occasions if he is refuting a claim of discrimination.

In *Steere* v. *Morris Bros* (1977) an employer operating a delivery service was able to refute the allegation of discrimination by showing that in the past he had employed women as drivers and the reason why the plaintiff was not appointed on this occasion was because she lived too far away from the place of employment.

4. In the way a person offers, or refuses or omits to offer the claimant access to opportunities for promotion, transfer or training or any other benefits facilities or services.

To deny a woman an opportunity for a promotion or to restrict her training opportunities would be discriminatory, although an imbalance of the sexes in a job training programme is not in itself discriminatory.

5. By dismissing a person, or subjecting them to any other detriment

A dismissal on grounds of a person's sex is unlawful, even though the employer is under pressure from other employees (*Munro* v. *Allied Suppliers* (1977)). A detriment may exist although the employee is compensated for it. In *Jeremiah* v. *Minister of Defence* (1979) the mere fact that men received extra pay for a particular job which was of a dirty nature did not prevent there being unlawful discrimination. The dismissal of a woman on the grounds that a male employee who is an alternative candidate for dismissal is the breadwinner of his family may amount to discrimination.

Exceptions to the Sex Discrimination Act 1975

It is permissible to discriminate on grounds of a person's sex:

(*a*) where the employment is for the purpose of a private household; or (*b*) the number of employees does not exceed five; or

(*c*) because the sex of the person is a genuine occupational qualification for the job.

It is permissible to discriminate on grounds of sex if a person's sex is a genuine occupational qualification, for example the nature of the job calls for authentic male or female characteristics, or the job needs to be held by a man or woman in order to preserve decency or privacy, or where persons of one sex may reasonably object to the presence of the opposite sex, or where the employee is required to live in premises provided by the employer and those which are available are not equipped with separate accommodation, and it would be unreasonable to expect the employer to provide separate accommodation facilities, or where the job has to be done by a person in a hospital, prison or other establishment where people require special care.

Other unlawful acts

It is unlawful to give instructions to discriminate or attempt to induce such discrimination.

Employment advertisements

The EPCA, s. 38, provides that it is unlawful to advertise in a manner which may be taken as an indication of an intention to discriminate, and the use of terms such as "sales girl, waiter, postman" in an advertisement or job description will be assumed to be discriminatory. In order to determine whether an advertisement shows an intention to discriminate it must be read as a whole and given a meaning which a reasonable person without any special knowledge would attach to it.

Enforcement of the Sex Discrimination Act

Any person may complain to the industrial tribunal that another has committed an act of discrimination. The conciliation officer will attempt to reach a settlement and if that fails and the complaint is justified the tribunal may make an order declaring the rights of the complainant or order compensation to be paid by the respondent, or make an order compelling the respondent to reduce the effect on the complainant of any act of discrimination.

Equal pay

The Equal Pay Act 1970, as amended by the Sex Discrimination Act 1975, is concerned with the establishment of equal terms and conditions of employment for men and women. The Act provides that the contract of employment of all women is deemed to include an equality clause and it will operate when a woman is employed either on "like work", or on work which has been "rated as equivalent" with that of a man.

In order to determine whether a woman is employed on "like work", the Act provides that the work must be the same, or similar so that any differences between the work done are of no practical importance. If there are differences in the nature of the work the tribunal must determine if these are such that it is reasonable to expect them to be reflected in different wage scales. There are three types of differences which have been recognised as important.

Different duties
In *Electrolux* v. *Hutchinson* (1977) it was held that, as well as there being a contractual obligation to perform different duties, those duties must actually be performed to an extent which is significant enough to warrant different pay treatment.

Different hours
It has been held that where the work done by men and women is broadly similar and the hours are the same, the mere fact that the men work a night shift is not a bar to equal pay at the basic rate, although men can be compensated for working unsocial hours by a premium on the night shift.

Different responsibilities
It has been held that where the difference in pay between a man and a woman's earnings is because the man handles more expensive products with the result that he has more responsibility, the wage differentiation is justified.

Remedies under the Act
When a complaint has been made, the industrial tribunal should consider the contract of employment and reach its own decision. The complainant may choose the male employee with whom she wishes her work to be compared and the tribunal cannot substitute another man for the purpose of comparison. Thus, a woman whose pay is equal with some men can still seek equal pay with a man who is paid at a higher rate if his work is the same as or similar to hers. It is also possible to compare the complainant with a former employee.

Racial discrimination
The Race Relations Act 1976 provides that it is unlawful to discriminate against a person on grounds of race. This discrimination may arise in one of three ways.

1. Direct discrimination
There is direct discrimination if a person treats another person less favourably than he would treat someone of another race. If the discrimination is on grounds of race, the actual race of the person discriminated against is irrelevant. In *Zarczynska* v. *Levy* (1979) a barmaid who alleged she had been dismissed for refusing to obey an order not to serve drinks to coloured persons in a pub was held to have been less favourably treated on racial grounds, and was held entitled to pursue her claim.

2. Indirect discrimination

This occurs when a person applies a requirement or condition which is such that a proportion of persons of a particular racial group cannot comply.

3. Victimisation

It is unlawful to show prejudice to a person because he has brought proceedings under the Act, or given evidence or information connected with proceedings brought by another person, or done anything under the Act in relation to the discriminator, or made allegations that a person has committed acts of racial discrimination.

Racial grounds

The Race Relations Act 1976, s. 3, defines racial grounds as meaning colour, race, nationality or other ethnic or national origins. Thus, to advertise for a "Scots cook" would be discriminatory.

Racial discrimination in employment

It is unlawful to discriminate against a person on grounds of race in any arrangement for determining who will be offered employment. Moreover, once a person is employed it is unlawful to discriminate against him on racial grounds, i.e., by refusing him access to opportunities to promotion, or transfer, or training, or any other benefit or facilities.

It is, however, permissible to discriminate against a person on racial grounds where being a member of a particular racial group is a genuine qualification for the job. There are four grounds on which discrimination will be permissible namely:

(*a*) the job involves participation in a dramatic performance or other entertainment in a capacity for which a person of that group is required for authenticity; or

(*b*) the job involves participation as a photographic or artistic model for which a person of that racial group is required; or

(*c*) the job involves working in a place where food or drink is provided to the public in a particular setting (e.g. a Chinese restaurant) for which a person of that racial group is required; or

(*d*) the holder of that job provides persons of that racial group with personal services of a nature best provided by a member of that group.

Other unlawful acts

There are a number of other acts which are made unlawful by the Act, namely:

(*a*) it is unlawful to apply a discriminatory practice under s. 28 of the Act (e.g. if it is well known that an ethnic minority need not apply for jobs in a certain factory). This type of conduct amounts to a discriminatory practice although no–one actually applies or is discriminated against;

(*b*) s. 29 provides that it is unlawful to publish an advertisement which indicates an intention to discriminate unless the advertisement is permitted under s. 5 of the Act;

(c) by s. 30 it is unlawful for a person to instruct or authorise another to do a discriminatory act; and

(d) it is unlawful to induce a person to act in an unlawful manner, i.e. to call a strike because of the appointment of a person with certain racial origins.

Remedies

A claim in respect of racial discrimination in employment must be brought before an industrial tribunal within three months of the discriminatory act, unless it is just and equitable to extend the time period. A copy of the complaint will be sent to the conciliation officer, whose job it is to try and promote a settlement. If this is unsuccessful the matter will then go for hearing and if the tribunal finds for the complainant, it can make one of the following orders:

(a) a declaration of the rights of the complainant; or

(b) an order that the respondent will pay compensation up to a maximum of £6,250; or

(c) a recommendation that, within a specific period, the respondent should take such action as appears to the tribunal to be practical for the purpose of reducing the adverse affect on the complainant of the act complained.

The burden of proof is on the applicant to show that an act of racial discrimination has occurred. The fact that the employer already employs people of different ethnic groups is taken into consideration although it is not conclusive evidence of absence of racial discrimination.

Commission for Racial Equality

The Commission for Racial Equality is empowered to investigate formally any practices carried on by an individual or an organisation. The Commission will then report and may make recommendations. If the Commission concludes that a person or organisation has been acting unlawfully, it may serve a non–discrimination notice on him requiring changes to be made, and to report to it on the changes that are made in pursuance to the report. If there is a repetition of discriminatory practices within the five years following the issue of a non–discrimination notice, the commission may obtain an injunction.

EMPLOYMENT PROTECTION

The Employment Protection (Consolidation) Act 1978, lays down certain minimum legal requirements which, although they can be added to, cannot be denied to an employee.

Guarantee payments

An employee who has been employed for a minimum of four weeks by the same employer must be made a guarantee payment in respect of any full day for which the employee is not actually provided with work (e.g. because there is a diminution in the requirements of the employer's business or any other event which affects the employer's business). The Employment Protection

(Consolidation) Act 1978, s. 12, only applies to a diminution of work. It does not include religious holidays, and in such circumstances a guarantee payment cannot be claimed (*North* v. *Pauleigh Ltd* (1977)). If the contract of employment is not likely to last more than three months there is no right to a guarantee payment. A guarantee payment is not required to be made if any day when the employees are not working is the result of a trade dispute. In *Garvey* v. *May Bank (Oldham) Ltd* (1979) as a consequence of a national lorry drivers strike the employers failed to receive supplies, and the firm laid off the applicant. It was held that he was not entitled to a guarantee payment because he was laid off due to a trade dispute.

The employee is entitled to be paid at the guaranteed hourly rate (i.e. one week's pay divided by the number of normal working hours) for the number of normal working hours on the day he is laid off. The statutory maximum an employee is entitled to receive is £8 for a maximum of twenty days in each year. The guarantee payment will be taken into account to discharge any contractual entitlement of the employee to receive payments for days he is idle.

Suspension on medical grounds

An employee who is continuously employed for more than four weeks will be entitled to remuneration if he is suspended from work because the nature of his work constitutes a health risk and the work or process he is engaged in is suspended. In these circumstances, the employee affected is entitled to payment for a maximum of 26 weeks from the day of suspension. An employee is not entitled to payment if during the period the work or process is suspended the employee would have been unable to continue work because of illness.

Maternity

Maternity dismissal

A woman employee who has been in continuous employment for two years will be deemed to have been unfairly dismissed if the reason for the dismissal is her pregnancy, unless it can be shown that at the date of termination she is likely to be incapable of doing the work adequately, or that because of her condition she cannot or will not be able to continue her work without contravening restrictions imposed by the law. If the employer dismisses a woman employee for either of these reasons, the employer must offer her alternative suitable employment where possible.

If an employer dismisses a pregnant woman he must show that the dismissal was unconnected with the pregnancy.

Maternity pay

A female employee who is absent from work because of pregnancy, or confinement is entitled to receive maternity pay for a period of six weeks during which she is absent. She will only be entitled to maternity pay if she continues to be employed until immediately before the eleventh week prior to the expected week of confinement and at the beginning of the eleventh week she has been continuously employed for a period of two years.

An employee who has been fairly dismissed because of her pregnancy will still be entitled to maternity pay if, had she not been dismissed, she would have been in continuous employment for two years at the beginning of the eleventh week before her confinement. She will not be entitled to maternity pay unless she informs the employer at least three weeks prior to her absence that she will be absent from work because of her pregnancy. The amount of pay she will be entitled to will be nine–tenths of a week's pay for each week's absence after a deduction is allowed for any maternity allowance payable under the Social Security Act 1975. The maternity pay is payable whether or not the employee intends to return to work after her confinement.

Return to work after confinement

An employee who has been absent from work because of her pregnancy or confinement is entitled to return to work under her original contract of employment on the same terms and conditions. The right to return can be exercised at any time before the end of 29 weeks from the week of her confinement. Where a woman cannot return to work because of redundancy she is entitled, where there is a suitable vacancy, to be offered alternative employment under a new contract.

In order to qualify for the right to return to work, the woman must have been employed until immediately before the eleventh week of her confinement, and she must have been continuously employed for two years. She must also have informed her employers in writing three weeks prior to her absence that she will be absent from work because of her pregnancy or confinement, and that she intends to return to work and the expected date of confinement.

If a woman resigns so that her resignation becomes effective prior to the eleventh week before her confinement she has no right to change her mind, but if she does not resign until after the eleventh week prior to her confinement then, provided she gives the requisite notice three weeks prior to her leaving, she can change her mind and exercise her statutory option to return to her employment after her confinement.

Seven weeks after the expected week of confinement the employer may ask the employee for written confirmation of her intention to return to work. She must give this in writing within two weeks.

When a woman wants to return to work after her pregnancy she must give three weeks written notice of the date of her intended return, but the employer may postpone her return to work for up to four weeks beyond that date.

Where an employee is not permitted to return to work under these provisions, she will be treated as having been continuously employed until the notified date of return for purposes of redundancy and unfair dismissal. Her remedy will be by way of a complaint of unfair dismissal or a claim for a redundancy payment.

TRADE UNION MEMBERSHIP

An employer may not penalise (and that includes any action short of dismissal) an employee for joining a trade union, or in order to prevent his taking part in union activities, or to compel him to become a member of a trade union (Employment Act 1982, ss. 3 and 10).

An employer must permit an employee who is an official of an independent trade union time-off during working hours to enable him to undertake any duties concerned with industrial relations between the employer and employee, and to undertake training in industrial relations.

The employer must permit an employee who is a member of a union time-off to participate in any union activities, or as a representative of that union, for example to attend a conference as a union delegate, but the employer is under no obligation to allow the time for activities which are in furtherance of an industrial dispute.

Relief for dismissed trade unionists

An employee who believes he was unfairly dismissed because he was or intended to become a member of a trade union or to participate in union activities can ask an industrial tribunal for an order that he shall be re-instated or re-engaged by the employer, or if this is not possible, that he be suspended on full pay pending a settlement of the complaint. The employee must file the complaint prior to the end of seven days from the effective date of termination of his employment. This must be accompanied by a signed certificate issued by an authorised union official stating that the employee was, or had intended to become, a member of that union and that there are reasonable grounds to believe that the employee's dismissal was connected with these reasons.

The tribunal will give the employer seven days notice before the hearing and will thereafter hear the complaint as soon as practicable. If the tribunal decides to uphold the complaint it will make a preliminary finding and explain its powers to the parties. The tribunal should then give the employer an opportunity to re-instate the employee on the same terms and conditions he enjoyed pending the settlement of the complaint. The employee may be offered alternative employment, but if he is reasonable in refusing the offer, the tribunal will make an order for the continuation of his contract of employment. If the tribunal considers that an employee's refusal to accept alternative employment is unreasonable, a continuation order will not be made.

Under the EPCA 1978, s. 67, an employee who had been dismissed in connection with a strike or other industrial action could present a claim if any other employee who had also taken part in the strike was re-engaged at any time, provided he claimed within three month's of the offer of re-engagement being made. The Employment Act 1982, s. 9, amended the 1978 Act by providing that a claim can only be brought if the offer to re-engage is made within three months of the other employee's dismissal. Additionally, the claimant must make a claim within six months of his own dismissal. The employee who is dismissed for taking part in a strike will only be able to present a complaint if other employees who took strike action are not dismissed or are re–engaged.

Effect of a continuation order
The effect of an order for continuation of the contract of employment is that the employment will continue in force until the settlement of the complaint. The tribunal will determine the employee's pay from the time of dismissal until the complaint is settled but it will take into account any lump sum payments.

PERFORMANCE OF THE CONTRACT OF EMPLOYMENT

A contract of employment is one of personal service but the courts will not compel either the employer, or employee to carry out that contract by an order for specific performance or an injunction. In *Warner Bros.* v. *Nelson* (1937) an actress agreed to work for the plaintiffs and undertook not to work for any other film company. An injunction was granted to restrain her from working for a rival film company. The effect of the injunction would not be to compel her to work for the plaintiffs since she was able to earn a living in other ways. In *Chappell* v. *Times Newspapers* (1975) members of a trade union were carrying on a campaign in support of a wage demand. The employers' association sent a telegram to the union to the effect that unless the campaign was called off, the members would be regarded as having broken their contracts of employment and, therefore, as having terminated their engagements. A group of employees sought an injunction to restrain the employers from terminating their contracts. It was held an injunction would not be granted, for its effect would be to compel the employers to perform their obligations specifically.

The Trade Union and Labour Relations Act 1974, s. 16, provided that a court will not compel an employee to work, or attend a place of work by granting an order for an injunction to restrain a strike or other industrial action.

Implied duties of the employer
There are a number of duties and obligations which the law imposes on both parties during the continuance of the contract of employment. These duties arise at common law and by virtue of certain statutory provisions.

1. Implied duty of mutual respect
An employer has a legal duty to treat his employees with due respect and consideration. In *Donovan* v. *Invicta Airways Ltd* (1969) an employee resigned after a number of incidents where he thought the employer was being unfair and claimed damages for breach of contract. It was held that the employer's conduct, though irritating, was not substantial enough to amount to a breach, but it was stated that there was an implied duty that the parties to a contract of

employment should treat each other with such degree of consideration and courtesy as would enable the contract to be performed. In *Cox* v. *Phillips Industries Ltd* (1976) the plaintiff was promoted to the post of product leader. He was subsequently demoted, but his duties were vague and he was given no further responsibilities. He became depressed and ill, and accepted a redundancy payment. In an action against the employers for breach of contract, the employee was held entitled to £500 damages in respect of the frustration caused by the breach of contract.

The duty arises from the commencement of employment and continues during its performance until its termination. The employer is under an obligation to ensure that the employee is provided with an adequate job description, together with adequate facilities and support staff.

2. Duty to provide work

The general rule is that the employer is not under an obligation to provide work for his employee, but there are certain special circumstances where the employer's failure to provide work may result in a breach of his duties:

(*a*) where the failure to provide work can lead to a loss of reputation or publicity, i.e. where an actor is offered a lead role in a theatrical comedy, and is subsequently offered a lesser role although at the same salary. The nature of the work is as important as the salary and the employer is in breach of contract;

(*b*) if the failure to provide work leads to a reduction in the employee's actual or potential earnings, i.e. an employee must be given an opportunity to earn his commission if he is remunerated by commission, or to earn a reasonable amount if he is on piece–work;

(*c*) if a term in the contract of employment implies that the employer will provide suitable work for the employee in accordance with his personal characteristics (e.g. a handicapped person), the employer may be in breach of the contract if he fails to do so;

(*d*) if the employee needs training or practice to do the work he is employed to undertake the employer is under an implied obligation to provide a reasonable amount of work for this purpose, but this is not so if the employee claims to have the necessary skill or experience already.

3. Duty to pay wages or remuneration when there is no work

The express terms of the contract will usually provide expressly for the amount of remuneration to be paid to an employee. It is proposed to look at the employer's liability to pay the employee if he cannot provide work.

The general rule, at common law, is that an employer must pay the agreed wages of all employees who are ready and available for work even if the employer cannot provide work for them. In the case of a piece–worker, although he is paid for work actually done, he is entitled to expect that the employers will give him an opportunity to earn his minimum wages if such a wage is agreed upon.

The implied terms at common law can be varied by an express or implied term to the contrary. If the contract provides that the employee will not be paid in respect of short–time working or during a lay–off, the employer incurs no obligation to pay. In *Hulme* v. *Ferranti Ltd* (1918) the plaintiff was employed on terms that if there was no work, he would not be paid. It was held that he was not entitled to be paid during the period the employee was laid–off as a result of a strike by other workers in the plant where he was employed, and he was thereby prevented from doing his work.

However, in respect of hourly, or piece–workers there is an implied term that they will not be paid during a lay–off or short–time working and the suggestion by the Court of Appeal that an employer has an implied obligation to provide a skilled employee with work should be treated with caution (*Longston* v. *AUEW* (1974)).

4. Duty to indemnify

If the employee incurs expenses in the performance of his duties then he is entitled to be indemnified by his employer to the extent of the expense incurred. There may be an express term in the contract of employment entitling the employee to be so indemnified, but where the employee acts under his employer's explicit orders such a term will be implied in any case.

5. References

An employer is under no legal obligation to provide an employee or ex–employee with a reference to enable him to obtain employment, or for any other purpose. An employer who makes an untrue statement in a reference he gives may find himself liable to the person to whom the reference is given either for negligent misrepresentation, or if the employer knew the reference was untrue for deceit; alternatively, if the reference is derogatory, the employee may expose himself to an action for defamation by his employee or ex–employee.

6. Duty to ensure employee's safety

There are a number of common law and statutory rules which determine the scope of the employer's duty to take reasonable care to ensure the safety of his employees. If the employer does not comply with his duties to take certain specific safety precautions, an employee who is injured may bring an action for damages against the employer. The two actions may be brought concurrently, so that an employee may succeed both at common law and in an action for breach of statutory duty, although only one set of damages will be awarded.

The standard of care required from an employer was said in *Paris* v. *Stepney Borough Council* (1951) to be such as an "ordinary prudent employer would take in all the circumstances". The employer only undertakes to take reasonable care, and he will be liable if due to a failure to meet that standard an employee is injured. In *Vinnyey* v. *Star Paper Mills* (1965) it was held that the employer was not liable when the plaintiff slipped and injured himself on a factory floor which the foreman had instructed to be cleaned after a flood. If the employer did not know of the existence of a danger and could not be expected to foresee the danger he will not be liable. Thus, where the state of medical knowledge is such that it is not known that a particular process will cause a risk to health, the employer will not be liable at common law.

7. Duty to unborn children

An employer may be liable to an unborn child of an employee if the child born is disabled as a result of the employer's breach of duty to its mother. The child may, therefore, sue in respect of pre–natal injury suffered regardless of whether the employer knew of the existence of the foetus.

The nature of the duty

Although there is only a single duty of care imposed on the employer the duty can be examined under three heads, namely:

1. Safe plant and appliances

All equipment, tools, machinery and plant where the employee works must be reasonably safe. In *Bradford* v. *Robinson Rentals Ltd* (1967) an employee who suffered frost–bite as a consequence of driving an unheated van for 400 miles for his employer was held entitled to recover damages.

If an employer purchases tools or equipment from a normally reliable and reputable source and the employer has no knowledge of any defect in them, he will have discharged his duty to take care at common law. The Employers' Liability (Defective Equipment) Act 1969, however, provides that if an employee suffers personal injury in the course of his employment in consequence of a defect in equipment attributable to the fault of a third party, the employer will be liable for the fault of the third party.

2. Safe system of work

Here the layout, training and supervision, the provision of warnings, protective clothing, safety devices etc. are all relevant factors. In *Barcock* v. *Brighton Corporation* (1949) the plaintiff was employed at an electricity sub–station. A method of testing the electricity generator used by the employers was unsafe and the plaintiff was injured. The employers were held liable. If, however, the employer gives safety instructions which the employee fails to observe, the employer will not be liable for a subsequent injury.

If there are safety precautions taken by the employer, the employee must be notified of them and if safety equipment is provided it must be available for his use. In *Finch* v. *Telegraph and Maintenance Construction Co* (1949) the plaintiff was employed as a grinder. Although goggles had been provided, the employee was not told where he could obtain them and he was injured in the course of his work by metal flying off the grindstones. The employers were held liable for breach of their duty to provide a safe system of work. The more dangerous the process, the greater the need for safety precautions.

3. Reasonably competent fellow employees
An employer who engages an incompetent person who injures another employee is liable to the injured employee.

Personal nature of employer's duty

The duty of the employer is a personal one, and he cannot absolve himself by delegating the performance of the duty to someone else (e.g. a factory manager or a foreman). The employer cannot, therefore, escape liability for breach of a duty imposed on him by appointing a security officer whose work consists of ensuring that safety precautions are observed (*Wilsons & Clyde Coal Co Ltd* v. *English* (1938)). The employer's duty is owed to each employee individually, not to them all collectively. The employer must display a higher degree of care when dealing with new or inexperienced employees than with responsible trained staff.

IMPLIED OBLIGATIONS OF THE EMPLOYEE

The relationship between an employer and employee is one of confidence and trust, and the law implies a term that every employee will serve his employer faithfully. A serious or persistent course of conduct by the employee inconsistent with this obligation will amount to a breach of contract. The wrongful act need not confer a benefit on the employee personally. In *Dalton* v. *Burton's Gold Medal Biscuit Co Ltd* (1974) an employee who was dismissed for falsifying the clock–card of a fellow employee was held to have been fairly dismissed.

Duty to obey orders and to exercise care and skill and the duty of loyalty

The employee undertakes to obey all lawful and reasonable orders but he need not obey an order if it is unlawful. In *Morrish,* v. *Henley's Ltd* (1973) an employee was held to have been wrongfully dismissed when his employers dismissed him because he refused to falsify certain records which the employers were required to keep by law.

The employee undertakes to perform his obligations with reasonable skill and care, but this is a corollary of the employer's duty to provide all necessary equipment, and if an employer has done this then a dismissal for incompetence will normally be fair. The employee impliedly undertakes to take proper care of the employer's property, and if he negligently allows some of the employer's property to be stolen he will be liable.

The employee also impliedly undertakes not to accept any secret bribes or commissions, or gifts from third persons or any other reward in respect of his work other than his agreed remuneration from his employer. However, an employee who receives a tip does not have to disclose it to his employer, unless the size of the tip is so great that it must have been an inducement to the employee to favour the person who gave it, and to disregard the employee's duties to his employer.

The employee must not disclose any confidential information about the employer's business to an unauthorised person. If the employee is obliged by law to disclose confidential information (e.g. to give evidence in legal proceedings) then he cannot be made liable for breach of contract, or be dismissed.

Employer's vicarious liability

An employee who commits a wrongful act in the course of his employment which causes injury to a third party is personally liable to the person wronged, but the employer will also be vicariously liable to compensate the injured third party if the employee was acting within the scope of his employment (i.e. carrying out work which he was employed to do, or doing something reasonably incidental thereto).

Disciplinary powers of management

The exercise of disciplinary powers is a corrective function of the employer. The object should be to improve an employee's performance in the future and not to punish him.

Fines for misconduct: manual workers

The Truck Act 1896 applies to "workmen" and shop assistants. An employer may lawfully impose a fine for misconduct, or indiscipline, i.e. for fighting, breach of works rules or lateness. These powers must be exercised within the terms of the Truck Act which provides that the power to fine must be provided for expressly by a written contract signed by the employee, or in a notice displayed conspicuously at his place of work. The fine can only be imposed in respect of acts which cause a loss to the employer, or which amount to an interference with the proper conduct of his business. The rules must specify the offence for which the fine can be imposed and either the amount of the fine must be specified, or it must be capable of calculation. Finally, the amount of the fine must be fair and reasonable, and on each occasion when a fine is imposed the workman must be given written particulars.

Similar rules apply where an employer wishes to deduct amounts for bad or negligent workmanship.

Other employees: fines and deductions

In respect of employees not governed by the Truck Act (e.g. clerical and secretarial employees) the imposition of fines and similar deductions depends on the terms of the contract of employment. The employer's power to fine or make deductions should be contained expressly in the terms of the contract.

Suspension without pay for misconduct

The courts will uphold a suspension of an employee from work provided that the employer is permitted by the terms of the contract of employment to suspend the employee for certain specific reasons, and that the suspension is carried out in accordance with the procedure laid down (if any). If the grounds and procedure for suspension are laid down in the works rules, they will be binding to the extent to which those rules form part of the individual contract of employment. Alternatively, the grounds for suspension and procedure to be adopted may be contained in a collective agreement, in which case the right to suspend may be embodied in the contract of employment by express or implied incorporation.

If an employer lawfully suspends an employee, the contract of employment is put temporarily into abeyance with a right for the employee to be reinstated at the end of the suspension period. If the suspension is wrongful, the employee is entitled to treat the suspension as a repudiation of the contract of employment by the employer. The employee is entitled to resign and sue for wrongful dismissal.

Warnings

An employer does not need a contractual power to issue warnings to employees (e.g. for unsatisfactory work) but this may be subject to a disciplinary code, or part of the works rules. If the procedure is formally laid down there then the procedure specified must be strictly followed. A warning can deal with specific conduct which is the cause of the complaint, or it may deal with general matters so that the employee's total record of conduct can be taken into account so as to justify his subsequent dismissal.

The warning should refer to past conduct which is the subject of a complaint and warn against future similar conduct. The warnings should be given by a person in authority and be clear, incisive and firm. They should make clear the nature of conduct which will not be tolerated, and should clarify that a failure to heed the warning may result in dismissal.

Reprimand

The tribunals have held that misconduct which is not gross should be punished by a reprimand, rather than dismissal.

Demotion

An employer who has lost confidence in the ability of an employee may demote him, whether with or without the possibility of review, and whether or not at a lower rate of earnings. If there is an express power to demote an employee under the terms of the contract then, provided the sanction is fairly exercised, it should not present any legal problems. In the absence of such a power the demotion of an employee may amount to constructive dismissal if the employee gives up his employment.

DISMISSAL

An employee now has a statutory right not to be unfairly dismissed. The relevant provisions are contained in the Employment Protection (Consolidation) Act 1978, as amended by the Employment Acts 1980 and 1982. However, it is still necessary to deal with the common law provisions, because they still apply to situations where the statutory provisions are inapplicable for any reason.

Summary dismissal

There are a number of established grounds on which an employer may dismiss an employee summarily, i.e. gross misconduct, or a wilful refusal to obey a lawful or reasonable order, or dishonesty, or gross negligence causing substantial damage. In *Ross* v. *Aquascutum Ltd* (1973) a person who was employed as a night–workman was absent from the building when he was supposed to be on guard for two hours every night. It was held that his conduct amounted to a serious breach of contract which justified summary dismissal. Similarly, in *Peppery* v. *Webb* (1969) a gardener was asked to do certain work but refused to do so in a manner which was insolent. It was held that his summary dismissal was justified for by refusing to obey a lawful and reasonable order he was in serious breach of his contract.

A breach of an express term of the contract of employment or of a provision in the works rules may justify summary dismissal, provided that it has been brought to the employee's attention that there are certain types of conduct which the employer will not tolerate, e.g. certain airlines have a rule that any pilot who takes drugs (other than on medical prescription), or is discovered drunk, whether on or off duty, will be liable for instant dismissal.

Lawful dismissal

Where an employer has a legal right to dismiss an employee (although not summarily) the employee is entitled to the period of notice specified by the contract, or implied into the contract of employment. An employer may alternatively dismiss an employee immediately, and pay his wages or salary in lieu of notice. If the contract of employment expressly states the period of notice which an employee is entitled to receive, then that is the minimum notice required, but if there is no provision in the contract then reasonable notice must be given. The Employment Protection (Consolidation) Act 1978, s. 49(1), provides that a certain minimum period of notice must be given to all employees (e.g. after four weeks' employment an employee is entitled to one week's notice, and when an employee has completed two years' service he is entitled to two weeks' notice). Thereafter, an employee is entitled to one additional week's notice in respect of each year's employment up to a maximum of twelve. During the period of his notice the employee is entitled to be paid his average wages for any period where no work is provided by the employer, or if the employee is absent due to illness.

Unfair dismissal

The statutory provisions relating to unfair dismissal contained in the

Employment Protection (Consolidation) Act 1978 do not apply to certain types of employees:

(*a*) where an employee is employed by his or her spouse;

(*b*) any employee registered as a dock worker;

(*c*) any contract of employment where the employee ordinarily works outside Great Britain;

(*d*) any employment where the employee has been continuously employed for less than 52 weeks;

(*e*) an employee who has reached the age of retirement laid down in the contract of employment;

(*f*) any employment covered by a dismissal procedure; and

(*g*) employees who work for a foreign government.

What amounts to dismissal

There are three ways in which a dismissal may be effected under the Employment Protection (Consolidation) Act 1978, namely:

(*a*) where the contract of employment is terminated by the employer, with or without notice; but if the employee resigns of his own volition there is no dismissal. In *Elliott* v. *Waldair (Construction) Ltd* (1975) the applicant resigned because he was moved from driving a heavy lorry to a smaller van by his employers. It was held that where the employee lost an opportunity to work overtime as a result of a change in the type of vehicle he would drive, that did not constitute dismissal by the employer. Where, however, the employer invites an employee to resign this will constitute a dismissal;

(*b*) where the employee is employed for a fixed term a dismissal takes place if that term expires without the employment's being renewed. The employer's action in not renewing the contract is still subject to the test of reasonableness. A fixed term contract is one which must run for a fixed period, even if it may be terminated by notice. However, the Employment Protection Consolidation Act 1978 provides that a fixed term contract must state the date on which the contract will expire;

(*c*) where the employee himself terminates the contract, with or without notice, in circumstances where he is entitled to terminate it, by reason of the employer's conduct, this amounts to constructive dismissal because it is the employer's conduct which constitutes a repudiation of the contract. Thus, where an employer by a unilateral act attempts to alter the terms of employment, i.e. by making a change in the job or salary or a significant change of location, an employee will be entitled to resign.

Fair and unfair dismissal

The Employment Protection (Consolidation) Act 1978, s. 57, lays down five grounds on which a dismissal may be justified as being fair: if the dismissal relates to the capability or qualifications of the employee in relation to the work he is employed to do; if the dismissal relates to the conduct of the employee, i.e. if the dismissal is in consequence of the redundancy of the employee; if the dismissal was because the employee could not continue to work in the position in which he is employed without contravening restrictions imposed by the law; if there is some other substantial reason which justifies the dismissal of the employee. In *Early* v. *Slater & Wheeler (Airlyne) Ltd* (1973) the question which arose was whether an employee who had been dismissed without being given an opportunity to rebut or explain allegations made against him had been unfairly dismissed. The court held that the employee had been unfairly dismissed as the employers failed to give an opportunity to the employee to explain the allegations against him, and because of this the dismissal was unfair. The court said that, in considering whether a dismissal is fair or unfair, the tribunal should adopt the common sense and common fairness approach, and ask whether the dismissal is reasonable or not. The court however held that, since the employee could not prove that he had actually suffered a loss, he was not entitled to compensation.

Whether or not a dismissal which is based on one of the grounds in s. 57 is fair depends on whether the employer has acted reasonably in the circumstances. If the employee challenges the fairness of the dismissal, the burden is on the employer to prove that the reason for dismissal falls into one of the five categories. It is then for the industrial tribunal to determine whether or not the employer has acted reasonably in the circumstances. If the employer fails to show that the ground for dismissal falls within one of the five reasons mentioned above the dismissal is automatically unfair. In *Raynor* v. *Remploy Ltd* (1973) a group general manager was dismissed for an alleged lack of business judgment and general inefficiency. He had been employed for five years. The tribunal rejected the company's allegations, since there was no evidence of incapability and held that the dismissal was unfair. In *Castledine* v. *Rothwell Engineering Ltd* (1973) the tribunal refused to accept allegations of incompetence against the employee because the employer had, subsequent to the dismissal, given favourable references to other prospective employers.

To dismiss an employee who is incapable of performing his job properly will be fair, provided the employer acts reasonably in the circumstances. Thus, he must inquire why an employee cannot do the job properly and must ensure that the employee has been given proper instructions and is properly supervised. In *Davison* v. Kent Meters Ltd (1975) the applicant was dismissed for assembling nearly 500 components in a manner she claimed to have been shown by her supervisor. The supervisor denied this, but it was held that the dismissal was unfair because, if she had not been shown how to assemble the components, she should have been and if she had assembled them wrongly she could not be held responsible.

The employer must consider alternative work which can be offered to the employee before he dismisses the employee.

An employee who is absent from work for a long time due to ill health may be fairly dismissed if the employer can no longer be reasonably expected to keep the employee's post open for him. An employee who is persistently absent from work for short periods due to illness can be warned about his absences and told to improve his performance. If, however, the absences persist, the employer may be entitled to dismiss the employee and will act reasonably in doing so. Where an employee's persistent absences due to illness may become a hazard to his fellow employees, or likely to cause damage to property then, provided the employer consults with the employees first, his dismissal will be fair.

Where an employee does not have the proper qualifications for the job or cannot obtain the necessary qualification after repeated attempts, his dismissal may be considered fair. In *Blackman* v. *Post Office* (1974) a telegraph officer was required to pass an aptitude test, but he failed after the maximum number of attempts allowed to pass the examination. It was held that his dismissal was fair on the ground of his lack of qualification. However, the employer must still act reasonably in dismissing an employee on this ground.

The conduct of an employee outside the course of the employment and outside working hours may be taken into account in appropriate cases. The seriousness of the misconduct must be commensurate with the penalty imposed by the employer, and he must show that he gave the matter a prompt and thorough investigation and that the employee was given an opportunity to state his case and, where necessary, that witnesses were interviewed.

Inadmissible reasons for dismissal

The Employment Protection (Consolidation) Act 1978, s. 58, as amended by the Employment Act 1982, provides that a dismissal may be unfair for a number of reasons. By s. 58 of the 1978 Act, the dismissal was unfair if the reason for the dismissal was that the employee was, or proposed to become, a member of an independent trade union, or had taken part in or proposed to take part in the activities of an independent trade union or if he refused to become or remain a member of the appropriate trade union where a closed shop was in operation.

In addition, an employee will be unfairly dismissed if the dismissal is for one of the following reasons:

(*a*) if he is dismissed for non–membership where there is no union membership (closed shop) agreement applying;

(*b*) where those dismissed do not fall within the conscientious objectors or existing membership exemptions, but where the closed shop agreement has not been approved by a ballot in the five years preceding their dismissal;

(*c*) where those who wished to belong to the union have commenced proceedings for unreasonable exclusion from the union; and

(*d*) where employees with professional obligations embodied in a written code are expelled from their union for failure to take part in industrial action which would be in breach of that code.

The Employment Act 1982, s. 3, introduces a periodic review requirement; dismissal of a non–member will automatically be unfair unless the closed shop agreement has been validated by a ballot within five years preceding the dismissal. Where an employee's claim is based on a failure to hold a ballot within the preceding five years, it may be important to know the exact date on which the last ballot was held. The Act therefore provides that ballots held over several days will be treated as having been held on the first day when votes were cast.

TERMINATION OF THE CONTRACT OF EMPLOYMENT

A contract of employment can be terminated in a number of other ways which do not amount to dismissal in law.

Resignation
If an employee resigns voluntarily he has not been dismissed. If the words used by the employee are ambiguous, then the question is whether a reasonable employer would have understood the words as amounting to a resignation. Where the employee is given the alternative either of resigning or being dismissed, a consequent resignation will amount to a dismissal.

Constructive resignation
If an employee acts in a manner so that his conduct shows he no longer intends to be bound by his contract of employment then that amounts to a repudiation of the contract and the employer may terminate the contract. There is a constructive resignation only when the sole reasonable inference that can be drawn from the employee's conduct is that he no longer intends to carry out his obligations under his contract of employment.

Frustration of the contract
Where the performance of the contract of employment becomes impossible because of some intervening event the contract is terminated by frustration, not by dismissal. In *Hare* v. *Murphy Bros Ltd* (1973) it was held that an employee who was imprisoned could not after serving his sentence seek his old job back because his contract of employment had been frustrated by his non–availability during his imprisonment. In order to decide whether or not a contract of employment is terminated because it is frustrated, regard must be had to the length of time the employee is likely to be absent from his work or unable to perform his contract and the need for the employer to obtain a replacement. The mere fact that an employee is absent due to illness does not necessarily frustrate the contract. In *Egg Stores* v. *Leibovicis* (1977) it was said that, among the other matters to be taken into consideration, the employer must take into account the length of employment, the nature of the job, the length and nature of sickness, the necessity of appointing a permanent replacement, the risk of the employer in incurring further obligations in respect of redundancy payment or unfair dismissal, whether sick pay is still being paid and whether in the circumstances it is reasonable for the employer to keep the job for the employee.

Consensual termination
A contract of employment is terminated if the parties have expressly agreed

that the happening or non–occurrence of an event will terminate the contract. In *British Leyland Ltd* v. *Ashraf* (1978) the applicant was granted five weeks' unpaid leave to visit his sick mother, in Pakistan. He was informed that if he failed to return by the end of the five week period, his employment would be treated as terminated, and he agreed to this. It was held there had been consensual termination of the contract when he did not return in time and that he had not been dismissed.

Project termination

If a person is employed for a specific project then, on its completion, the employment will cease and he will not have been dismissed. The contract is discharged by performance.

REMEDIES

An employee who wants to obtain a remedy for a breach must present his claim within the appropriate time limit. If he is dismissed for redundancy, he must apply for a redundancy payment within six months of the dismissal, although the tribunal has a discretion to extend the period for a further six months if it thinks just and equitable. The employee's complaint must be in writing and must contain a statement of the grounds on which relief is sought. An employer is similarly entitled to give a reply in writing of the grounds on which he intends to resist the claim. A settlement between the parties will not prevent an employee's bringing his case before an industrial tribunal although the agreement was one which purported to be a final settlement. However, a settlement reached between the parties through a conciliation officer is binding on all the parties and can be enforced in the same way. If a settlement is not reached, an industrial tribunal will hear the case and the burden of proof is on the applicant. If the industrial tribunal finds that the employee has been unfairly dismissed it can make a number of orders:

1. Re–instatement and re–engagement orders
The industrial tribunal has the power to make an order that the former employee be re–instated or re–engaged if the employee so wishes. If an order for re–instatement is made, the employer must treat the employee as if he had not been dismissed and the tribunal may specify the amount of arrears in salary payable to the employee. His rights and privileges, including seniority, pension rights and any improvement in his terms and conditions of employment had he not been dismissed must be restored to him. If the tribunal makes an order in respect of arrears of pay, any sums received by the applicant between the date of dismissal and the date of re–instatement, or by way of wages in lieu of notice or ex gratia payments must be taken into account.

In considering the question whether an order for re–instatement is to be made, it must take three considerations into account:
 (*a*) whether the applicant wishes to be re–instated;

(b) whether it is practical for the employer to comply with an order of re–instatement; and

(c) whether the applicant was the cause, or to some extent contributed to the dismissal and whether it would be just to order the re–instatement.

If the employer has engaged someone else to replace the dismissed employee the tribunal will not take this into account unless the employer can show that it was not practical for the dismissed employee's work to be done without engaging a permanent replacement, or that he engaged the replacement after the lapse of a reasonable time without having heard from the dismissed employee that he wished to be re–instated or re–engaged.

2. Compensation awards

If an order for re–instatement or re–engagement is made, but its terms are not fully complied with, the tribunal may make an award of compensation. Where an employee is dismissed for reason of redundancy, but is not entitled to a redundancy payment because of the operation of the EPCA, ss. 85(5) or (6) (e.g. where he unreasonably refuses alternative employment, terminates the new contract during the trial period, or is not entitled to be treated as having been dismissed under s. 84 (e.g. if there is a renewal of his contract or re–engagement under a new contract)) then a basic award of two weeks' pay with a maximum limit of £20 per week will be paid. The basic award will depend on the number of years during which the employee has been employed. A compensatory award will be the amount the tribunal considers just and equitable in all the circumstances, having regard to the loss sustained by the complainant, including all expenses reasonably incurred by him or the loss of any benefit which he may reasonably be expected to have gained. In such cases the tribunal may consider the immediate loss of wages, the manner of dismissal, if it causes some financial loss, loss of future earnings, loss of any benefits, loss of protection against future unfair dismissal and any loss of entitlement to a redundancy payment. The tribunal may reduce the amount of the award if the applicant fails to mitigate his loss (i.e. by taking reasonable steps to obtain other employment). Any ex gratia payments will be deducted from the compensatory award and any conduct on the part of the employee which leads to his dismissal will be taken into consideration and the award reduced accordingly.

An additional award will be made if the employer totally ignores the order of the tribunal.

REDUNDANCY

An employee who is dismissed for reason of redundancy can claim compensation under the EPCA. A dismissal will be for reasons of redundancy if it is attributable in any way to:

(a) the fact that the employer has ceased, or intends to cease carrying on the business for which the employee was employed;

(b) the employer has ceased or intends to cease carrying on that business in the place where the employee was employed; or

(c) the fact that the requirements of that business for employees to carry out work of a particular kind, or for them to carry out that work in the place where they were so employed have ceased or diminished, or are expected to cease or diminish.

If the employer makes an offer to re–engage him under a new contract which is to take effect on the expiry of the old contract, or within four weeks of the previous contract's terminating, or to renew the contract of employment and the employer unreasonably refuses that offer, he will not be entitled to redundancy payment.

Claims for redundancy payments

A claim to an industrial tribunal must be made six months from the date of notice to terminate the employment, or from the date when the contract expires, but no claim will be allowed after twelve months have lapsed. The employee must have been continuously employed for two years or more by the same employer, for more than 16 hours a week. The claim for payment, if admitted or successful must be met by the employer, but he is entitled to a 41 per cent rebate from the redundancy fund, which is adminstered by the Secretary of State for Employment and funded by contributions made by both employers and employees.

Procedure for handling redundancies

If an employer recognises an independent trade union he must consult with representatives of that union about any proposal to dismiss as redundant any employee who is covered by that recognition agreement. If he proposes to make ten or more employees redundant at one place of work within thirty days or less, he must enter into consultation at least 30 days before the first dismissals take effect. The actual notice of dismissals can be issued during the consultation period, provided the dismissals do not take effect until after the consultation period has lapsed. In the consultations the employer must disclose, amongst other things, the reasons for his proposals, the number of employees he proposes to dismiss as redundant, the proposed method of selecting the employees to be dismissed and the proposed method of carrying out the dismissals, including the period over which dismissals are to take effect.

The employer must consider any representations made by the trade union, and if necessary reply to them.

Redundancy may be a ground for dismissal, but three considerations must be taken into account where an employer is faced with a situation where he has made some or most of his work force redundant. As a reasonable employer he must consider whether such action is necessary or whether the situation can be dealt with in some other way (e.g. by restricting recruitment, cutting down on overtime, introducing work–sharing or short–time working). In *Allwood* v. *William Hill Ltd* (1974) the employers made a number of managers at their betting shops redundant without any prior warning and without investigating the alternative courses of action available to them. It was held that, although there was a redundancy situation, it did not automatically follow that the employees had to be made redundant.

The employer must also make some attempt to find the dismissed employee alternative employment within the same concern or organisation.

The employer may dismiss the employee for redundancy only after proper consultation and warning, although a failure to consult the appropriate unions does not necessarily make the dismissal unfair.

The industrial tribunal must examine whether the employer's selection procedure for redundancies is fair. The tribunal must discover who made the decisions as to which employees were to be selected for redundancy, what information was taken into account by the employer, and by what criteria the information was assessed. If these requirements are complied with the dismissal will be fair.

PROBLEMS

1. Explain the requirements of the Employment Protection (Consolidation) Act 1978, s. 1.

2. What kinds of sex discrimination are declared to be unlawful under the Sex Discrimination Act 1975? What are the five kinds of actions which will amount to discrimination by the employer under the Act?

3. The Equal Pay Act 1970, as amended by the Sex Discrimination Act 1975, implies an equality clause with regard to a female employee's pay where she is employed on work which is the same or similar to that undertaken by a man. Under what circumstances have the industrial tribunals recognised a difference in pay as justifiable?

4. Explain the provisions of the Race Relations Act 1976.

5. Explain the law relating to maternity leave under the Employment Protection (Consolidation) Act 1978.

6. What obligations for the safety of his employees are imposed on an employer at common law under a contract of employment?

7. Explain the nature of duties imposed at common law on an employee under a contract of employment.

8. What disciplinary powers can an employer exercise over his employees?

9. Explain the law relating to unfair dismissal.

10. How may a contract of employment be terminated?

Appendix

Specimen Examination Questions

CONTRACT

Univerity of Liverpool—LL.B 1976–1980

1. Explain the nature and usefulness of the rules governing the "ostensible authority" of an agent. Distinguish ostensible authority from the other types of authority which may be conferred on an agent.

2. Peter Bloggs owns a sweetshop over the door of which is inscribed "Bloggs: Tobacconist and Confectioner"; Peter employs his son Albert as an assistant in the shop.

One day Albert is left in charge of the shop and, in pursuance of an agreement with Vincent, a neighbouring greengrocer (who has gone for the day to the seaside), takes delivery of a number of packets of frozen vegetables which he places in an ice cream cabinet. Soon afterwards the cabinet ceases to function and Albert, in the belief that the contents will begin to deteriorate, agrees with his aunt (who runs a shop some miles away) to sell and deliver the ice cream and frozen vegetables to her forthwith at a low price.

Later in the same day Albert is visited at Peter's shop by a travelling salesman who represents the Greyleaf Cigar Company and who asks whether he is "Mr Bloggs". On Albert's replying "Yes" the salesman persuades him to buy on credit 50 boxes of cigars.

Consider the possible liabilities of Bloggs and of Albert if Bloggs and Vincent disown Albert's actions.

3. Describe the nature and scope of an agent's fiduciary status.

4. Gold is appointed by Silver as his agent
   (*a*) to sell his country house; and
   (*b*) to purchase a cottage at Elleston–on–Sea as cheaply as possible.

Gold sells the country house to his sister at a price substantially lower than the actual value of the house and tells Silver that, in the present state of the market, he has obtained the best price. He purchases a cottage at Elleston–on–Sea and is paid a 10 per cent commission as an incentive to purchase. The price, however, is fair and not affected by the 10 per cent commission.

Advise Silver as to his remedies on his discovery of these facts.

Institute of Bankers—Banking Diploma Examination 1976

5. (*a*) "A contract consists in a concurrence of intention in two parties, each of whom promises something to the other, who in turn accepts such promise."

Consider this statement as a definition of contract.

(*b*) Thomas wrote to Bertie on 9th March offering his stamp collection to Bertie for £500. Consider whether a contract was concluded between them in each of the following different sets of circumstances:

- (*i*) Bertie wrote to Thomas on 14th March, accepting the offer, but the letter was lost in the post;
- (*ii*) Bertie wrote to Thomas on 14th March, accepting the offer, but changed his mind and telephoned Thomas and told him so before the letter arrived.

6. Although tickets may often appear to be mere receipts, yet they frequently cover attempts by those who issue them to relieve themselves from liability for loss or damage to goods or injury to the ticket holders. What measures have the courts been forced to adopt in order to prevent injustice to the ticket holders?

University of Liverpool—Business studies students 1973

7. (*a*) In 1970, Dum lent Dee £1,000 on the understanding that this sum would be repaid to Dum's widow, Mrs Dum, within 6 months of Dum's death. Dum died in November 1972 but Dee has refused to pay anything to Mrs Dum.

Advise Mrs Dum.

(*b*) In January of this year, V agreed to let his caravan to T for the month of July in consideration of a payment of £50 which T paid to V. In May, V sold the caravan to P subject to the agreement but P has now written to T informing him that the caravan will not be available for his use in July.

Advise T, whose primary concern is to obtain the use of the caravan.

8. (*a*) Equitable relief for mistake may take the form of rescission of the contract. In granting such relief, however, the court will insist the mistaken party does justice to the other party to the contract.

Discuss.

(*a*) Andrew advertises that he has for sale a "very fine old grand piano". Barbara inspects the piano and, believing it to be a *Bumler,* of which only about ten still exist, offers Andrew £10,000. Andrew, who believes the piano to be a *Stammer,* a good but not quite so rare make of piano, immediately accepts the offer. When Barbara comes to collect and pay for the piano two days later it is discovered that it is a *Manobe,* of which only two others are known to be in existence. Andrew refuses to allow Barbara to have the piano.

Advise Barbara as to her legal rights, if any.

9. (*a*) Distinguish between innocent and fraudulent misrepresentation leading to the formation of a contract and consider the differences (if any) in the remedies available to the party acting upon the misrepresentation.

(*b*) Jones advertised his petrol–filling station for sale stating that there was no other similar station within 10 miles. This statement was true at the date of the advertisement. Robinson read the advertisement and decided to purchase the garage at an agreed price of £50,000. A binding contract was entered into between Jones and Robinson on 1st June, but, unknown to Robinson, a competing petrol–filling station had been opened up within one mile on 30th May, in consequence of which the value of Jones' station was reduced by £10,000.

Advise Robinson.

COMPANY LAW

University of Liverpool—Business Studies students 1981

10. "The company is at law a different person altogether from the subscribers ... and, although it may be that after incorporation the business is precisely the same as it was before, and the same persons are managers, and the same hands receive the profits, the company is not in law the agent of the subscribers or trustee" per Lord MacNaghten.

Discuss the extent to which this statement is a true reflection of the courts attitude to the status of companies and shareholders.

11. Compare the distinguishing features of a preference share with those of a debenture. What are the rights of a preference shareholder and to what extent are these rights different from those of a debenture holder?

12. What remedies has a person who subscribes for shares in a company in response to a prospectus published by it addressed to the public at large if

(*a*) the prospectus sets out incorrectly the profits earned and dividends paid by the company for its preceding 5 financial years;

(*b*) the prospectus contains a forecast of the company's profits for its current financial year, and in the event it earns only one–tenth of the profits forecast;

(*c*) the prospectus fails to set out the company's profits and dividends for any of those years?

13. "It is an inflexible rule that a director is not, unless otherwise expressly provided, entitled to make a profit out of his office, he must not put himself in a position where his own interests and his duty to the company conflict."

Discuss.

14. (*a*) What is meant by the requirement that an alteration of the memorandum or articles must be for the benefit of the company as a whole?

(*b*) Discuss the effectiveness of the following alterations made by a company to its memorandum of association:

   (*i*) Z Ltd is a company formed to "manufacture rubber tyres, vehicles using rubber parts and any other rubber goods". The company passes a special resolution that it will in future also purchase shares and invest in other companies manufacturing these products.

   (*ii*) Z Ltd is a company formed to manufacture aeroplane engines.

It passes a special resolution that it will in future cease manufacturing aeroplane engines and instead commence the business
of coal–mining.

Institute of Chartered Secretaries and Administrators 1978

15. D. is the Company Secretary of F Ltd, a company formed to carry on, and
operating, a hardware business. D (who is heavily in debt) orders several
consignments of dustbins from G in the name of F Ltd which he then sells on
his own stall in the local market. He also persuades H to invest in F Ltd and in
return for the subscription price issues him with a share certificate with F Ltd's
seal affixed. D keeps for himself both the proceeds of sale of the dustbins and
the subscription moneys. He had signed his own name as one of the witnesses
to the affixing of the seal and had also signed one of the directors' names
without his authority. F Ltd is now in liquidation.
  Advise G and H.

16. (a) What are the differences between a share and a debenture?
  (b) X owns 100 shares in A Ltd, a public company. He mislays the share
certificate which is found by Y, who then forges X's signature and procures a
registered transfer of the shares to Z who is issued with a new share certificate
by the company. Z has since transferred the shares to B in the usual manner. X
has now discovered the loss of his certificate.
  Advise the company.

17. "The restrictions placed by the courts on petitions under section 210 [of
the Companies Act 1948] seem unduly harsh when compared with judicial
attitudes towards a winding up on the just and equitable ground." Discuss.

18. X Ltd is a private company. A was appointed company secretary for ten
years in 1970 but his contract makes no mention of his salary. B, who made a
substantial loan to the company in 1972, has a contractual right to appoint one
director to the board of X Ltd until the loan is repaid in 1980. C owns 50 shares
in X Ltd and wishes to sell his shares to the directors of the company who are
unwilling to buy them. The articles include the following clauses:

  (i) The company secretary shall be paid £5,000 per annum.
  (ii) All shareholders who wish to sell their shares must offer them to
       the directors who must buy them at a price agreed by the
       company's auditors.

The directors, who own 80 per cent of the shares of Z Ltd, wish to alter
Article (i) to provide that the company secretary shall be paid £3,000 per
annum and to include a new clause whereby all directors shall be appointed by
the general meeting.
  Advise A, B and C.

19. Write notes on TWO of the following:
  (a) the fiduciary duties of a promoter;

(*b*) fraudulent preferences;

(*c*) bonus shares;

(*d*) the right to give notice of and to propose resolutions at company meetings.

Institute of Bankers—Banking Diploma Examination Part II 1977

20. The East Bank had been worried for some time about the overdraft of its customer Go–Slow Ltd. On 1st February 1977, under pressure from the bank, the company gave an unlimited debenture to the bank to secure its overdraft, then £35,000. The debenture contained a fixed first charge on the company's factory, and a first floating charge on all other assets. On 1st July 1977 the company passed an extraordinary resolution to wind–up voluntarily because it could not, by reason of its liabilities, continue in business. At that time the company owed the bank £45,000.

There were also:

(*a*) unpaid wages and salaries totalling £6,000;

(*b*) two years' arrears of taxes totalling £4,500 (being £2,500 for the earlier year, and £2,000 for the more recent year);

(*c*) unpaid rates for the previous 12 months totalling £1,000;

(*d*) ordinary trade creditors amounting to £55,000.

Assume that the liquidation expenses will be £500, the factory will fetch £25,000, and the remaining assets £30,000. State the order of priority of the various claims.

What difference, if any, would it make if the liquidator was able to prove that the company was already insolvent on 1st February 1977?

University of Nottingham—BA Degree 1974

21. Cotton, Silk and Rayon have carried on a business in partnership for the past five years. The partnership deed states that any partner may be dismissed, inter alia, for immoral conduct if his fellow partners so decide. Any dispute in relation to the dismissal of any partner should be settled by arbitration.

Cotton has recently discovered that Silk is to be prosecuted for alleged acts of indecency and that Rayon has lent some money to a rival firm and is being repaid out of the profits of that firm.

Advise Cotton.

SALE OF GOODS

University of Liverpool—Business Studies & Accountancy Students 1981

22. William agreed to buy for his son a secondhand Cannonball car from David, a dealer. There was a condition, however, that David would fit a new exhaust pipe and have the car ready for delivery within fourteen days. At the same time David allowed William to take a new Alpino car on approval for the same length of time with a view to William purchasing it for his own use.

What is the position if, within the fourteen day period, David fits a new exhaust pipe to the Cannonball, which is stolen from David's garage before delivery to William, and the Alpino is badly damaged by a fire in William's garage?

23. Mrs Lewis (who is a vegetarian) bought some steak labelled "Prime Angus Steak" for her husband and meat pies for her two children. Mr Lewis complained that the meat was very tough and unappetising. Mrs Lewis subsequently discovered that it came from the Argentine, not Scotland as she had believed. Both the children became violently ill and it is proved that the remaining meat pie contains salmonella germs.

Has the butcher incurred any liability?

24. Discuss the remedies of a seller under a contract for the sale of goods against a buyer who refuses to accept and pay for them.

25. What is the legal distinction between hire purchase, credit sale and conditional sale?

How are these transactions classified in the Consumer Credit Act 1974?

26. On Monday Harry sold his car to Chris. Chris produced a stolen cheque book and means of identification, and persuaded Harry to let him have possession of the car and log book in return for a cheque. Later the same week Chris sold the car to Edward, and Harry discovered that the signature on Chris's cheque was forged so he informed the police. The police have now traced the car to Edward. Chris has disappeared.

Consider the circumstances in which Edward will have a good title to the car.

University of Nottingham—BA 1974

27. Mendit Ltd contracted to buy one gross of brushes from Shine Ltd. The brushes were to be used by Mendit Ltd in applying cleaning fluid to components being reconditioned in their factory. When some of the brushes were used it was discovered that the special brand of cleaning fluid used by Mendit Ltd adversely affected the bonding of the bristles rendering the brushes unusable, although they would have been suitable for applying paint, lubricants and other types of cleaning fluid.

Advise Mendit Ltd.

BANKING

Institute of Bankers—Banking Diploma Examination Part II 1978

28. (a) When is a bill of exchange deemed to be overdue, and what significance does this have as regards its negotiation?

(b) On 20th January 1978 Oswald drew a bill of exchange for £500 on Philip payable to bearer three months after date. Whilst being sent to Philip, the bill was amongst items of mail stolen by thieves, who threw it away. It was found by Roger, who passed it on to Sam in settlement for goods supplied. When Sam presented the bill to Philip at maturity, it was dishonoured. Advise Sam as to his legal rights, if any.

29. What statutory protection is afforded to a banker when paying cheques drawn by customers? Outline the circumstances in which this protection may be lost. Does the legal position alter at all if the paying banker is also the collecting banker?

30. Codd visits the Dogger Bank with his friend, who is posing as Bloater, a famous television personality, whom he closely resembles. Codd asks to open a current account, offering "Bloater" as a referee. Thereupon "Bloater" gives a favourable reference in respect of Codd, which the banks accepts without further inquiry. Codd then pays in a cheque for a large amount and after it has been cleared, he withdraws almost all the proceeds. The true owner of this cheque now claims its value from the bank, and Codd cannot be found. Advise the bank.

Would you change your advice if in fact the bank had allowed Codd to draw against the cheque whilst still uncleared, and payment of it was stopped by the drawer?

COMMERCIAL LAW

University of Birmingham—International Trade 1978

31. (a) S & Co English merchants acquire 10,000 tonnes horse beans afloat the *Cycle Star* owned by UCS Ltd and sell 9,000 tonnes and 1,000 tonnes to B & Co and C & Co respectively cif Sydney. Bills of lading covering these goods are duly tendered and accepted by those buyers. C & Co, whilst the goods are in transit sell their consignment to B & Co re–indorsing their bill of lading. The goods are and remain unseparated in the hold of the *Cycle Star*. During the voyage, sea water enters the hold due to an improperly fitted hatch cover and 500 tonnes of the beans are contaminated.

B & Co seek your advice as to the claims they may maintain. What would be the position if the 1,000 tonnes originally bought by C & Co, had been resold as to 500 tonnes to B & Co and 500 tonnes to D & Co?

(b) Explain the factors which might influence the choice of an fob contract rather than a cif contract.

32. (a) Burger & Co bought from Soy Inc 5,000 tons soyabean meal fob New York at US$10 per ton, shipment May 1980. Burger & Co duly nominated their vessel and gave notice on 1st May of her probable arrival on 15th May. Soy Inc brought the goods on to the quay but on 14th May, Burger & Co telexed that the vessel had been delayed by strikes and substituted a second ship they had chartered. This vessel arrived and berthed at New York on 28th May but only 2,500 tons could be loaded by midnight on 31st May and she then sailed. Burger & Co, rightly suspecting that the goods had begun to deteriorate whilst awaiting loading, refuse to pay for them.

Advise Soy Inc (assume English law applies).

(b) "It is proved beyond all doubt... that when goods are sold in London "free on board" the cost of shipping them fall on the seller but the buyer is considered the shipper" *Cowasjee* v. *Thompson* (1845) per Lord Brougham. How far does this statement of the law remain true?

University of Birmingham—Insurance LL.B.—Commercial Law paper 1976

33. "If a moral certainty be a ground of insurable interest, there are hundreds perhaps thousands, who would be entitled to insure" (*Lucan* v. *Crauford* (1806), per Lord Eldon).

How does English law avoid Lord Eldon's fears in relation to life insurance?

What criticisms would you make of the present English approach to insurable interest in lives?

34. (a) In 1975 Rogers applied for motor insurance and completed a proposal form which contained, among others, the following questions.
  (i)   Do you suffer from defective vision, defective hearing or any other ailment? Give details.
  (ii)   Have you made a claim against any insurance company resulting from a road accident? Give details.
  (iii) Date of birth.

In reply to these three questions, Rogers answered:
  (i)   No. (In fact he wore contact lenses at all times).
  (ii)   Yes. I claimed £75 in 1973 when I skidded in the snow into my garage door. (In fact he had successfully claimed £8,000 for personal injuries in a car accident in 1970 when he had been an innocent victim.)
  (iii) 22nd September. (This was correct and would make him 36. But in the personal details box at the top of the proposal form he had incorrectly put his age as 35.)

How will the court deal with these answers if the insurance company claimed to avoid liability in the event of a claim by Rogers for damage to his car when he ran into the back of a bus?

(b) If the proposal form contained a "basis of the contract" clause, how would that affect your answer in (a)?

EMPLOYMENT

University of Liverpool—LL.B paper 1975

35. AB Ltd have announced plans for large scale redundancies. The Regional Officer of the Engineering Workers Trade Union (EWTU) advises his members at AB to concentrate on negotiating favourable severance pay agreements. However, at a mass meeting, the employees decide, by a show of hands, to begin an immediate strike in protest at the proposed redundancies. A

Strike Committee is elected by the employees to run the strike fund and to organise pickets.

AB receive supplies from X. One of AB's main customers for the finished products is Y. At each of the three entrances to AB's factory a group of pickets is stationed to persuade drivers of lorries employed by X not to deliver to AB and drivers employed by Y not to collect goods destined for Y. There are eight pickets at each of the two side entrances and ten at the main front entrance. Initially the pickets are orderly but later there are disturbances. The first occurs at the main entrance when a driver from X shouts abuse at the pickets and a brick is thrown at the lorry. The second is at a side entrance when a police constable asks some of the pickets to leave and they refuse. In each case, several pickets are arrested.

The next day a mass picket of 200 appears at the main gate. Included in this number is the Regional Officer of the EWTU and EWTU representatives from local factories, together with a local MP. A meeting at the factory gates calls for all EWTU members to support the dispute at AB. Industrial action subsequently begins at several local factories including that of Z Ltd, where members of the EWTU begin sympathetic action.

AB is forced to cancel orders from X and cease deliveries to Y. AB, X, Y and Z are considering legal action against the EWTU and its members to prevent further interference with their businesses. What are the legal principles involved?

Institute of Chartered Secretaries and Administrators 1975

36. Eric, owner of the Velour Bees, a Cardiff night club, enters into contracts of service with the following:

(a) Cariad, a flamenco dancer, for a period of six months. It is agreed that Cariad is not to appear anywhere else in the capacity of a dancer during the period of the contract and that Eric is to have an option to extend the contract for a further six months if he so wishes.

(b) Bronwen, a strip-tease artiste, for a period of six months. Her contract states that she will not appear in any other club nor work anywhere else in any capacity during the period of the contract.

(c) Clem, a female impersonator, for a period of one year. Eric agrees that he will not employ anyone else in that capacity during the contract period.

After two months Cariad tells Eric that she will be leaving at the end of the six months, but Eric informs her that he intends to take up the option in her contract. At the same time Bronwen tells Eric she has had a much better offer from Cecil, owner of The Nos-y-Gogo night club, and that she is leaving. Clem, who finds the cold wet Welsh weather affects him rather badly, is suffering from chilblains and has been unable to perform for three weeks. Eric tells Clem that he is terminating the contract and that he will be employing Cyril, Clem's main rival, instead. Advise Eric as to his legal rights and liabilities in respect of the above agreements.

37. "The product of collective bargaining is the collective agreement, the legal effect of which varies according to whether one views it from the point of view of the trade union or the individual union member."

Discuss.

University of Liverpool—LL.B. 1980

38. (*a*) Explain the remedies which are available to an employee whose complaint of unfair dismissal succeeds.

(*b*) Angus works for M Sporran Ltd, which produces jackets made of Harris tweed. He has been there for 6 years. Because of a boom in trade, in 1980 his employers decide to introduce Saturday working. Angus, who is a known malingerer, objects to this, but he is warned that, unless he agrees within a fortnight, he will be dismissed for "malingering". A few days later, he finds another job and resigns. After he has left, his employers discover that for the past year he has been stealing jackets and giving them to all his friends.

Angus has presented a complaint of unfair dismissal and seeks your advice as to its chances of success.

Index